Artificial Intelligence in the 21st Century

Artificial Intelligence in the 21st Century

Edited by **Akira Hanako**

New York

Published by Willford Press,
118-35 Queens Blvd., Suite 400,
Forest Hills, NY 11375, USA
www.willfordpress.com

Artificial Intelligence in the 21st Century
Edited by Akira Hanako

Contents

Permissions

List of Contributors

Preface

The purpose of the book is to provide a glimpse into the dynamics and to present opinions and studies of some of the scientists engaged in the development of new ideas in the field from very different standpoints. This book will prove useful to students and researchers owing to its high content quality.

Artificial intelligence is a rapidly emerging branch of computer science which deals with intelligent behavior adaptation in machines. This book presents the complex subject of artificial intelligence in the most comprehensible and easy to understand language. From theories to research to applications, case studies related to all contemporary topics of relevance to this field have been included in this book. The various advancements in genetic algorithms and robotics are glanced at and their applications as well as ramifications are looked at in detail. It will help the readers in keeping pace with the rapid changes in this field.

At the end, I would like to appreciate all the efforts made by the authors in completing their chapters professionally. I express my deepest gratitude to all of them for contributing to this book by sharing their valuable works. A special thanks to my family and friends for their constant support in this journey.

Editor

High speed performance of semiconductor electrooptic modulators for multi Gigahertz communication systems operation

Abd El–Naser A. Mohamed, Ahmed Nabih Zaki Rashed*, Mohammed A. Metwae'e and Amira I. M. Bendary

Electronics and Electrical Communications Engineering Department, Faculty of Electronic Engineering, Menouf 32951, Menoufia University, Egypt.

The effects of electrodes geometry and temperature on high frequency radio frequency transmission characteristics are deeply investigated against semiconductor material based electro optic modulator devices such as aluminum gallium arsenide (AlGaAs) and optical waveguide parameters. On the other hand, we have developed the optimization of the electro-optic modulator parameters where the effective index plays an essential role in the evaluation of the bandwidth structure. Therefore, a theoretical analysis of the capacitance, the characteristic impedance and the effective index determine how to increase the bandwidth. The effects of design parameters on the modulating voltage and optical bandwidth are also investigated for different materials based electro-optic modulators by using rigorous transmission modeling techniques. The low-loss wide-bandwidth capability of optoelectronic systems makes them attractive for the transmission and processing of microwave signals, while the development of high capacity optical communication systems has required the use of microwave techniques in optical transmitters and receivers. These two strands have led to the development of the research area of microwave photonics.

Key words: Electrooptic modulator, semiconductor material, optical bandwidth, high transmission performance.

INTRODUCTION

Present communication technology relies on fiber-optic systems which include light sources such as a laser, optical fiber, integrated optical components such as modulators and switches, and optical detectors. The lasers and detectors are fabricated using semiconductor materials, and the integrated optical components are generally fabricated using electrooptic single crystal materials such as lithium niobate (LiNbO$_3$). Among the integrated optical components, the contribution from electrooptic modulators using LiNbO$_3$ waveguide structures has been significant in the last several decades due to their high speed and chirp-free nature (Soref, 2006). The essential requirements for efficient electrooptic modulation are low half-wave (switching)

voltage and broad 3-dB bandwidth. The optical modulator is a key component for photonics. Optical fiber communications, microwave photonics, instrumentation, and optical signals processing all require optical modulators. Several different technology platforms can be used for the realization of optical modulators. Of these, LiNbO$_3$ based ferroelectric electrooptic modulators provide the most mature technology. Electro-optic polymers and compound semiconductors are also attractive technologies for optical modulators. High-speed integrated electro-optic modulators and switches are the basic building blocks of modern wideband optical communications systems and represent the future trend in ultra-fast signal processing technology. As a result, a great deal of research effort has been devoted to developing low-loss, efficient and broadband modulators in which the radio frequency signal is used to modulate the optical carrier frequency (Liu et al., 2004). Most of the

*Corresponding author. E-mail: ahmed_733@yahoo.com.

work done in the area of designing electrooptic modulators has been strongly focused on using LiNbO$_3$ (Liao et al., 2005). Interest in research in this field has arisen as lithium niobate devices have a number of advantages over others (Gu et al., 2007), including large electro-optic coefficients, low drive voltage, low bias drift, zero or adjustable frequency chirp, and the facility for broadband modulation with moderate optical and insertion losses and good linearity. However, on the other hand, LiNbO$_3$ devices cannot be integrated with devices fabricated using other material systems such as semiconductors and as a result they are best suited to external modulation applications. However, with the recent developments in semiconductor technology, modulators based on semiconductor materials have been receiving increasing attention. In particular, AlGaAs/GaAs material offers the advantage of technological maturity and potential monolithic integration with other optical and electronic devices in creating better optoelectronic integrated circuits (OEIC). Recently, electrooptic polymer modulators have also emerged as alternatives for optical modulators, particularly for low-cost applications for the next-generation metro and optical access systems. Today 2.5 Gb/s and 10 Gb/s modulators are standard commercial products and 40 Gb/s modulators are also being developed for the market after successful prototype demonstrations: however, the continuous demand to increase the data rate further will push their operating frequency well into the millimeter wave range Kim and (Gnauck, 2002).

High-speed optical modulators are essential for dealing with the current explosive growth in network traffic. These modulators are based on two types of physical effect: the electro absorption (EA) effect and the electro-optic (EO) effect. EA modulators have been widely used in recently developed 2.5 and 10 Gb/s optical transmission systems, because they have a small driving voltage of around 2 Volt Tsuzuki et al. (2004), a small size and can be easily integrated with laser sources. However, it is difficult to apply EA modulators to high-bit-rate transmission systems because of their chirp characteristics. EA modulators can only be applied to very-short-reach (VSR) systems at 40 Gb/s (Tsuzuki et al., 2003; 2004). In contrast, the interferometric Mach Zehnder (MZ) modulator provides more flexibility than the EA modulator in terms of chirp controllability. Moreover, MZ modulators are capable of controlling the optical phase. The MZ modulator is the most widely used device employing the EO effect. The optical phase can be controlled by supplying the EO waveguides with a voltage (Tsuzuki et al., 2004). High-bit rate transmission systems require a phase controlled modulation format, such as a carrier-suppressed return-to-zero (CS-RZ) or optical duo binary signal format (Tsuzuki et al., 2005; Cui and Berini, 2006; Shin et al., 2007). These formats are capable of improving the transmission performance because of their dispersion tolerance resulting from the fact that there is less spectral width broadening during modulation.

In the present study, aluminum gallium arsenide (AlGaAs) semiconductor material based electrooptic external modulators have been developed for extensive use in high speed and long distance optical fiber transmission systems. This is because they can offer the advantages of modulation exceeding multi Gb/sec combined with a low driving voltage, and they can eliminate the dynamic laser wavelength chirping which limits the span-rate system product due to their fiber dispersion characteristics. Modulators fabricated on semiconductor substrates such as (AlGaAs) and silicon doped materials are particularly attractive in that there exists the possibility of monolithic integration of these devices with other optoelectronic components.

MODELING ANALYSIS

For Al$_x$Ga$_{(1-x)}$As, the parameters required to characterize the ambient temperature and operating signal wavelength dependence of the refractive-index, where Sellmeier empirical equation is under the form of Ibrahim et al. (2011):

$$n^2 = C_1 + \frac{C_2}{\lambda^2 - C_3} - C_4 \lambda^2$$

(1)

The set of the parameters is recast and dimensionally adjusted as the following Tsuzuki et al. (2004; 2005): C_1= 10.906-2.92x, C_2= 0.97501, C_3=c_3T^2; c_3= (0.52886-0.735x/T$_o$)^2, for x < 0.36. And C_4=c (0.93721+ 2.0857x10^{-4}T); c_4 = 0.002467(1.14x+1). We have taken into account the value of x=0.2, then the first and second differentiation of above empirical equation with respect to operating optical signal wavelength λ gives:

$$\frac{dn}{d\lambda} = -(\lambda/n)\left[\frac{C_2}{\left(\lambda^2 - C_3\right)^2} + C_4\right]$$

(2)

$$\frac{d^2 n}{d\lambda^2} = \frac{-1}{n}\left[\frac{C_2\left(\left(\lambda^2 - C_3^2\right) - 4\lambda^2\right)}{\left(\lambda^2 - C_3^2\right)^3} - C_4\right],$$

(3)

The switching voltage V$_\pi$ or the voltage required to change the output light intensity from its maximum to minimum value can be expressed as the following (Abd El-Naser et al., 2011; Seo and Fetterman, 2006; Abd El-Naser et al., 2009):

$$V_\pi = \frac{\lambda d}{2\Gamma n^3 r_{41} L_m},$$

(4)

Where λ is the operating optical signal wavelength in μm, Γ is the confinement factor, d is the modulator thickness in μm, L$_m$ is the modulator length in μm, and r$_{41}$ is the electrooptic coefficient for used semiconductor material.

Under the perfect velocity matching condition (Allocation and Service Rules, Federal Communications Commission, Washington

DC, 2005; Abd El-Naser et al., 2009), achievable modulation bandwidth f_m is:

$$f_m = \frac{6.84}{\alpha L_m} \quad , \; GHz \tag{5}$$

Where α is the power absorption coefficient in dB/µm.

Therefore the device performance index (DPI) can be expressed as the following expression (Abd El-Naser et al., 2009; Tazawa and Steier, 2006):

$$DPI = \frac{f_m}{V_\pi} \quad , \; GHz/Volt \tag{6}$$

If a modulating voltage V_m in z-direction is applied, the change in index for the TM polarization is:

$$\Delta n_e = \frac{0.5 V_m n^3 r_{41}}{L_m} \quad , \tag{7}$$

Therefore the product of the sensitivity and the bandwidth is not related to the signal quality factor and is given by Abd El-Naser et al. (2009):

$$SBP = \frac{0.65 n^2 \Gamma r_{41} c}{d \lambda} \quad , \tag{8}$$

Where r_{41} is the electro optic coefficient for aluminum gallium arsenide material based EO modulator devices.

The total system rise time is the square root of the sum of the squares of the transmitter, optical fiber connection, and receiver rise times. That is given by Xu, et al. (2005):

$$\tau_s = \sqrt{\tau_t^2 + \tau_{mat.}^2 + \tau_r^2} \quad , \tag{9}$$

The material dispersion time of the single mode fiber $\tau_{mat.}$ is given by the following equation:

$$\tau_{mat.} = -\left(\frac{L_m . \Delta\lambda . \lambda}{c}\right) . \left(\frac{d^2 n}{d\lambda^2}\right) \quad , \tag{10}$$

In addition to providing sufficient power to the receiver, the system must also satisfy the bandwidth requirements imposed by the rate at which data are transmitted. A convenient method of accounting for the bandwidth is to combine the rise times of the various system components and compare the result with the rise time needed for the given data rate and pulse coding scheme. The system rise time is given in terms of the data rate for non return to zero pulse code by the expression (Abd El-Naser and Ahmed, 2009):

$$B_R(NRZ) = \frac{0.7}{\tau_s} , \tag{11}$$

Then the bandwidth length product within electrooptic modulator device is given by Abd El-Naser et al. (2009; 2011):

$$P_R(NRZ) = B_R . L_m \quad , \; Gbit.µm/sec \tag{12}$$

The bandwidth for single mode operation within electrooptic modulator length L_m is given by:

$$B.W_{sig.} = \frac{0.44}{\tau_s . L_m} \quad , \; GHz \tag{13}$$

The signal to noise ratio (SNR) is a measure of signal quality at the receiver end, it is given by Michalak et al. (2006):

$$SNR = \frac{(G P_0 \rho)^2 R_L}{4 k T B.W_{sig.} + 2 e R_L B.W_{sig.} G^n (I_D + \rho P_0)} \quad , \tag{14}$$

$$(SNR)_{dB} = 10 \log SNR \quad , \tag{15}$$

Where P_0 is the received or output optical power, ρ is the detector's unamplified responsivity, G is the detector gain if an avalanche photodiode (APD) is used, n accounts for the excess noise of the APD (usually between 2 and 3), $B.W_{sig.}$ is the signal bandwidth at the receiver, k is Boltzmann's constant (k = 1.38 x 10^{-23} J/K), e is the magnitude of the charge on an electron (1.6 x 10^{-19} coulomb), T is the ambient temperature in K, I_D is the detector's dark current, and R_L is the resistance of the load resistor that follows the photodetector. The maximum transmission bit rate or capacity according to modified Shannon technique is given by Abd El-Naser et al. (2011):

$$B_{R(SH)} = BW_{sig.} \log_2 (1 + SNR) \quad , \tag{16}$$

Where $B.W_{sig.}$ is the actual bandwidth of the optical signal, and SNR is the signal to noise ratio in absolute value (that is, not in dB). The Shannon Bit rate length product P_{SH} can be given by:

$$P_{SH} = B_{R(SH)} . L_m \quad , \tag{17}$$

SIMULATION RESULTS AND PERFORMANCE ANALYSIS

We have investigated ultra high speed semiconductor electrooptic modulator devices for gigahertz system operation over wide range of the affecting operating parameters as shown in Table 1.

Based on the model equations analysis, assumed set of the operating parameters, and the set of the Figures (1 to 14), the following facts are assured:

i) As shown in the series of Figures (1 to 3), as both modulator length and confinement factor increase, and operating optical signal wavelength decreases, resulting in decreasing of switching voltage.

ii) Figure 4 has assured that as both modulator length and relative refractive index difference increase, this leads to increase in modulating voltage.

iii) Figure 5 has demonstrated that as power absorption coefficient and modulator length increase, this result in decreasing of modulation device bandwidth.

Table 1. Proposed operating parameters for our suggested electrooptic modulator device.

Parameter	Definition	Value and unit
T	Ambient temperature	$300\ K \leq T \leq 330\ K$
L_m	Modulator length	$2\ \mu m \leq L_m \leq 5\ \mu m$
d	Modulator thickness	$0.1\ \mu m \leq w \leq 0.5\ \mu m$
τ_t	Rise time of the transmitter	0.8 nsec
τ_r	Rise time of the receiver	1 nsec
P_0	Output power	$0.1 \leq P_0,\ Watt \leq 0.6$
T_0	Room temperature	300 K
λ	Signal operating wavelength	$1.3\ \mu m \leq \lambda \leq 1.65\ \mu m$
$\Delta\lambda$	Spectral line width of the optical source	0.1 nm
r_{41}	Electoptic coefficient for $Al_xGa_{(1-x)}As$	18 Pm/volt
L	Inductance	20 μH
C	Capacitance	0.2 pF
R_L	Load resistance	5 kΩ
G	Detector gain	20 dB
α	Power absorption coefficient	0.1–0.5 dB/μm
Δn_e	Effective refractive index difference	$0.01 \leq \Delta n_e \leq 0.09$
Γ	Confinement factor	$0.8 \leq \Gamma \leq 0.95$
I_D	Detector dark current	8 nA
ρ	Detector responsivity	0.8 A/Watt
η	Modulator efficiency	90 %
c	Speed of light	3×10^8 m/sec

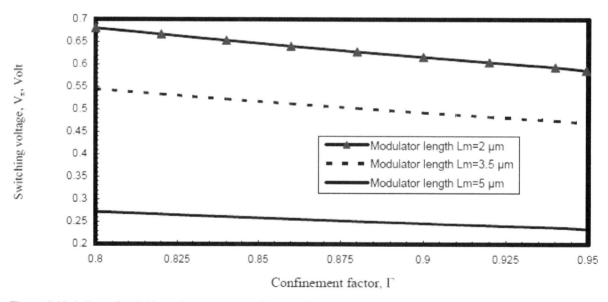

Figure 1. Variations of switching voltage versus confinement factor at the assumed set of parameters.

i) Figures (6 and 7) have indicated that as both operating optical signal wavelength and modulator thickness increase, and confinement factor decreases, this leads to decrease in device performance index.
ii) Figure 8 has assured that as operating optical signal wavelength increases and confinement factor
iii) Decreases, this result in decreasing of device

sensitivity bandwidth product.
iv) Figure 9 has proved that as modulator length and optical output power increase, this result in increasing of signal to noise ratio.
v) As shown in Figures (10 and 11) have demonstrated that as modulator length and output power increase, this result in increasing of transmission bit rate length

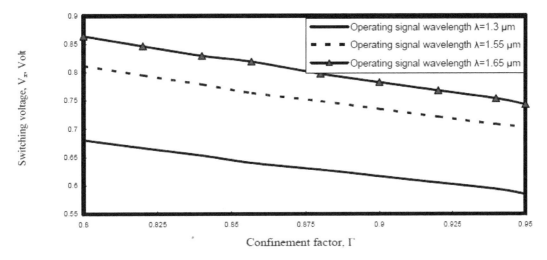

Figure 2. Variations of switching voltage versus confinement factor at the assumed set of parameters.

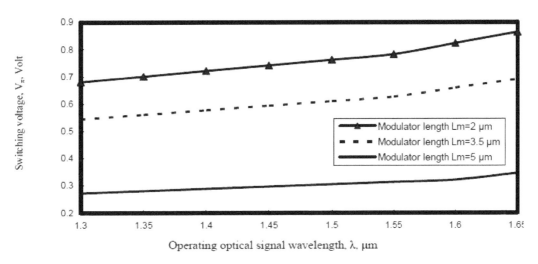

Table 3. Variations of switching voltage versus signal wavelength at the assumed set of parameters.

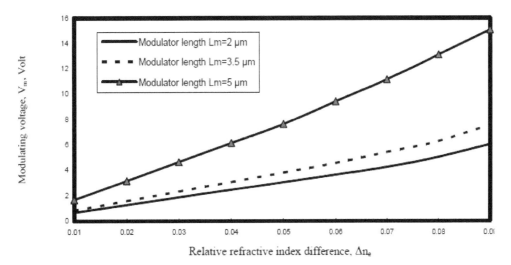

Table 4. Variations of modulating voltage against relative refractive index difference at the assumed set of parameters.

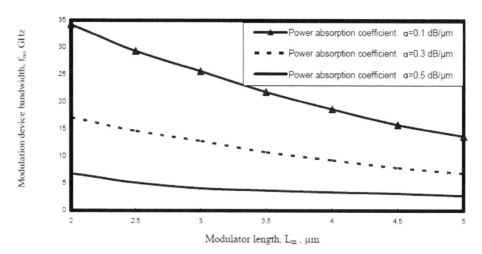

Figure 5. Variations of modulation bandwidth against modulator length at the assumed set of parameters.

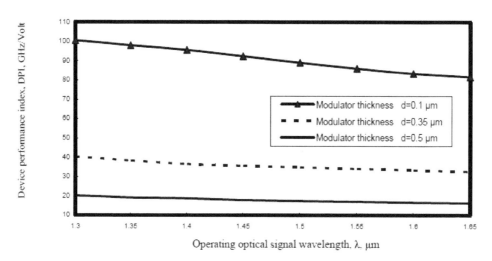

Figure 6. Variations of device performance index against optical signal wavelength at the assumed set of parameters.

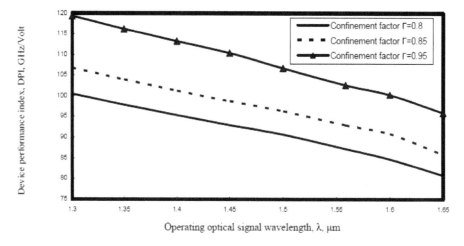

Figure 7. Variations of device performance index optical signal wavelength at the assumed set of parameters.

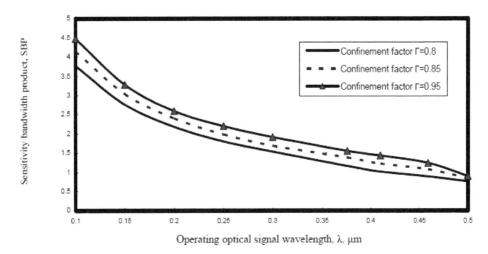

Figure 8. Variations of sensitivity bandwidth product against optical signal wavelength at the assumed set of parameters.

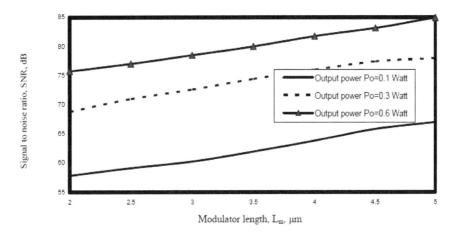

Figure 9. Variations of signal to noise ratio against modulator length at the assumed set of parameters.

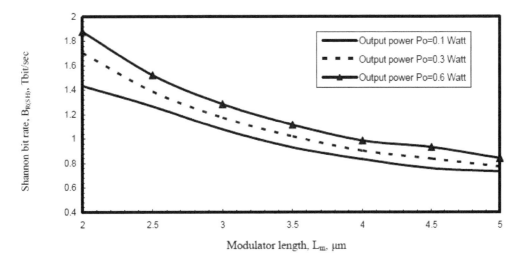

Figure 10. Variations of Shannon transmission bit rate against modulator length at the assumed set of parameters.

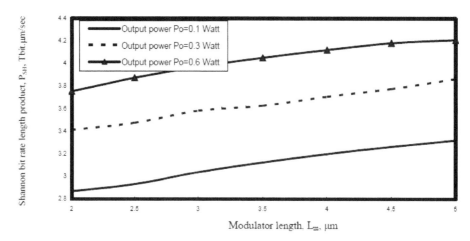

Figure 11. Variations of Shannon bit rate length product against modulator length at the assumed set of parameters.

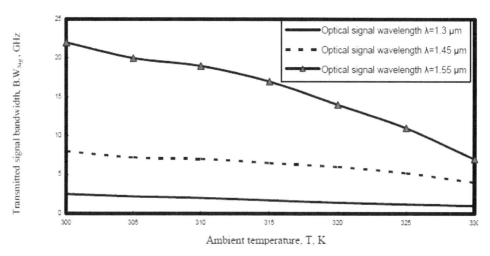

Figure 12. Variations of transmitted signal bandwidth versus ambient temperature at the assumed set of parameters.

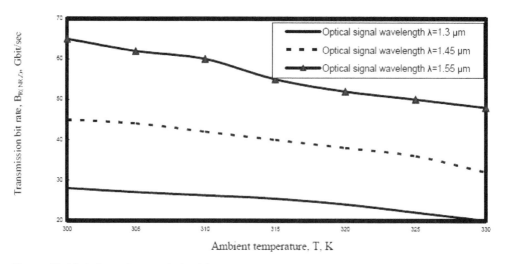

Figure 13. Variations of transmission bit rate versus ambient temperature at the assumed set of parameters.

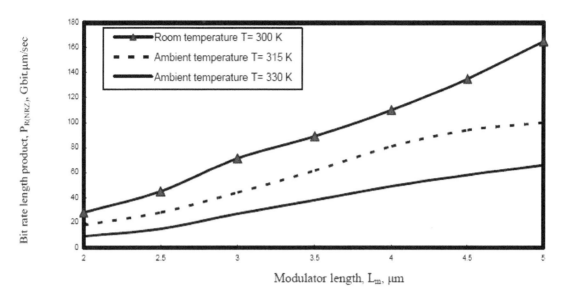

Figure 14. Variations of transmission bit rate length product against modulator length at the assumed set of parameters.

product. As well as modulator length increases, and output power decreases, this leads to decrease in transmission bit rates with Shannon transmission technique.

vi) Figure 12 has indicated that as ambient temperature decreases operating optical signal wavelength increases, this leads to increase in transmitted signal bandwidth.

vii) Figures (13 and 14) have demonstrated that as both modulator length and operating optical signal wavelength increase, and ambient temperature decreases, this result in increasing transmission bit rate length product. As well as both modulator length and ambient temperature increase and operating optical signal wavelength decreases, this result in decreasing of transmission bit rates with non return to zero coding formats.

Conclusions

In summary, we have presented ultra high speed semiconductor electrooptic modulator devices for multi gigahertz operation systems. It is theoretically found that the increased confinement factor and modulator length, and the decreased operating optical signal wavelength, this leads to the decreased switching device voltage. It is evident that the decreased operating optical signal wavelength and modulator thickness, and the increased confinement factor, this results in increasing of device performance index. As well as the increased output received power and modulator length, and the increased operating optical signal wavelength, and the decreased ambient temperature, this results in the increased transmission bit rate length product with using both Shannon transmission technique and NRZ coding formats.

REFERENCES

Soref R (2006). "Silicon Photonics Technology: Past, Present, and Future," IEEE J. Sel. Topics Quantum Electron., 12(6): 1678–1687, Nov/Dec.

Liu A, Jones R, Liao L, Rublo DS, Rubin D, Cohen O, Nicolaescu R, Paniccia M (2004). "A high Speed Silicon Optical Modulator Based on A metal Oxide Semiconductor Capacitor," Nature Photonics, 42(7): 615–617.

Liao L, Samara-Rubio D, Morse M, Liu A, Hodge D, Rubin D, Keil UD, Franck T (2005). "High Speed Silicon Mach–Zehnder Modulator," Opt. Exp., 13(3): 3129–3135.

Gu L, Jiang W, Chen X, Wang L, Chen RT (2007). "High Speed Silicon Photonic Crystal Waveguide Modulator for Low Voltage Operation," Appl. Phys. Lett., 90(2): 5-8.

Kim H, Gnauck AH (2002). "Chirp Characteristics of Dual Drive Mach-Zehnder Modulator with A finite DC Extinction Ratio," IEEE Photonics Technol. Lett., 14(3): 298–300.

Tsuzuki K, Yasaka H, Ishibashi T, Ito T, Oku S, Iga R, Kondo Y, Tohmori Y (2004). "10-Gbit/s, 100-km SMF Transmission Using an InP Based n-i-n Mach-Zehnder Modulator with A driving Voltage of 1.0 Vpp," Proc. Optical Fiber Communication 2004 (OFC'04) Postdeadline Papers.

Tsuzuki K, Ishibashi T, Ito T, Oku S, Shibata Y, Iga R, Kondo Y, Tohmori Y (2003)."40 Gbit/s n-i-n InP Mach-Zehnder Modulator with a peak voltage of 2.2 V," Electron. Lett., 39(20): 1464–1466.

Tsuzuki K, Ishibashi T, Ito T, Oku S, Shibata Y, Ito T, Iga R, Kondo Y, Tohmori Y (2004). "1.6 V-driven 40-Gbit/s n-i-n Mach-Zehnder modulator based on InP substrate," Proc. 9th Optoelectronics and Communication Conference 2004 (OECC'04), 15E3-2, pp. 706–707.

Tsuzuki K, Ishibashi T, Ito T, Oku S, Shibata Y, Ito T, Iga R, Kondo Y, Tohmori Y (2005). "A 40-Gb/s InGaAlAs-InAlAs MQW n-i-n Mach-Zehnder Modulator with A drive Voltage of 2.3 V," IEEE Photon. Technol. Lett., 17(1): 46–48, January.

Cui Y, Berini P (2006). "Modeling and Design of GaAs Traveling Wave Electrooptic Modulators Based on the Planar Microstrip Structure," J. Lightw. Technol., 24(6): 2368–2378, June.

Shin J, Wu S, Dagli N (2007). "35-GHz Bandwidth, 5-V-cm Drive Voltage, Bulk GaAs Substrate Removed Electrooptic modulators," IEEE Photon. Technol. Lett., 19(18): 1362–1364, September.

Ibrahim MEI-d, Abd El-Naser AM, Ahmed Nabih ZR, Mahomud MEid (2011). "Ultra Wide Wavelength Multiplexing/Demultiplexing Conventional Arrayed Waveguide Grating (AWG) Devices for Multi Band Applications," Int. J. Comp. Intelligence Information Security,

2(2): 20-32, February.

Abd El-Naser AM, Ahmed NZR, Mahomud MEid (2011). "Rapid Progress of a Thermal Arrayed Waveguide Grating Module for Dense Wavelength Division Multiplexing Applications," Int. J. Computational Intelligence and Information Security, 2(2): 39-50, February.

Seo BJ, Fetterman HR (2006). "True-time-delay element in lossy environment using EO waveguides," IEEE Photon. Technol. Lett., 18(1): 10–12, January.

Abd El-Naser AM, Abd El-Fattah AS, Ahmed NZR (2009). "Matrices of the Thermal and Spectral Variations for the fabrication Materials Based Arrayed Waveguide Grating Devices," Int. J. Phy. Sci., 4(4): 205-211, April.

Allocation and Service Rules for the 71–76 GHz, 81–86 GHz, and 92–95 GHz Bands, Federal Communications Commission, Washington, DC, March. 2005.

Abd El-Naser AM, Abd El-Fattah AS, Ahmed NZR (2009). "Thermal Sensitivity Coefficients of the Fabrication Materials Based A thermal Arrayed Waveguide Grating (AWG) in Wide Area Dense Wavelength Division Multiplexing Optical Networks," Int. J. Eng. Technol. (IJET), 1(2): 131-139, June.

Abd El-Naser AM, Abd El-Fattah AS, Ahmed NZR (2009). "Characteristics of the Fabrication Materials Based Arrayed Waveguide Grating (AWG) in Passive Optical Networks (PONs)," Int. J. Mater. Sci. Res., 1(6): 89-97, June.

Tazawa H, Steier WH (2006). "Analysis of Ring Resonator Based Traveling Wave Modulators," IEEE Photon. Technol. Lett., 18(1): 211–213, January.

Abd El-Naser AM, Abd El-Fattah AS, Ahmed NZR (2009). "Study of the Thermal and Spectral Sensitivities of Organic-Inorganic Fabrication Materials Based Arrayed Waveguide Grating for Passive Optical Network Applications," J. Eng. Technol. Res., 1(5): 81-90, August.

Xu G, Liu Z, Ma J, Liu B, Ho S-T, Wang L, Zhu P, Marks TJ, Luo J, Jen AK (2005). "Organic Electro-optic Modulator Using Transparent Conducting Oxides as Electrodes," Opt. Expr., 13(2): 7380–7385, September.

Abd El-Naser AM, Ahmed NZR (2009). "Ultra Wide Band (UWB) of Optical Fiber Raman Amplifiers in Advanced Optical Communication Networks," J. Media Communication Studies, 1(4): 56-78, October.

Abd El-Naser AM, Mohammed AM, Ahmed NZR, Mohamoud MEid (2009). "Distributed Optical Raman Amplifiers in Ultra High Speed Long Haul Transmission Optical Fiber Telecommunication Networks," IJCNS Int. J. Comp. Network Security, 1(1): 1-8, October.

Abd El-Naser AM, Mohammed AM, Ahmed NZR, Amina MEl-nabawy (2011). "Unguided Nonlinear Optical Laser Pulses Propagate in Waters With Soliton Transmission Technique," IJMSE Int. J Multidisciplinary Sci. Eng., 2(1): 1-10, March.

Michalak M, Kuo Y, Nash F, Szep A, Caffey J, Payson P, Haas F, Mckeon B, Cook P, Brost G, Luo J, Jen A, Dalton L, Steier W (2006) "High Speed Polymer Modulator," IEEE Photon. Technol. Lett. 18(11): 1207–1209, June.

Abd El-Naser AM, Mohamed MEEl-H, Ahmed NZR, Mohammed SFT (2011). "High Transmission Performance of Radio over Fiber Systems over Traditional Optical Fiber Communication Systems Using Different Coding Formats for Long Haul" International Journal of Computer Science and Telecommunications (IJCST), 2(3): 29-42 June.

Abd El-Naser AM, Abd El-Fattah AS, Ahmed NZR, Hazem MH (2011). "Low Performance Characteristics of Optical Laser Diode Sources Based on NRZ Coding Formats under Thermal Irradiated Environments" Int. J. Comp. Sci. Telecommunications (IJCST), 2(2) 20-30, April.

2

Brain fingerprinting

Dhiraj Ahuja* and Bharat Singh

Department of Electrical and Electronics Engineering, YMCA University of Science and Technology, Faridabad-121006 (Haryana), India.

Brain finger printing is based on finding that the brain generates a unique brain wave pattern when a person encounters a familiar stimulus. Use of functional magnetic resonance imaging in lie detection derives from studies suggesting that persons asked to lie show different patterns of brain activity than they do when being truthful. Issues related to the use of such evidence in courts are discussed. In the field of criminology, a new lie detector has been developed in the United States of America called "brain finger printing". This invention is supposed to be the best lie detector available as on date and is said to detect even smooth criminals who pass the polygraph test (the conventional lie detector test) with ease. The new method employs brain waves, which are useful in detecting whether the person subjected to the test, remembers finer details of the crime. Even if the person willingly suppresses the necessary information, the brain wave is sure to trap him, according to the experts, who are very excited about the new kid on the block.

Keywords: Polygraph, electroencephalography, Farwell brain fingerprinting, electroencephalography (EEG) signals.

INTRODUCTION

Brain fingerprinting is an investigative technique which measures recognition of familiar stimuli by measuring electrical brain wave responses to words, phrases, or pictures that are presented on a computer screen. Brain fingerprinting was invented by Lawrence Farwell. Its theory explains that the suspect's reaction to the details of an event or activity will reflect if the suspect had prior knowledge of the event or activity (Farwell and Donchin, 1991). Farwell's brain fingerprinting originally used the well known P300 brain response to detect the brain's recognition of the known information (Farwell and Donchin, 1986, 1991; Farwell 1995a). Later Farwell discovered the "memory and encoding related multifaceted electroencephalographic response" (MERMER), which includes the P300 and additional features and is reported to provide a higher level of accuracy than the P300 alone (Farwell and Smith, 2001; Farwell, 1994, 1995b). One of the applications is lie detection. Farwell brain fingerprinting has been proven 100% accurate in over 120 tests, including tests on FBI agents, tests for a US intelligence agency and for the US Navy, and tests on real-life situations including actual crimes. In peer-reviewed publications Farwell and colleagues report over 99% accuracy in laboratory research (Farwell and Donchin, 1991; Farwell and Richardson, 2006b) and real-life field applications (Farwell and Smith, 2001; Farwell and Richardson, 2006a). In independent research William Iacono and others who followed identical or similar scientific protocols to Farwell's have reported a similar high level of accuracy (Allen and Lacono, 1997).

The technique can be applied only in situations where investigators have a sufficient amount of specific information about an event or activity that would be known only to the perpetrator and investigator. In this respect, brain fingerprinting is considered a type of guilty knowledge test, where the "guilty" party is expected to react strongly to the relevant detail of the event of activity. Existing (polygraph) procedures for assessing the validity of a suspect's "guilty" knowledge rely on measurement of autonomic arousal (for example, palm sweating and heart rate), while brain fingerprinting measures electrical brain activity via a fitted headband

*Corresponding author. E-mail: dahuja8978@yahoo.com.

Figure 1. Person being tested wearing a special headband with electronic sensors.

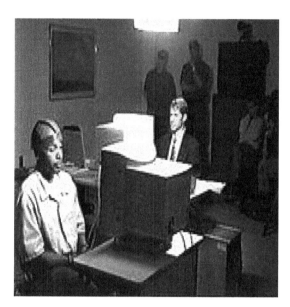

Figure 2. Victim's facial expression.

containing special sensors. Brain fingerprinting is said to be more accurate in detecting "guilty" knowledge distinct from the false positives of traditional polygraph methods, but this is hotly disputed by specialized researchers and has been criticized on a number of fronts (Abdollah, 2003; Fox 2006b). Although independent scientists who have used the same or similar methods as Farwell's brain fingerprinting have achieved similar, highly accurate results (Allen and Lacono, 1997; Harrington v. State), different methods have yielded different results. J. Peter Rosenfeld used P300-based tests incorporating fundamentally different methods, resulting in as low as chance accuracy (Rosenfeld et al., 2004) as well as susceptibility to countermeasures, and criticized brain fingerprinting based on the premise that the shortcomings of his alternative technique should generalize to all other techniques in which the P300 is among the brain responses measured, including brain fingerprinting.

OPERATION OF THE TECHNIQUE

The person to be tested wears a special headband with electronic sensors that measure the electroencephalography from several locations on the scalp (Figure 1). In order to calibrate the brain fingerprinting system, the testee is presented with a series of irrelevant stimuli, words, and pictures, and a series of relevant stimuli, words, and pictures. The test subject's brain response to these two different types of stimuli allow the tester to determine if the measured brain responses to test stimuli, called probes, are more similar to the relevant or irrelevant responses.

The technique uses the well known fact that an electrical signal known as P300 is emitted from an individual's brain approximately 300 ms after it is confronted with a stimulus of special significance, for example, a rare vs. a common stimulus or a stimulus the subject is asked to count (Gaillard and Ritter, 1983; Picton, 1988). The novel interpretation in brain fingerprinting is to look for P300 as response to stimuli related to the crime in question for example a murder weapon or a victim's face (Figures 2 and 3).

Because it is based on EEG signals, the system does not require the testee to issue verbal responses to questions or stimuli.

Brain fingerprinting uses cognitive brain responses and do not depend on the emotions of the subject, nor is it affected by emotional responses (Farwell, 1994). Brain fingerprinting is fundamentally different from the polygraph (lie-detector), which measures emotion-based physiological signals such as heart rate, sweating, and blood pressure (Farwell and Smith , 2001; Farwell 1992a, 1995a). Also, unlike polygraph testing, it does not attempt to determine whether or not the subject is lying or telling the truth. Rather, it measures the subject's brain response to relevant words, phrases, or pictures to detect whether or not the relevant information is stored in the subject's brain (Farwell and Smith, 2001; Simon, 2005; Harrington v. State).

Four phases of Farwell brain fingerprinting

In fingerprinting and DNA fingerprinting, evidence is recognized and collected at the crime scene, and preserved properly until a suspect is apprehended, is scientifically compared with evidence on the person of the suspect to detect a match that would place the suspect at the crime scene. Farwell Brain fingerprinting works similarly, except that the evidence collected both at the crime scene and on the person of the suspect (that is, in the brain as revealed by electrical brain responses) is informational evidence rather than physical evidence. There are four stages to Farwell brain fingerprinting, which are similar to the steps in fingerprinting and DNA fingerprinting:

1. Brain fingerprinting crime scene evidence collection;
2. Brain fingerprinting brain evidence collection;
3. Brain fingerprinting computer evidence analysis; and
4. Brain fingerprinting scientific result.

In the crime scene evidence collection, an expert in Farwell brain fingerprinting examines the crime scene and other evidence connected with the crime to identify detail of the crime that would be known only to the perpetrator. The expert then conducts the brain evidence collection in order to determine whether or not the evidence from the crime scene matches evidence stored in the brain of the suspect. In the computer evidence analysis, the Farwell

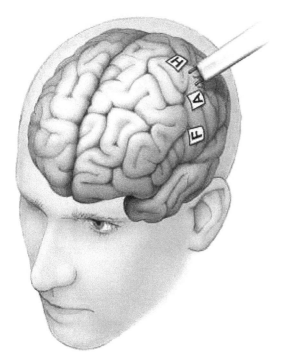

Figure 3. Victim's stimulus.

brain fingerprinting system makes a mathematical determination as to whether or not this specific evidence is stored in the brain, and computes a statistical confidence for that determination. This determination and statistical confidence constitute the scientific result of Farwell brain fingerprinting: either "information present" – the details of the crime are stored in the brain of the suspect – or "information absent" – the details of the crime are not stored in the brain of the suspect (Figure 4).

APPLICATIONS

Counter terrorism

Brain fingerprinting can help in addressing the following critical elements in the fight against terrorism:

1. Aid in determining who has participated in terrorist acts, directly or indirectly.
2. Aid in identifying trained terrorists with the potential to commit future terrorist acts, even if they are in a "sleeper" cell and have not been active for years.
3. Help to identify people who have knowledge or training in banking, finance or communications and who are associated with terrorist teams and acts.
4. Help to determine if an individual is in a leadership role within a terrorist organization.

In a terrorist act, there may or may not be peripheral evidence such as fingerprints or DNA, but the brain of the perpetrator is always there, planning, executing, and recording the crime (Figure 3). The terrorist has knowledge of organizations, training and plans that an

innocent person does not have. Until the invention of Brain fingerprinting testing, there was no scientific way to detect this fundamental difference.

Brain fingerprinting testing provides an accurate, economical and timely solution to the central problem in the fight against terrorism. It is now possible to determine scientifically whether or not a person has terrorist training and knowledge of terrorist activities. With this technology, now, terrorists and those supporting terrorism can be identified quickly and accurately.

A brain fingerprinting test can determine with an extremely high degree of accuracy those who are involved with terrorist activity and those who are not. In a study with the FBI, Dr. Farwell and FBI scientist Drew Richardson, former chief of the FBI's chem-bio-nuclear counterterrorism unit, used brain fingerprinting to show that test subjects from specific groups could be identified by detecting specific knowledge which would only be known to members of those groups (Farwell, 1993; Farwell and Richardson, 2006b). A group of 17 FBI agents and 4 non-agents were exposed to stimuli (words, phrases, and acronyms) that were flashed on a computer screen. The probe stimuli contained information that would be common knowledge only to someone with FBI training. Brain fingerprinting correctly distinguished the FBI agents from the non-agents.

Criminal justice

A critical task of the criminal justice system is to determine who has committed a crime. The key difference between a guilty party and an innocent suspect is that the perpetrator of the crime has a record of the crime stored in their brain, and the innocent suspect does not. Until the invention of Brain Finger printing testing, there was no scientifically valid way to detect this fundamental difference. This exciting technology gives the judge and jury new, scientifically valid evidence to help them arrive at their decision. DNA evidence and fingerprints are available in only about 1% of major crimes. It is estimated that Brain fingerprinting testing will apply in approximately 60 to 70% of these major crimes. The impacts on the criminal justice system will be profound. The potential now exists to significantly improve the speed and accuracy of the entire system, from investigations to parole hearings. Brain Fingerprinting testing will be able to dramatically reduce the costs associated with investigating and prosecuting innocent people and allow law enforcement professionals to concentrate on suspects who have verifiable, detailed knowledge of the crimes. Brain Fingerprinting testing was also "instrumental in obtaining a confession and guilty plea" from serial killer James B. Grinder, according to Sheriff Robert Dawson of Macon County, Missouri. In August 1999, Dr. Farwell conducted a brain fingerprinting test on Grinder, showing that information stored in his brain matched the details of the murder of Julie Helton

USING BRAIN WAVES TO DETECT GUILT

Brain fingerprinting uses brain waves to test memory. A crime suspect is given words or images in a context that would be known only to police or the person who committed the crime.

HOW IT WORKS
A suspect is tested by looking at three kinds of information represented by different colored lines:

— **Red:** Information the suspect is expected to know.
— **Green:** Information not known to suspect.
— **Blue:** Information of the crime that only perpetrator would

NOT GUILTY
Because the blue and green lines closely correlate, suspect does not have critical knowledge of the crime.

GUILTY
Because the blue and red lines closely correlate, suspect has critical knowledge of the crime.

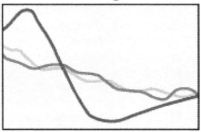
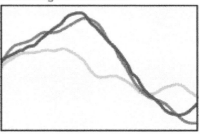

For more information see: www.brainwavescience.com.

SEATTLE POST-INTELLIGENCER

Figure 4. Use of Brain waves to detect guilt.

(Dalbey, 1999). Faced with a certain conviction and almost certain death sentence, Grinder then pled guilty to the rape and murder of Julie Helton in exchange for a life sentence without parole. He is currently serving that sentence and has also confessed to the murders of three other women.

Medical

'Brain fingerprinting' is the patented technology that can measure objectively, for the first time, how memory and cognitive functioning of Alzheimer sufferers are affected by medications. A 30 min test involves wearing a headband with built-in electrodes; technicians then present words, phrases and images that are both known and unknown to the patient to determine whether information that should be in the brain is still there. When presented with familiar information, the brain responds by producing MERMERs, specific increases in neuron activity. The technician can use this response to measure how quickly information is disappearing from the brain and whether the drugs they are taking are slowing down the process.

In a study funded by the CIA, Farwell and colleagues

(Farwell and Richardson, 2006b) used brain fingerprinting to detect which individuals had US Navy military medical training. All 30 subjects were correctly determined to have or not to have the specific information regarding military medicine stored in their brains.

Additional applications

In advertising, Brain fingerprinting laboratories will offer significant advances in measuring campaign and media effectiveness. Most advertising programs today are evaluated subjectively using focus groups. We will be able to offer significantly more advanced, scientific methods to help determine the effectiveness of campaigns and be very cost competitive with current methodologies. This technology will be able to help determine what information is actually retained in memory by individuals. For example, in a branding campaign do people remember the brand, the product, etc. and how do the results vary with demographics? We will also be able to measure the comparative effectiveness of multiple media types.

In the insurance industry, brain fingerprinting laboratories will be able to be helpful to reduce the incidence of insurance fraud by determining if an individual has knowledge of fraudulent or criminal acts. The same type of testing can help to determine if an individual has specific knowledge related to computer crimes where there is typically no witness or physical evidence. In a CIA-funded study, brain fingerprinting correctly detected which individuals had participated in specific real-life events, some of which were crimes, based on the record stored in their brains. Accuracy again was 100% (Farwell and Richardson, 2006a). Dr. Farwell collaborated with FBI scientist Sharon Smith in a further study in which brain fingerprinting detected real-life events that was published in the Journal of Forensic Sciences (Farwell and Smith, 2001).

COMPARISON WITH OTHER TECHNOLOGIES

Conventional fingerprinting and DNA match physical evidence from a crime scene with evidence on the person of the perpetrator. Similarly, brain fingerprinting matches informational evidence from the crime scene with evidence stored in the brain. Fingerprints and DNA are available in only 1% of crimes. The brain is always there, planning, executing, and recording the suspect's actions.

Brain fingerprinting has nothing to do with lie detection. Rather, it is a scientific way to determine if someone has committed a specific crime or other act. No questions are asked and no answers are given during Farwell brain fingerprinting. As with DNA and fingerprints, the results are the same whether the person has lied or told the truth at any time.

Admissibility of brain fingerprinting in court

The admissibility of brain fingerprinting in court has not yet been fully established. The following well established features of brain fingerprinting, however, will be relevant when the question of admissibility is tested in court. 1) Brain fingerprinting has been thoroughly and scientifically tested. 2) The theory and application of brain fingerprinting have been subject to peer review and publication. 3) The rate of error is extremely low -- virtually nonexistent -- and clear standards governing scientific techniques of operation of the technology have been established and published. 4) The theory and practice of brain fingerprinting have gained general acceptance in the relevant scientific community. 5) Brain fingerprinting is non-invasive and non-testimonial. There are examples where court has considered the brain finger printing reports. Farwell's brain fingerprinting has been ruled admissible as evidence in court in the reversal of the murder conviction of Terry Harrington (Harrington v. State, Farwell and Makeig, 2005). Following a hearing on post-conviction relief on November 14, 2000, an Iowa District Court held that Dr. Farwell's brain fingerprinting

P-300 test results were admissible as scientific evidence as defined in Congress Ruling 702 and in the Daubert standard. Harrington was freed by the Iowa Supreme Court on constitutional grounds.

LIMITATIONS OF BRAIN FINGERPRINTING

1. Brain fingerprinting detects information-processing brain responses that reveal what information is stored in the subject's brain. It does not detect how that information got there, be it a witness or a perpetrator.
2. Brain fingerprinting detects only information, and not intent. The fact that the suspect knows the uncontested facts of the circumstance does not tell us which party's version of the intent is correct (Simon, 2005).
3. Brain fingerprinting is not applicable for general screening, for example, in general pre-employment or employee screening wherein any number of undesirable activities or intentions may be relevant. If the investigators have no idea what crime or undesirable act the individual may have committed, there is no way to structure appropriate stimuli to detect the telltale knowledge that would result from committing the crime. Brain fingerprinting can, however, be used for specific screening or focused screening, when investigators have some idea what they are looking for. For example, brain fingerprinting can be used to detect whether a person has knowledge that would identify him as an FBI agent, an Al-Qaeda-trained terrorist, a member of a criminal organization or terrorist cell, or a bomb maker (Farwell and Richardson, 2006b).
4. Brain fingerprinting does not detect lies. It simply detects information. No questions are asked or answered during a brain fingerprinting test. The subject neither lies nor tells the truth during a brain fingerprinting test, and the outcome of the test is unaffected by whether he has lied or told the truth at any other time. The outcome of "information present" or "information absent" depends on whether the relevant information is stored in the brain, and not on what the subject says about it (Farwell, 1994; Simon, 2005; PBS 2004).
5. Just as all witness testimony depends on the memory of the witness, brain fingerprinting depends on the memory of the subject.
6. Like all forensic science techniques, brain fingerprinting depends on the evidence-gathering process which lies outside the realm of science to provide the evidence to be scientifically tested. A DNA test determines only whether two DNA samples match, it does not determine whether the investigator did an effective job of collecting DNA from the crime scene. Similarly, a brain fingerprinting test determines only whether or not the information stored in the suspect's brain matches the information contained in the probe stimuli.
7. Brain fingerprinting is not a substitute for effective

investigation on the part of the investigator or for common sense and good judgment on the part of the judge and jury (PBS 2004).

REFERENCES

AbdollahT (2003). Brain Fingerprinting – Picture-perfect crimes. Berkeley Med. J. Issues, Spring 2003. Accessed July 20, 2008.

Allen JJB, Lacono WG (1997). A comparison of methods for the analysis of event-related potentials in deception detection. Psychophysiol., 34: 234-240.

Dalbey B (1999). Brain Fingerprinting Testing Traps Serial Killer in Missouri. The Fairfield Ledger. Fairfield, IA, August, p. 1.

Farwell LA, Donchin E (1986). The brain detector: P300 in the detection of deception. Psychophysiology, 24: 434.

Farwell LA, Donchin E (1991). The Truth Will Out: Interrogative Polygraphy ("Lie Detection") With Event-Related Brain Potentials. Psychophysiol., 28: 531-547.

Farwell LA (1992a). The brain-wave information detection (BID) system: A new paradigm for psycho physiological detection of information (unpublished doctoral dissertation). Urbana-Champaign (IL): University of Illinois.

Farwell LA (1993). Brain MERMERs: Detection of FBI Agents and crime-relevant information with the Farwell MERA system. Proceedings of the International Security Systems Symposium, Washington, D.C.

Farwell LA (1994). Method and Apparatus for Multifaceted Electroencephalographic Response Analysis (MERA). U.S. Patent #5,363,858, Nov. 15.

Farwell LA (1995a). Method and Apparatus for Truth Detection. U.S. Patent #5,406,956, April 18.

Farwell LA (1995b). Method for Electroencephalographic Information Detection. U.S. Patent #5,467,777, Nov. 21.

Farwell LA, Smith SS (2001). Using Brain MERMER Testing to Detect Concealed Knowledge Despite Efforts to Conceal. J. Forens. Sci., 46(1): 135-143.

Farwell LA, Makeig T (2005). Farwell Brain Fingerprinting in the case of Harrington v. State. Open Court X, 3: 7-10. Indiana State Bar Association.

Farwell LA, Richardson DC (2006a). Brain Fingerprinting in Field onditions. Psychophysiology, 43: 5 S37-S38.

Farwell LA, Richardson DC (2006b). Brain Fingerprinting in Laboratory Conditions. Psychophysiol., 43: S38.

Fox C (2006b). Brain Fingerprinting Skepticism. American Observer, March 29.

Gaillard AKW, Ritter W (1983). Tutorials in event-related potential research: endogenous components. Amsterdam: North-Holland.

Harrington v. State, Case No. PCCV 073247. Iowa District Court for Pottawattamie County, March 5, 2001.

PBS Innovation Series (2004). Brain Fingerprinting May 4, 2004. Brain Fingerprinting: Ask the Experts. Accessed July 20, 2008.

Picton TW (1988). Handbook of electroencephalography and clinical neurophysiology: Human event-related potentials. 3: Amsterdam: Elsevier.

Rosenfeld JP, Soskins M, Bosh G, Ryan A (2004). Simple, Effective Counter measures to P300-based Tests of Detection of Concealed Information. Psychophysiol., 41: 205–219.

Simon S (2005). What you don't know can't hurt you. Law Enforcement Technology, Sept., 2005.

3

Design and simulation study of a simple ion injector

M. M. Abdelrahman*, N.I. Basal and S.G. Zakhary

Accelerators and Ion Sources Department, Nuclear Research Center, Cairo Egypt.

The stated purpose of this manuscript is to study the parameters of a single-gap accelerator system with a view to optimizing the transport of a beam of argon ions. A study is made for the main factors that must be considered on the design of an ion injector taking into account the appropriate design of the single gap accelerator column by doing such study both analytically and with ion beam simulation. These study shows the dependence of the optimal voltage ratio which is related to the minimum beam emittance depends on the column dimension. Study of analytical calculations was done without space charge while simulation processes with space charge effect. Study of optical ion beam properties for a single gap accelerating column was done by using a SIMION computer program. A series of simulation studies were made in order to determine optimum conditions for acceleration of space-charge-dominated argon ion trajectories with incident energy of 50 keV from a distance 150 mm of the ion source at constant gradient acceleration system.

Key words: SIMION computer program, single gap tube acceleration system, beam emittance, injector system.

INTRODUCTION

Along with the development of computer and calculation techniques, numerical simulation has been a main tool to assist design and research of ion beam system. With high accuracy and velocity, numerical computation can study the effects of ion extraction system on characteristics of ion beams such as ion beam emittance. Also, simulation of ion beam injection into the accelerating tube for appropriate design of tube radius which determines the accelerator acceptance to match the beam emittance of the beam that exits from the ion source. Also, the simulation of beam trajectory inside the accelerating column is necessary to avoid ion beam aberration such as crossover inside and outside of the accelerating tube. The applications of accelerators include various branches of science and technology, medical treatment, and industrial processing. Accelerator scientists proposed many advanced technologies to produce beams with qualities required for each application (Lee 2000; Humphires 2002; Prakash et al 2012). Computer modeling of charged particle beam is

important part in investigation of processes that take place in different electro-physical equipments and has been used for about 50 years (Litovko and Oks 2006). The aim of these simulations is always to investigate the beam quality, which is necessary to adjust the beam conditions for the required applications. In this work, beam simulation is carried out to reveal the influence of the space charge effect on both the beam emittance and beam diameter. Also, influence of the tube diameter on the ion beam quality (beam emittance and beam diameter) was studied. Indeed, the influence of both charge state of the argon and mass of different elements on beam emittance and beam diameter for the singly charged argon ion trajectories was investigated. Samples of ion beam simulation with potential distributions inside the accelerating column with different tube diameters of 15, 20, and 30 mm were performed.

OPTIMIZATION OF THE ION BEAM CHARACTERISTICS (INTENSITY AND EMITTANCE) PRODUCED FROM THE ION SOURCE

To keep aberration as low as possible, the aspect ratio S

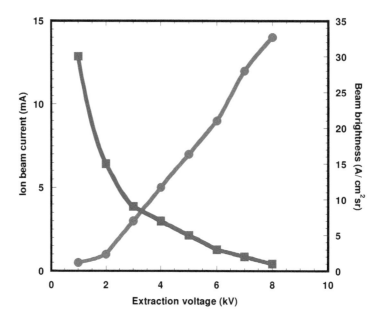

Figure 1. Influence of the extraction voltage on both the extracted ion current and beam brightness.

(the ratio of aperture radius to the electrode distance) should be of the order. S = 0.5, with the breakdown limit in mind (d in mm, V in kV); d $\geq$ 0.015 V$^{1/2}$, the extracted current is given by (Spadtke 1992):

$$I_{Ch} = \frac{\pi}{9} \, \chi \, V^{3/2}$$

Where

$$\chi = 2\varepsilon_0 \sqrt{\frac{2q}{m}}$$

On the other hand the emittance ε can be estimated to first order by the aperture radius and a certain divergence angle of the beam if a waist is assumed at the exit of the extraction system:

$$\varepsilon = \alpha \, r_0,$$

as mentioned before the aperture radius depends on the extraction voltage with the aspect ratio:

$\varepsilon = \alpha S d$, using the breakdown limit, the emittance can be estimated

$$\varepsilon = 2.37 \times 10^{-7} \alpha_0 \, V^{3/2}$$

The brightness is defined as, $B = I/\Omega$ A, where I is the current, A the area from which it is emitted, and Ω the solid angle into which the current is emitted.; we have (Spakudo and Hashi 1996):

$$B = \frac{1.24 x 10^{13} \varepsilon_0 \sqrt{2q/m}}{\alpha_0^2 V^{3/2}}$$

Figure 1 shows the influence of the extraction voltage on both the beam current and beam brightness extracted from hydrogen with assumed beam divergence α_0=20 m.rad (Kunze et al 2003). It might be surprising that the current increases with the extraction voltage, whereas the brightness decreases with the extraction voltage. These dependences make clear why the optimization of extraction systems is necessary.

ESTIMATION OF THE OPTIMAL VALUE OF THE ACCELERATING FIELD FOR BEST BEAM FOCUSING AND TRANSPORT WITHOUT ABERRATION

Estimation of the optimal value of the accelerating field can be obtained from studying the motion of the ion beam through a single accelerating gap. From the study one can deduce the influence of the accelerating field on tracing the beam line within the gap and on the transverse beam emittance at the gap exit. The variation of the cross section of a beam propagating along the Z axis of an accelerating column shown in Figure 2 can be determined using Equation 1 (Wilson and Brewer 1973, Abdelaziz et al

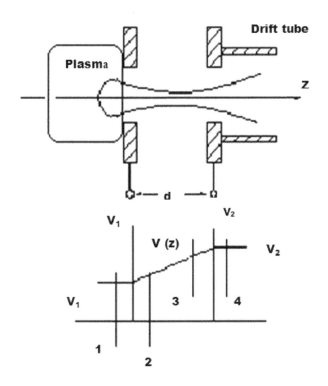

Figure 2. Schematic diagram of the single gap accelerating column with the variation of the potential distribution along the beam line.

1996, Abdelrahman and Zakhary 2011):

$$\frac{\partial^2 r}{\partial z^2} + \frac{V_o}{2V_o}\frac{\partial r}{\partial z} + \frac{V_o}{4V_o} = -Q\frac{r}{4V_o\varepsilon_o}$$

where V_o is the potential on the Z axis and the primes denotes the derivatives with respect to Z axis, Q represents the space charge density (which is assumed to be uniform over the beam cross section) and ε_o is the dielectric permittivity of the free space . Neglecting the space charge effect, the right hand side of Equation 1 is set equal to zero. This equation was solved to determine the ray path between two planes representing the input and output of the accelerating column shown in Figure 2, located at a given distance apart (d) a long the Z axis. Defining the input and output of an ion optical element (r_1, r_1, V_1) refer to condition of beam radius, half angle of beam divergence, and the voltage at the input, (r_4, r_4, V_4) are the conditions of the beam at the outlet . The solution is given by (Kirstein et al 1967, Reiser 1985):

Tracing the beam line within the gap (as shown in Figure 3) shows decrease of the beam outlet radius with the increase

$$\begin{bmatrix} r_4 \\ \sqrt{V_4}\,r_4 \end{bmatrix} = M_{14} \begin{bmatrix} r_1 \\ \sqrt{V_1}\,r_1 \end{bmatrix}$$

where

$$M_{14} = \begin{bmatrix} \dfrac{3\sqrt{V_1} - \sqrt{V_2}}{2\sqrt{V_1}} & \dfrac{2d}{\sqrt{V_1} + \sqrt{V_2}} \\[4mm] \dfrac{3(V_2 - V_1)(\sqrt{V_1} - \sqrt{V_2})}{8d\sqrt{V_1}\sqrt{V_2}} & \dfrac{3\sqrt{V_1} - \sqrt{V_1}}{2\sqrt{V_2}} \end{bmatrix}$$

of the accelerating ratio up to a certain optimal value. Higher than the optimal value the beam radius starts to increase and the aberration appears. Figure 3 shows the variation of the beam outlet radius with the accelerating ratio and Figure 3 also shows the variation of the transverse emittance of the beam outlet from a single gap with the voltage acceleration ratio applied to the gap. The optimal value of the accelerating ratio is found at the minimum beam emittance and with the beam transport without aberration (cross over).

ION BEAM SIMULATION FOR SINGLE GAP ACCELERATION COLUMN

A series of simulation studies were made in order to determine optimum conditions for acceleration of space-charge-dominated argon gas with different incident energies at constant gradient acceleration system. The curvature of the plasma-emission surface tends to converge/diverge extracted ion beams. The optimum radius of curvature can be achieved by carefully balancing the plasma density in relation to the strength of the electric field. Under this condition, the angular divergence is minimum. As clearly illustrated, the curvature of the ion-emission boundary is critically dependent on the position of the extraction electrode relative to the emission aperture for fixed plasma density, charge-state distribution, and extraction-potential difference. The space charge force acts as a diverging force because particles of the same charge repel each other. The influence of space charge effects for both the quality and intensity of the extracted ion beams.

SIMION 3 D Version 7.0 (Dahl 2000, Dahl et al 1990) is a software package primarily used to calculate electric fields and the trajectories of charged particles in those fields when given a configuration of electrodes with voltages and particle initial conditions, including optional RF (quasistatic), magnetic field, and collisional effects. This program provides extensive supporting functionality

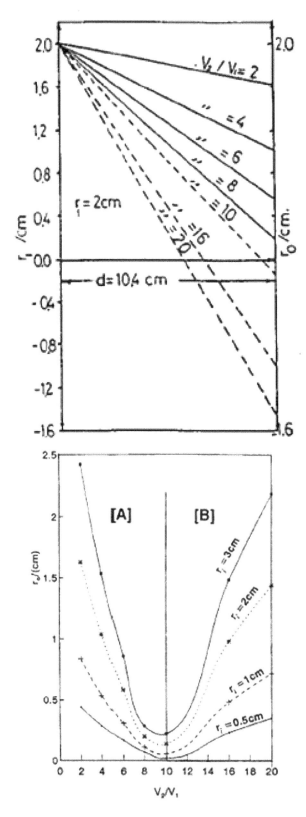

Figure 3. Schematic diagram of the single gap accelerating column with the variation of the potential distribution along the beam line

Table 1. Relation between voltage ratio and beam emittance and beam radius for a single gap accelerating column.

Voltage ratio (V_2 / V_1)	Beam emittance/ 10 (cm mrad)	Beam radius (mm)
2	0.19	7.39
4	0.04	6.12
6	0.15	3.65
8	0.38	0.68
10	2.17	8.64
12	7.30	20.95
14	26.91	41.75
16	87.36	83

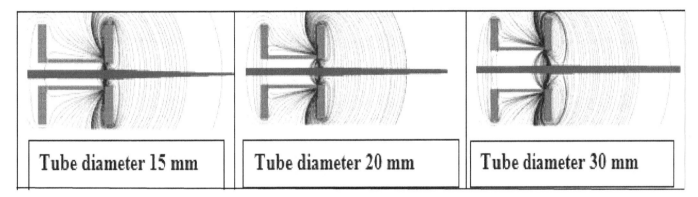

Tube diameter 15 mm | Tube diameter 20 mm | Tube diameter 30 mm

Figure 4. Single gap accelerating column as simulated by SIMION computer program for different tube diameters.

in geometry definition, user programming, data recording, and visualization. Simulation of the singly charged argon ion trajectories for flat plasma was studied with and without space charge effect using a model of constant gradient acceleration system with the aid of SIMION computer program. The simulation process was carried out at an assumption of a constant plasma density. In this work, beam simulation is carried out to reveal the influence of the space charge effect on the beam emittance and beam radius. Also, influence of the incident energy on the ion beam quality (beam emittance and beam radius) was studied. Indeed, the influence of the tube diameter on beam emittance for the singly charged argon ion trajectories was investigated.

Table 1 shows the relation between the voltage ratio applied to the single gap accelerating column system and both beam emittance and beam radius for a single charged argon ions with incident energy of 50 keV from a distance 150 mm of the ion source. The first one of the single gap accelerating column was applied on a fixed voltage of 5 kV; where the second one was changed according to obtain several of voltage ratios of 2, 4, 6, 8,10,12,14 and 16. It is clear from this table, minimum beam emittance was found at voltage ratio of 4 (output

voltage applied is 20 kV) whereas maximum one at voltage ratio of 16 (output voltage applied is 80 kV). Also, minimum beam radius was found at voltage ratio of 8 (output voltage applied 40 kV), whereas maximum one at 16 (output voltage applied is 80 kV).

Sample of ion beam simulation inside the accelerating column with different input diameters of 15, 20, and 30mm (Figure 4 a, b, c) were performed. This figure shows that the influence of variation of input tube diameter on both the beam emittance and beam radius for the argon ion trajectories passed through the single gap accelerating column system. It was seen that from this figure, minimum of beam emittance and beam radius is obtained at input diameter of 15 mm. This can be attributed to the variation of the electric field inside the accelerating tube.

Figure 5 a and b show the influence of the voltage ratio on both the beam emittance and beam diameter of the argon ion trajectories passed through the accelerator system. It was seen that from this figure, minimum beam emittance and beam diameter is obtained, at 4 cm mrad, 8 mm, respectively. This can be attributed to the variation of the electric field inside the accelerating tube. Figure 6 a and b show the influence of the inner tube diameter on

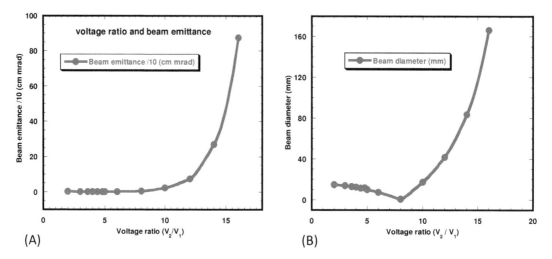

Figure 5. Influence of the voltage ratio on both beam emittance and beam diameter of the accelerator system for singly charged argon ion trajectories with space charge of 0.1mA. (A) Beam emittance with voltage ratio. (B) Beam diameter with voltage ratio.

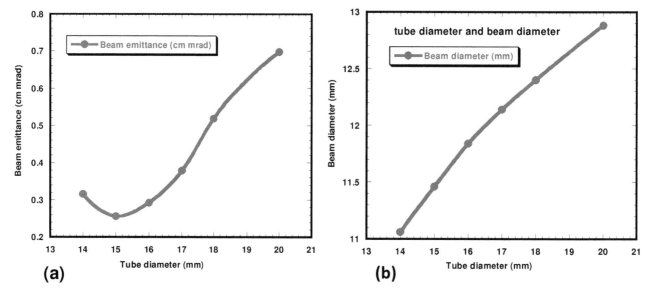

Figure 6. Beam emittance and beam diameter as a function of the diameter of the accelerator system (A) Beam emittance with tube diameter and (B) Beam diameter with tube diameter.

both the beam emittance and beam diameter of the argon ion trajectories passed through the accelerator system. It was found that, minimum beam emittance at diameter of 15 mm is gotten. An increase of the inner tube diameter was accompanied by an increase of the beam diameter.

Space charge depends on the geometry of the electrodes, applied potentials and ion current. Therefore, the change of the ion current has a clear influence where other parameters were fixed. The space charge force charge repel each other. It was found that space charge

has no influence on the ion beam envelope at currents of micro amperes.

The space charge started to have a clear influence on the ion beam envelope at currents of 1×10^{-4} A (Figure 7 a, b). Space charge depends on the geometry of the electrodes, applied potentials and ion current. Therefore the change of the ion current has a clear influence where other parameters were fixed. The space charge force acts as a diverging force because particles of the same charge repel each other.

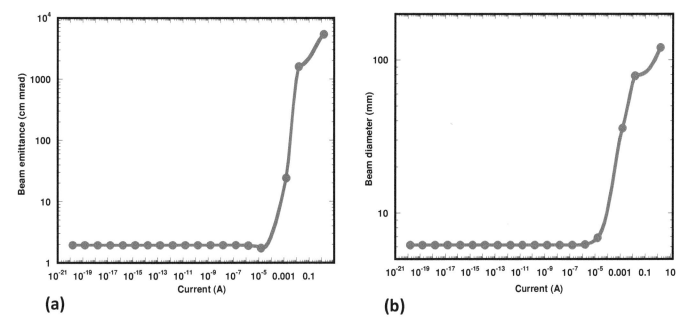

Figure 7. Influence of space charge on both beam emittance and beam diameter of the accelerator system for singly charged argon ion trajectories (a) Beam emittance with space charge and (b) Beam diameter with space charge.

Influence of the charge states of argon atom on both the beam emittance and beam diameter for the accelerator system has been investigated with current of 0.1 mA (Figure 8 a, b). Minimum beam emittance has been obtained for argon of highly charged ions (charge = 5^+). The same behaviour was found for the beam diameter where, minimum beam diameter was obtained for a highly charged argon ions (charge = 5^+).

Influence of atomic masses of different elements (hydrogen, helium, lithium, carbon, nitrogen, oxygen, neon and finally argon) on both the beam emittance and beam diameter for the single gap tube accelerator system has been investigated (Figure 9 a, b). It was found that, an increase of the atomic masses of the chosen elements was accompanied by an increase of the beam emittance and then started to have a minimum for argon.

Whereas for beam diameter, an increase of the chosen elements was accompanied by a decrease of the beam diameter and started to have a minimum for carbon and then increased to the highest beam diameter and finally have a minimum point for argon atom.

Conclusion

Study of optical ion beam properties for a single gap accelerating column was done by using a SIMION computer program. A series of simulation studies were made in order to determine optimum conditions for acceleration of space-charge-dominated argon ion

trajectories with incident energy of 50 keV from a distance 150 mm of the ion source at constant gradient acceleration system. The new achievement given by both beam simulation and analytical treatment are useful tools for designing of constant gradient acceleration system. The influence of the voltage ratio on both the beam emittance and beam diameter of the argon ion trajectories passed through the accelerator system was done. It was seen that, minimum beam emittance and beam diameter is obtained, at 4 cm mrad, 8 mm, respectively. Also, the influence of the inner tube diameter on both the beam emittance and beam diameter of the argon ion trajectories passed through the accelerator system. It was found that, minimum beam emittance at diameter of 15 mm is gotten. An increase of the inner tube diameter was accompanied by an increase of the beam diameter. Furthermore, influence of the charge states of argon atom on both the beam emittance and beam diameter for the accelerator system has been investigated with current of 0.1 mA. Minimum beam emittance was obtained for argon of highly charged ions is studied for the accelerator system. Minimum beam emittance is found at a current of 10^{-4} A, and started to have a large effect at current higher than 10^{-4} A. Minimum beam diameter for the system is also found at a current of 10^{-5} A, and is started to have a large effect at current higher than 10^{-5} A. Influence of atomic masses of different elements on both the beam emittance and beam for the accelerator system is investigated. Minimum beam emittance for accelerator system is obtained for argon (m

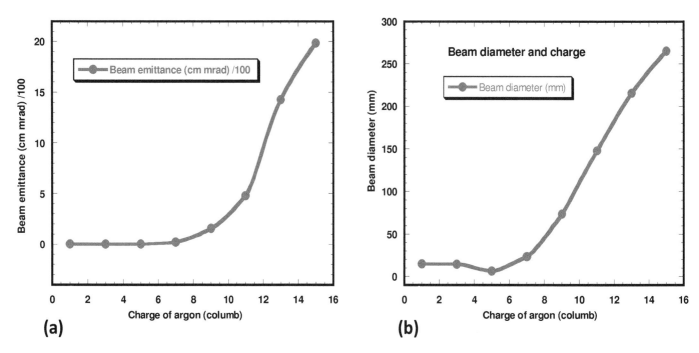

Figure 8. Beam emittance and beam diameter as a function of the charge states of argon atom (a)   Beam emittance with charge **and** (b) Beam diameter with charge

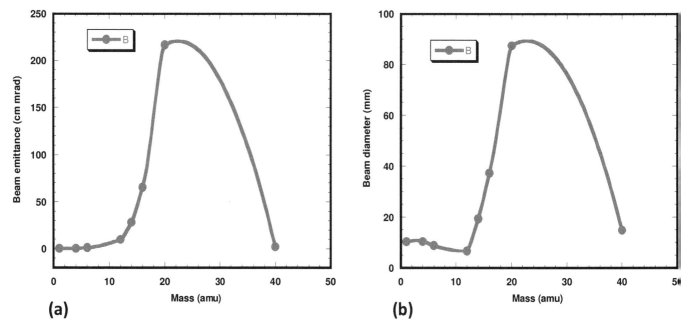

Figure 9. Beam emittance and beam diameter as a function of atomic mass for different elements (a)   Beam emittance with atomic mass and (b) Beam diameter with atomic mass.

= 40). The influences of inner tube diameter and accelerating voltage ratio slightly have the same effect on output beam emittance.

ACKNOWLEDGMENTS

Authors are grateful to both reviewers for their valuable

comments towards improving the quality of the work. The authors gratefully acknowledge Prof. M. E. Abdelaziz, Ex-President of Egypitation Atomic Energy Authority, Egypt for his valuable discussions and scientific help.

REFERENCES

Abdelaziz ME, Zakhary SG, Ghanem AA (1996). Factors affecting the design of a single gap accelerating column, "Rev. Sci. Instrum." 67:3.

Abdelrahman MM, Zakhary SG (2011). Proposed design of DC low voltage acceleration system. Int. J. Phys. Sci. 6:5492-5497.

Dahl DA (2000). SIMION 3 D Version 7.0 User's Manual INEEL–95 / 0403, Idaho National Engineering and Environmental Laboratory; I D 83415.

Dahl DA, Delmoreand JE, Appelhans AD (1990). SIMION PC/PS2 electrostatic lens design program. Rev. Sci. Instrum. 61:607.

Humphries S (2002), Charged Particle Beams, John Wiley and Sons, USA.

Kirstein PT, Kino CS, Waters WE (1967). Space Charge Flow, McGraw-Hill, New York.

Kunze HJ, El-Khalafawy T, Hegazy H (2003).First Cairo conf. on plasma physics and applications. p. 34.

Lee SY (2000). Accelerator Physics, World Scientific Publishing Co. Pte. Ltd, 5 Toh Tuck Link, Singapore 596224.

Litovko I, Oks E (2006). 33rd EPS Conference on Plasma Phys. Rome, 19 - 23 June ECA .30l(2):104.

Prakash NP, Amit RP (2012). Design of a superconducting low beta niobium resonator J. Phys. 78:4.

Reiser M (1985). Particle Accelerator Conf., Accelerator Engineering and Technology, Vancouver, Canada. p. 3.

Spadtke P (1992), Numerical simulation of ion beam related problems, Rev. Sci. Instrum. 63:(4)2647-2651.

Spakudo P, Hashi K (1996). Exact energy values of "low-energy ion beams' Rev. Sci. Instrum. 67:3.

Wilson RG, Brewer GR (1973). "Ion Beams with Applications to Ion Implantation", John Wiley and Sons, New York.

4

Using structured analysis for the control of real-time systems

M. N. LAKHOUA

Department of Electrical Engineering, ESTI, University of Carthage, Tunisia Laboratory of Analysis, Design and Command of Systems, ENIT, Tunisia. E-mail: MohamedNajeh.Lakhoua@enit.rnu.tn.

After a presentation of the real time system analysis and design, we present the Structured Analysis for Real Time Systems, or SA-RT. This graphical design notation is focusing on analyzing the functional behaviour and information flow through a system. In fact, the modeling of the real time systems helps us to understand its working, without eliminating its complexity. Then, we present the graphic and textual formalism of the SA-RT method on the one hand and we apply this method on a practical case of an ABS braking system, on the other hand.

Key words: Real time systems, SA-RT method, ABS braking system.

INTRODUCTION

Domains of development of real time systems are various. Classically, one recovers the levels network and transport of the heterogeneous communication systems in the domain of telecommunications; the embarked software; the aerial control for what concerns the aerospace domain; the follow-up of production processes or the control of the manufacture in factories; electronics or the convivial software interfacings for the user in the domain of the micro computing (Dorseuil and Pillot, 1993).

The first essential characteristic of a real time system must be its reliability and its safety. Two parameters are to consider: the frequency of failings and consequences of these last in presence of no controlled entrance data (Gomaa, 1994; Ryan and Heavey, 2006).

An operator's behavior facing a critical situation is not still foreseeable. If techniques of redundancies of information and resources have the tendency to encourage a reliable and sure working, they degrade in counterpart the temporal performances of the whole of the system. Otherwise, difficulties of test in true size remain an essential question for teams of development working on projects of big span (Jane and Liu, 2000; Tschirhart, 1990).

In real time systems, the formal methods enable us to clear essential functionalities of the system to achieve (Cottet, 2005). For this type of real time system, we can identify five essential phases in the development of the system: the development of the load notebook; the functional analysis phase; the design phase; the coding phase; the test and clarification phase.

The object of this article is to present the interest of the structured analysis approach based on the method SA-RT (Structured Analysis Real Time). So, we present the different tools of representation exploited by this method. A practical case study of an ABS (Anti-lock Braking) braking system was presented and discussed.

METHODOLOGY

Real time systems analysis and design

The specification of systems supposes the two essential characteristics: the temporal evolution of components of the system and the interaction system - environment. Indeed, the complexity of relations between a system and its environment is especially verified in the domain of process conduct (Attiogbe and Vailly, 1996).

Among techniques of system specification, we mention: the methods of analysis that enable to systematise and to canalise the various perceptions of the needs; the languages of specification possessing syntax and a very definite semantics and the languages of simulation enabling to develop tools for the help of the decision (Drix and Robin, 1992).

Methods of analysis and design provide standard notations and convenient advices that enables to lead to the reasonable conceptions, but one will always make call to the inventor's creativeness (Melese, 1990; Vautier, 1999).

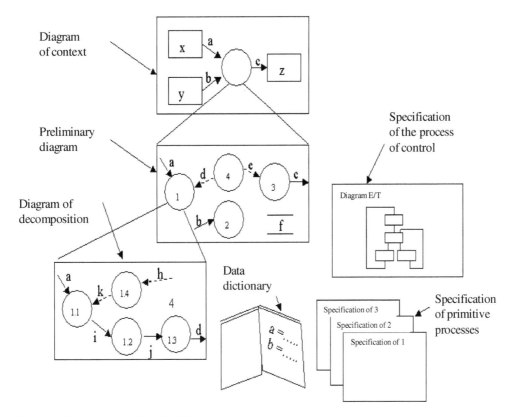

Figure 1. Organization of the SA-RT model.

In the functional strategy, a system is seen like a whole of units in interaction, having each a clearly definite function. Functions arrange a local state, but the system has a shared state, that is centralized and accessible by the whole of the functions (Sticklen and William, 1991).

Oriented-object strategies consider that the system is a whole of interacted objects. Every object arranges a whole of attributes describing its state and the state of the system is described by the state of the whole (Larvet, 1994).

Contrary to most of the functional methods, the oriented-object methods are considered the methods of analysis and design (Budgen, 1995; Lecardinal et al., 1999).

We are interested in this work to the different methods of structured analysis. We cam mention, for instance, the methods: SA (Structured Analysis), SADT (Structured Analysis and Design Technique) and SA-RT. These methods can be used in order to lead to a global functional analysis of a system (Jaulent, 1992; Sommerville, 1988).

In the methods of structured analysis, the highest level is called Context Diagram (CD). Indeed, the box of Data Flows Diagram (DFD) represents a process and must be decomposed. Every process (or treatment) not decomposed is described by the "mini-specification". The dictionary specifies the definition of data, processes and storage zones.

For example the SADT method (Jaulent, 1989; Lissandre, 1990) enables to produce a model of the software under a coherent following and hierarchies of diagrams gotten by successive decompositions.

The structured analysis was insufficient to express constraints of time and synchronization; extensions have been brought to this effect: addition of the graph of Control Flows and specifications of control: information of process activation-deactivation; utilization of diagrams states-transitions.

Presentation of the SA-RT method

Structured Analysis for Real-Time Systems, or SA-RT, is a graphical design notation focusing on analyzing the functional behaviour and information flow through a system. SA-RT, which in turn is a refinement of the structural analysis methods originally introduced by Douglass Ross and popularized by Tom DeMarco in the seventies, was first introduced by Ward and Mellor in 1985 and has thereafter been refined and modified by other researchers, one well-known example being the Hatley and Pirbhai proposal (Hatley and Pirbhai, 1991).

Among the graphical methods most commonly used in industry, two of the leading methods are SA-RT and Statecharts. SA-RT is a short name for Structured Analysis Methods with extensions for Real Time. The model is represented as a hierarchical set of diagrams that includes data and control transformations (processes). Control transformations are specified using State Transition diagrams, and events are represented using control flows. The other graphical and state based paradigm for specification of real time systems is Statecharts. The system is represented as a set of hierarchical states instead of processes. Each state can be decomposed into sub states and so on. The statecharts notation is more compact than the SA-RT notation and has been formally defined.

Thus, SA-RT is a complex method for system analysis and design. This is one of the most frequently used design method in technical and real-time oriented applications adopted by various Case-Tools. It is a graphical, hierarchical and implementation independent method for top-down development (Figure 1).

SA-RT method enables us to identify an entrance and an exit of data in an algorithm or a computer program. It is divided in three modules: Context Diagram (CD), Data Flows Diagram (DFD) and Control Flows Diagram (CFD). Every module includes in its graphic

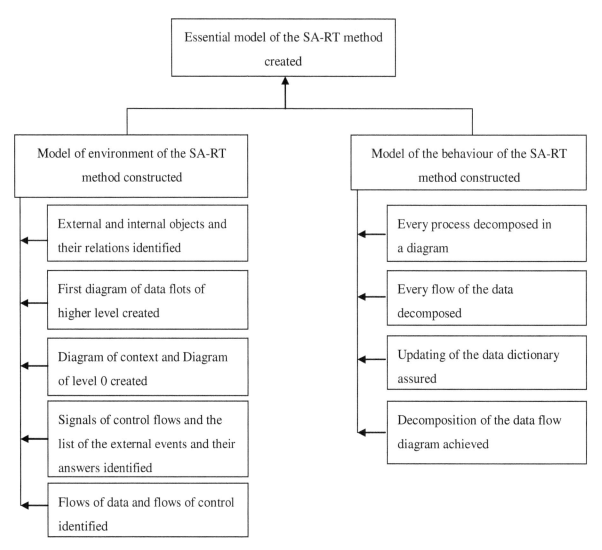

Figure 2. Essential model of the SA-RT.

interpretation different symbols (Hatley and Pirbhai, 1991).

Indeed, the CD in the SA-RT method is going to enable us to identify a process in a program in relation to the entered and exits of data. This process can have different units. This process will be able to be identified per seconds, in term of constant or variable but as this process will be able to be material type (Process interfacing).

The different symbols used in a CD of the SA-RT method are:

1. The terminator is the element in end, final element that encloses the action.
2. The flow of data is the final element that opens up on a last action.
3. The flow of control is generally a tie back of the process toward the terminator. It can be a main element of the process.

The termination is generally a direct tie between a terminator and the process. The DFD is an under-process of the CD. One can analyze every element of the CD and more especially terminators and flows of data. It is going to concern entrances and exits of process exclusively.

The CFD is the last stage of the SA-RT analysis. The CFD

represents in fact a summarized of the Diagram of Context and the DFD while integrating the new exits and entrances.

The Process of control is going to either define a function, a procedure or a place with its internal or external parameters. It can happen that a process of control corresponds to a structure. It can be carrier of parameters in the setting of function or procedure but it is especially a tie between the process of control and the under-process.

Figure 2 presents Essential model of the SA-RT composed two models: a model of environment of the SA-RT method constructed; a model of the behaviour of the SA-RT method constructed.

Practical case of an ABS braking system

The braking knew undoubtedly the most spectacular important evolutions concerning the unblocking of wheels: the ABS (Anti-lock Braking); a system that made its apparition in 1952 on planes, then since 1978, on cars; thanks to the Bosch, inventor of the process. Reliable and efficient, one finds it in series today on all ranges of vehicles. Let's recall that the ABS acts as soon as a wheel wants to block itself. It does not brake shorter on the distance. Its role is the

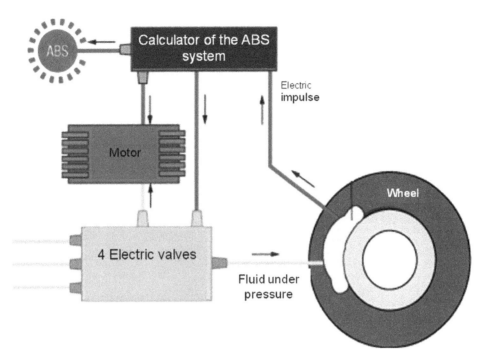

Figure 3. ABS braking system.

unblocking of wheels to help to avoid the obstacle while braking (Figure 3).

When there is blocking of wheels to the braking, it is not more possible to preserve the control of the trajectory of the vehicle, for example, to avoid an obstacle. The ABS system is going to avoid this blockage therefore while using the maximal adhesion of the air. The advantage for the driver is an optimal braking on difficult road, while limiting risks of skid and while keeping the possibility to direct his vehicle.

In a situation of normal braking, the electric valves are opened. When the ABS enters in action, it starts with closing a first electric valve that stops the consignment of the brake liquid. If the blockage persists, a second electric valve is closed, and so on. Stirrups of brake loosened wheels are freed. As soon as the wheel begins to take the speed, the pressure is sent back, still by stages, until the moment where the wheel reaches the speed of others rotation or until a next beginning of blockage.

This operation can take place until 12 times by second, to assure a pretty much homogeneous braking. The ABS requires a regulator therefore extremely sophisticated: it must not only react on the news very precise way that arrive him, but also to take in account the different inertias of the braking system, or same the diameter different of a spare wheel that would not have the same diameter.

RESULTS

In this paragraph, we present an SA-RT analysis of an automotive braking system composed on the one hand of a classic whole of a brake pedal (braking demand) and a brake (braking actuator) and on the other hand of an ABS system (Cottet, 2005). A sensor sliding of wheel is associated to this ABS system. To simplify, the working of the ABS is based on a stop of braking when a sliding is detected on the wheels and it even though the driver's

demand is always efficient. The driver has the possibility to either activate this ABS system with the help of a specific button (button to two steady states: switch). A seer permits to indicate it the activation of the ABS system. But then, it is not possible to deactivate the ABS system during braking that is during the support on the brake pedal.

The whole of data or events exchanged with the outside of the functional process that represents the application, constitute specifications of entrances and exits of the application. The description of these Inputs/Outputs will be made in the dictionary of data.

The context diagram (Figure 4) is constituted of the functional process "to control the braking system" and of five terminators:

1. "Brake pedal" providing the data "braking demand ";
2. "Activation Button of the ABS" providing the data "ABS activation ";
3. "Sliding sensor" providing the data "Wheel sliding ";
4. "Braking system" consuming the data "Braking command";
5. "ABS light" consuming the data "Display ABS".

This context diagram perfectly defines the interfacing between the inventor and the customer that is data to either provide or to generate.

The preliminary diagram is constituted of five functional processes (Figure 5). We can immediately underline at the level the obligatory consistency between the context diagram and the preliminary diagram at the level of the data flows in entrance and in exit. The passage of data

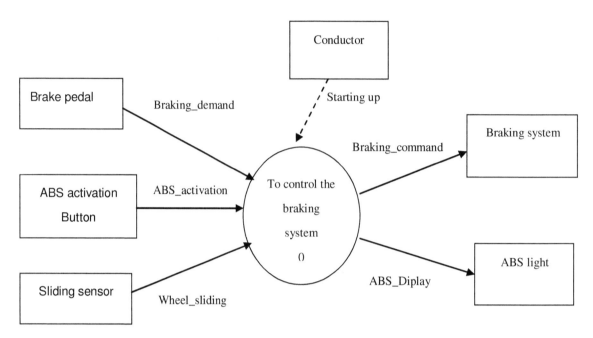

Figure 4. Context diagram.

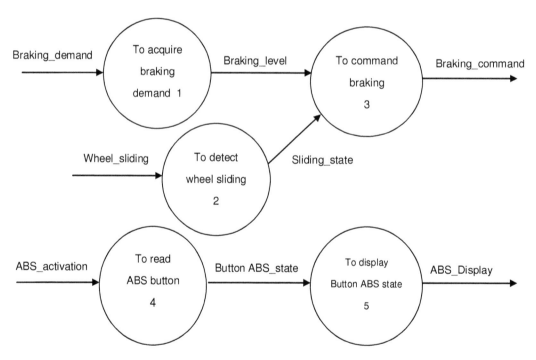

Figure 5. Data flow diagram.

between the functional processes is done in a direct way. It is important to note that the data "Sliding_state" and the data "Button_ABS_state" are Boolean type.

We implanted a control process in the preliminary diagram in order to coordinate the different functional process execution (Figure 6). This control process will therefore interact with a functional process either to

launch or to activate its execution and, in return, the functional process will provide if necessary an event indicating the result of its treatment in order to give some useful information to change the control states.

In order to specify the control process of the application, we present the representation of the state-transition diagram (Figure 7).

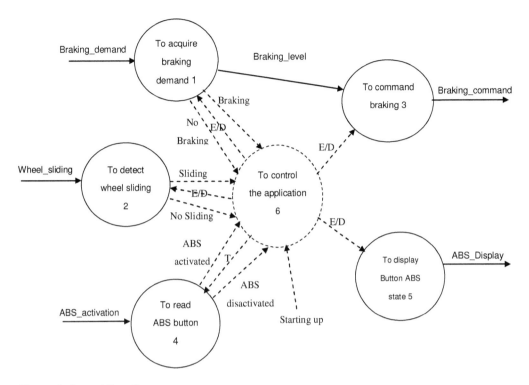

Figure 6. Control flow diagram.

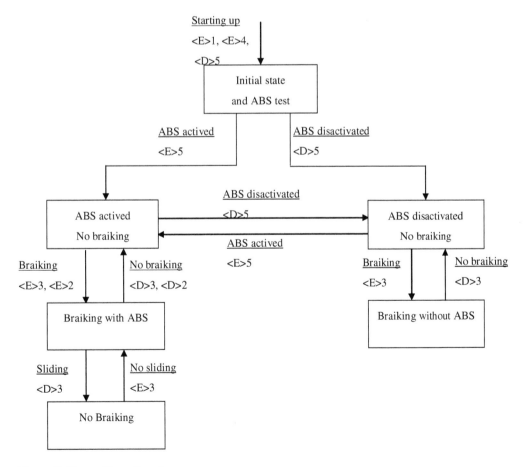

Figure 7. State – Transition diagram.

Conclusion

The modeling of real time systems helps us to understand its working, without eliminating its complexity. In fact, different methods are used for the specification of real time systems. These methods are characterized by their graphic and textual formalism that are necessary to understand and to exploit with a coherent and a correct manner.

In this paper, we present on the one hand the method SA-RT and on the other hand an application of this method on a practical case of an ABS braking system. This application shows the interest of the graphic and textual formalism of SA-RT for the analysis and design of a real time system.

REFERENCES

Attiogbe C, Vailly A (1996). Multi-formalism specifications. AFCET. Paris.

Budgen D (1995). Design models from software design methods. Des. Stud., 16(3): 293 - 325.

Cottet F (2005). Real time systems of control command. Dunod. Paris.

Dorseuil A, Pillot P (1993). The Time in the industrial environment. Dunod. Paris.

Drix P, Robin L (1992). Modeling of the knowledge. Formel methods and specifications. IRIN. University of Nantes. France.

Gomaa H (1994). Software design methods for the design of large-scale real-time systems. J. Syst. Softw., 25(2): 127 - 146.

Hatley D, Pirbhai I (1991). Specifications strategies of real time systems (SA-RT), Masson. Paris. France.

Jane W, Liu S (2000). Real-time Systems. Prentice Hall.

Jaulent P (1989). SADT a langage for communication. IGL Technology. Eyrolles. Paris.

Jaulent P (1992). Software engineering the methods: SADT, SA, E-A, SA-RT, SYS-P-O, OOD, HOOD. Armand Colin. Paris.

Larvet P (1994). Analysis of systems: from functional approach to object approach. Inter Editions. Paris.

Lecardinal J, Mekhileg M, Bocquet JC (1999). A systemic decision approach for capitalizing disfunctions in design processes. ASME. USA.

Lissandre M (1990). To understand SADT. Editions Armand Colin. Paris.

Melese J (1990). Systemic approaches of the organizations. Editions d'organisation. Paris. France.

Ryan J, Heavey C (2006). Process modeling for simulation. Comput. Ind., 57: 437-450.

Sommerville I (1988). The software engineering and its applications. Inter Editions. France.

Sticklen J, William E (1991). Functional Reasoning and Functional Modelling. IEEE Expert: Intelligent Systems and Their Applications. pp. 20-21.

Tschirhart D (1990). Command in real time. Dunod. Paris.

Vautier JF (1999). Systemic methods applied to human factors. Techniques of engineers.

5

Predictive modeling for an industrial naphtha reforming plant using a recurrent-layer artificial neural network

Sepehr Sadighi and S. Reza Seif Mohaddecy

Catalysis and Nanotechnology Division, Catalytic Reaction Engineering Department, Research Institute of Petroleum Industry (RIPI), Iran.

In this research, a layered-recurrent artificial neural network (ANN) using back-propagation method was developed for simulation of a fixed-bed industrial catalytic-reforming unit, called Platformer. Ninety-seven data points were gathered from the industrial catalytic naphtha reforming plant during the complete life cycle of the catalyst (about 919 days). A total of 80% of data were selected as past horizontal data sets, and the others were selected as future horizontal ones. After training, testing and validating the model using past horizontal data, the developed network was applied to predict the volume flow rate and research octane number (RON) of the future horizontal data versus days on stream. Results show that the developed ANN was capable of predicting the volume flow rate and RON of the gasoline for the future horizontal data with the AAD% of 0.238 and 0.813%, respectively. Moreover, the AAD% of the predicted octane barrel against the actual values was 1.447%, confirming the excellent capability of the model to simulate the behavior of the under study catalytic reforming plant.

Key words: Modeling, simulation, artificial neural network, catalytic reforming, naphtha cycle life.

INTRODUCTION

The need for transportation fuels, especially gasoline, will show a steady growth in the future, contributing to demand petroleum processes. Catalytic naphtha reforming is a very important process for producing high octane gasoline, aromatic feedstock and hydrogen in petroleum refining and petrochemical industries (Hu et al., 2002). This unit uses naphtha as feedstock to produce high octane value liquid, hydrogen (H_2) and liquefied petroleum gas (LPG) as by-products (Liang et al., 2005). To design new plants and optimize existing units, an appropriate mathematical model for simulating the industrial catalytic reforming process is needed (Weifeng et al., 2006).

Besides of kinetic-based models which are classified as deterministic or first principal models, the use of an artificial neural network (ANN), a 'black box' model, can be also beneficial, especially when the first principal approach cannot appropriately describe a system. In particular, neural networks are nonlinear, and they learn (or train) by examples. The user of a neural network gathers representative data, and then invokes training algorithms to learn the structure of them (Chaturvedi, 2010). ANN has been previously applied for modeling of refinery processes, such as hydro desulfurization, hydrocracking, delayed coking, and thermal cracking of naphtha processes (Bellos et al., 2002; Arce-Medina et al., 2009; Sadighi et al., 2010; Zahedi et al., 2009; Niaei et al., 2007). Due to its ability to model the complex and nonlinear problems, the ANN can be a useful approach to model the complex behavior between input and output

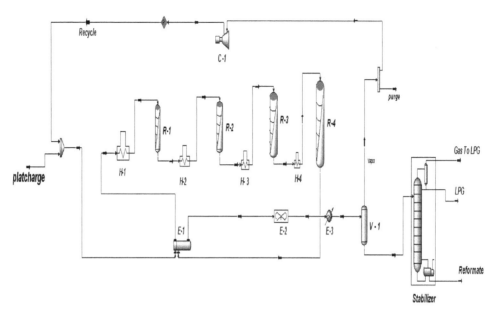

Figure 1. Block flow diagram of the catalytic reforming unit of the target oil refinery.

in the catalytic processes, such as catalytic–dielectric barrier discharge plasma reactors (Istadi et al., 2006; Istadi et al., 2007; Istadi et al., 2007). In the field of modeling catalytic reforming plant using ANN (Manamalli et al., 2006) developed an artificial neural network to maximize the aromatics yield subject to constraints in inlet temperature of the reactors. Two neural networks one in the forward path and the other in the feedback path were trained to give set points for temperature control. Zahedi et al. (2008) developed two ANN models using the back-propagation and radial basis function (RBF) methods for simulating an industrial catalytic-reforming unit. The proposed models predict the volume flow rate of hydrogen, gasoline, and liquid petroleum gas (LPG), outlet temperature of reactors, gasoline specific gravity, Reid vapor pressure (RVP) and research octane number (RON) of gasoline. In this case, 97 data sets were collected from an industrial naphtha reforming plant, and all data sets were used to train, test and validate the ANN architecture. After using ANN model, a set of optimized operation conditions leading to a maximized volume flow rate of produced gasoline were obtained. But, there were no reports to compare the optimized volume flow rate of product estimated by model against the actual results. Furthermore, the life of the catalyst or days on streams was not included in the model which was a crucial factor for a commercial scale fixed-bed reactor.

The present study was aimed at investigating the predictability of artificial neural network (ANN) models for an industrial naphtha reforming unit, called Platformer. This investigation discusses about the usage of mathematical models to find the behavior of the Platformer that is, yield and research octane number

(RON) of the product from the existing data. This work can be significant because of considering the life of the catalyst or days on stream to predict the significant output variables.

Process description

A catalytic naphtha reforming unit licensed by Chevron research cooperation with the nominal capacity of 16,500 barrel per day was chosen as a case study. The feed of the plant prior to entering the catalytic reformer should undergo hydro desulphurization (HDS) reaction in the hydrotreatment unit. Then, the produced naphtha, called Platcharge is introduced to the catalytic reforming process. The most commonly types of catalytic reforming units have three or four reactors that each has a fixed catalytic bed. For such a unit, the activity of the catalyst is reducing during the operation due to depositing coke and losing chloride. Hopefully, the activity of the catalyst can be periodically regenerated or restored using in situ high temperature oxidation of the coke followed by chlorination process (Weifeng et al., 2006; Chaturvedi et al., 2010). Therefore, the catalyst of the semi-regenerative catalytic reforming is regenerated during routine shutdowns of the process occurring once each 18 to 24 months. Normally, the catalyst can usually be regenerated 3 or 4 times, and then it must be returned to the manufacturer for reclamation of the valuable platinum and/or rhenium elements.

As shown in Figure 1, Platcharge is first preheated by the output stream of the last reactor in effluent heat exchanger (E-1), and after passing through the first furnace (H-1), it enters the first reactor (R-1) where

Table 1. Catalyst distribution in reforming reactors.

Parameter	1st reactor	2nd reactor	3rd reactor	4th reactor
Catalyst weight (kg)	5077.25	7615.87	12693.13	25386.25
Catalyst distribution (wt %)	10	15	25	50

Table 2. Operating conditions in the catalytic reforming of the target oil refinery.

Process variable	Value
Inlet temperature (°C)	490 - 515
Hydrogen/hydrocarbon ratio (mol/mol)	3-7
LHSV (h^{-1})	1- 2
Yield (vol %)	70 - 85

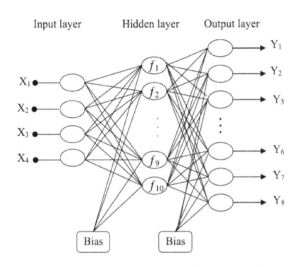

Figure 2. Schematic diagram of a typical structure layer.

naphthenes are dehydrogenated to aromatics. Then, the product stream from the first reactor passes through the second reactor (R-2), and the outlet stream of that enters the third reactor (R-3). Similarly, the product stream from the third reactor enters the fourth reactor (R-4). Due to endothermic nature of naphtha reforming reaction, furnaces that is, H-1, H-2, H-3 and H-4 should essentially be provided before each corresponding reforming reactor.

The product stream from the fourth reactor, after exchanging heat with fresh feed in heat exchanger (E-1), enters a separator (V-1) wherein the produced hydrogen during reforming process (gas stream) is recycled, and it then mixed with the Platcharge. Finally, the liquid product leaving the separator is introduced to the gasoline stabilizer in which the LPG and light gases are separated from the gasoline. So, the vapor pressure of the gasoline can be set according to the market requirement. The final product from the stabilizer is called Reformate.

The catalyst distribution of reactors in an industrial catalytic naphtha reforming process is revealed in Table

1. Moreover, the normal operating conditions of this unit are presented in Table 2.

DEVELOPMENT OF ARTIFICIAL NEURAL NETWORK MODEL

Although the subject of ANN modeling was discovered 50 years ago, it is only in the last 2 decades that ANN software have been presented to tackle with practical problems. ANN is a parallel structure composed of nonlinear nodes which are connected by fixed weights and variables. ANNs are different from the classic modeling approaches in that they are trained to learn solutions instead of being programmed to model an individual problem in the classic way. The advantages of ANN compared to classical methods are speed, simplicity, and capacity to learn from examples. Moreover, its ability to learn by experimental data makes ANNs very flexible and powerful than any other parametric approaches (Zahedi et al., 2008).

Figure 2 shows the scheme of a typical ANN structure. A typical network consists of an input layer, at least one hidden layer, and an output layer. The most widely employed networks have one hidden layer only (Hagan et al., 1995). For a feed-forward ANN, the information propagates in only the forward direction. In this case, each node within a given layer is connected to all of the nodes of the previous layer. The node sums up the weighted inputs and a bias and passes the result through a linear or nonlinear function (Haykin et al., 1998). The training of ANN is carried out by introducing it with a set of known inputs and outputs. Then, it learns the trend of these known data by manipulating the weights and biases. The ANN parameters that is, weights and biases are adjusted up to the minimization criterion reached. The most widely used criterion is the mean square error (MSE) as follows (Demuth et al., 2007):

$$MSE = \frac{1}{N}\sum_{i=1}^{N}(P_{i,actual} - P_{i,model})^2 \qquad (1)$$

where N is the total number of known values; P is the output values; actual refers to the measured outputs from the plant, and model refers to the simulated values by ANN.

To create an ANN model, 110 data sets during the life cycle of the catalyst (about 919 days) were gathered from the understudy catalytic reforming plant. All data were selected from the normal condition when no abnormalities, such as tower flooding, emergency depressurization and pump or compressor shut down were happen in the operation. Before using these data to build the

Table 3. The input variables and their ranges used for building the ANN model.

Variable	Ranges
Days on streams (DOS)	154-919
Naphtha feed flow rate (m³/h)	125.76-149.18
Recycle gas flow rate (m³/h)	112200-135100
Hydrogen to hydrocarbon molar ratio	3.52-4.963
Inlet temperature to reactor 1 (°C)	500-518
Inlet temperature to reactor 2 (°C)	500-518
Inlet temperature to reactor 3 (°C)	500-518
Inlet temperature to reactor 4 (°C)	500-518

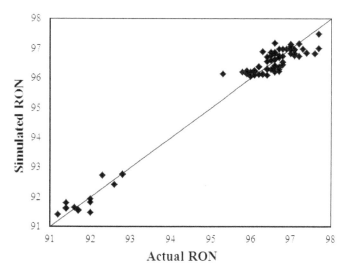

Figure 3. Parity plot for the trained, tested and validated RON simulated by ANN model.

ANN, it was necessary to validate them. If a reasonable overall mass balance (±5%) could not be calculated, the validity of test run was compromised. According to this strategy, 97 data points were obtained. The variables and their operating ranges are presented in Table 3.

Among 97 data points, 80 data (up to the day of 800) were selected for building the ANN model. So, 48 data points were selected for training the ANN (60%), 17 data points for testing (20%), and the remained ones for validating the developed network. These data were called the past horizontal data supposed to show the behavior of the Platformer from start of run to the day of 800. The other data points, that is, from the day of 800 to the end of run (day of 919) were called the future horizontal data that were chosen to evaluate the ability of the ANN model as a reliable tool to predict the cycle life of the catalyst.

The ANN model of Platformer was developed by using the neural network toolbox (newlrn function), presented in MATLAB 2010a. A layered-recurrent neural network consisting of 7 neurons in the input layer and 2 neurons in the output layer was built. Determination of nodes in a hidden layer was very important for the ANN model. Too small a number of hidden nodes may not train the network well to reach an acceptable error. On the other hand, too many hidden nodes make the ANN to memorize the data instead of learning them. For the developed model in this work, 3 nodes were

selected for the ANN model. So, it was found that the required coefficients that is, weights and biases of the designed network using 3 hidden nodes were limited to 80 parameters, less than the number of training data (97 sets). Therefore, the over learning of the model can be prevented.

The transfer or activation function used in the hidden and output nodes is the Tangent sigmoid function as follows:

$$f(x) = \frac{e^x - e^{-x}}{e^x + e^{-x}} = \tan sig(x) \tag{2}$$

where x is the sum of the weighted inputs to the neuron and f(x) represents the output of the node.

The input neurons of the ANN consisted of days on stream (DOS), naphtha feed flow rate, recycle gas flow rate, hydrogen to hydrocarbon molar ratio, and inlet temperature to reactors 1 to 4 (7 neurons). The output layer of that was the research octane number (RON) and the product flow rate that is, gasoline or reformate (2 neurons). Training of the ANN was carried out using the function 'trainlm' which applied Levenberg-Marquardt optimization method to estimate weights and biases. Training was performed until finding the minimum MSE between the simulated and actual output variables that is, all past horizontal data points. Detailed of the ANN model used for the under study naphtha catalytic reforming plant is presented in Table 4.

RESULTS AND DISCUSSION

Developing the neural network using past horizontal data

The described procedure for developing the artificial neural network was followed to train, test and validate the model for 80 points of past horizontal data. The MSE and AAD% of model obtained for RON and gasoline flow rate are presented in Table 5. Additionally, the parity plots for the RON and gasoline flow rate simulated by the ANN models are presented in Figures 3 and 4. From these results, it can be found that the deviation of simulated values in comparison to the measured data is acceptable for the output values of past horizontal data points. It is supposed that the main source of deviation was the possibility of error measurements in gathering data obtained with some faults, such as signal transmission, calibration and power fluctuation of instruments which could not be excluded from the actual data. However, from the presented simulation results, it can be concluded that the developed simulation program was reliable enough to be applied for predicting the behavior of the under study catalytic reforming unit.

Predicting the future horizontal outputs

After building the ANN, the outputs corresponding to the future horizontal data, that is, RON and gasoline flow rate were extrapolated. It is obvious that the predicted outputs are related to the days on streams from day of 800 to the end of run (day of 919).

Table 4. Detailed of ANN algorithm build for the Platformer.

Variable	Value
Number of hidden layers	1
Number of neurons in the hidden layer	3
Number of data used for training (60%), Testing (20%) and validating (20%)	80
Type of network	Layered-recurrent
Number of model parameters	40
Transfer function of hidden layers	Tangent Sigmoid
Transfer function of output layer	Tangent Sigmoid
Algorithm used for training	Levenberg-Marquardt
Performance function	MSE

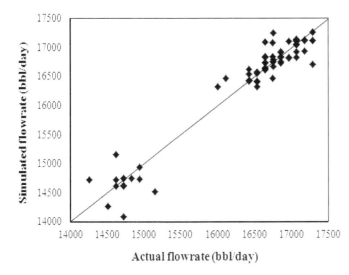

Figure 4. Parity plot for the trained, tested and validated gasoline flowrate simulated by ANN model

As an important parameter for a naphtha catalytic reforming unit, the octane barrel of the unit (that is, RON × gasoline flow rate) was studied using the validated ANN model. This variable is so important to distinguish the end of the life cycle, and also it is always monitored to estimate the catalyst life. The results showed that AAD% of the predicted octane barrel for the future horizontal data using the ANN-based model was 1.477%. Additionally, the AAD% of the prediction for the octane barrel at the end of run (day of 919) was about 0.3%. From Figure 7, close mappings between the measured and simulated octane barrels for both past and future horizontal data can be understood. These results confirm that the presented approach can be applied by the refineries to monitor the operation of the catalytic reforming plant, and it can be used to estimate the octane, flow rate of gasoline and life cycle with an acceptable accuracy.

Table 5. AAD% and MSE of ANN model after training, testing and validating procedure.

Variable	AAD%	MSE
RON of gasoline	0.238	0.084
Flow rate of gasoline	0.813	1.787

Figures 5 and 6 show the comparisons between the RON and flow rate of the produced gasoline against the actual values, respectively. As it can be seen from these figures, there are close mappings between the measured and the predicted (or extrapolated) output variables. It should be mentioned that the AAD% of predictions for the RON and gasoline flow rate were 0.52 and 1.62%, respectively. It is concluded that the ANN-based model is also good for extrapolating the behavior of the catalytic naphtha reformer.

Conclusions

In this work, a recurrent layer neural network model was developed for the simulation of an industrial fixed-bed catalytic naphtha reformer. The collected data from the under study plant was divided to the past horizontal data (80 points from start of run to the day of 800), and the future horizontal ones (from the day of 800 to end of the life cycle). The built ANN model was trained, tested and validated on the basis of the past horizontal data. The results showed that the ANN model could simulate the RON, the flow rate of the produced gasoline, and the octane barrel of the past horizontal data with the AAD% of 0.238, 0.813 and 0.853%, respectively. Finally, the developed ANN model were applied to predict the RON, gasoline flow rate and octane barrel of the future horizontal data which were significant for estimating the life of the catalyst. The comparison between the model predictions (or extrapolation) and the future horizontal data confirmed that the developed ANN model could predict these momentous outputs with the AAD% of 0.52, 1.62 and 1.477%, respectively.

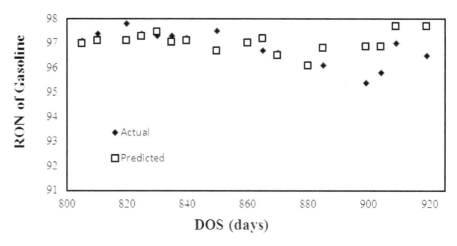

Figure 5. Actual RON of gasoline against predicted values vs. days of streams.

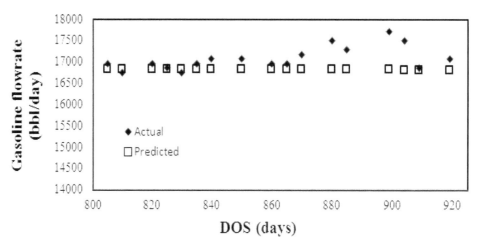

Figure 6. Actual flowrate of gasoline against predicted values vs. days of streams.

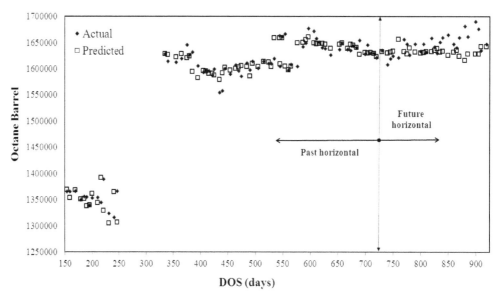

Figure 7. Octane barrel of past and future horizontal data against actual values vs. days of streams.

REFERENCES

Arce-Medina E, Paz-Paredes JI (2009). Artificial neural network modeling techniques applied to the hydrosulfurization process. Math. Comp. Model. 49:207-214.

Bellos GD, Kallinikos LE, Gounaris CE, Papayannakos NG (2005). Modeling the performance of industrial HDS reactors using a hybrid neural network approach. Chem. Eng. Process. 44:505-515.

Chaturvedi DV (2010). Modeling and Simulation of Systems Using MATLAB and Simulink. CRC Press, Taylor & Francis Group, New York.

Demuth H, Beale M (2007). User's Guide: Neural Network Toolbox for Use with Matlab. The Mathworks, Inc., Natick, MA.

Hagan MT, Demuth HB, Beale M (1995). Neural Network Design. PWS Publishing Company, Boston, MA.

Haykin S, Hamilton O (1998). Neural Networks. 2nd ed., Prentice Hall International, Inc. Upper Saddle River, NJ.

Hu YY, Su HY, Chu J (2002). The research summarize of catalytic reforming unit simulation. Contr. Instrum. Chem. Ind. 29(2):19-23.

Istadi I, Amin NAS (2006). A Hybrid Artificial Neural Network - Genetic Algorithm (ANN-GA) Technique for Modeling and Optimization of Plasma Reactor. Ind. Eng. Chem. Res. 45:6655-6664.

Istadi I, Amin NAS (2007). Catalytic-Dielectric Barrier Discharge Plasma Reactor For Methane And Carbon Dioxide Conversion. Bull. Chem. React. Eng. Catal. 2(2-3):37- 44.

Istadi I, Amin NAS (2007). Modeling and Optimization of Catalytic-Dielectric Barrier Discharge Plasma Reactor for Methane and Carbon Dioxide Conversion Using Hybrid Artificial Neural Network – Genetic Algorithm Technique. Chem. Eng. Sci. 62:6568–6581.

Liang KM, Guo HY, Pan SW (2005). A study on Naphtha Catalytic Reforming Reactor Simulation and Analysis. J. Zhejiang Univ. Sci. 6B(6):590-596.

Manamalli D, Kanagasabapathy P, Dhivya K (2006). Expert Optimal Control of Catalytic Reformer Using ANN. Chem. Eng. Comm. 193:729–742.

Niaei A, Towfighi J, Khataee AR., Rostamizadeh K (2007). The Use of ANN and the Mathematical Model for Prediction of the Main Product Yields in the Thermal Cracking of Naphtha. Petrol. Sci. Technol. 25:967–982.

Sadighi S, Ahmad A, Irandoukht A (2010). Modeling a Pilot Fixed-bed Hydrocracking Reactor via a Kinetic Base and Neuro-Fuzzy Method. J. Chem. Eng. Jap. 43:174-185.

Weifeng H, Hongye SU, Yongyou HU, Jian CHU (2006). Modeling, Simulation and Optimization of a Whole Industrial Catalytic Naphtha Reforming Process on Aspen Plus Platform. Chin. J. Chem. Eng. 14(5):584–591

Zahedi G, Lohiy A, Karami Z (2009). A Neural Network Approach for Identification and Modeling of Delayed Coking Plant. Int. J. Chem. React. Eng. 7:1-25.

Zahedi G, Mohammadzadeh S, Moradi M (2008), Enhancing Gasoline Production in an Industrial Catalytic-Reforming Unit Using Artificial Neural Networks. Energy Fuels 22:2671–2677.

6

Performance evaluation of wireless multipath/shadowed *G*-distributed channel

Govind Sharma*, Ankit Agarawal and Vivek K. Dwivedi

ECE Department, Jaypee Institute of Information Technology, Noida, Uttar Pradesh, India-201307.

In wireless communication the effect of multipath as well as shadowing takes place simultaneously over the channel and this phenomena leads to composite fading. G-distribution is frequently encountered distribution in wireless fading environment. Combination of multipath fading and shadowing model are used as composite fading model. This composite fading model is named as G-distribution. G-distribution is a combination of the Inverse-Gaussian distribution and the distribution. In this paper the Pade approximation approach is used to analyze the performance of composite multipath/shadowed fading channel. This distribution is used to approximate any system in form of closed form solution as well as for accurate approximation in several shadowing conditions. The Pade approximation is applied over the general expression that is given in terms of moment generating function and results are obtained by varying shadowing parameters as well as signal to noise power threshold ratio. Our study start by deriving the moment generating function of the G-distribution and approximate them by using the Pade approximation for the calculation of bit error rate and outage probability for different values of average Signal to noise ratio (SNR). All simulations are done using Maple-13 software tool and results are obtained for outage probability and bit error rate versus average SNR.

Key words: Pade's approximation, G-distribution, moment generating function, inverse Gaussian distribution, Nakagami distribution and composite distributions, average signal to noise ratio, outage probability, bit error probability.

INTRODUCTION

Wireless is the fastest growing communication system for communication that provides high data rates and lesser complexity for global coverage. In wireless communication multipath fading and shadowing phenomenon are encountered in different scenario. Multipath fading and shadowing reduces the performance of wireless communication system. In this case receiver does not mitigate the effect of multipath fading as well as shadowing.

The composite distribution is used for the perfect modeling for these channels. In case of outdoor communication an electromagnetic signal experiences the effect of reflection, diffraction, scattering as well as path loss and shadowing. These effects can be modeled in terms of composite multipath/shadowing fading distribution (Jeffrey and Goldsmith, 2004; Homayoun, 1993). One of the best known distributions is shadowed Nakagami fading distribution (Ho and Stuber, 1993). This is the generalized distribution of combined Rayleigh-Lognormal distribution model (also called Suzuki model)

(Suzuki, 1977; Amine et al., 2009).

The main drawback of this distribution is that the probability density function (PDF) of this distribution does not provide closed form solution for performance evaluation of communication channel such as bit error probability, outage probability and channel capacity. So this log-normal distribution is substituted by the closed form gamma distribution function and obtained the K-distribution (Abdi and Kaveh, 1998). In K-fading log-normal distribution is substituted with Inverse-Gaussian pdf and this composite Rayleigh-Inverse Gaussian distribution approximate more accurately as compared to K-distribution. There are several composite fading models that have been presented in literature (Stüber, 1996).

In this paper, we constraint a very general form of distribution function which is combination of general Nakagami-Inverse Gaussian model considered as a composite distribution model. We demonstrated that this combination gives birth to a closed form composite distribution called the G-distribution (Homayoun, 1993; Amine et al., 2009). This distribution is used to approximate any system in form of closed form solution as well as for accurate approximation in several shadowing conditions. We approximate the G-distributed function using the Pade approximation and evaluate the bit error rate and outage probability performance of single user communication system using different modulation schemes.

Our analysis starts from closed form expression for composite pdf and then, the moment generating function has been solved. The outage probability and bit error rate for different values of SNR have been analyzed by using the relation of outage probability versus moment generating function and bit error rate versus moment generating function.

PADE APPROXIMATION (PA)

To analyze the performance of wireless fading channel we always deal with different complicated mathematical function like infinite power series, exponential function, Bessel's functions and Gamma functions etc., which are not easy to handle by simple mathematical approaches. So we require an alternative approach to work with infinite power series functions. PA is a well known method that is used to approximate infinite power series that are either not guaranteed to converge, converge very slowly or for which a limited number of coefficients is known. The approximation is given in terms of a simple rational function of arbitrary numerator and denominator orders (Mahmoud and Mustafa, 2006). Let $g(s)$ be an unknown function given in terms of a power series in the variable $s \in \mathbb{C}$, the set of complex numbers, namely (Mahmoud and Mustafa, 2006; Baker, 1971).

$$g(s) = \sum_{n=0}^{\infty} c_n s^n, \quad c_n \in \mathbb{R} \tag{1}$$

where $\mathbb{R}$ is the set of real number. There are several reasons to look for a rational approximation to a series, the series might be divergent or converging too slowly to be of any practical use. PA gives result in a transfer function form thus it can be used easily for any computation and one of the major reasons is that only few coefficients of the series may be known and that is why a good approximation is needed which represents the properties of the function.

The one point PA of order $[N_p/N_q]$, $P^{[N_p/N_q]}(s)$, is defined from the series $g(s)$ as a rational function by (Hansen and Mano, 1977).

$$P^{[N_p/N_q]}(s) = \frac{\sum_{n=0}^{N_p} a_n s^n}{\sum_{n=0}^{N_q} b_n s^n} \tag{2}$$

Where the coefficients $\{a_n\}$ and $\{b_n\}$ are defined such that,

$$\frac{\sum_{n=0}^{N_p} a_n s^n}{\sum_{n=0}^{N_q} b_n s^n} = \sum_{n=0}^{\infty} c_n s^n + \mathcal{O}(s^{N_p+N_q+1}) \tag{3}$$

Where $\mathcal{O}(s^{N_p+N_q+1})$ representing the term of order higher than N_p/N_q. For better approximation the value of Np should be lesser than the value of Nq. It is straightforward to see that the coefficients $\{a_n\}$ and $\{b_n\}$ can be easily obtained by matching the coefficients of like powers on both sides of the above Equation. Specifically, taking $b_0=1$, without loss of generality, one can find that the values of all coefficients (Mahmoud and Mustafa, 2006).

G- DISTRIBUTION

The probability density function of the composite multipath/shadowing channel is given by (Amine et al., 2009)

$$f_X(x) = \int_0^{+\infty} f_{X/Y}(x/Y = y) f_Y(y) dy, \tag{4}$$

where $f_{X/Y}$ is the Nakagami-m multipath fading distribution and it is given by

$$f_{X/Y}(x/Y = y) = \frac{2 m^m x^{2m-1} \exp\left(\frac{-mx^2}{y}\right)}{\Gamma(m) y^m}, \quad x > 0 \tag{5}$$

And $f_Y(y)$ is the inverse- Gaussian (IG) distribution which is given by

$$f_Y(y) = \sqrt{\frac{\lambda}{2\pi}} y^{-\frac{3}{2}} \exp\left(-\frac{\lambda(y-\theta)^2}{2\theta^2 y}\right), \quad y > 0 \tag{6}$$

On substituting (5) and (6) in (4) the closed form of composite envelope is expressed as follows

$$f_X(x) = \left(\frac{\lambda}{\theta^2}\right)^{m+\frac{1}{2}} \sqrt{\frac{\lambda}{2\pi}} \frac{4m^m x^{2m-1} exp\left(\frac{\lambda}{\theta}\right)}{\Gamma(m)\left(\sqrt{g(x)}\right)^{m-\frac{1}{2}}} K_{m+\frac{1}{2}}\left(\sqrt{g(x)}\right) \quad (7)$$

Where $g(x) = \frac{2\lambda}{\theta^2}\left(mx^2 + \frac{\lambda}{2}\right)$ and $K_v(\bullet)$ is the modified Bessel (Gradshteyn and Ryzhik, 1994) function of the second kind of order v. At $m = 1$, this distribution reduces to the Rayleigh-Inverse Gaussian.

The probability density function of the instantaneous composite signal to noise power ratio $f_\gamma(\gamma)$ can be easily deduced from (7) as

$$f_\gamma(\gamma) = A \frac{\gamma^{m-1}}{\left(\sqrt{\alpha+\beta\gamma}\right)^{m-\frac{1}{2}}} K_{m+\frac{1}{2}}\left(b\sqrt{\alpha+\beta\gamma}\right) \quad (8)$$

Terms used in Equation (8) can be expressed as:

$$A = \frac{(\lambda\gamma)^{\frac{1+2m}{4}}}{\Gamma(m)} \sqrt{\frac{2\lambda}{\pi\theta}} \exp\left(\frac{\lambda}{\theta}\right)\left(\frac{m}{\gamma}\right)^m \quad , \quad b = \frac{1}{\theta}\sqrt{\frac{\lambda}{\gamma}} \quad , \alpha = \lambda\bar{\gamma}, \beta = 2m\theta$$

From (Abdi and Kaveh, 1998), $\gamma = \frac{\bar{\gamma}}{E[x^2]}x^2$, where γ represents instantaneous SNR, $\bar{\gamma}$ represents average SNR, $E[\bullet]$ is the expectation operator and λ, θ are the shadowing parameters.

Moment generating function

In probability theory and statistics, the MGF of any random variable is an alternative definition of its probability distribution. Thus, it provides the basis of an alternative route to analytical results compared with working directly with probability density functions or cumulative distribution functions. There are particularly simple results for the moment-generating functions of distributions defined by the weighted sums of random variables. The moment-generating function does not always exist even for real-valued arguments, unlike the characteristic function. There are relations between the behavior of the moment-generating function of a distribution and properties of the distribution, such as the existence of moments. Thus, MGF is nothing but the Laplace transform of the PDF with argument reversed in sign.

The MGF of an CRV, $\gamma > 0$ is defined as (Mahmoud and Mustafa, 2006; Athanasios, 1989)

$$\mathcal{M}_\gamma(s) = E(e^{-s\gamma}) = \int_0^\infty e^{-s\gamma} f_\gamma(\gamma)\, d\gamma \quad (9)$$

Where $\mathcal{M}_\gamma(s\bullet)$ is the moment generating function and $f_\gamma(\gamma)$ is the probability density function (PDF) of γ. Using the Taylor series expansion of $e^{-s\gamma}$ the MGF can be expressed as (Mahmoud and Mustafa, 2006)

$$\mathcal{M}_\gamma(s) = \sum_{n=0}^\infty \frac{(-1)^n}{n!} E[\gamma^n] s^n \quad (10)$$

For composite PDF the n_{th} moment is given by Equation (11) and on using the power series expansion for Bessel function (Gradshteyn and Ryzhik, 1994, Equation 8.468)

$$E[\gamma^n] = \sqrt{\frac{2\lambda}{\pi\theta}} e^{\frac{\lambda}{\theta}} \left(\frac{\gamma}{m}\right)^m \frac{\Gamma(m+n)}{\Gamma(m)} K_{n-\frac{1}{2}}\left(\frac{\lambda}{\theta}\right) \quad (11)$$

$$K_{n-\frac{1}{2}}\left(\frac{\lambda}{\theta}\right) = \sqrt{\frac{\pi\theta}{2\lambda}} e^{-\frac{\lambda}{\theta}} \sum_{k=0}^{n-1} \frac{(n+k-1)!}{k!\left(n-K_{n-\frac{1}{2}}\left(\frac{\lambda}{\theta}\right)=k-1\right)!\left(\frac{2\lambda}{\theta}\right)^k} \quad (12)$$

On substituting (11) and (12) in (10), the moment generating function for specific number of numerator and denominator order is given by

$$\mathcal{M}_\gamma(s) = \sum_{n=0}^{N_p+N_q+1}\left[\frac{(-1)^n}{n!}\left(\frac{\gamma}{m}\right)^m \frac{\Gamma(m+n)}{\Gamma(m)}\sum_{k=0}^{n-1}\left(\frac{(n+k-1)!}{k!(n-k-1)!\left(\frac{2\lambda}{\theta}\right)^k}\right)s^n\right] \quad (13)$$

On solving the Equation (12) for the value of $m = 5$ in case of frequent heavy shadowing MGF is represent in power series which is order of N_p+N_q+1. Pade approximation of this power series is represent by the Equation (14)

$$P^{[\frac{5}{6}]}(s,m,\bar{\gamma}) = \frac{1+14.93\,\bar{\gamma}S+74.51\,\bar{\gamma}^2S^2+143.23\,\bar{\gamma}^3S^3+82.97\,\bar{\gamma}^4S^4-6.59\,\bar{\gamma}^5S^5}{1+15.93\,\bar{\gamma}S+89.29\,\bar{\gamma}^2S^2+215.98\,\bar{\gamma}^3S^3+220.85\,\bar{\gamma}^4S^4+76.17\,\bar{\gamma}^5S^5+2.29\,\bar{\gamma}^6S^6} \quad (14)$$

Table 1 shows the value of coefficient at the nominator and denominator for different fading parameter. As we change the value of fading parameter the value of coefficient is also changed. Coefficient of approximation for different fading parameter value (m=1, 2, 4, 5) are given in Table 1.

Outage probability

For reliable wireless communication the received power level should be greater than the minimum power level which is required for uninterrupted communication between transmitter and receiver. This minimum level is

Table 1. Value of coefficient of nominator and denominator in moment generating function for different fading parameter (m).

Shadowing	Numerator coefficients (a_n), (a_0=1)	Denominator coefficients (b_n), (b_0=1)
Frequent heavy shadowing		
m=1	{53.786, 966.572, 6970.783, 18904.747, 13580.563}	{54.78, 1019.44, 7891.57, 25156.42, 28532.05, 7965.94}
m=2	{26.775, 223.313, 602.796, 36.947, -867.123}	{27.7748, 249.65, 815.69, 571.43, - 913.44, - 698.914}
m=5	{14.934, 74.507, 143.239, 82.976, -6.591}	{15.9337, 89.292, 215.976, 220.8524, 76.175, 2.295}
Average shadowing		
m=1	{6.8597, 18.0859, 22.8953, 13.9043, 3.2379}	{7.8597, 24.919, 40.829, 36.487, 16.8715, 3.1550}
m=2	{2.9102, 3.0314, 1.3226, 0.1992, 2.3447}	{3.9102, 6.172, 5.02539, 2.22, 0.50517, 0.04609}
m=4	{1.0846, 0.286, -0.000262, 0.000021, -0.000001015}	{2.0846, 1.7296, 0.730, 0.16503, 0.0189, 0.00085}
m=5	{0.46227, 0.016074, -0.0010309, 0.00005115, -0.0000014938}	{1.463, 0.8625, 0.2638, 0.0444, 0.00394, 0.000147}

known as received power threshold. Due to the effect of fading received signal value fluctuates therefore it is important to calculate the probability of outage of any communication system when the received power level goes below then the certain threshold level. In terms of moment generating function the outage probability is given by (Karagiannidis, 2004).

$$P_{out} = \frac{1}{2\pi j} \int_{\varepsilon-j\infty}^{\varepsilon+j\infty} \frac{[\mathcal{M}_\gamma(s)]}{s} e^{s\gamma} \, ds \qquad (14)$$

or in the terms of Laplace transform this is given by (8, 17)

$$P_{out} = \mathcal{L}^{-1}\left(\frac{\mathcal{M}_\gamma(-s)}{s}\right)\Big|_{\gamma_{th}} \qquad (15)$$

On using Pade approximation it can be solved for fixed number of numerator and denominator coefficients and which is as follows

$$\mathcal{M}_\gamma(s) = \frac{\sum_{n=0}^{N_p} a_n s^n}{1+\sum_{n=1}^{N_q} b_n s^n} = \sum_{n=1}^{N_q} \frac{\lambda_n}{s+p_n} \qquad (16)$$

$$P_{out} = 1 - \sum_{n=1}^{N_q} \frac{\lambda_n}{p_n} e^{-p_n \gamma_{th}} \qquad (17)$$

where p_n are the poles of the approximated result and λ_n are the residue (Stüber, 1996; van Nee et al., 1992). By using Pade approximated MGF we plotted the result for outage probability versus normalized outage threshold that is, $\frac{\gamma_{th}}{\bar{\gamma}}$ in later section (Karagiannidis, 2004).

Table 2 shows the value of coefficient at the nominator and denominator for different fading parameter for calculation of outage probability. As we change the value of fading parameter the value of coefficient is also changed.

Amount of fading

Amount of fading is a statistical characterization of fading environment. On varying the fading parameter m for a particular range the effectiveness of fading can be measured through the wireless channel. AF = 0 (for higher values of m) represents ideal Gaussian channel and AF = ∞ (for very small values of m) represents severe fading environment.

$$AF = \frac{E[\gamma^2]}{E[\gamma]^2} - 1 ; \qquad (18)$$

On using (11) and (12) it represents by following Equation

$$AF = \frac{\Gamma(m+2)\Gamma(m)}{\Gamma^2(m+1)}\left(1+\frac{\theta}{\lambda}\right) - 1 \qquad (19)$$

Bit error rate

Bit error rate or bit error probability (BEP) is an important performance analysis measurement of any digital communication system. Compute of bit error rate for any system is very difficult as compare to other parameter. BEP is one of the most relevant methods to show about the nature of any system (Mahmoud and Mustafa, 2006). Moment generating function plays a key role for evaluating the average BEP for several modulation schemes. For differently coherent detection of binary phase shift keying (DPSK) and non coherent frequency shift keying (FSK), the average BEP is given as (Simon and Alouini, 2004).

$$P_b(E) = C_1 \mathcal{M}_\gamma(a_1) \qquad (20)$$

Where M(•) is moment generating function and c_1 and a_1 are constant depend on the modulation scheme

$$P^{[4/5]}(s,m,\bar{\gamma}) = \frac{1+4.3857s+3.984\bar{\gamma}^2}{1+5.3847s+8.2739\bar{\gamma}^2 s^2+3.9137\bar{\gamma}^3 s^3+.4395\bar{\gamma}^4 s^4} \qquad (21)$$

Table 2. Value of coefficient of nominator and denominator in outage probability for different value of fading parameter (m).

Shadowing		Residue of the approximated MGF (λ_n)	Poles of the approximated MGF (p_n)
Frequent shadowing	heavy		
m=1		{4.91×10⁻⁹, 1.460, 3.05×10⁻⁶,0.231, 3.25×10⁻⁴, 0.0123}	{0.039, 2.448, 0.066, 0.658, 0.119, 0.248}
m=2		{ .0012, 5.77 ×10⁻⁸, 0.0027, 3.22 ×10⁻⁵, 1.151, 0.0846}	{-1.014, 0.074, 0.224, 0.124, 1.418, 0.478}
m=5		{ 1.365, -4.447, 2.59×10⁻⁴, 7.51×10⁻⁷,0.0127, 0.197}	{ 1.645, 30.098, 0.229, 0.146, 0.376, 0.697}
Average shadowing		**Residue of the approximated MGF (λ_n)**	**Poles of the approximated MGF (p_n)**
m=1		{0.4602, 0.421, 0.0729, 8.878 ×10⁻⁷, 0.0018, 0.0699}	{1.153, 0.929, 0.752, 0.445, 0.6023, 1.464}
m=2		{0.039, 3.475, 0.918, -0.675, 1.444 ×10⁻⁴, -3.757}	{1.172, 1.722, 1.426, 3.166, 0.938, 2.534}
m=4		{-7.767, 5.5×10⁻⁴, 1.204, 27.224, 214.88, -235.55}	{7.286, 1.593, 2.141, 2.643, 4.372, 4.0
m=5		{45.447, 0.687,-0.625-j4.68, -0.625+j4.68, -22.44+j52.36, - 22.44-j52.36 }	{2.972, 2.379, 6.48-j3.06, 6.48+j3.06, 4.23-j0.85, 4.23+j0.85 }

After putting the value of s=a_1

$$P_b(E) = C_1 \left(\frac{1+4.385\bar{\gamma}a_1+3.984\bar{\gamma}^2a_1^2}{1+5.384\bar{\gamma}a_1+8.2739\bar{\gamma}^2a_1^2+3.9137\bar{\gamma}^3a_1^3+.4395\bar{\gamma}^4a_1^4} \right) \quad (22)$$

Where C_1=1/2 and a_1=1 for coherent DPSK and $C_1 = \frac{1}{2}$ and a_1=1/2 for noncoherent FSK.

The average BER for BPSK/BFSK modulation scheme is given as (Simon and Alouini, 2004; Vivek and Ghanshyam 2011)

$$P_b(E) = \frac{1}{\pi} \int_0^{\frac{\pi}{2}} M_{\bar{\gamma}} \left(\frac{g}{\sin^2 \theta} \right) d\theta \quad (23)$$

By putting $\sin^2\theta = x^2$ and simply (23) for pade's approximation $P^{[2/5]}$ is expressed as

$P_b(E)$

$$= \frac{1}{\pi}\int_0^1 \frac{.1857}{\bar{\gamma}\left(\frac{g}{x^2}\right)+.651} \times \frac{1}{\sqrt{1-x^2}}dx + \frac{1}{\pi}\int_0^1 \frac{.003}{\bar{\gamma}\left(\frac{g}{x^2}\right)+.3203} \times \frac{1}{\sqrt{1-x^2}}dx + \frac{1}{\pi}\int_0^1 \frac{2.015}{\bar{\gamma}\left(\frac{g}{x^2}\right)+6.163} \times \frac{1}{\sqrt{1-x^2}}dx + \frac{1}{\pi}\int_0^1 \frac{1.826}{\bar{\gamma}\left(\frac{g}{x^2}\right)+1.77} \times \frac{1}{\sqrt{1-x^2}}dx \quad (24)$$

where g=1/2 for BFSK and g=1 for BPSK and g=.715 for coherent BFSK with minimum correlation.

$$P_b(E) = \frac{.1857}{\pi}\left(2.4134 - \frac{2.99153}{\sqrt{1.53644+\frac{1}{\bar{\gamma}}}}\right) + \frac{.003}{\pi}\left(4.9029 - \frac{8.6621}{\sqrt{3.1213+\frac{1}{\bar{\gamma}}}}\right) - \frac{2.01519}{\pi}\left(.254857 - \frac{.102656}{\sqrt{.162247+\frac{1}{\bar{\gamma}}}}\right) + \frac{1.8261}{\pi}\left(.887262 - \frac{.66683}{\sqrt{.5648+\frac{1}{\bar{\gamma}}}}\right) \quad (25)$$

RESULTS AND DISCUSSION

Figure 1 shows the outage probability for different fading environment frequent heavy ($\lambda = 0.03019$, $\theta = 0.02762$) shadowing and average ($\lambda = 34.38756$, $\theta = 0.902993$) shadowing for different pade approximated function. These models were widely used in wireless environment (van Nee et al., 1992; Chau and Sun, 1996). From this figure we notice that as we move for higher order rational function, the proposed method provides best match to reference (Amine et al., 2009). In all approximation, N_p has chosen to be equal to ($N_q - 1$) as these guarantees the convergence of Pade approximation (Mahmoud and Mustafa, 2006). In this paper, we took N_q such that it 'm' increase the value of outage probabilty reduces

guarantees the uniqueness of the all approximations and that is given at $N_p = (N_q - 1)$.

Figure 2 shows the plot between outage probability versus average SNR for different values of fading parameter 'm'. In this case of frequent heavy shadowing we take $\mu = -3.914$ and $\sigma = 0.806$ (Amine et al., 2009). Result depicts that as the value of fading parameter 'm' increase, the value of outage probabilty get reduce for higher values of average SNR. In Figure 3 we draw a plot between outage probability and average SNR for different values of threshold SNR. Plot depicts that as the threshold SNR increase then the value of outage probability also increases. In Figure 4 plots are shown for average shadowing environment by using $\mu = -0.115$ and $\sigma = 0.161$. It reflects that as the value of Figure 5 provides best match between proposed

rapidly after the 5 dB average SNR value.

method results and reference (Amine et al., 2009).

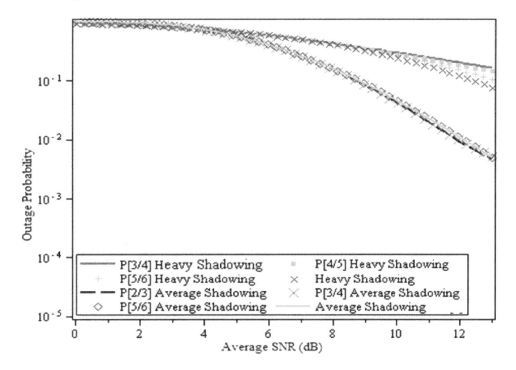

Figure 1. Outage probability for different Pade approximations with $m = 4$ and $\gamma_{th} = 5 dB$ in frequent heavy shadowing and average shadowing environment.

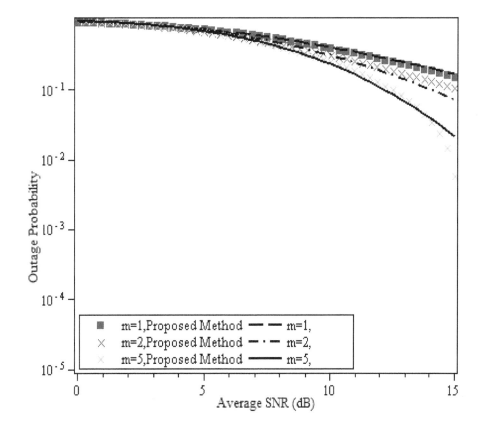

Figure 2. Outage probability for P[5/6], $\gamma_{th} = 5dB$ in frequent heavy $(\lambda = 0.03019, \theta = 0.02762)$ shadowing environments using different value of fading parameter m.

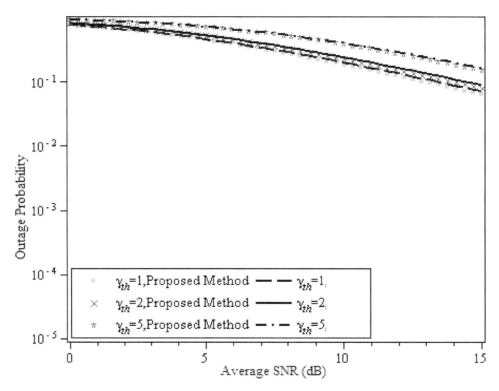

Figure 3. Outage probability for P[5/6], $m = 1$ in heavy $(\lambda = 0.03019, \theta = 0.02762)$ shadowing environments using different value of γ_{th}.

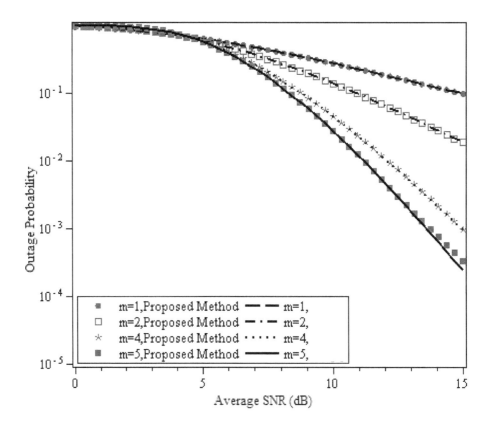

Figure 4. Outage probability for P[5/6], $\gamma_{th} = 5dB$ in average $(\lambda = 34.38756, \theta = 0.902993)$ shadowing environments using different value of fading parameter m.

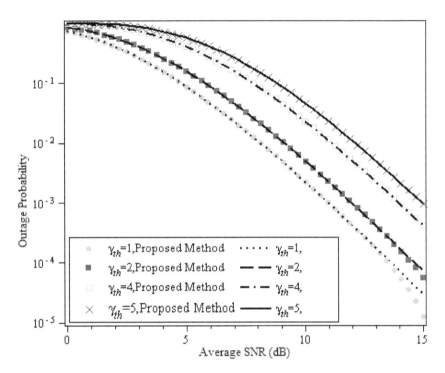

Figure 5. Outage probability for P[5/6], $m = 4$ in average $(\lambda = 34.38756, \theta = 0.902993)$ shadowing environments using different value of γ_{th}.

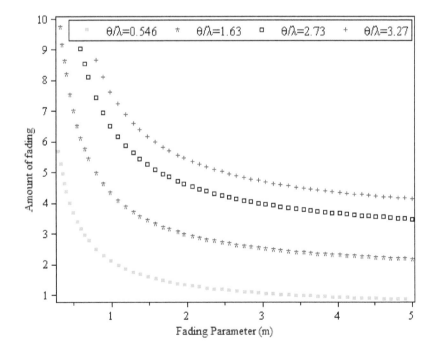

Figure 6. Amount of fading as a function of m for different values of θ/λ.

results. As γ_{th} increase, it reflects an increment in the value of outage probability. The impact of fading parameter m over amount of fading is shown in Figure 6. From this figure it can be notice that as the value of

fading parameter approaches to infinity then the fading severity approaches to zero. So this figure reflects the results over different fading and shadowing situation by varying the value of μ and σ and fading parameter 'm'.

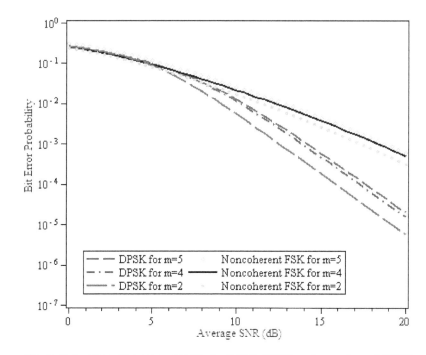

Figure 7. Average bit error probability for BFSK, BPSK and noncoherent BFSK for different value of fading parameter(m=7 and m=4) in frequent heavy shadowing environment (μ= -3.914 and σ= 0.806).

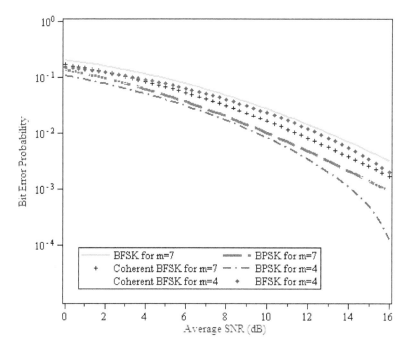

Figure 8. Average bit error probability for DPSK and noncoherent FSK for different value of fading parameter(m=5, m=4 and m=2) in frequent heavy shadowing environment (μ= -3.914 and σ= 0.806).

Figure 7 shows the plot between bit error probability and average SNR for different modulaton scheme for different fading parameter. From this we analysis that as we increase the value of fading parameter the bit error probability is also increases for a value of average SNR and also conclude that when we move from BFSK to BPSK and than coherent BFSK modulation system performance is also enhanced. Figure 8 shows the plot

between bit error probability and average snr curve for DPSK and noncoherent FSK modulation scheme and estimate the performance of system that in which modulation scheme system performance is better. From plot we conclude that as DPSK modulation scheme is better as compare to Noncoherent FSK because in DPSK bit error rate is less.

Conclusion

From the whole analysis we concluded that the Pade approximation provide a best match to the reference results. In this paper we have done the composite analysis of Nakagami- Inverse Gaussian model and calculate the outage probability and bit error rate using Pade approximation. By using the Pade approximation method calculation is much easier as compare to analytical expression. As we know that to analyze the performance of wireless channel we deal with different PDF function that contains complex mathematical function like Bessel function of different kinds and orders, exponential function, Gamma function and other mathematical infinite series which makes the analysis very difficult. Hence Pade approximation provides a simple solution to this problem and it creates a way to very easy system modeling. There is a lot of work has been done using Pade approximation over the different areas like finance, image theory etc and now it also has been used in performance analysis of short term faded wireless channels but in this paper we are suggested this method to performance analysis over the composite (multipath/shadowed) wireless fading channels. For future analysis this method can be used for approximation of other wireless channel which also have the consideration of diversity, equalization etc. This analysis concludes that the Pade approximation provides a better approximation as compare to other approximation method.

REFERENCES

Abdi A, Kaveh M (1998). K distribution an appropriate substitute for Rayleigh-log-normal distribution in fading-shadowing wireless channels. IEEE Electron. Lett. 34(9): 851-852.

Amine L, Mohomed SA, Sofiene A, Alex S (2009). On the Performance Analysis of Composite Multipath/Shadowing Channels Using the G-distribution. IEEE Trans. Comm. 57(4):1162-1170.

Athanasios P (1989). Probability and Statistics. Prentice Hall, Facsimile ed.

Baker GA (1971). Essentials of Pade's Approximants. Academic Press.

Chau YA, Sun JT (1996). Diversity with distributed decision combining for direct-sequence CDMA in a shadowed Rician-fading land-mobile satellite channel. IEEE Trans. Veh. Technol. 45(2):237-247.

Gradshteyn IS, Ryzhik IM (1994). Table of Integrals, Series and Products. 5th ed. San Diego, CA: Academic.

Hansen F, Mano FI (1977). Mobile fading-Rayleigh and log-normal superimposed. IEEE Trans. Veh. Technol. 26:332-325.

Ho MJ, Stuber GL (1993). Co-Channel interference of microcontroller systems on shadowing Nakagami fading channels. IEEE Veh. Technol. Conf. pp. 568-571.

Homayoun H (1993). The indoor radio propagation channel. IEEE 81(7).

Jeffrey GA, Goldsmith AJ (2004). Multicarrier Modulation, 2nd ed. Wiley, Stanford University.

Karagiannidis GK (2004). Moments-based approach to the performance analysis of equal gain diversity in Nakagami-m fading. IEEE Trans. Commun. pp. 685-690.

Mahmoud HI, Mustafa MM (2006). On the Use of Pade's Approximation for Performance Evaluation of Maximal Ratio Combining Diversity over Weibull Fading Channels. J. Wireless Commun. Netw. pp. 1-7.

Simon MK Alouini MS (2004). Digital Communication over Fading Channels. 2nd ed. New York: John Wiley & Sons, Inc.

Stüber GL (1996). Principles of Mobile Communications. Norwell, MA: Kluwer Academic Publishers.

Suzuki H (1977). A statistical model for urban multipath propagation. IEEE Trans. Commun. 25:673-680.

van Nee RDJ, Misser HS, Prasad R (1992). Direct sequence spread spectrum in a shadowed Rician fading land-Mobile satellite channel. IEEE J. Sel. Areas Commun. 10:350-357.

Vivek KD, Ghanshyam S (2011). Error-rate analysis of the OFDM for correlated Nakagami-m fading channel by using maximal-ratio combining diversity. Int. J. Microw. Wireless Technol. pp. 1-10.

7

Implementation of neural network for monitoring and prediction of surface roughness in a virtual end milling process of a CNC vertical milling machine

Hossam M. Abd El-rahman[1] , R. M. El-Zahry[2] and Y. B. Mahdy[3]

[1]Sohag University, Sohag, Egypt.
[2]Mechanical Engineering Department, Faculty of Engineering, Assiut University, Assiut, Egypt.
[3]Dean of Faculty of Computer Information Science, Assiut University, Egypt.

This paper presents a real time simulation for virtual end milling process. Alyuda NeuroIntelligence was used to design and implement an artificial neural network. Artificial neural networks (ANN's) is an approach to evolve an efficient model for estimation of surface roughness, based on a set of input cutting conditions. Neural network algorithms are developed for use as a direct modeling method, to predict surface roughness for end milling operations. Prediction of surface roughness in end milling is often needed in order to establish automation or optimization of the machining processes. Supervised neural networks are used to successfully estimate the cutting forces developed during end milling processes. The training of the networks is preformed with experimental machining data. The neural network is used to predict surface roughness of the virtual milling machine to analyze and preprocess pre measured test data. The simulation for the geometrical modeling of end milling process and analytical modeling of machining parameters was developed based on real data from experiments carried out using Prolight2000 (CNC) milling machine. This application can simulate the virtual end milling process and surface roughness Ra (μm) prediction graphs against cutting conditions simultaneously. The user can also analyze parameters that influenced the machining process such as cutting speed, feed rate of worktable.

Key words: Surface roughness, virtual reality, simulation, surface roughness, virtual end milling process, neural network.

INTRODUCTION

Milling process is classified as material removal process. This process and its machine tools are capable of producing complex shapes with the use of multi-tooth, cutting tools. In the milling process, a multi-tooth cutter rotates along various axes with respect to the work piece. Applications of the end milling process can be found in almost every industry ranging from large aerospace industry to small tool and die makers. One reason for the popularity of the end milling process is that it can be used for both rough and finish machining of components. The major problem, which may result from the end milling process, is the generation of a finished part surface which does not satisfy product design specifications. A finished part surface might be too rough or poor dimension accuracy. An undesirable part surface may require additional machining, thus lowering productivity and increasing the cost of the production. In order to produce parts, which conform to design specifications, proper machining conditions (spindle speed, feed rate, depth of cut, cutter diameter, number of cutting flutes, and tool geometry), must be selected (Boothroyd, and Knight, 1989).

Machining processes such as turning, milling, drilling and grinding can be visualized using Virtual Reality (VR). VR technology can also be used to evaluate the feasibility of a design, selection of process equipment and to allow a user to study the factors affecting the quality, machining time and costs. It is important to note that a virtual reality system is essentially an interactive simulation that can represent a real or abstract system. The simulation is a representative computer based model, which provides appropriate data for visualization or representation of the system. The virtual environment can take many forms and for example, it could be a realistic representation of a physical system (Schofield, 1995).

Some of the machine operator using 'trial and error' method to set-up milling machine cutting conditions. This method is not effective or efficient and the achievement of a desirable value is a repetitive and empirical process that can be very time consuming thus, a mathematical model using statistical method provides a better solution. Multiple regression analysis is suitable to find the best combination of independent variables, which is spindle speed, feed rate, and the depth of cut in order to achieve desired surface roughness. Unfortunately, multiple regression model is obtained from a statistical analysis which requires large sample data. The advantages of ANN-based prediction systems are as follows:

(i) ANN is faster than other algorithms because of their parallel structure.
(ii) ANN does not require solution of any mathematical model.
(iii) ANN is not dependent on the parameters, so the parameter variations do not affect the result.

Instead of attempting to find analytical relationships between machining parameters by the use of statistics, machine learning is used. In the present paper, a different approach that is based on advanced artificial intelligence techniques is implemented and tested. More specifically neural networks are used to predict the surface roughness developed during end milling. The advantages of proposed system over the traditional estimation methods are: simple complementing of the model by new input parameters without modifying the existing model structure, automatic searching for the non-linear connection between the inputs and outputs.

According to the comparisons on the testing results, it has been shown that the neural network approach is more accurate and faster than the other methods. Compared to traditional computing methods, the ANNs are robust and global. ANNs have the characteristics of universal approximation; parallel distributed processing, hardware implementation, learning and adaptation. Because of this, ANNs are widely used for system modeling function optimizing and intelligent control. ANNs give an implicit relationship between the input(s) and output(s) by learning from a data set that represents the behavior of a system.

Tandon and Mounayri (2001) also proposes a back propagation (BP) ANN for on-line modeling of forces in end milling. In (Zuperl and Cus, 2003), a more efficient model is created using BP ANN (using Levenberg–Marquardt approach). This approach has the disadvantage of requiring too many experiments to train the ANN. This, in terms of industrial usability, is unattractive and expensive. Researchers (Lee and Lin, 2000), in their ANN implementations, evolve knowledge of the machining environment by training these networks on run-time data. Researches (Szecsi, 1999) also propose a modified back propagation ANN which adjusts its learning rate and adds a dynamic factor in the learning process for the on-line modeling of the milling system. The learning rate is adjusted by the divided method and a dynamic factor is used during the learning process so as to develop the convergence speed of the back propagation ANN. A much larger set of input machining parameters is considered than in other work reported so far.

In this paper the Multi-Layer back propagation (BP) network is a supervised, continuous valued, multi-input and single-output feed forward multi-layer network that follows a gradient descent method interfaced with the virtual environment to predict surface roughness in the end milling process. ANN based model is developed with using the optimized network for this particular case (100 networks are tested) that the most accurate model will be suggested for in-process part surface roughness prediction. Computer numerical control or better known as CNC has been used as a model for the virtual end milling process simulation. The application will simulate an end milling process as well as perform analytical modeling of machining parameters such as surface roughness on machined work piece. Real time graphs of the surface roughness Ra (µm) against cutting conditions will be displayed simultaneously during the simulation of the end milling process. The mechanism behind the formation of surface roughness in CNC milling process is very dynamic, complicated, and process dependent. Several factors will influence the final surface roughness in a CNC milling operations such as controllable factors (spindle speed, feed rate and depth of cut) and uncontrollable factors (tool geometry and material properties of both tool and work piece).

RELATED WORKS

Manufacturing industries have gained benefit from VR applications in several ways. The use of VR to build prototypes will reduce the costs of finished products, changes in the physical product can be costly but modifications can be made in the virtual prototypes inexpensively.

Virtual reality has been applied to many areas of manufacturing. It provides 3D visualization of manufacturing environment and has great potential in manufacturing applications to solve problems and help in important decision-making.

A desktop virtual shop floor containing a 3-axis numerical control milling machine and a 5-axis robot for painting has been developed. The user can mount a work piece on the milling machine, choose a tool and perform direct machining operations, such as axial movements or predefined sequences (Bayliss et al., 1994). Java, Virtual Reality Modeling Language (VRML) and the External Authoring Interface (EAI) have been employed to perform Numerical Control (NC) machining simulation in a networked VR environment (Qiu et al., 2001).

The geometry of the work piece being cut will be updated dynamically A number of applications of VRML exist on the Web in various areas. One of them is a method for simulating basic manufacturing operations such as unload, load, process, move and store in a 3D virtual environment. The virtual environment provides a framework for representing a facility layout in 3D that consists of the static and dynamic behavior of the manufacturing system (Chawla and Banerjee, 2001).

Another VR application is a virtual machining laboratory for knowledge learning and skill training in an interactive environment. This virtual laboratory is specifically designed for helping students to virtually operate a lathe or set machining parameters and input CNC G-code program to turn the work piece automatically (Fang et al., 1998). Yuzhong and Altintas (2007) have developed an integrated model of the spindle bearing and machine tool system, consisting of a rotating shaft, tool holder, angular contact ball bearings, housing, and the machine tool mounting. The model allows virtual cutting of a work material with the numerical model of the spindle during the design stage. The proposed model predicts bearing stiffness, mode shapes, frequency response function (FRF), static and dynamic deflections along the cutter and spindle shaft, as well as contact forces on the bearings with simulated cutting forces before physically building and testing the spindles.

Delmia's Virtual NC is also an interactive 3D simulation environment for visualizing and analyzing the functionality of an NC machine tool, its CNC controller and the material removal process (Delmia, 2001).

A prototype of 3D virtual environment which is based on the standalone concept has been developed using AutoCAD 2002, VRML Out, VRML Pad, JavaScript and Java (CUS et al., 2003). AutoCAD 2002 was used to model the 3D objects and then the models were transformed into VRML format using VRML Out. Java, JavaScript and VRML were used to develop the animation of end milling process simulation and machining parameters simulation such as the flank wear on cutting tools. The simulation for the geometrical modeling of end milling process and analytical modeling of machining parameters was developed based on real data from some experiments using Computer Numerical Control (CNC) milling machine (Haslina and Zainal, 2008).

An Adaptive neuro-fuzzy inference system (ANFIS) to predict the surface roughness in the end milling process has been developed (Haslina and Zainal, 2008). Surface roughness was used as dependant variable while cutting speed, feed rate and depth of were used as predictor variables. Normal and feed forces were used as predictor variables to verify the ANFIS model. Different membership functions were adopted during the training process of ANFIS. Surface roughness was measured in an off line manner. The normal and feed forces were measured in an on-line manner using two components dynamometer (Soltan et al., 2007).

DEVELOPMENT OF THE SIMULATION ENVIRONMENT

In developing the application, there are some important stages and these are clearly illustrated by Figure 1. These stages will begin with static object (machine parts), which covered the authoring of the 3D model up to the creation of virtual environment. Details of the processes are explained in 3D world in solid works (static objects) part of the work. In the next stage, assembly of dynamic objects is constructed and their coordinates or positions are generated accordingly. Details of the interfacing activities are explained in 3D world in solid works (static objects) as part of this research.

3D World in solid works (static objects)

Initially, this paper reports the research surrounding the development of a virtual machine tool designed to simulate a typical actual machine implemented to predict several parameters in the virtual environment. The actual machine tool details were not developed in complete structure of a typical CNC machine within this paper; however, the major constituents of the machine were reconstructed to a point where it could be implemented and become the subject of research in the virtual environment. Only selected parts of the CNC machine that are involved in the end milling process are created instead of developing a complete structure of a typical CNC machine. The machine table system that which

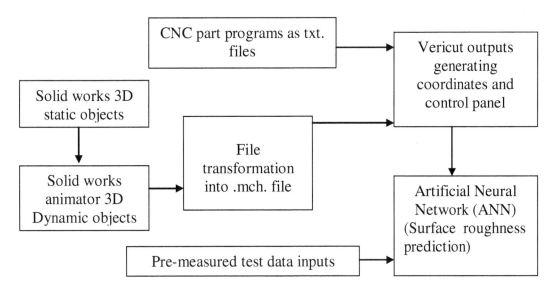

Figure 1. Framework of Real Time Simulation for Virtual Milling Process.

linear bearings are subject, typically due to the actual traversals, also the same friction and mass is generally found in actual slides. The three dimensional model for the static objects (machine parts) was first created using Solid works 2008 to form a 3D world of end milling process.

Construction of the virtual machine

Design requirements demanded the use of commercially available cutters to produce the same actual work pieces. Spindle speeds (revolutions per minute) rpm and drive system specifically for use with the same actual materials.

The saddle engages the linear rods that are attached to the base of the machine. A ball screw moves the saddle along the Y axis. The linear rods running through the top of the saddle engage the cross slide. Another ball screw moves the cross slide along the X and Z axis (Figure 1). The spindle motor on the movable machine head is a 1hp DC permanent magnet motor (regarding to the machine power requirements). The spindle motor drives the spindle shaft with a timing belt. The axis drive belts are located between the motors and balls crews on each axis. The developed virtual machine has the following major specifications: Steeples 0 to 5,000 rpm spindle speed range, X Travel: 12", Y Travel: 6", Z Travel: 8", Motor: 1 hp. Table: 25 1/2" x 6 1/4" and Power: 230 volt, single phase. The three dimensional model of CNC milling machine has been drawn in a wire frame form before the solid model of the machine is displayed as shown in Figure 2. When this stage is completed, the translation process begins where a group of few objects representing the components of the machine is being

exported to the solid works animator tools. For example, the detailed worktable would be exported as one group. This procedure is repeated with the other groups (column, bed, head, etc) until the entire model has been translated into the solid works animator. The entire translation process as shown in Figure 3 was released by Solidworks2008 to allow the exporting of any 3D solid model to be animated. Finally, all the groups of file are gathered once again with solid works animation editor, to form a complete animated model as previously seen in the Solidworks2008 drawing. Now, the virtual end milling process world is completed and ready to be explored through the Vericut browser and to be equipped with the control panel CNC part program inputs. In this application, programming is to transform the final model of extension (.sld.) to typical file extension: (.mch.) It is an ASCII file that contains data describing the construction, kinematics, and other properties of an NC machine tool. Machine file can be loaded into VERICUT via the Configuration menu > Machine > Open function. NC machine configurations are changed via other "Machine" functions in the Configuration menu. Save the new file via Configuration menu >Machine > Save as.

MACHINING TESTS

All the machining tests were carried out on the Prolight 2000 CNC milling machine as shown in Figure 4. The work piece tested is 60/40 Brass (80 mm × 40 mm × 40 mm). The end milling and four flutes high speed steel is chosen as the machining operation and cutting tool. The diameter of the tool is D=7/16 inch (11 mm.). End milling experiment were performed under dry machining condition. Seventy-five readings were used as training

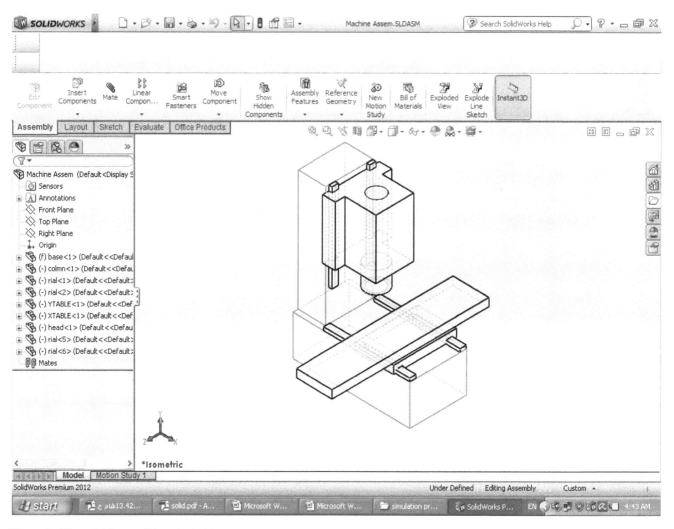

Figure 2. 3D model from solid works 2008.

data set and thirty two readings were used as testing data set. The range selected of speed is 750, 1000, 1250, 1500 and 1750 rpm, for feed rate is 50, 100, 150, 200 and 250 mm/min, and for depth of cut is 0.3, 0.5 and 0.7 mm. Every test was repeated three times, measurements were taking the average value for the roughness parameter Ra, as shown in Tables 1 and 2. Surface Roughness Ra, was observed and measured by using a stylus-based profile-meter (Surtronic 3+, accuracy of 99%) (Figure 5). The direction of measurement of the surface roughness is perpendicular to the direction of the lay. The measurement length of each specimen equals to 12.5 mm divided into five cuts; of length; 2.5 mm each.

THE INTERFACE OF ARTIFICIAL NEUROINTELLIGENCE

Generally, the interface of NeuroIntelligence is optimized to solve forecasting, classification and function approximation problems. NeuroIntelligence is neural network software designed to assist experts in solving real-world problems. Aimed at solution of engineering problems, NeuroIntelligence features only proven algorithms and techniques, is fast and easy-to-use. NeuroIntelligence supports all stages of neural network application. It is used in this work to:

1. Analyze and preprocess the pre measured test results,
2. Find the best neural network architecture that represents the end milling process trend accurately,
3. Test and optimize the selected network,
4. Apply the optimum network to predict surface roughness (Ra) for the designed virtual CNC end milling process (Cus and Balic, 2000). The prediction is much faster with easy-to-use interface and unique time-saving features. All processes on the machine are automated and we can easily understand the underlying machine

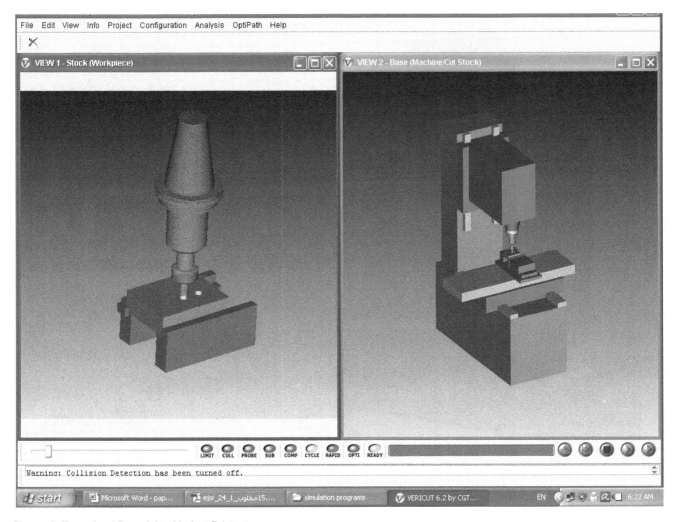

Figure 3. Exporting 3D model to Vericut Printout.

behavior with graphs, statistics and reports. Machining parameters are represented to be intelligible, comprehensive and accessible with the overall virtual environment as in Figure 6.

Predictive surface roughness modeling

Artificial neural networks are systems with inputs and outputs composed of many simple interconnected parallel processing elements, called neurons. These systems are inspired by the structure of the brain. Computing with neural networks is no algorithmic (Yang and Park, 1991) and they are trained through examples rather than programmed by software. Some of the key features of ANN's are their processing speed due to their massive parallelism, their proven ability to be trained, to produce instantaneous and correct responses from corrupted inputs once trained, and their ability to generalize information over a wide range. The Multi-Layer BP

network is a supervised, continuous valued, multi-input and single-output feed forward multi-layer network that follows a gradient descent method. The gradient descent method alters the weight by an amount proportional to the partial derivative of the error with respect to the weight in question. The back propagation phase of the neural network alters the weights so that the error of the network is minimized. This is achieved by taking a pair of input/output vectors and feeding the input vector into the net which generates an output vector, which is compared to the output vector supplied, thus gaining an error value. The error is then passed back through the network (back propagation process), modifying the weights due to this error using the equations. Hence, if the same sets of input/output vectors are presented to the network, the error would be smaller than previously found. For modeling the surface roughness, three-layer feed-forward neural network was used as in Figure 7, because this type of neural network which was used gives the most accurate results. The detailed topology of the used ANN

Figure 4. ProLight 2000 CNC end milling machine.

with optimal training parameters is shown on Figure 7. The ANN was trained with the following parameters: cutting speed (n rpm), feed (f mm/min), radial depth of cut (t mm), The first layer of processing elements is the input layer (buffer), where data are presented to the network (Feng and Menq, 1996). The last layer is the output layer (buffer) which holds the network response (surface roughness Ra). The layers between the input and output layers are called hidden layers. The activation of the multilayer feed forward network is obtained by feeding the external input to the first layer, using the corresponding input function to activate the neurons, and then applying the corresponding transfer function to the resulting activations. The vector output of this layer is then fed to the next layer, which is activated in the same way, and so on, until the output layer is activated, giving the network output vector. This is called the feed forward phase, because the activations propagate forward through the layers.

Developing the ANN predictor

To develop the optimal neural network predictor the following steps must be accomplished:

1. Collecting the experimental data through the measurements of surface roughness.
2. Preparation of data for training and testing of ANN is carried out as follows: Cutting conditions and measured surface roughness Ra are listed into a data matrix (text file or excel file), where cutting conditions as input vectors and roughness values as output vector.
3. Optimization process: where the optimal network configuration is determined and training of parameters is done by simulations.
4. Training and testing of ANN.
5. Putting the estimator into operation. Graphic representation of results and prediction of statistic are obtained.

Details of neural network and its adaptation to surface roughness modeling problem

For the BP network, the choice of the training parameters is the most important criteria that determine the degree of success of a network used to perform the specific task. Even if a set of training parameters and a corresponding architecture have been selected and successfully implemented, the question of whether or not the selected

Table 1. Measured Ra in microns (training data set).

n (rpm)	750			1000			1250			1500			1750		
t (mm) f (mm/min)	0.3	0.5	0.7	0.3	0.5	0.7	0.3	0.5	0.7	0.3	0.5	0.7	0.3	0.5	0.7
50	1.1	1.36	1.9	0.96	1.12	1.36	1.18	1.6	1.08	0.6	0.82	1.02	0.84	0.82	1.54
100	1.28	2.06	2.22	1.02	1.44	1.78	1.18	1.3	1.14	0.86	1.02	1.24	0.98	1.16	1.22
150	1.42	2.63	2.96	1.54	1.54	2.24	1.24	1.34	1.22	1.32	1.36	1.38	1.1	1.26	1.62
200	1.54	3.5	3.52	1.16	2.28	2.64	1.26	1.5	1.44	1.56	1.56	1.4	1.32	1.62	1.6
250	1.82	2.5	5.5	1.58	2.96	3.14	1.66	1.38	1.62	1.32	1.26	1.42	1.48	1.74	1.56

Table 2. Measured Ra in microns (testing data set).

n (rpm)	875		1125		1375		1625	
t (mm) f (mm/min)	0.4	0.6	0.4	0.6	0.4	0.6	0.4	0.6
75	1.42	1.86	1.02	1.36	1.02	1.18	0.76	1.22
125	1.96	2.36	1.28	1.62	1.14	1.33	1.16	1.32
175	2.42	2.66	1.36	1.92	1.22	1.32	1.22	1.38
225	2.06	2.88	1.56	1.96	1.26	1.52	1.3	1.44

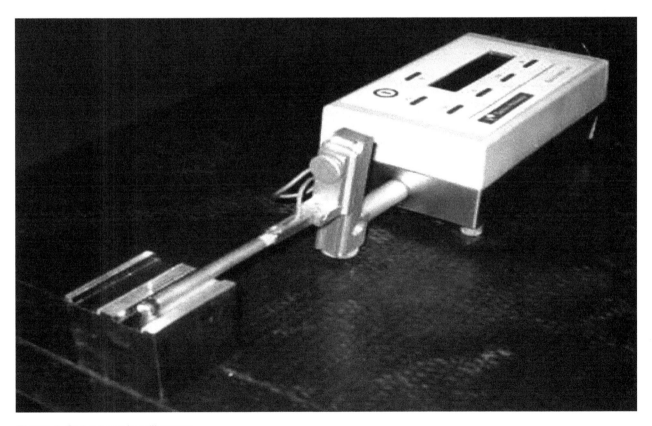

Figure 5. Stylus-based profilometer.

parameters are the optimum for that task will still remain to be answered. The important questions are: How many hidden layer neurons, should be assigned to a given network? What values should be picked for the learning rate (a) and momentum rate (b)? The selection of these training parameters is more art than science and is

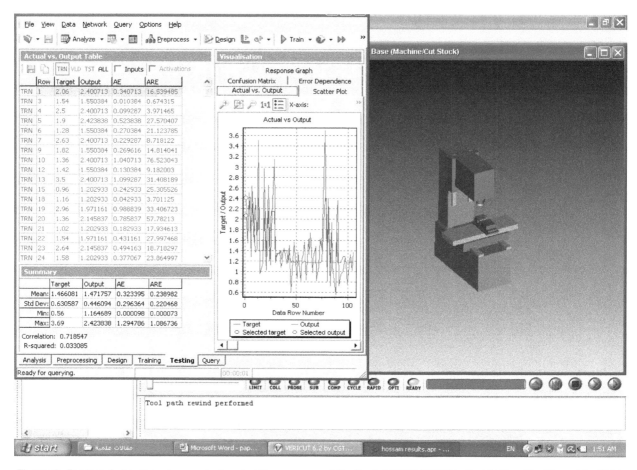

Figure 6. Designed virtual environment of end milling process of the Prolight2000 CNC Vertical Milling Machine while ANN predict Ra.

reported to be depended on application (El Mounayri et al., 1998). In researches three groups of simulations were executed to study systematically the individual influences of training parameters on the performance of back propagation networks used for predicting surface roughness in end milling. The individual effects of varying each of these parameters were kept at (or near) their optimum values (CUS et al., provide year). To evaluate the individual effects of training parameters on the performance of neural network 100 different networks were trained, tested and analyzed using actual machining data. From the results of all simulations the following conclusions can be drawn:

(i) Learning rates below 0.3 give acceptable prediction errors while learning rates must be between 0.01 and 0.2 to minimize the number of training cycles and obtain low predictions errors. Therefore, learning rates that will give an overall optimum performance are any value between 0.01 and 0.2;

(ii) To minimize the estimation errors, momentum rates between 0.001 and 0.005 are good. However, the momentum rate should not exceed 0.004 if the number of training cycles is also to be minimized;

(iii) The optimum number of hidden layer nodes is 3 or 6. Networks with between 2 and 15 hidden layer nodes, other than 3 or 6, also performed fairly well but resulted in higher training cycles;

(iv) Networks trained with the (tanh) transfer function in all their processing elements give the least prediction errors, while those employing sigmoid and sine give the highest and next highest prediction errors respectively;

(v) Networks that employ the sine function require the lowest number of training cycles followed by the Arctangent, while those that employ the hyperbolic tangent require the highest number of training cycles; Figures 8 to 16 shows the network information details implemented in this paper.

DISCUSSION

The interface of this application is a page that briefly explains the project as shown in Figure 6 which has some description about the CNC milling machine and the milling process. The machining equipment menu will

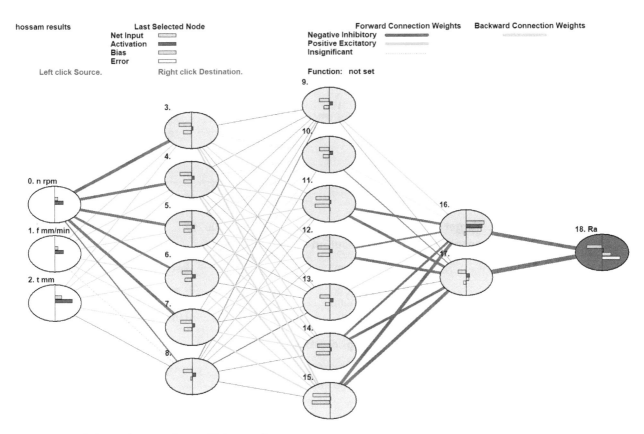

Figure 7. Predictive surface roughness (Ra) network.

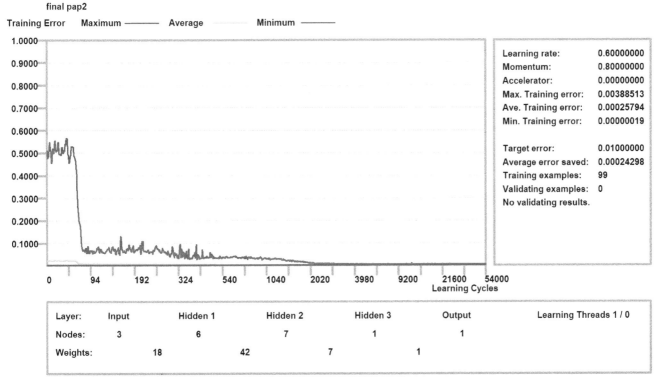

Figure 8. Training error curve of modeling surface roughness (Ra.) after 54000 cycles.

hossam results   78250 cycles. Target error 0.0100 Average training error 0.007451
The first 3 of 3 Inputs in descending order.

Column	Input Name	Importance	Relative Importance
0	n rpm	1.5562	
1	f mm/min	1.4925	
2	t mm	1.2772	

Figure 9. Effect weights of cutting conditions.

final pap2   54239 cycles. Target error 0.0100 Average training error 0.000258
The first 3 of 3 Inputs in descending order.   Output column 3 Ra

Column	Input Name	Change from	to	Sensitivity	Relative Sensitivity
0	n rpm	750.0000	1750.0000	0.242541335	
1	f mm/min	50.0000	250.0000	0.024277320	
2	t mm	0.3000	0.7000	0.002490710	

Figure 10. Sensitivity of Surface Roughness (Ra) to cutting conditions.

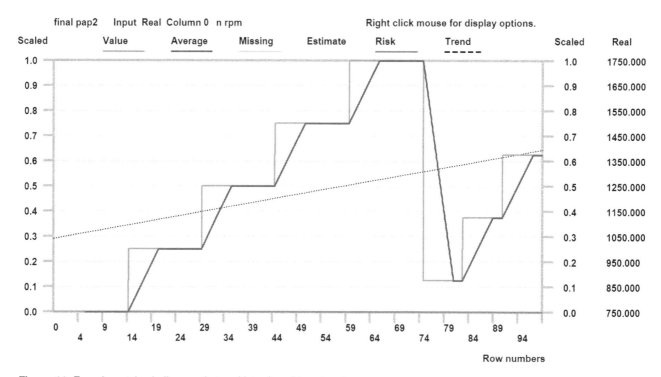

Figure 11. Experimental spindle speeds trend introduced to network.

describe and displays the cutter and example of CNC milling machine processes. In this application, VR has made it easy to perform the simulation of the geometrical modeling of end milling process and analytical modeling of machining parameters. By clicking the Simulation button, it would link the user to the page where two windows comprising of control panel (user input) and ANN browser displaying the surface roughness predictions in a 3D environment. The control panel shows information on the machining process such as

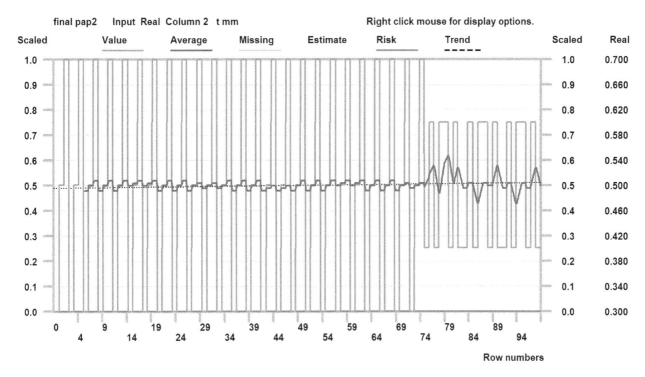

Figure 12. Experimental radial depth of cut trend introduced to network.

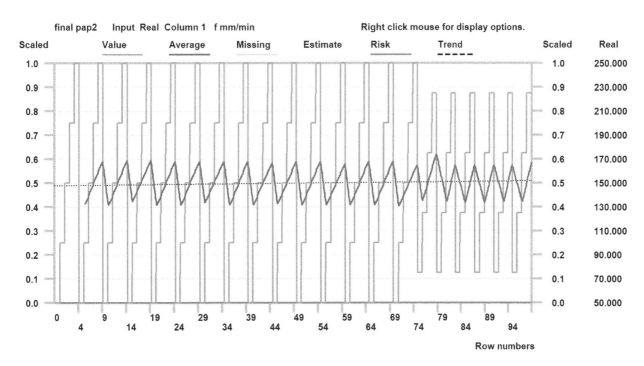

Figure 13. Experimental feed rates trend introduced to network.

specification of the machine, cutting condition and manual description on how to use this application. To run the simulation, the user has to input the CNC part program in G & M coding as a text file as shown in Figure 17. The coding program specifies the size of the work piece and chooses the milling process parameters such

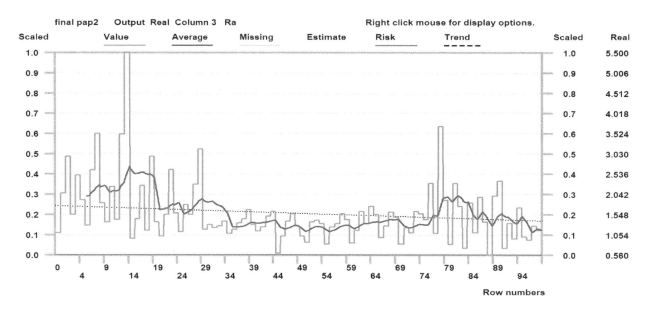

Figure 14. Experimental surface roughness (Ra) trend introduced to network.

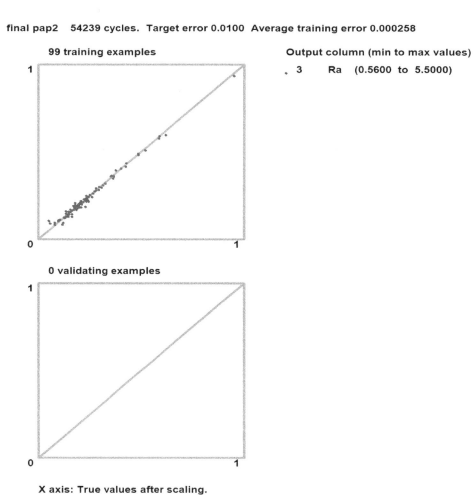

Figure 15. Network scatter diagram.

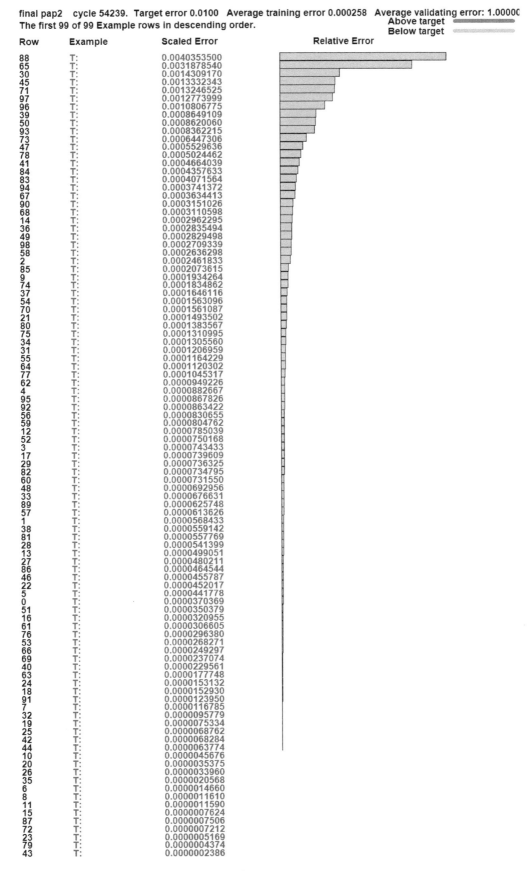

Figure 16. Error distribution along input row values.

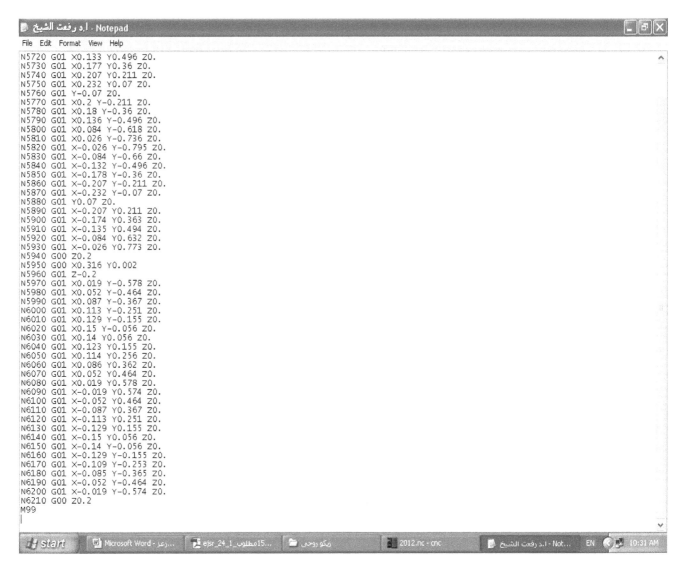

Figure 17. Optimized G& M Coding CNC Program as a Text Format.

as cutting speeds, radial depth of cut and the feed rate of worktable. Simulation of the virtual end milling process and surface roughness on machined work pieces are generated simultaneously. The predictive capability of using neural network approaches are compared using statistics, which showed that neural network predictions for surface roughness were for 1.8% closer to the experimental measurements, compared to 8% using analytical (depending on empirical equations) method.

CONCLUSIONS

Virtual Milling Process has been successfully developed. This application shows a simulation of the end milling process in the virtual reality environment and simulation of the machining parameters such as surface roughness

on machined work pieces. It is developed with the purpose of providing useful information on the end milling process and the related parts of the CNC machine to the user. As a prototype, Real time simulation for virtual milling process is implemented using, Solidworks2008, Vericut6.2, and Alyuda NeuroIntelligance, are interfaced as the animation and prediction engine making the virtual milling machine controllable. This simulation software interface can be used in training students on operation of CNC milling machine and increase the understanding of the milling process. This will save money in purchasing the actual equipment and hence accidental damage on the actual machine due to programming errors or mishandling can be avoided. Supervised neural networks are used to successfully estimate the surface roughness developed during end milling process. It can be claimed that the results obtained from the neural model and of the experimental results confirms the efficiency and accuracy of the model for predicting the surface roughness. In testing the model, the surface roughness was predicted to an accuracy of ±1.8% (more accurate for this particular case compared with other techniques such as multiple regression or genetics). An effort is made to include as many different cutting conditions as possible that influence the surface roughness value extensive experimentation forms the basis of the model developed. The procedure should be used for the fast approximate determination of optimum cutting conditions on the machine, when there is not enough time for deep analysis. Due to high speed of processing, low consumption of memory, great robustness, possibility of self-learning and simple incorporation into chips the approach ensures estimation of the surface roughness in real time.

REFERENCES

Bayliss GM, Bowyer A, Taylor RI, Willis PJ (1994). Set-theoretic Solid Modelling Techniques and Applications. Virtual Manufacturing Proceedings, CSG 94, Winchester, UK, pp. 353-365.

Boothroyd G, Knight WA (1989). Fundamentals of Machining and Machine Tools. Marcel Dekker, Inc.

Chawla R, Banerjee A (2001). A Virtual Environment For Simulating Manufacturing Operations in 3D. Proceeding of the 2001 Winter Simulation Conference pp. 991-997.

Cus F, Balic J (2000). "Selection of cutting conditions and tool flow in flexible manufacturing system". Int. J. Manuf. Sci. Technol. 2:101-106.

Delmia (2001). Delmia Machining Solution. (online) http://www.delmia.com/ (20 April 2003).

El Mounayri H, Spence AD, Elbestawi, MA (1998). "Milling Process Simulation-A General Solid Modeller Based Paradigm". ASME J. Manuf. Sci. Eng. 120:213-221.

Fang XD, Luo S, Lee NJ, Jin F (1998). Virtual Machining Lab for Knowledge Learning and Skill Training. Computer Appl. Eng. Educ. 6(2):89-97.

Feng HY, Menq CH (1996). "A Flexible Ball-End Milling System Model for Cutting Force and Machining Error Prediction". ASME J. Manuf. Sci. Eng. 118:461-469.

CUS F, ZUPERL U, MILFELNER M (2003). University of Maribor, Slovenia Dynamic Neural Network Approach for Tool Cutting Force Modeling of End Milling Operations.

Haslina A, Zainal R, Mahayuddin Y (2008). Flank Wear Simulation of a Virtual End Milling Process, Eur. J. Sci. Res. 24(1):148-156. ISSN 1450-216X, © EuroJournals Publishing, Inc. 2008 http://www.eurojournals.com/ejsr.htm

Qiu ZM, Chen YP, Zhou ZD, Ong SK, Nee AYC (2001). Multi-User NC Machining Simulation Over the WWW. Int. J. Adv. Manuf. Technol. 18:1-6.

Schofield D (1995). Virtual Reality Technology and its Application.

Soltan IM, Eltaib MEH, El-Zahry RM (2007). Surface Roughness Prediction in End Milling using Adaptive Neuro-Fuzzy Inference System, Fourth International Conference on Advances in Production Engineering (APE)., Warsaw-Poland.

Tandon V, El-Mounayri H, Kishawy H (2002). "NC End Milling Optimization Using Evolutionary Computation. Int. J. Mach. Tools Manuf. 42:595-605.

Yang M, Park H (1991) "The Prediction of Cutting Force in Ball-End Milling". Int. J. Mach. Tools Manuf. 31:45-54.

Yuzhong C, Altintas Y (2007). Modeling of spindle-bearing and machine tool systems for virtual simulation of milling operations. Int. J. Mach. Tools Manuf. 47(9):1342-1350.

8

Development of a realtime microcomputer-based logging system for diagnosis and research

Ogidan O. K.[1]*, Bamisaye[2], A. J. and Adeloye V. S. A.[3]

[1]Department of Electrical Engineering, Cape Peninsula University of Technology, South Africa.
[2]Department of Electrical and Electronics Engineering, Federal University of Technology, Akure, Nigeria.
[3]Department of Electrical and Electronics Engineering, Ekiti State University, Ado Ekiti, Nigeria.

In this research, a realtime temperature logging system that logs human temperature into the computer over a period was developed and the temperature chart produced is useful for diagnosis and research purposes. The graphical representation within the threshold temperature (36°C) depicts normal body temperature of a healthy person. An upshot beyond this temperature makes the logger to signal an audible alarm for medical attention. It consists of hardware and software units. The hardware consists of sensor NTC (negative coefficient of temperature) thermistor, pre-amp; analog to digital converter, buffer between analog to digital converter and computer interface port. The software was developed in Visual Basic 6.0 for interfacing through the parallel port of the computer and the program designed to provide a user-friendly environment where the measurement can be read. There is high correlation between the approach developed by this study and other standard measuring equipments — correlation of 0.994574 with standard thermistor, and correlation of 0.997785 with standard thermocouple. The temperature logged to the PC can also be viewed from another PC remotely located over a network thus providing a good framework for telemedicine.

Key words: Diagnosis, remote logging, temperature measurement, thermistor, thermocouple.

INTRODUCTION

A realtime system is "any system where a timely response by the computer to external stimuli is vital"; it is a system in which the total correctness of an operation depends not only upon its logical correctness, but also upon the time in which it is performed. In other words, the completion of an operation after its deadline is considered useless - ultimately, this may cause a critical failure of the complete system (Ben-Ari, 1990). It can be hard realtime or soft realtime and has its application in different fields including manufacturing, process controls, high-speed data acquisition devices, medical monitoring equipment, aircraft "fly-by-wire" controls to mention a few (Juvva, 1998). In this work, the monitoring of human temperature is considered. Temperature is one of the parameters used to determine the health status of an individual (Medline, 2008). It is regarded as one of the vital signs. Vital signs include the heartbeat, pulse rate, temperature, and blood pressure. These signs are measured and monitored to check an individual's level of physical functioning (Gao et al., 2005; Medline, 2009). In

Medicare, temperature is important and it is often one of the first examinations carried out on a patient. Most ailments common to mammals are accompanied by temperature increase. A normal human temperature is between 36 and 37.4°C; body temperature rising above this range indicates fever.

REALTIME TEMPERATURE LOGGING SYSTEM

The developed Realtime Logging System is portable and battery powered. It is used to monitor the human temperature for a period of time. It has a user-friendly computer program that facilitates the viewing, digital recording and plotting of the logged temperature. The plot within the threshold temperature (36°C for a healthy person) depicts normal body temperature. An upshot beyond this temperature makes the logger to signal an audible alarm to alert the medical personnel. The recording and graphical representations are done per second and in realtime.

HARDWARE DESIGN AND SOFTWARE DEVELOPMENT

The device developed contains a temperature sensor – negative temperature coefficient (NTC) thermistor, which transduced the temperature measured into electronic analog signal. The analog signal was then passed into an analog-to-digital converter (ADC).

---

*Corresponding author. E-mail: gbengaogidan@yahoo.com.

Figure 1. Circuit under construction.

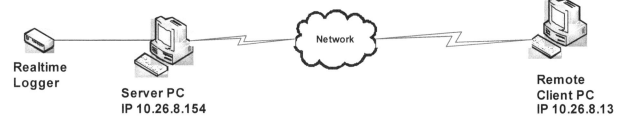

Realtime Logger

Server PC IP 10.26.8.154

Network

Remote Client PC IP 10.26.8.13

Figure 2. Diagram of developed logger measurement being accessed remotely over a network.

The converted signal was received and transmitted (using a transceiver) to the microcomputer through the parallel port (Axelson, 2000). In the laboratory setting, a personal computer (server PC) was used (Intel™ i3 CPU, 3.06 GHz processor, 2 GB RAM, 160 GB HDD, Windows Xp professional service pack 3 OS). A computer program in Visual Basic 6.0 was then written to address the parallel port and to log the measured temperature into a user-friendly interface where the temperature was both interpreted and analyzed. The program was written to be able to:

(a) measure and log human temperature into the computer in realtime;
(b) start and stop logging automatically and
(c) raise an audible alarm or give a visual message when the reading is beyond a pre-set (threshold) value.

Figure 1 shows the logger during construction. The server PC was networked to a client PC (Genuine Intel (R) CPU, 1.2 GHz Intel Processor, 2 GB RAM, 80 GB HDD, Windows7 OS) using the University Intranet (Figure 2).

PERFORMANCE TESTING AND ANALYSIS

After the individual circuit stages and the software were tested; the assembly was then tested connecting to a human being. The temperature was logged into the computer over a period of time. This was done also with a mercury thermometer and the readings were found to be almost exactly the same with a difference of 0.02°C. The software was tested and found to be able to

i) measure and log human temperature into the computer in realtime;
ii) start and stop logging automatically and
iii) raise an audible alarm or give a visual message when the reading is beyond a pre-set (threshold) value.
iv) give the temperature reading as well as details of the date, time (minute, second)
v) log temperature over the network into a remote client

Table 1. Measurement of temperature of the atmosphere. Table of data recorded every 30 s using standard thermistor, standard thermocouple and developed datalogger.

Time (s)	Developed	Standard TH	Standard THC
30	25.42	25.53	25.51
60	25.62	25.69	25.65
90	25.64	25.67	25.65
120	25.62	25.69	25.67
150	25.66	25.65	25.51
180	25.62	25.65	25.65
210	25.64	25.67	25.65
240	27.54	27.58	27.55
270	27.56	27.61	27.58
300	27.62	27.6	27.64
330	27.62	27.68	27.72
360	27.6	27.64	27.55
Correlation with developed thermometer		0.9945748	0.997785

PC (in realtime) using the remote desktop connection in windows operating system.

In order to validate the developed logger measurement, it was used (at room temperature) to measure atmospheric temperature alongside standard temperature sensors (thermistor and thermocouple) for about one hour.

It must be noted however that the temperature sensor would have to be attached to the patient being monitored in order to take the reading for a period of time. In this paper, the temperature measurement device was used (at room temperature) to measure atmospheric temperature alongside standard temperature sensors (thermistor and thermocouple) for about one hour. Table 1 shows the table of data recorded every 30 s and the graphs of the comparison are shown in Figure 4.

DISCUSSION

The human body temperature measured was logged into a user-friendly interface that facilitates the viewing, digital recording plotting of the measured temperature. The graph within the threshold temperature (36°C) depicts normal body temperature of a healthy person with the plotting in colour blue. An upshot beyond this temperature makes the logger to signal an audible alarm thus alerting the medical personnel. The colour of the graph also changes from blue to red colour (Figure 3). The alarm and change of plotting colour depends on the threshold monitor temperature set by the user as seen in Figure 3. Using the Windows operating system Remote Desktop Connection (RDC) to access the server PC with Internet Protocol (IP) address 10.26.8.154 located at the Department of Electrical CPUT (Figure 2), the measured temperature logging could be viewed from client PC with IP address 10.26.8.13 located at the PG residence,

CPUT over the Intranet. The remote user is able to operate (start/stop) the logger, however, the alarm system was not audible from the remote PC (Figures 2 and 5).

Figure 4 shows the graph of the comparison results of the developed logger having a correlation of 0.9945 with standard thermistor and 0.9977 with thermocouple. In both cases the correlation tends towards unity (Jain RK 2004). This indicates a high degree of measurement closeness/reliability.

Conclusion

This work has developed a Realtime microcomputer-based logging system for diagnosis and research purposes that successfully logs human temperature into a remote PC over a network (Intranet).The result obtained was compared with that of the standard digital thermometers and found to extremely close with a difference of 0.02. It compares favourably with standard thermistor and standard thermocouple with a correlation of 0.9945 and 0.9977 respectively. It would be very useful to medical personnel in gathering data to be used in diagnosis and research and offers a high potential for telemedicine. It would be of immense importance to pediatricians who have to treat children, many of whom cannot talk, the dumb or even animals (mammals) in veterinary medicine. The device is capable of raising audible alarm and as such, it would be very useful in Intensive Care Unit (ICU) of the hospital where prompt responses are needed to save lives of patients under critical conditions. The device is portable and compatible with most computers (laptop and desktop) running windows. This makes it useful not only in the hospital but in the homes and offices thus bringing Medicare to your door. However it could be improved in future to transmit

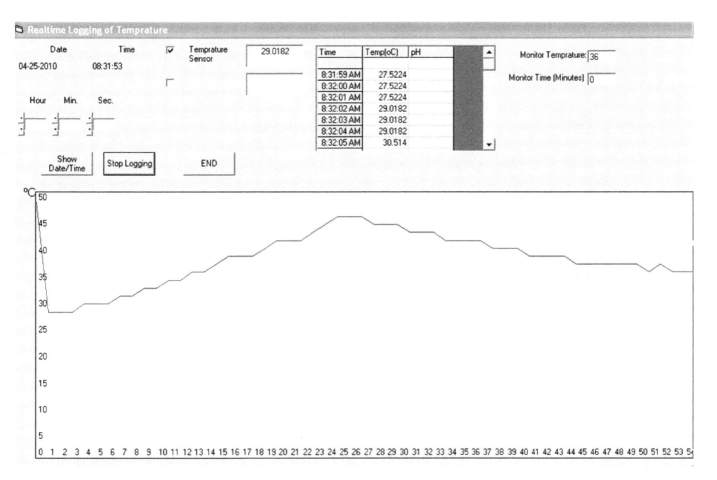

Figure 3. User-friendly interface on server PC showing plotting of temperature measured by the logger with (threshold temperature set at 36°C).

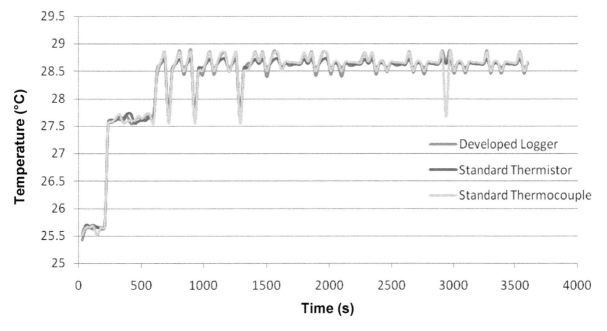

Figure 4. Graph of developed logger compared with standard thermistor and thermocouple when used to measure atmospheric temperature.

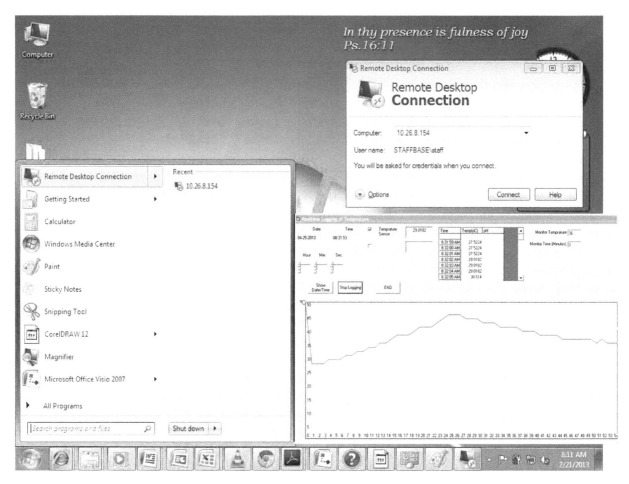

Figure 5. Diagram showing Remote Desktop Connection and user-friendly interface accessed on remote client PC.

measured temperature wirelessly to the PC instead of cable thus making it more convenient for users.

REFERENCES

Axelson J (2000). Parallel Port Complete. Lakeview Research Publishers, Madison USA pp. 10-30.

Ben-Ari M (1990). Principles of Concurrent and Distributed Programming. Prentice Hall p. 164.

Gao T, Greenspan D, Welsh M, Juang RR, Alm A (2005). Vital Signs Monitoring and Patient Tracking Over a Wireless Network. Proceedings of the 27th Annual International Conference of the IEEE EMBS, Shanghai, p. 4.

Jain RK (2004). Mechanical and Industrial Measurements. Khanna Publishers, India pp. 857-891.

Juvva K (1998). Topics in Dependable Embedded Systems. Carnegie Mellon University Electrical and Computer Engineering Department.http://www.ece.cmu.edu/~koopman/des_s99/real_time/index.html, accessed 20/02/2013.

Medline P (2008). http://www.nlm.nih.gov/medlineplus/ency/article/003400.htm accessed 2010-06-06.

Medline P (2009).http://www.nlm.nih.gov/medlineplus/ency/article/002341.htm accessed 2010-06-06.

9

Spiking neural network-based control chart pattern recognition

Medhat H. A. Awadalla[1]*, I. I. Ismaeil[1] and M. Abdellatif Sadek[2]

[1]Communications and Electronic Department, Faculty of Engineering, Helwan University, Egypt.
[2]Information Technology Department, High Institute of Engineering, Shorouk Academy, Egypt.

Due to an increasing competition in products, consumers have become more critical in choosing products. The quality of products has become more important. Statistical process control (SPC) is usually used to improve the quality of products. Control charting plays the most important role in SPC. Control charts help to monitor the behavior of the process, to determine whether it is stable or not. Unnatural patterns in control charts mean that, there are some unnatural causes for variations in SPC. Spiking neural networks (SNNs) are the third generation of artificial neural networks that consider time as an important feature for information representation and processing. In this paper, spiking neural network architecture is proposed to be used for control charts pattern recognition (CCPR). Furthermore, enhancements to the SpikeProp learning algorithm are proposed. These enhancements provide additional learning rules for the synaptic delays, time constants and for the neurons thresholds. Experiments have been conducted and the achieved results show a remarkable improvement in the overall performance compared with artificial neural networks.

Key words: Spiking neural network, control chart pattern recognition, SpikeProp algorithm,

INTRODUCTION

Traditionally, statistical process control (SPC) was used only for monitoring and identifying process variation. Advances in SPC charting have moved from merely statistical and economic control to diagnosis purposes through control chart pattern identification (Ibrahim and Adnan, 2010). Control charts are useful tool in detecting out-of-control situations in process data (Hui-Ping and Chuen-Sheng, 2009). A process is considered out of control, if a point falls outside the control limits or a series of points exhibit an unnatural pattern (also known as nonrandom variation). There are seven basic CCPs, normal (NOR), systematic (SYS), cyclic (CYC), increasing trend (IT), decreasing trend (DT), upward shift (US) and downward shift (DS), as shown in Figure 1. All other patterns are either special forms of basic CCPs or mixed forms of two or more basic CCPs.

Advances in manufacturing and measurement technology have enabled real-time, rapid and integrated gauging and measurement of process and product quality (Indra et al., 2010). A typical control chart consists of a centre line (CL) corresponding to the average statistical level and two control limits, upper (UCL) and lower (LCL) normally located at $\pm 3\sigma$ of this statistic, where σ is a measure of the spread, or standard deviation in a distribution. Selection of CCPs parameters is important for training and testing the ANN recognizers. Among the important parameters included window size, random noise, mean shift (for shift patterns), trend slope (for trend patterns), cycle amplitude and cycle period (for cyclic pattern), and systematic departure (for systematic pattern), Table 1 shows the equations that described all patterns in CCPs. The following equations were used to create the data points for the various patterns.

Control chart pattern recognition has the capability to recognize unnatural patterns (Jenn-Hwai et al., 2005). Pattern recognition is an information-reduction process which aims to classify patterns based on a priori knowledge or based on statistical information extracted from the patterns. The patterns to be classified are usually groups of measurements or observations come from process or event (Samir, 2009).

Currently, most researchers in artificial neural networks are interested in spiking neural networks (SNNs). SNNs

---

*Corresponding author. E-mail: awadalla_medhat@yahoo. co.uk.

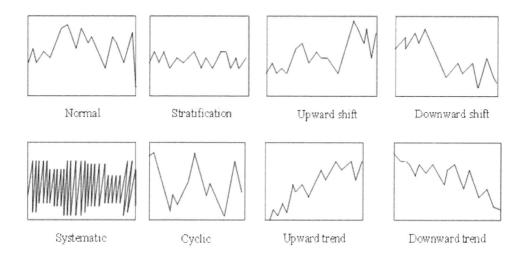

Figure 1. Common CCPs for univariate process.

Table 1. Equations for simulation control charts.

Patterns class	Description	Equations
1	Systematic	$P(t) = \eta + r_i(t)\sigma + d \times (-1)^i$
2	Cyclic	$P(t) = \eta + r_i(t)\sigma + a \sin(2\pi t/T)$
3	Increasing Trend	$P(t) = \eta + r_i(t)\sigma + gt$
4	Decreasing Trend	$P(t) = \eta + r_i(t)\sigma - gt$
5	Upward Shift	$P(t) = \eta + r_i(t)\sigma + bs$
6	Downward Shift	$P(t) = \eta + r_i(t)\sigma - bs$

where η is the nominal mean value of the process variable under observation (set to 80), σ is the standard deviation of the process variable (set to 5), a is the amplitude of cyclic variations in a cyclic pattern (set to 15 or less), g is the gradient of an increasing trend pattern or a decreasing trend pattern (set in the range 0.2 to 0.5), b indicates the shift position in an upward shift pattern and a downward shift pattern ($b = 0$ before the shift and $b = 1$ at the shift and thereafter), s is the magnitude of the shift (set between 7.5 and 20), $r_i(.)$ is a function that generates random numbers normally distributed between -3 and 3, t is the discrete time at which the monitored process variable is sampled (set within the range 0 to 20), T is the period of a cycle in a cyclic pattern (set between 4 and 12 sampling intervals) and $P(t)$ is the value of the sampled data point at time t.

are often referred to as the third generation of neural networks which have potential to solve problems related to biological stimuli. They derive their strength and interest from an accurate modeling of synaptic interactions between neurons, taking into account the time of spike emission. SNNs overcome the computational power of neural networks made of threshold or sigmoid units. Based on dynamic event-driven processing, they open up new horizons for developing models with an exponential capacity of memorizing and a strong ability to fast adaptation. Moreover, SNNs add a new dimension, the temporal axis, to the representation capacity and the processing abilities of neural networks (Meftah et al., 2008).

One of the key problems with spiking neural networks is the training algorithm. Much research relied on biologically inspired local learning rules, but these rules can only be implemented using unsupervised learning. However, in supervised learning SpikeProp algorithm operates on networks of spiking neurons, that use exact spike time temporal coding. This means that the exact spike time of input and output spikes encode the input and output values (Bohte et al., 2000). SpikeProp is an error-back propagation learning rule suited for supervised learning of spiking neurons that use exact spike time coding. SpikeProp assumes a special network topology. Globally the network looks like a classical feedforward network, but every connection consists of a fixed number of delayed synaptic terminals, different weights and different delays. However, the delays are fixed, and only the weights can be trained. Because the delayed synaptic terminals are fixed, this network topology has to be largely over-specified to make all possible weight/delay combinations possible (Natschlager and Ruf, 1998).

Enhancements to the SpikeProp algorithm such that, the delay and the time constant of every connection and the threshold of the neurons can be trained; because the delays can be trained, fewer synaptic terminals are necessary, effectively will reduce the number of weights and thus, the simulation time of the network.

SPIKING NEURAL NETWORKS ARCHITECTURE

Spiking neural networks (SNNs) have a similar architecture to traditional neural networks. Elements that differentiate in the architecture are the numbers of synaptic terminals between each layer of neurons and also there are synaptic delays. Several mathematical models have been proposed to describe the behavior of spiking neurons such as Leakey Integrate-and-Fire model (LIFN) (Mass, 1997) and Spike Response model (SRM) (Bialek et al., 1991). Figures 2(a) and (b) show the network structure proposed by Natschlager and Ruf (1998).

This structure consists of a feedforward fully connected spiking neural network with multiple delayed synaptic terminals. The different layers are labeled H,I and J for the input, hidden, and output layer respectively as shown in Figure 3. The adopted spiking neurons are based on the Spike Response Model (SRM) to describe the relationship between input spikes and the internal state variable. Consider a neuron J, having a set Dj of immediate pre-synaptic neurons, receives a set of spikes with firing times firing times $t_i, i \in D_j$. It is assumed that any neuron can generate at most one spike during the simulation interval and discharges when the internal state variable reaches a threshold. The dynamics of the internal state variable xj (t) are described by the following function:

$$x_j(t) = \sum_{i \in D_j} w_{ij} y_j(t) \qquad (1)$$

yj (t) is the un-weighted contribution of a single synaptic terminal to the state variable which described as a pre-synaptic spike at a synaptic terminal k as a PSP of standard height with delay d^k.

$$y_i^k = \varepsilon(t - t_i - d^k) \qquad (2)$$

The time t_i is the firing time of pre-synaptic neuron i, and d^k the delay associated with the synaptic terminal k. by considering the multiple synapses per a connection, the state variable $x_j(t)$ of neuron j is receiving inputs from all preceding neurons and then described as the weighted sum of the pre-synaptic contributions as follow:

$$x_j(t) = \sum_{i \in D_j} \sum_{k=1}^{m} w_{ij}^k y_i^k(t) \qquad (3)$$

The effect of the input spikes is described by the function ε(t) and so is called the spike response function, and w_{ij} is the weight describing the synaptic strengths. The spike response function ε(t) is modeled with the α- function, thus implementing a leaky-integrate-and-fire spiking neuron, is given by:

$$\varepsilon(t) = \frac{t}{\tau} e^{1 - \frac{t}{\tau}}, \text{ for } t > 0, \text{ else } \varepsilon(t) = 0 \qquad (4)$$

Where τ is the time constant, which defines the rise and the decay

time of the postsynaptic potential (PSP). The individual connection described in Jenn-Hwai and Miin-Shen (2005), consists of a fixed number of m synaptic terminals.

Each terminal serves as a sub-connection that is associated with a different delay and weight (Figure 3b). The delay d^k of a synaptic terminal k is defined as the difference between the firing time of the pre synaptic neuron and the time when the postsynaptic potential starts rising. The threshold θ is constant and equal for all neurons in the network.

An overview of neural coding schemes

In real biological systems, signals are encoded by information using specific coding methods. Basically, there are three different coding methods: rate coding, temporal coding, and population coding. Rate coding is the earliest neural coding method. The essential information is encoded in the firing rates and the rate is counted as a spike in an interval T divided by T (averaged over time). More recently, there has been growing recognition that the traditional view of mean firing encoding is often inadequate. Experiments on the visual system of a fly and studies of the middle temporal (MT) area of the monkey have indicated that the precise timing of spikes can be used to encode information. Such a scheme is called temporal coding (Bohte, 2002; Bohte et al., 2000). In temporal coding, the timing of single spikes is used to encode information. It is considered that, the timing of the first spike contains most of the relevant information needed for processing. Population coding is another coding scheme in which information is encoded in the activity of a given population of neurons firing within a small temporal window. This work adopts temporal coding as the code used by neurons to transmit information.

Spiking neural network for supervised learning procedure

Authors worked on supervised learning (Rumelhart et al., 1986) proposed a network of spiking neurons, that encodes information in the timing of individual spike times. They derived a supervised learning rule, SpikeProp, akin to traditional error back propagation. They utilized a fully connected feed-forward spiking neural network with layers labeled H(input), I (hidden) and J (output). Each connection between two neurons corresponds to multi sub-connections. Each sub-connection is characterized with a different delay and weight. They demonstrated how networks of spiking neurons with biologically reasonable action potentials can perform complex non-linear classification in fast temporal coding just as well as rate-coded networks and the resulting algorithm can be applied equally well to networks with many hidden layers. The target of the algorithm is to learn a set of target firing times, denoted at the output neurons j∈J for a given set of input patterns

$$\{P[t_1, t_2, \ldots, t_h]\}$$

where defines a single input pattern described by single spike-times for each neuron h∈H. The least mean squares error is choosing as the error-function. Given the desired spike times $\{t_j^d\}$ and actual firing times $\{t_j^a\}$, this error-function is defined by:

$$E_v = \frac{1}{2} \sum_j (t_j^a - t_j^d)^2 \qquad (5)$$

The general form of the error derived by a connection's weight is:

$$\frac{\partial E}{\partial w_{ij}^k} = \frac{\dfrac{\partial E}{(\partial t_j)(t_j^a)(\partial t_j)}}{\dfrac{(\partial a_j t)(t_j^a)(\partial a_j(t))}{(\partial w_{ij}^k)(t_j^a)}}$$

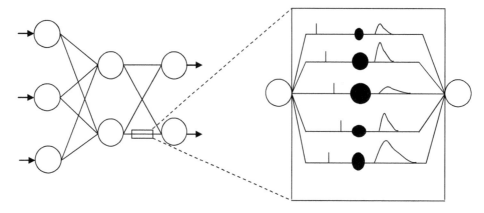

Figure 2. a) Feed forward spiking neural network b) Connection consisting of multiple synaptic terminals.

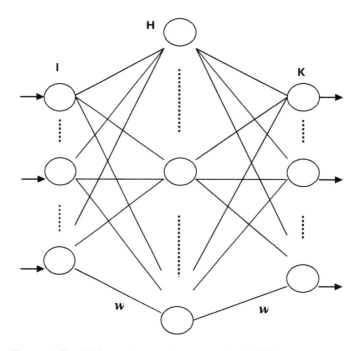

Figure 3. The MLP neural network structure for CCPR.

$$= \varepsilon_{ij}^{k}\left(t_{j}^{a} - t_{i}^{a} - d_{ij}^{k}\right)\delta_{j} \qquad (6)$$

Here δ_j is not the same for neurons in the output layer and neurons in the hidden layers. The set is used to represent all the direct pre-synaptic neurons of neuron j, while the set represents all the direct successors of neuron j. For a neuron in the output layer, $j \in o$, δ_j is equal to:

$$\delta_j = \frac{-\left(t_j^a - t_j^d\right)}{\sum_{i \in \Gamma_j} \sum_k w_{ij}^k \dfrac{\partial \varepsilon_{ij}^k}{\partial t}\left(t_j^a - t_i^a - d_{ij}^k\right)} \qquad (7)$$

For hidden neurons $j \in H$, is equal to:

$$\delta_j = \frac{\sum_{i \in \Gamma_j} \delta_i \sum_k w_{ij}^k \dfrac{\partial \varepsilon_{ij}^k}{\partial t}\left(t_i^a - t_j^a - d_{ij}^k\right)}{\sum_{i \in \Gamma_j} \sum_k w_{ij}^k \dfrac{\partial \varepsilon_{ij}^k}{\partial t}\left(t_j^a - t_i^a - d_{ij}^k\right)} \qquad (8)$$

Here, the error-backpropagation is clearly visible because is dependent on all 's of the successors neuron j.

The adaptation rule for weights is

$$w_{ij}(T+1) = w_{ij}(T) + \Delta w_{ij}(T). \qquad (9)$$

Where T is the Tth step of algorithm (T^{th} is simulation interval), and

$$w_{new} = w_{old} + \Delta w_{ij} \qquad (10)$$

Table 2. Control chart patterns and neural network outputs.

Pattern class	Description	ANNs outputs Node 1	2	3	4	5	6
1	Systematic	1	0	0	0	0	0
2	Cyclic	0	1	0	0	0	0
3	Increasing trend	0	0	1	0	0	0
4	Decreasing trend	0	0	0	1	0	0
5	Upward shift	0	0	0	0	1	0
6	Downward shift	0	0	0	0	0	1

$$\Delta w_{ij}(T) = -\eta \frac{\partial E}{(\partial w_{ij})(T)} \quad (11)$$

The symbol η is the learning rate. The error is minimized by changing the weight according to the negative local gradient.

Enhancements to SpikeProp algorithm

The following enhancements have been proposed to provide additional learning rules for the synaptic delays, time constants and the neurons' thresholds.

Learning synaptic delays

The partial derivative of the error function to the synaptic delay d_{ij}^k is determined:

$$\frac{\partial E}{\partial d_{ij}^k} = \frac{\dfrac{\partial E}{(\partial t_j)}(t_j^a)(\partial t_j)}{(\partial a_j(t))(t_j^a)(\partial a_j(t))}{(\partial d_{ij}^k)(t_j^a)} \quad (12)$$

The first two terms are the same as for the weight update rule, only the last term is different:

$$\frac{\partial a_j(t)}{\partial d_{ij}^k}(t_j^a) = -w_{ij}^k \frac{\partial \varepsilon_{ij}^k}{\partial t (t_j^a - t_i^a - d_{ij}^k)}$$
$$= -w_{ij}^k \varepsilon_{ij}^k (t_j^a - t_i^a - d_{ij}^k)\left[\frac{1}{t_j^a - t_i^a - d_{ij}^k} - \frac{1}{\tau_{ij}^k}\right] \quad (13)$$

By substitution and using the definition of in Equation 8 (which is different for output neurons and hidden neurons) we can get:

$$\frac{\partial E}{\partial d_{ij}^k} = -w_{ij}^k \frac{\partial \varepsilon_{ij}^k}{\partial t (t_j^a - t_i^a - d_{ij}^k)} \delta_j \quad (14)$$

The final update rule for the delays is:

$$\Delta d_{ij}^k = -\eta_d \frac{\partial E}{\partial d_{ij}^k} \quad (15)$$

Where η_d is the learning rate for the delays.

Learning synaptic time constants

The partial derivative of the error function to the time constant of the α-function

$$\frac{\partial E}{\partial \tau_{ij}^k} = \frac{\partial E}{\partial t_j}(t_j^a)\frac{\partial t_j}{\partial a_j(t)}(t_j^a)\frac{\partial a_j(t)}{(\partial \tau_{ij}^k)(t_j^a)} \quad (16)$$

The third term can be written as:

$$\frac{\partial a_j(t)}{\partial \tau_{ij}^k}(t_j^a) = w_{ij}^k \frac{\partial \varepsilon_{ij}^k}{(\partial \tau_{ij}^k)(t_j^a - t_i^a - d_{ij}^k)}$$
$$= w_{ij}^k \varepsilon_{ij}^k (t_j^a - t_i^a - d_{ij}^k)\left[\frac{(t_j^a - t_i^a - d_{ij}^k)}{(\tau_{ij}^k)^2} - \frac{1}{\tau_{ij}^k}\right] \quad (17)$$

By substitution and using the definition of δ_j in Equation 8 we can get:

$$\frac{\partial E}{\partial \tau_{ij}^k} = w_{ij}^k \varepsilon_{ij}^k (t_j^a - t_i^a - d_{ij}^k)\left[\frac{(t_j^a - t_i^a - d_{ij}^k)}{(\tau_{ij}^k)^2} - \frac{1}{\tau_{ij}^k}\right]\delta_j \quad (18)$$

The final update rule for the synaptic time constants becomes:

$$\Delta \tau_{ij}^k = -\eta_\tau \frac{\partial E}{\partial \tau_{ij}^k} \quad (19)$$

Where η_τ is the learning rate for the synaptic time constants.

Learning neuron's threshold

Last we derive the error function for the neuron's threshold:

$$\frac{\partial E}{\partial \theta_j} = \frac{\partial E}{\partial t_j}(t_j^a)\frac{\partial t_j}{(\partial \theta_j)(t_j^a)} \quad (20)$$

$$\frac{\partial t_j}{\partial \theta_j}(t_j^a) = \frac{1}{\dfrac{\partial a_j(t)}{\partial t}(t_j^a)}$$
$$= \frac{1}{\sum_{i\in\Gamma_j}\sum_k w_{ij}^k \dfrac{\partial \varepsilon_{ij}^k}{\partial t (t_j^a - t_i^a - d_{ij}^k)}} \quad (21)$$

Table 3. The network parameters for CCPR.

Parameters	Values
Number of input neurons	20
Number of hidden neurons	6
Number of output neurons	6
Threshold ϑ	0.3
Goal error	0.001
Coding interval ΔT	0-20 ms
Synaptic time constant τ	170 ms
Number of synaptic terminals k	3
Learning rate for weight updating η_w	0.0075
Learning rate for delay updating η_d	0.0065
Learning rate for synaptic time constant updating η_τ	0.0055
Learning rate for neuron threshold updating η_ϑ	0.0035

Table 5. Targeted recognizer based on weight update with ANNs.

Pattern class	Description	Targeted recognizers outputs (%) Node					
		1	2	3	4	5	6
1	Systematic	86	2	0	0	0	12
2	Cyclic	1	84	0	3	12	0
3	Increasing trend	0	0	87	0	13	0
4	Decreasing trend	0	0	10	88.1	0	1.9
5	Upward shift	12	0	0.8	0	87.2	0
6	Downward shift	0	0	10	1.7	0	88.3

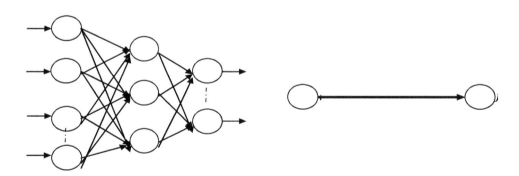

Figure 4. The proposed SNNs for CCPR with single synaptic termanial.

By adding the first term, we can get the negative of δ_j as learning rule:

$$\frac{\partial E}{\partial \theta_j} = -\delta_j \qquad (22)$$

The final update rule for the neuron threshold is:

$$\Delta\theta_j = -\eta_\theta \frac{\partial E}{\partial \theta_j} \qquad (23)$$

Where η_θ is the learning rate for the neuron's threshold.

ANN-Based CCPR schemes

First, an artificial neural network has been developed for control chart pattern recognition for comparison with the spiking neural network. A multilayer perceptions (MLPs) architecture comprises an input layer with 20 neurons, one hidden layer with 6 neurons and an output layer with 6 neurons, one for each patterns of CCPs is used, as shown in Figure 3. Table 2 depicts the control chart patterns and representation of the desired neural network outputs.

Table 6. Targeted recognizer based on weight update with SNNs single synaptic.

| | | Targeted recognizers outputs (%) | | | | | |
| | | Node | | | | | |
Pattern class	Description	1	2	3	4	5	6
1	Systematic	90	2	0	0	0	8
2	Cyclic	1	89	0	0	10	0
3	Increasing trend	0	0	92.5	0.5	7	0
4	Decreasing trend	0	0	2.9	91.1	0	6
5	Upward shift	9	0	0.8	0	90.2	0
6	Downward shift	0	0	7	0	0	93

Table 7. Targeted recognizer based on synaptic delay update with SNNs single synaptic.

| | | Targeted recognizers outputs (%) | | | | | |
| | | Node | | | | | |
Pattern class	Description	1	2	3	4	5	6
1	Systematic	92	0.8	0	0	0	7
2	Cyclic	3	90	0	0	7	0
3	Increasing trend	0	0	94.5	0.5	5	0
4	Decreasing trend	0	0	0.8	93.2	0	6
5	Upward shift	9	0	0	0	91	0
6	Downward shift	0	0	6	0	0	94

Sample patterns

Sample patterns should be collected from a real manufacturing process. Since, a large number of patterns are required for developing and validating a CCP recognizer, and as those are not economically available, simulated data are often used. Since a large window size can decrease the recognition efficiency by increasing the time required to detect the patterns, an observation window with 20 data points is considered here. A set of 720 (120 x 6) sample patterns are generated from 120 series of standard normal variants. It may be noted that each set contains equal number of samples for each pattern class. The equations used for simulating the six CCPs. Table 3 shows the network parameters that were used in our simulations for two proposed networks.

SNN-Based CCPR schemes

SNN with single connection and multi-synaptic terminals have been developed, as shown in Figures 4 and 5, respectively. Table 4 depicts the control chart patterns and representation of the desired spiking neural network outputs.

The proposed SNN network architecture

Here, we proposed a new architecture for spiking neural network in application to control charts. The proposed architecture consists of a fully connected feed-forward network of spiking neurons. An individual connection consists of a fixed number of synaptic terminals, where each terminal serves as a sub-connection that is associated with a different delay and weight between the input, hidden and output layers. The weights of the synaptic terminals are set randomly between -1 to +1. The network adopted 20 input neurons in the input layer which mean that, the input patterns consisted of the 20 most recent mean values of the process variable to be controlled, therefore, one input neuron was dedicated

for each mean value, six output neurons with one for each pattern category, and six hidden neurons where the numbers of the hidden neurons here adopted on the number of classes.

RESULTS AND DISCUSSION

CCPR using artificial neural networks

Table 5 shows the obtained results of control chart pattern recognition based on artificial neural network. It was noted during training that ANN-based recognizers were more easily trained. This table shows that 86.76% of the patterns were correctly recognized.

CCPR using single synaptic terminals SNN

Synaptic weights update

First, the synaptic weights only are updated while the other parameters are fixed. The achieved results are presented in Table 6. It is obviously that there is an improvement in the performance accuracy for all recognized patterns compared with ANN, the performance accuracy is increased to 90.9%.

Updating of the synaptic delay

Again, synaptic delays are updated while the other parameters are fixed and the values of the synaptic weights are optimum weights w_opt obtained from the

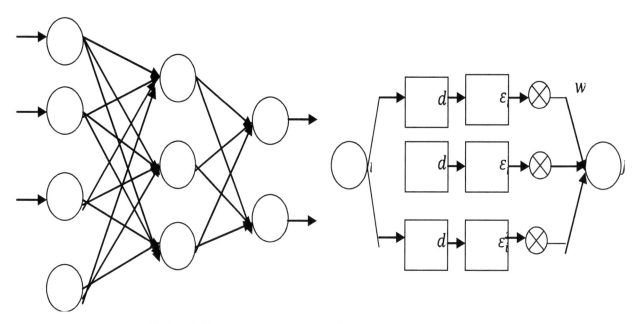

Figure 5. The proposed SNNs for CCPR with multi synaptic termanial.

Table 8. Targeted recognizer based on synaptic time constant update with SNNs single synaptic.

		Targeted recognizers outputs (%)					
		Node					
Pattern class	Description	1	2	3	4	5	6
1	Systematic	94	0.8	0	0	0	5.2
2	Cyclic	2	91	0	0	7	0
3	Increasing trend	0	0	94.8	0.2	5	0
4	Decreasing trend	0	0	0.7	94.3	0	5
5	Upward shift	7	0	0.7	0	92.3	0
6	Downward shift	0	0	5.4	0	0	94.6

Table 9. Targeted recognizer based on neurons threshold update with SNNs single synaptic.

		Targeted recognizers outputs (%)					
		Node					
Pattern class	Description	1	2	3	4	5	6
1	Systematic	95	0.8	0	0	0	4.2
2	Cyclic	3	91.4	0	0	5.6	0
3	Increasing trend	0	0	9	0.2	4.8	0
4	Decreasing trend	0	0	0.8	95.2	0	4
5	Upward shift	7	0	0.2	0	92.8	0
6	Downward shift	0	0	5	0	0	95

previous learning part. Table 7 shows the obtained results based on the adaptation of the synaptic delay. The achieved results show that 92.4% of the patterns were correctly recognized. It is obviously that there is an increment in the performance accuracy for all recognized patterns; the performance accuracy is getting better.

Table 10. Targeted recognizer based on weight update with SNNs multi synaptic.

| Pattern class | Description | Targeted recognizers outputs (%) | | | | | |
| | | Node | | | | | |
		1	2	3	4	5	6
1	Systematic	97	0.8	0	0	0	2.2
2	Cyclic	3	93	0	0	4	0
3	Increasing trend	0	0	96	4	0	0
4	Decreasing trend	0	0	0.8	96.2	0	3
5	Upward shift	4	0	0.6	0	95.4	0
6	Downward shift	3	0	0.5	0	0	96.5

Table 11. Targeted recognizer based on synaptic delay update with SNNs multi synaptic.

| Pattern class | Description | Targeted recognizers outputs (%) | | | | | |
| | | Node | | | | | |
		1	2	3	4	5	6
1	Systematic	98	0.6	0	0	0	1.4
2	Cyclic	3	95	0	0	5	0
3	Increasing trend	0	0	96.4	3.6	0	0
4	Decreasing trend	0	0	0.2	96.8	0	3
5	Upward shift	3	0	0.6	0	96	0.4
6	Downward shift	3	0	0.1	0	0	96.9

increased to 92.4%.

Synaptic time constant update

The synaptic time constant is updated only while other parameters are fixed, synaptic weights are the optimum weights w_opt and the synaptic delay is the optimum synaptic delay d_opt obtained in previous steps. Table 8 shows the obtained results based on the adaptation of the synaptic time constant.

Again, the performance accuracy for all recognized patterns is improved; the performance accuracy is increased to 93.5%.

Neuron threshold update

The neuron's threshold is updated while the other parameters are fixed. Synaptic weights, synaptic delay, and synaptic time constant are the optimum values previously obtained; the obtained results are shown in Table 9. Also there is a remarkably improvement especially for downward shift pattern. From Table 9, we can observe that the recognition rate is still increasing with neuron threshold updating about 94.06%.

SNNs for CCPR with multi synaptic terminals

The existence of multiple synapses is biologically plausible, since in brain areas like the neocortex a single pre-synaptic axon makes several independent contacts with the pot-synaptic neuron. Instead of a single synapse, with its specific delay and weight, this synapse model consists of many sub-synapses, each one of them has its own weight and delay as shown in Figure 2b. The use of multiple synapses enables an adequate delay selection using the learning rule. In this proposed SNN, multiple synapses per a connection are used. The network topology is feed-forward SNN with multiple synaptic (seven sub-connections per synaptic terminal, k=3) terminals per connection with different weights and delays.

Again the same procedure conducted in the SSN with single synaptic connection is repeated with the same chosen parameters.

Synaptic weights update

The obtained results with the proposed architecture and the SpikeProp learning procedure for control chart pattern recognition are presented in Table 10. It is obviously that there better performance accuracy for all recognized patterns. The results from Table 10 shows that, the accuracy of the network is still increasing from 94.06 to 95%.

Updating of the synaptic delay

Again Table 11 shows the obtained results based on the

Table 12. Targeted recognizer based on synaptic time constant update with SNNs multi synaptic.

Pattern class	Description	Node					
		1	2	3	4	5	6
1	Systematic	98	0.6	0	0	0	1.4
2	Cyclic	3	96	0	0	4	0
3	Increasing trend	0	0	97	3	0	0
4	Decreasing trend	0	0	0	98	0	2
5	Upward shift	3	0	0.5	0	96.5	0
6	Downward shift	3	0	0	0	0	97

Table 13. Targeted recognizer outputs based on neuron's threshold update.

Pattern class	Description	Node					
		1	2	3	4	5	6
1	Systematic	99	0.6	0	0	0	1
2	Cyclic	2	98.2	0	0	0.8	0
3	Increasing trend	0	0	98	0	0	2
4	Decreasing trend	0	0	0	98.5	0	1.5
5	Upward shift	0	0	1	0	99	0
6	Downward shift	0.4	0	0	0.6	0	99

adaptation of the synaptic delay. From the results shown in Table 11, there is an increment in the performance accuracy for all recognized patterns. The network performance still increases.

Synaptic time constant update

Table 12 shows the obtained results based on the adaptation of the synaptic time constant. The obtained results show that, there is an improvement in the performance accuracy.

Neuron threshold update

The obtained results are shown in Table 13. Also,

there is an improvement especially for downward shift pattern. Generally, the results of the overall percentages of correct recognition of random patterns in Tables 10 (95.68%), 11 (96.51%), 12 (97.08%) and Table 13 (98.61%) suggest that, there are better performance accuracy for all recognized patterns with the proposed architecture of SNNs with multi-connection compared with SNN-based recognizers with single connection. Table 14, shows the comparison between three networks topologies for performance accuracy of six unnatural patterns.

Furthermore, Table 15 shows the comparison between spiking neural networks based on LVQ

algorithm and the work presented in this paper for control chart pattern recognition. From Table 15, it can be summarized that the SNNs with three synaptic terminals achieve better performance in the control chart pattern recognition.

Conclusion

In this paper, a spiking neural network architecture is developed and used for control charts pattern recognition (CCPR). It has a good capability in data smoothing and generalization. The overall mean percentages of correct recognition of SNN-based recognizers were 98.61%. This shows clearly that, the superior

Table 14. Recognition performance comparison between ANN and SNN recognizers.

Patterns	ANNs (%)	Percentage correction recognition							
		SNNs single connection				SNNs Multi Connections			
		Weight (%)	Delay (%)	Time constant (%)	Neuron threshold (%)	Weight (%)	Delay (%)	Time constant (%)	Neuron threshold (%)
Systematic	86	90	92	94	95	97	98	98	99
Cyclic	84	89	90	91	91.4	93	95	96	98.2
Inc. Trend	87	92.5	94.5	94.8	95	96	96.4	97	98
De. Trend	88.1	91.1	93.2	94.3	95.2	96.2	96.8	98	98.5
Up. Shift	87.2	90.2	91	92.3	92.8	95.4	96	96.5	99
Dow. Shift	88.3	93	94	94.6	95	96.5	96.9	97	99

Table 15. Results of four different pattern recognizers applied to control chart data set.

Pattern recognizers	No. of training epochs	Learning performance (%)	Test performance (%)
SNN-based LVQ	20	100	97.70
ANN-based CCPR	100	98	86.76
SNN-based CCPR Single Connection	150	99	94.06
SNN-based CCPR Multi Connection	200	100	98.61

performance of the spiking neural networks technique in an application to control chart data over the other procedures using traditional neural network. Furthermore, enhancements to the SpikeProp learning algorithm are presented. These enhancements provide additional learning rules for the synaptic delays, time constants and for the neurons thresholds. Experiments have been conducted and the achieved results show a remarkable improvement in the overall performance. This work can also be extended to investigate online learning and address the effect of costs on the decisions in terms of computational time and complexity.

REFERENCES

Bialek W, Rieke F, Steveninck R, Warland D (1991). Reading a neural code. Science, 252(5014): 1854-1857.

Bohte M (2002). Unsupervised clustering with spiking neurons by sparse temporal coding and multilayer RBF networks. IEEE Transaction on Neural Networks, 13(2): 426-435.

Bohte M, la Poutre H, Kok JN (2002). SpikeProp: Error-Backpropagation for networks of spiking neurons. ESANN'2000, Bruges (Belgium), pp. 419-425.

Bohte SM, Poutre HL, Kok JN (2002). Error-backpropagation in temporally encoded networks of spiking neurons, NeuroComputting, 48: 17-37.

Hui-Ping C, Chuen-Sheng C (2009). Control Chart Pattern Recognition Using Wavelet Analysis and Neural Networks, J. Qlty., 16(5): 311-319.

Ibrahim M, Adnan H (2010). Issues in Development of Artificial Neural Network- Based Control Chart Pattern Recognition Schemes, Eur. J. Sci. Res., 39(3): 336-355.

Indra K, Pramila DM, Lakshmi G (2010). Effective Control Chart Pattern Recognition Using Artificial Neural Networks, IJCSNS Int. J. Compt. Sci. Network Security, 10(3): 194-198.

Jenn-Hwai Y, Miin-Shen Y (2005). A Control Chart Pattern Mass W (1997). Networks of spiking neurons: the third generation of neural network models; Neural Networks, 10(9): 1659-1671.

Meftah B, Benyettou A, Lezoray O, Debakla M (2008). Image

Natschlager T, Ruf B (1998). Spatial and Temporal Pattern analysis Via Spiking Neurons, Network: Computation in Neural Systems. 9(3): 319-332.

Recognition System Using a Statistical Correlation Coefficient method, Comput. Ind. Eng., 48: 205-221.

Rumelhart DE, Hinton GE, Williams RJ (1986). Learning representations by back-propagation errors, Nature, 323: 533-536.

Samir BB (2009). Fast and Accuracy Control Chart Pattern Recognition Using a New Cluster-K-Nearest Neighbor, World Academy of Science, Engineering and Technology, 49: 1022-1025.

Segmentation with Spiking Neuron Network, 1st Mediterranean Conference on Intelligent Systems and Automation, pp. 15-18.

10

Educational software for radial power system protection

Nasr-Eddine BOUHENNA

Department of Electrical and Electronics Engineering Technology, Higher Colleges of Technology, ADMC - United Arab Emirates.

This paper presents a set of analysis tools for self learning for radial power system protection training (Bouhenna 2010). It automates a radial feeder for an overcurrent protection that would include fault calculations, fuse-fuse co-ordination, current transformer, relay-relay and fuse-relay co-ordination, directional overcurrent protection, ground fault protection, automatic recloser and sectionalizer. The software explains the function of all these protective elements and provides the students with the skills and knowledge necessary to understand and comprehend radial power system protection.

Key words: Set of analysis tools, radial power system protection, fault calculations, co-ordination, protective elements.

INTRODUCTION

Many existing materials cover most of the power system protection topics in a very deep manner which may be difficult for a new learner. Without any support, the student will have difficulties in understanding the topics. Protection coordination is based on devices' operating characteristics where students are able to select and configure protection devices and display their corresponding time-current characteristics. Different scenarios can be applied with different combinations from simple network to advanced coordination schemes. After completing this course, the student will have accumulated enough skills to be able to do the protection design of a complex radial network.

Some previous related work was developed which does not seem to help a new learner to understand the concepts of the coordination in power system protection. Three of them are mentioned as follow: *A Matlab /GUI Based Fault Simulation Tool for Power System Education* (Koç and Aydoğmu, 2009), (covers only the fault calculations); *Computer Assisted Learning in Power System Relaying* (Lai, 2002) (does not cover all the

different protection schemes, it is suitable for students who already know the basic schemes); *Easy Power* (ESA, 2009), (delivers a full lineup of powerful Windows-based electrical software tools for intelligently designing, analyzing, and monitoring electrical power systems, but it does not explain in details how the fault currents have been calculated or how the coordination time interval between two protective devices has been found).

METHODOLOGY

The software developed in this paper is based on Excel/Visual Basic Applications to allow learning and analysis. This user-friendly educational software presents a comprehensive and systematic description of the concepts and principles of operation and application of protection schemes for radial power system. It covers the calculation of the per-unit and power system faults for small scale systems. It is followed by the basic protection functions of the fuse, current transformer, and different types of protective relays.

Most of the students are quite familiar with the main functions of excel worksheet when they have to enter data and write formulae. A set of tools consisting of multiple choice questions, true or false applications, animated circuits, correct or wrong answer applications, and plotting curves make the software really interactive and helps considerably the student to understand the concept of the protective devices.

This software which has been developed contains the essential material to cover the basic concepts of radial power system protection. It is developed in such a way that the students need no extra resources to understand the principles of protection systems. Most of the circuit diagrams in this software are animated and the student is guided through to the correct answer. A variety of networks for different situations are presented in this program to further enhance the understanding of the subject matter.

The software developed is a training model and teaching tool for radial power system protection. The model will serve as supplementary material or training tool for engineers entering this field.

RESULTS AND DISCUSSION

Software description

A user-friendly Excel /GUI based software has been developed to present a set of analyses tools for self contained study that will help students / trainees understand the radial protection schemes in electric power systems. It aims to provide the student with enough skills to understand the concept of the main protective devices and their operation in electrical power systems. Definitions and formulae are well presented. For each of the topics below, the student animate the circuit as an introduction to the problem he or she has to solve as it is explained in part 3. The software covers the following topics (Stenven 2010; John and Jan, 2010; Areva and Alstrom, 1995; Keit, 2008; Ron, 2008; Soman, 2008; John and William, 2003).

(a) Per-unit section
(b) Fault section
(c) Fuse section
(d) Current Transformers section
(e) Relay Part (1) section
(f) Relay Part (2) section

The menu in (Figure 1) represents all the applications which have been developed using Excel/Based Visual Basic Applications. There are six sections which are: Per-Unit, Fault, Fuse, Current Transformer, Relay Part 1 and Relay Part 2.

There are a total of 44 applications. The student can switch from one section to another by just clicking on the button 'Back to Menu'.

The applications of the six topics are detailed in the Table 1.

Five assessment models have been developed to cover all the chapters which have been detailed as follows:

(i) Model 1: Multiple Choice Questions
(ii) Model 2: True or False

(iii) Model 3: Animated Graphics
(iv) Model 4: Correct or Wrong answer
(v) Model 5: Data Setting

Assessment model of the software

Five assessment models are made to help the student to understand each application of each topic.

Model 1: Multiple choice questions

A set of multiple choice questions (Figure 2) is presented to the student to check his or her knowledge after reading the topic related to the fuse from the material given.

Model 2: True or false

Ten questions are presented to the student (Figure 3). The student has to select either True or False. The response is correct if all the 10 answers are correct.

Model 4: Animated graphics

An example of a relay–relay coordination as shown in Figure 4 will help the student to understand the coordination between the primary relay and the backup relay when a fault occurs at different locations. The characteristics are displayed for each step that will help the student to understand the importance of the coordination time interval between the two relays.

Operational logic of two-count sectionalizer can be summarized with reference to Figure 5, which illustrates the responses to a transient fault and permanent fault when the fuse saving scheme is used. Step by step the student can display the operation by just clicking on the sequence button. The animated circuits/graphics as an introduction to the application help the student to understand better the topic so that he or she will not have problem answering the questions presented just below the graphic.

The animated graphic in Figure 6a shows the operation of the directional relays R3 and R5. The animated circuit shows the two scenarios, one with the directional relays and the other one without the directional relays. When there is a fault at F2, only the directional relay R3 sees the fault and disconnects the feeder 1. The load is still getting energy from feeder 2 as shown in Figure 6b. All the information during this short time is displayed on the screen. The operation of the directional relays is shown at three different locations.

Model 3: Correct or wrong answer

A set of applications to be solved is presented to the

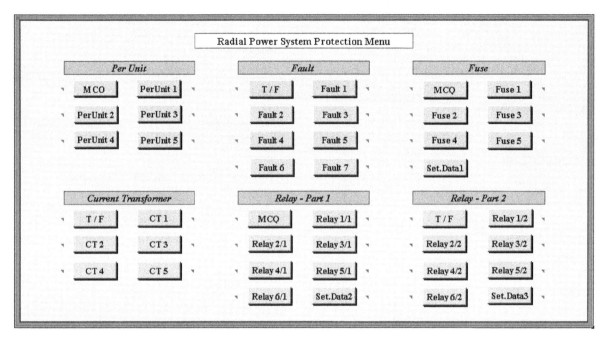

Figure 1. Radial power system protection menu.

Table 1. Software content.

(a) Per-unit section:	(d) Current transformer section:
. Multi-choice questions	. True / false
. Use of per-unit	. Current transformer - relay
. Transformer per-unit calculations	. Current transformer performance calculation
. Per-unit value of a . transmission line	. Current transformer saturation
. Transmission system per-unit calculations	. Multi-ratio current transformer performance
. Per-unit impedances in single phase transformer circuits	. Effect of saturation on current transformer

(b) Fault section:	(e) Relay part (1) section:
. True / false	. Multi-choice questions
. Balanced system 3-phase fault (1)	. Relay operation
. Balanced system 3-phase fault (2)	. Relay - relay coordination
. Symmetrical components of unsymmetrical phasors	. Setting - up the relay
. Operator "a" and unbalanced system	. Getting familiarized with setting data (2)
. Various types of short-circuit faults	. Fault calculations and relay - relay coordination
. Line - to - line ground fault	. Plug setting multiplier and phase relay coordination
. Line - to - line fault and line - to - line – to - ground fault	. Setting data (2): Relay characteristics display

(c) Fuse section:	(f) Relay part (2) section:
. Multi-choice questions	. True / false
. Clearing - melting time	. Fuse - MCCB - relay coordination
. Fuse selectivity ratio	. Directional relay coordination
. Fuse - fuse coordination	. Earth fault relay coordination
. Fuse type selection	. Current transformer - burden relay
. Low voltage fault - case study	. Auto - reclosing relay selection
.Setting data (1): Fuse characteristics display	. Recloser - sectionalizer operation
	. Recloser - sectionalizer - fuse coordination
	. Setting data (3): fuse - relay characteristics display
	.Challenge problem.

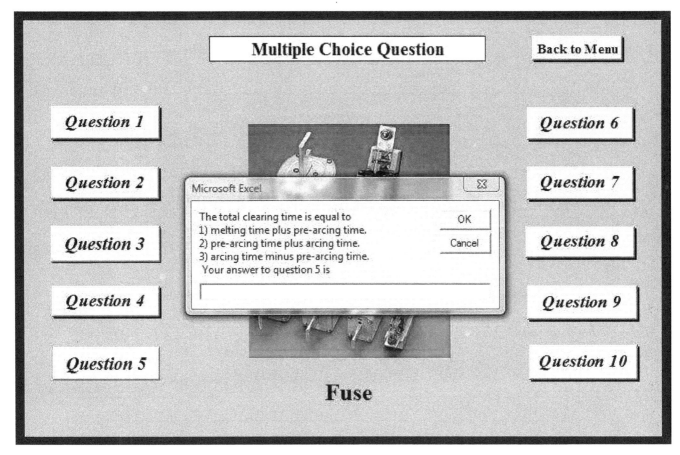

Figure 2. Fuse multiple choice questions.

student for each topic as it is shown in Figure 7. After an animated introduction, the student has to solve a problem by entering values or selecting good answers from the selection box. The application question and some notes can be displayed on the screen by just clicking on the appropriate button. Correct or wrong answer can be checked after entering each answer.

Model 5: Setting data

It's important to display the characteristics of the protective devices such as fuse and relay so that the coordination becomes easier to check.

A total of 6 data tables are presented to the student, which means 6 different curves to plot. Once the data of the protective fuse is entered in the proper locations (white cells) as shown in the data table of Figure 8, a simple click on "Do Calcs" button will display the time – current characteristics of the protective device and the fault current line will show the corresponding tripping time response. Three setting data are made, one for fuse (setting data 1), one for relay (setting data 2) and the third one is for fuse-relay combined together (setting data 3).

Conclusion

Protection system's main function is to quickly clear faults from the power system by minimizing the time for which a fault remains in the circuit. This helps enhance people's safety and minimize equipment damage while maintaining power system stability. Protection of power systems requires an understanding of system faults and their detection, and the safe isolation of the faulted device from the system.

This educational software will explain the function of all the protective elements in detail and provide the students with the skills and knowledge necessary to calculate fault currents, coordinate fuses, select and coordinate relays and associated instrument transformers.

The software covers the calculation of the balanced and unbalanced faults using the symmetrical components. The grading between two fuses has been detailed so that the grading between the downstream and upstream fuses will generally be achieved if the current rating ratio between them is equal or greater than two or by using the $I^2 t$ Let-through Energy condition. The grading between two relays has been applied in many applications using the formulae of the four standard current time characteristics – standard inverse (SI), very

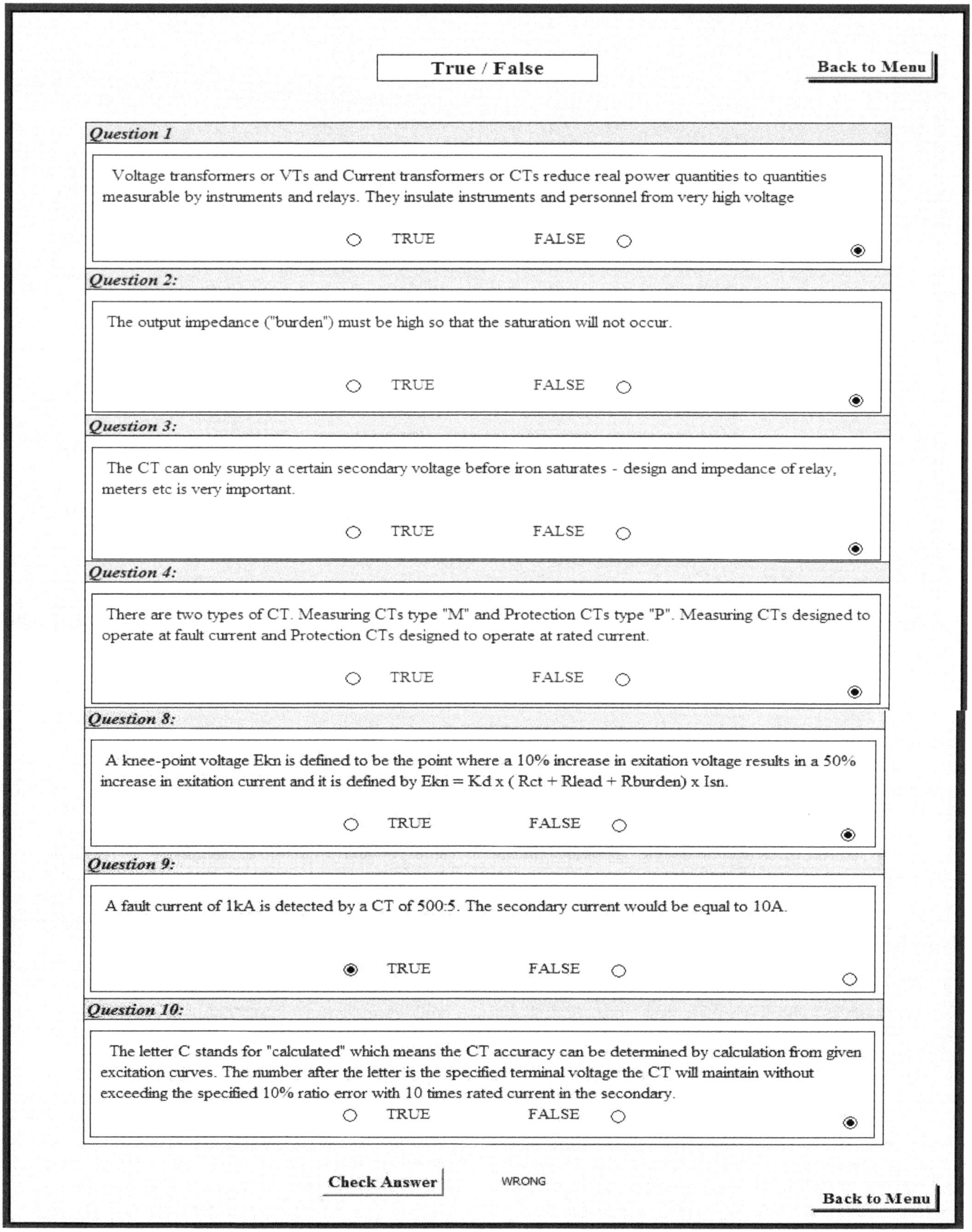

True / False

Back to Menu

Question 1

Voltage transformers or VTs and Current transformers or CTs reduce real power quantities to quantities measurable by instruments and relays. They insulate instruments and personnel from very high voltage

○   TRUE   FALSE   ○

◉

Question 2:

The output impedance ("burden") must be high so that the saturation will not occur.

○   TRUE   FALSE   ○

◉

Question 3:

The CT can only supply a certain secondary voltage before iron saturates - design and impedance of relay, meters etc is very important.

○   TRUE   FALSE   ○

◉

Question 4:

There are two types of CT. Measuring CTs type "M" and Protection CTs type "P". Measuring CTs designed to operate at fault current and Protection CTs designed to operate at rated current.

○   TRUE   FALSE   ○

◉

Question 8:

A knee-point voltage Ekn is defined to be the point where a 10% increase in exitation voltage results in a 50% increase in exitation current and it is defined by Ekn = Kd x (Rct + Rlead + Rburden) x Isn.

○   TRUE   FALSE   ○

◉

Question 9:

A fault current of 1kA is detected by a CT of 500:5. The secondary current would be equal to 10A.

◉   TRUE   FALSE   ○

○

Question 10:

The letter C stands for "calculated" which means the CT accuracy can be determined by calculation from given excitation curves. The number after the letter is the specified terminal voltage the CT will maintain without exceeding the specified 10% ratio error with 10 times rated current in the secondary.

○   TRUE   FALSE   ○

◉

Check Answer   WRONG

Back to Menu

Figure 3. Current transformer true or false.

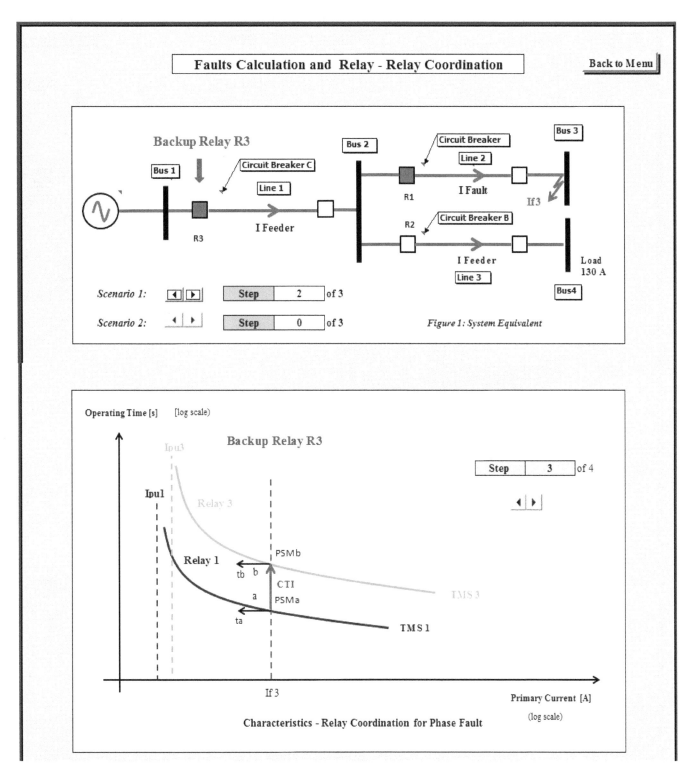

Figure 4. Relay – relay coordination (animated graphic)

inverse (VI), extremely inverse (EI) and long-time inverse (LTI). The curves can be displayed to verify if the coordination is achieved.

The student will also learn how to adjust the setting of the relays using the standard operating characteristics so that the relays closest to the fault will operate and clear the fault faster than the backup devices and also how to successfully coordinate the fuses and relays with both

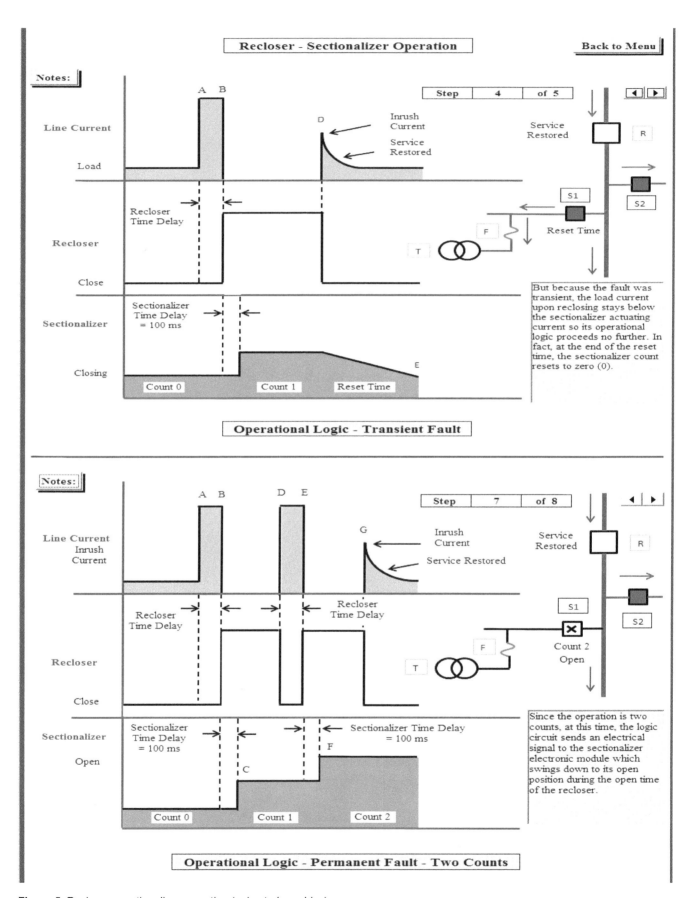

Figure 5. Recloser - sectionalizer operation (animated graphics)

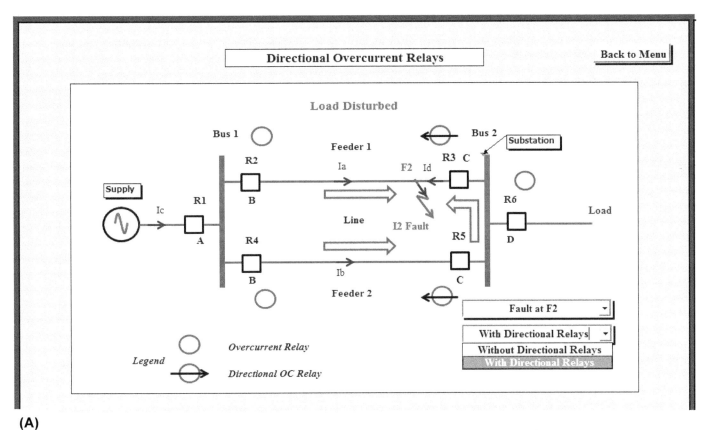

(A)

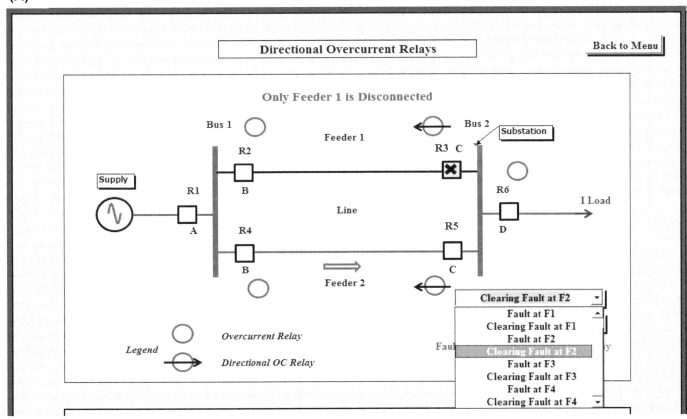

(B)

Figure 6. (a) Operation of directional relays at fault location F2. (b) Clearing the fault by the directional relay R3 at fault location F2.

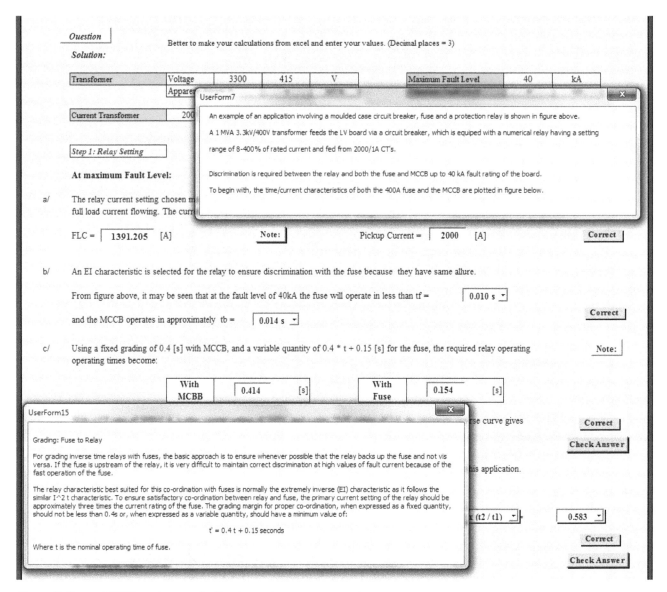

Figure 7. Fuse – MCCB – relay coordination (correct or wrong answer).

source-side and load-side protective devices, as well as the coordination of the other types of relays such as directional relays, earth fault relays, and recloser relays.

The software can be extended to cover distance protection, differential protection, and pilot relaying protection. With more complex systems, it is necessary to detect the point of fault precisely and trip only those sections affected by the fault while the rest of the system can continue to function normally. This requirement necessitates different forms of relaying apart from the simple current sensing relays. Equipment such as generators, transformers and motors also need special forms of protection characterized by their design and operating principles.

The software will become complete and will then emphasize advanced protection schemes required for practical systems experienced in industrial plants, distribution, transmission and generation systems.

In summary, at the end of the course, the student/trainee will have a solid background in protection concepts to apply them to protective devices for radial protection schemes in electric power systems. After completing all the topics, a challenge problem is given the student to check his or her knowledge on a radial network system.

ACKNOWLEDGMENT

Author would like to sincerely thank and acknowledge the following people for their assistance, guidance and support throughout the duration of this project: firstly, the

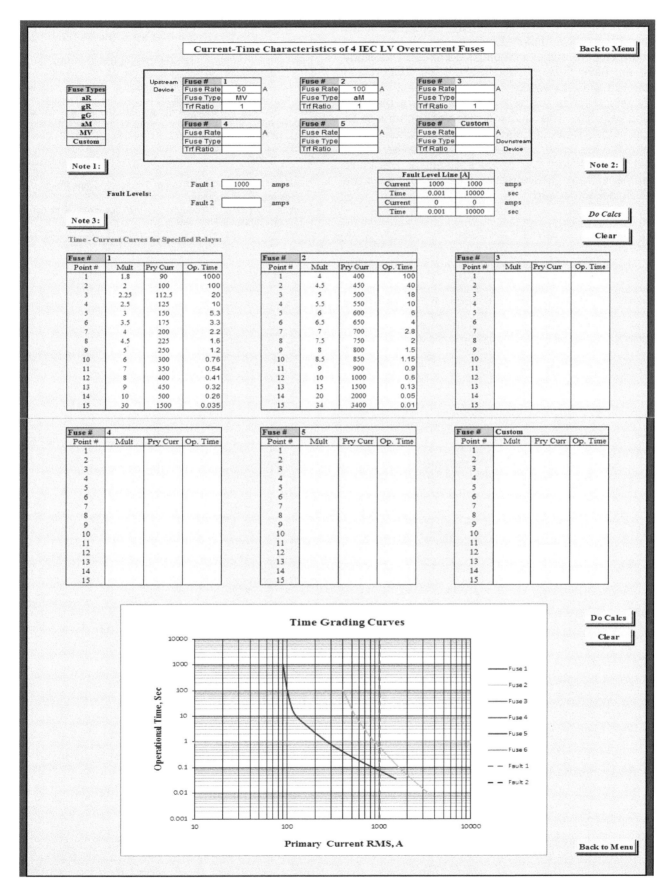

Figure 8. Fuse characteristics display (setting data 1).

supervisor Dr Tony Ahfock, Deputy Head (Electrical, Electronic and Computer Engineering, University of Southern Queensland, Toowoomba Campus). This study would not have been possible without his support and advice. His wide knowledge has been of great value to the development of this study. It has been a pleasure working with him. The author is also very grateful to Dr Shakib Farhat, Dean of Engineering at Abu Dhabi Men's College for the continued support and interest in this project. The support and encouragement of Electronic Department Team, his immediate family, and friends are gratefully acknowledged.

REFERENCES

Areva TD, Alstrom P (1995). Network Protection and Automation Guide. 1st edn.

Bouhenna N (2010). Radial Power System Protection Training Software. Project and Dissertation Submitted in Fulfillment of the Requirements for the degree of Master of Engineering Technology (Power System Engineering) at The University of Southern Queensland, Faculty of Engineering and Surveying, Australia.

ESA (2009). EasyPower, viewed on Mars 2009.

John JG, William DS (2003). Power System Analysis. Tata McGraw-Hill, New Delhi.

John W, Jan KP (2007). Microsoft Office Excel 2007 VBA Programming for DUMMIES. Willey Publishing, Inc., USA.

Keit M (2008). Power System Protection, Electrical and Information Engineering, viewed Apr. 08.

Koç S, Aydoğmu Z (2009). A Matlab /GUI Based Fault Simulation Tool for Power System Education, University Technical Education Faculty.

Lai LL (2002). Computer Assisted Learning in Power System Relaying. IEEE Education Society.

Ron S (2008). Electrical Plant. University of Southern Queensland, Toowoomba.

Soman SA (2008). Power System Protection, Department of Electrical Engineering IIT Bombay,

Stenven CC (2010). Introduction to VBA for Excel. 2nd edn. Pearson Higher Education, New Jersey.

11

Improving Web Content Management System: Template personalization approach

Hebah ElGibreen[1]* and Samir El-Masri[2]

[1]Information Technology Department, College of Computer and Information Sciences, King Saud University, Saudi Arabia.
[2]Information Systems Department, College of Computer and Information Sciences, King Saud University, Saudi Arabia.

Web Content Management System (WCMS) has been developed to facilitate different aspects of website development. However, up until now, designing of web pages is accomplished by the website developers. Even though WCMS might suggest a number of templates, but it does not consider the nature of the website that will be developed. Many designers have complained about designing the right structure, and different users have complained about poor website structure. Thus, this manuscript will present a new approach that extracts personalized templates by applying web personalization in order to facilitate WCMS and increase its scalability and flexibility. In specific, a new technique that mixes hybrid Evolutionary Algorithm (Genetic Algorithm and Ant Colony Clustering) with Cluster Tree Matching is developed. Moreover, an experiment has been conducted to prove the quality of the proposed approach, which confirmed the good quality of the algorithm concerning speed, precision, and accuracy.

Key words: Web personalization, Web Content Management System, group profiling, evolutionary algorithm, document object model.

INTRODUCTION

Nowadays, the Web emerged and became the most-wanted method for information sharing and communication. Websites grow daily to serve different visitors for different purposes with its own structure. Due to such a rapid and hectic growth, Web access and effective design have become a challenge. It has been noticed that websites that have poor information and structure makes the visitors get lost and feel disoriented (Eirinaki et al., 2006). To respond to such challenges, web personalization has emerged to better fit the information access and design to the user's needs (Shen et al., 2006). Web personalization can be defined as providing the right content to the right person on behalf of the user.

Originally, web personalization was used in advertisement and promotion personalization for different visitors. Currently, it focuses more on visitors to provide the appropriate information and service access to make the websites more useful (Flesca et al., 2004). However, website developers are usually neglected when it comes to personalization, such that, web personalization is used to personalize websites based on visitors' needs and none for the developers of such websites (Eirinaki et al., 2006). It mainly focuses on visitors' behaviors and concentrates on what contents should be presented to them during their navigation; while developers have to customize everything by themselves to build the website before it can be used by the visitors. Note that visitors are the users of the website while developers are the builder and owner of the website. For example, in www.Amazon.com, one type of the visitors is the customers who purchase books while the developers, on the other hand, are the people that built the page of purchase.

Web Content Management Systems (WCMS), on the other hand, is a tool that allows a variety of centralized and decentralized non-technical people to manage, edit, create, and control a large and dynamic collection of HTML contents (He and Chen, 2010). Thus, it concentrates more on website developers' needs rather than the visitors of the website. However, current WCMS provides customization of web pages instead of personalization; such that developers customize the web page design by themselves. Sometimes it provides template samples, but such samples do not automatically consider the need of developers or the purpose of the website to be developed.

Accordingly, using web personalization in WCMS can help both WCMS and website developers. When using web personalization, WCMS developers would not have to provide a large repository of templates and, thus, no need for studying of templates' usability or updating it every period of time. Additionally, using personalization will reduce the website developers' time for checking similar websites and studying the visitors' needs to choose which structure is more appropriate for them. For example, if the website is for children, then WCMS can retrieve the template of other similar websites and, most probably, retrieve templates with simple structure that uses buttons instead of drop down menus. Moreover, no matter how much WCMS providers searched, studied, and analyzed web pages it is difficult to guarantee covering all cases, especially since the web users' demand is very dynamic and changes excessively. Thus, instead of studying Human Computer Interaction strategies, repeatedly, and searching for usable page structure, using personalization will automatically take advantage of others' experiences.

To further motivate the use of personalization in WCMS, it has been found that the spread of the World Wide Web and the increase of website development increased the necessity for WCMS to tailor itself for different website developers designing preferences. However, it has been noticed that most of the studies conducted to improve WCMS have only concentrated on increasing the usability without the flexibility or scalability. On the contrary, using personalization in WCMS will increase its scalability and flexibility; by automatically updating the templates based on the current trends and matched users' needs.

Regardless of the advantages stated above, there are some challenges when personalizing a web page template in WCMS. The most challenging factor is time. New users must be profiled and compared with all others and matched with similar ones to collect the suitable web pages. In addition, after matching, collected web pages must be further refined to extract and generate templates. Such process may take some time, especially if the number of users is huge. Moreover, the quality of the matching measure, which is used to match the users, is also important. Appropriate similarity measure must be chosen to ensure that the personalization process is accurate. Moreover, random modification, in color and

images, of the extracted templates must be considered to guarantee a degree of individuality.

Consequently, this manuscript will present a new approach to improve WCMS using web personalization; such that WCMS can take advantage of previous developers' knowledge to offer different template designs for each website developer depending on their needs. Hence, static content of websites (that is, templates) will be automatically built without the intervention of website developers or WCMS. Such an approach merges web personalization with automatic template extraction to improve the quality of WCMS and increase its flexibility and scalability. It mixes hybrid Evolutionary Algorithm (Genetic Algorithm and Ant Colony Clustering) with Cluster Tree Matching in order to accomplish the process of personalization.

Ultimately, it can be said that the proposed approach will increase the website's productivity and WCMS scalability and flexibility by considering the static content of web pages to personalize template extraction and, thus, automate the process of website design. Nevertheless, it must be noted that this manuscript is an extended version of a short paper that has been published as a work in progress by ElGibreen and El-Masri (2012). However, sufficient details of the application, method, analyses and results achieved is indicated and explained in this manuscript.

LITERATURE REVIEW

In this part of the paper, the main aspects needed to understand the proposed approach are defined. First, Web personalization is explained and its steps are discussed. Then, user profiling is presented. After that, HTML web pages are defined, and its representation is described. Finally, Evolutionary Algorithm is identified and some of its main techniques are shown.

Web personalization

In Eirinaki et al. (2006) web personalization has been defined as "any action that adapts the information or services provided by a web site to an individual user, or a set of users." Personalization, in general, is different from customization. In customization, the effort is passed on to the users, that is, they have to choose what is appropriate and what is not. However, in personalization, all the work is done automatically on behalf of the users, based on their data. It uses different techniques to collect users' data and then personalize the services based on the similarity between the current data and other content or users of the website.

There are a lot of companies that offer and use web personalization in their websites. For example, Yahoo.com personalizes their online advertisement based on the users' behavior. If the user's log files showed that their interest is mostly in sport websites, then most of the advertisement ads will be focused on that area.

In general, web personalization requires a lot of efforts to gather the required information and data. It mainly includes four elements, as illustrated in Figure 1. First, web data must regularly be collected to be pre-processed and modeled. Then, such data must be analyzed and matched to finally determine what action should be performed (Eirinaki and Vazirgiannis, 2003).

In web personalization, different types of data are collected and used in the process of personalization. In specific, personalization data has been divided into four main categories, as follows (Eirinaki and Vazirgiannis, 2003). First, "Content" which is the directly retrieved data, such as text, images, or database information. Second, "Structure" which contains the content organization data, such as HTML tags and hyperlinks. Third, "Usage" which is the website usage data included in the Web access log, such as date and time of access, visitor IP address, and access paths. Finally, "User Profile" which is the website users' data, such as demographic information, preferences, or interests. Regardless of the type of data used, such data are collected in three different manners (Hildebrandt, 2008) depending on the type of the website and its visitors. It can be collected explicitly, that is, collected data are available and directly derived from its sources; or implicitly, that is, collected data are indirectly deduced from observing the user behavior; or in a hybrid manner where the collected data are gathered implicitly and explicitly.

In addition, the analysis of users' data to recommend a certain personalization has been categorized into four types: user-based, item-based, Web usage mining, and rule-based (Eirinaki and Vazirgiannis, 2003; Flesca et al., 2004). User-based (collaborative) personalization recommends and personalizes the website based on previous similar users' preferences. Item-based (content-based) personalization, on the other hand, recommends and personalizes the website for each user separately by relating their preferences with the available content. It recommends items similar to items previously liked by the user. Alternatively, Web usage mining analyzes and mines the Web log data to extract users' navigational behavior. Finally, rule-based personalization asks the users a series of questions, which are derived from a decision tree, to tailor the final result based on their answers. The focus of this manuscript will be on user-based personalization for the personalization process.

User profiling

Discovering users' difference is essential to provide the required personalized service. User profile has been defined in Hildebrandt (2008) as "the process of 'discovering' correlations between data in databases that

Figure 1. Web personalization elements.

can be used to identify and represent a human or nonhuman subject (individual or group) and/or the application of profiles (sets of correlated data) to individuate and represent a subject or to identify a subject as a member of a group or category." In general, user profiles vary in content and type, which usually depend on the application. The content gathered can be user interests, knowledge, background, skills, goals, behaviors, interaction preferences, characteristics, or context. However, the profile type itself can be grouped or individual, public or private, static or dynamic, distributed or non-distributed, explicit or implicit, feedback or stereotypes. These content and profile types have been discussed and further explained in Crossley et al. (2003) and Hildebrandt (2008). In addition, in order to build and use profiles, different techniques have been developed and further improved in the last few years (Schiaffino and Amandi, 2009), such as machine learning, genetic algorithm, and classification techniques.

Hypertext markup language (HTML) web pages

In order to understand how web page templates can be automatically extracted it is important to know the main aspects of HTML web pages and how it is handled. In general, web pages include static and dynamic content (Ravi et al., 2009). Dynamic content usually changes depending on the visitors' activities and does not have a fixed design or definition. On the other hand, static contents are the content that are usually fixed during the visitor navigation, and are usually designed by the website developers with the help of WCMS. Hypertext mark-up language (HTML) is one language that is used to define the static content. It has been defined in Wan Mohd Mahidin (2003) as "a web programming language used to display web pages." Usually, browsers provide web pages based on HTML files, which define the structure and represent the pages as tags and attributes. Thus, different web pages can be generated by extracting some nodes of the HTML tree (Christos et al., 2004).

In order to navigate, modify, add, or delete content or elements of HTML web pages, Document Object Model (DOM) has been developed by W3C as HTML standard interface ("What is the Document Object Model?," 2004). Specifically, HTML files are represented by DOM trees in order to apply different similarity measures and extract common templates (Chulyun and Kyuseok, 2011). DOM has been defined as *"a standard for accessing documents, like HTML"* and *"presents an HTML document as a tree structure"* (Chulyun and Kyuseok, 2011). Thus, DOM can be used, with any programming language as an interface to HTML web pages. Its representation aims to display and show the structure of HTML web pages rather than its content.

For example, Figure 2 illustrates how HTML tags can be represented in a DOM tree. The hierarchy of the tags is preserved, and the content of the page is stored at the leaf nodes.

Templates are usually used to take advantages of the static content of previous web pages and define a general structure that standardizes such content (Laahs et al., 2008). HTML template extraction, in specific, has been divided into two categories: site-level and page-level (Chulyun and Kyuseok, 2011). Site-level template extraction extracts the template from different pages in the same site while page-level extraction, on the other hand, extracts the template from a single page. In this manuscript, the focus will be on page-level extraction for HTML template extraction.

Nevertheless, HTML web page structure must be compared and, thus, DOM tree similarity must be measured. The most famous tree similarity measure used in DOM trees are Tree Edit Distance (TED) (Bille, 2005) and Simple Tree Measure (STM) (Ferrara and Baumgartner, 2011). TED measures between two trees returns editing operations' cost of turning one tree to the other (Bille, 2005). Such measure introduces high complexity, especially with large trees. On the other hand, STM measures the similarity between two trees by mapping and comparing the nodes and return its maximum value (Kim et al., 2007). A node mapping value is equal to one, assuming equal weights of all the nodes. Using STM will simplify the process of matching since, in contrast of TED, no inserting, deleting, or re-labeling operations are needed. However, the assumption of equal weight is not valid in HTML trees because HTML tags have different values depending on the data browsed in the web page. Thus, STM measure has been improved, and a new measure called Cluster Tree Matching (CTM) (Ferrara and Baumgartner, 2011) has been developed.

CTM measure was developed based on STM by Ferrara and Baumgartner (2011) to calculate the tree similarity recursively in a matrix and count the weight difference between two trees. Their measure divides the greater number of siblings between two trees over the match value between two nodes, level by level; thus, it cluster the matching process sub-tree by sub-tree. It assigns a weighted value to give less weight to insignificant sub-trees; such that deep levels of HTML

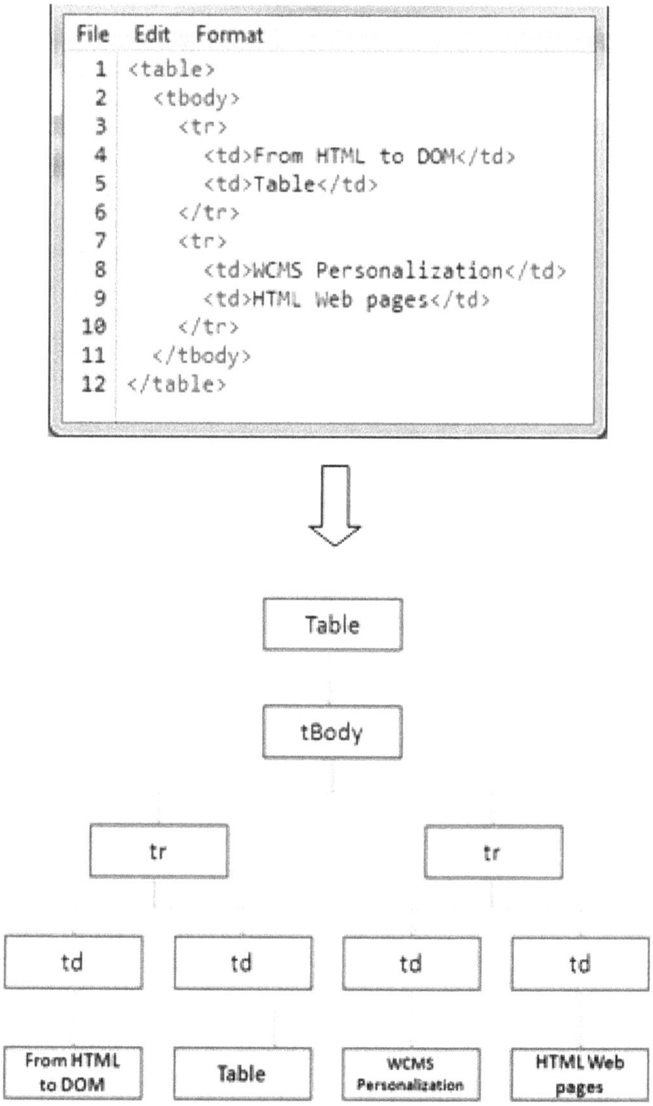

Figure 2. HTML to DOM tree representation.

trees usually indicate an insignificant component of the web pages like table rows or list of items. CTM increases the accuracy whenever the trees complexity and similarity increases. Thus, it is more effective than STM and less complex than TED. Figure 3 illustrates two trees (a) and (b) and circles the similar elements between them. The result of CTM will be equal to 0.375 (that is, 38%) which represent the division of 3 over 8. In this manuscript, the focus will be on CTM for tree matching, thus, more details will be explained later.

Evolutionary algorithms

Evolutionary Algorithms (EA) (Freitas, 2002) are artificial intelligent algorithms that have been inspired by nature. Such algorithms are used to solve any kind of problems

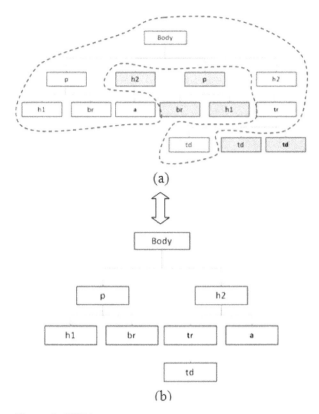

Figure 3. CTM tree measure.

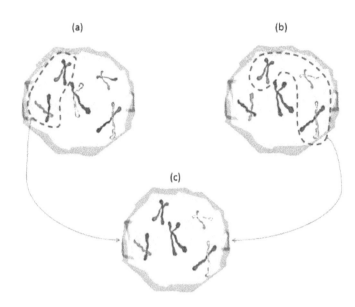

Figure 4. GA: (a) initialization (b) reproduction (c) selection.

and identify candidate solutions as fast as possible. It is useful when the best solution is unknown, and the data repository is very large. Different techniques have been developed under the umbrella of EA, such as Genetic Algorithm (GA) (Wook and Woo, 2005) and Ant Colony Clustering (ACC) (Deneubourg et al., 1991). Each technique has been tailored in different domains depending on the problem and solution required. In this manuscript, the focus will be on GA and ACC techniques for problem solving.

GA is considered as the most popular technique of EA. It is *"a general purpose search algorithm which use principles inspired by natural genetic populations to evolve solutions to problems"* (Wook and Woo, 2005). It typically starts from a collection of random solutions, called population, and then evolves it using selection and reproduction. The fittest solution is chosen based on the fitness function that measures the strength of the solution. The population contains elements, called individuals or chromosomes, to represent possible solutions. In GA, four steps are performed to match individuals (Russell and Norvig, 2003). First, it represents the available datasets to the required data type, such as text, character, or binary representation. Then it initializes the population by randomly assigning different values to the chromosomes. Afterward, it reproduces a new solution by mixing every chromosome with another to reproduce an offspring. Finally, it selects the best chromosomes based on their fitness value. Figure 4

illustrates how population of chromosomes starts reproduction, after the representation step, to produce a new solution and better results. GA can search potentially large spaces and, thus, it can solve the problem of large users' repository and improve the performance of profile matching, considering the time.

Alternatively, ACC method is a new type of clustering that is based on an algorithm called Ant Colony Optimization. Such an algorithm is an Evolutionary Algorithm that is built based on nature. In specific, it is developed based on how ants look for food by spreading their pheromone to find the food path (Wei et al., 2005). Figure 5 illustrates how the ants search for food. It starts updating its local pheromone (Figure 5b) and explores all possible roads to finally emphasize the shortest one. As a result, the global pheromone (Figure 5c) will be emphasized, while the other pheromone is fading, by communicating the local pheromone, that is, the best solution will be chosen.

ACC is developed to optimize the process of clustering and improve its time. It is mostly used in web usage mining (Lu et al., 2007) and basically divided into three steps (Dinh and Mamun, 2004). First, it updates the local pheromone, that is, update each ant solution with the suitable cluster. Then, it applies the state transition rule, that is, decide if a certain ant should be dropped in a cluster or out of it. Finally, it updates the global pheromone, that is, update the final solution which is the road map.

Related works in personalization and template extraction

To the best of our knowledge, no one yet has considered personalization in template extraction; it was treated

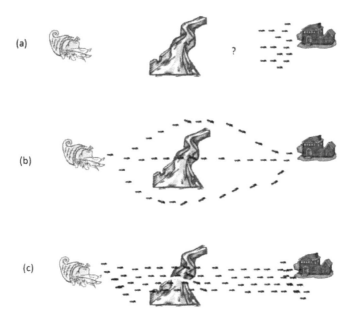

Figure 5. Ant colony optimization.

separately to handle dynamic content and website navigation. Thus, available work in personalization and template extraction is discussed here separately.

When it comes to web personalization, Yen and Kong (2002) proposed a Personalized Electronic Catalogue System to personalize e-commerce websites. Display, organization, and information content were personalized based on the interest and preference of each website visitor. Moreover, Flesca et al. (2004) proposed a new personalization strategy to use content and user interest similarity. The purpose of their strategy is to recommend web page navigation that is appropriate for each user. Thus, they presented a new methodology that allows users to personalize their web page navigation through websites by emerging content and usage mining techniques within the field of recommendation systems and analyzing users' preferences and related content in order to suggest the most relevant pages to users. Similarly, in Shen et al. (2006) web mining model that dynamically creates personalized web pages is presented. Their model was based on hidden Markov model and clustering; such that users with similar interest are grouped and their visited pages are related.

On the other hand, in Nasraoui et al. (2008) a complete framework is presented along with web usage mining of real websites. Their framework first profile users explicitly, using search query that is stored in the web log data, then the web content is described in the ontology, and the result is validated in terms of its adaptability to user behavior. Their profiling is done by clustering user sessions and group users based on their activities to extract profile of each group as a set of significant URLs. After the clustering process, website hierarchy is exploited to give similarity weight between URLs.

Moreover, for further improvement, a web personalization was proposed in Eirinaki et al. (2006) and applied to semantically annotate websites' content. They integrated content semantics with the user's activity patterns (navigational actions) and then represented both using ontology. Furthermore, to personalize the website, they used techniques of web mining and enhance the users' behaviors with semantic knowledge.

Additionally, in Munk et al. (2010), it was found that web log mining effect personalization because it is used to mine the websites visitors' activities and personalize the web based on in. Hence, techniques used for web log mining were evaluated to conclude a matrix that can be used to minimize the time of personalization. Moreover, Perugini (2010) tried to formalize the transformation of hierarchal website and built a toolkit to collect all possible transformations. The toolkit was used to make shortcuts to the desired information and to personalize the user navigation based on his previous interaction with the websites. In Rana (2012), however, a study was carried out to show the different web usage mining that is used to study the behavior of the visitors while interacting with a website. In Eslami et al. (2011), nevertheless, web services were personalized to allow non-technical users to use and create services in homecare domains without the need to go into the technical details of such services. Moreover, Carminati et al. (2012) proposed a multi-layer framework to personalize collaborative tagging, which is used as metadata when sharing online resources.

Alternatively, a new attempt of personalizing WCMS was found in CoreMedia (2012). CoreMedia Corporation has recently lunched a new solution that was added to their WCMS. This solution allowed media and entertainment companies to personalize their multimedia content based on social, historical, situational, and behavioral of audience data. Such personalization would reduce the need for developers to constantly update their websites. However, again, this personalization is based on visitors' behavior and considers the dynamic content of a website, not the static.

Consequently, it can be noticed that all the previous studies of web and WCMS personalization focus on the behaviour of the visitors and how to manage the dynamic content of the websites. However, the needs of the developer who come up with such websites were neglected, and the static contents of web pages were usually customized.

Alternatively, when it comes to template extraction, it was found that template matching has been applied to different domains. For example, in Chávez et al. (2012), template were extracted from laser pointer and matched to other templates, stored in the system, in order to discover how to interact with smart home users and activate the demanded service using laser pointer commands. However, since the scope of this manuscript is about web template, the focus will be on template extraction in the web domain.

In Ji et al. (2010) a new method suggested parsing

different websites into HTML Tag trees to extract the content of pages by identifying repeated patterns. The Tag tree was constructed based on certain rules in order to parse HTML web pages into a tag tree then extract the template by allocating the content in the leaf nodes. On the other hand, in Gui-Sheng (2010) another method is presented to induce web page template. Their method suggested to first select websites randomly, and then transforms it to DOM tree, judge its similarity, and cluster the web page to extract templates, correlate it, and extract other pages' content. Moreover, in Haikun (2010) an approach of three steps was proposed. First, pages are transformed into DOM trees to be fed to a tree clustering module that calculates trees' similarity. Then, the resulting trees will be presented to users as pages so that users can select interesting data in order to finally generate the desired template for data extraction. In addition, it was introduced in Shui-Lung (2004) a Tree Template Automatic Generator to learn template from given web pages. The template is generated using a top-down approach starting from the root and going down one level at a time.

Regardless of all the evaluation conducted in the previous works, some important deficiencies have been noticed. When it comes to personalization, all the works discussed have only considered the visitor behavior, and the focus was on the website/visitor relationship; such that the problem of navigation is only considered, thus, website designer has been neglected in web personalization. In addition, when it comes to filtering and recommending process of web personalization, most of the available works used only content based similarity. Consequently, even though it is called web personalization but the focus was mostly directed to navigation personalization and content similarity.

Alternatively, when it comes to template extraction, the available works have directed the focus to the dynamic content of the website rather than the template itself. Templates were generated only to identify the content of different websites without taking advantage of the semi-structured[1] knowledge that has already been extracted. In addition, time of template extraction and its accuracy was not fully considered in these works.

As a result, this work next proposes a new approach which considers personalization for template extraction in order to simplify the process of website designing on the developers and to further improve WCMS. Hence, users' similarity, time of template extraction, and its accuracy were considered when developing such an approach.

WCMS TEMPLATE PERSONALIZATION APPROACH

WCMS template personalization is a new approach to personalize the process of template extraction in WCMS.

Such an approach captures both structure and user profile data by mixing hybrid Evolutionary Algorithm (EA), specifically GA and ACC, with CTM. First, it regularly collects data from the developers' account. Then, it creates individual profiles for matching. After that, when developers choose to design their websites, profiles will be matched and common templates will be extracted. The steps of the proposed approach are illustrated in Figure 6 and its details are explained next.

Data collection

The data used to build the individual profiles are collected explicitly from the developer account. Such data would contain the developers'[2] country, religion, and their business scale (large company, small company, individual). In addition, more data are collected about the type of visitors, in which the website is targeting, including age (kid, adult, elderly), language, gender, ability (normal, mute, autism...), and nature (business, discussion forum, medical...).

Individual profiling

After collecting the required data, profiles will be generated. The profile of each website will be gathered in Extensible Markup Language (XML) file. XML is a standard language for describing the data in a tree structure. Thus, using such structure will increase the scalability of the proposed approach for any field, and it will be possible to profile any website as long as it has such XML tags in its metadata. The profile will contain the characteristics collected in the first step; such that each tag is a characteristic, and the data are its value. All websites that target the same age are grouped together in order to simplify and speed up the process of matching. An example of such a profile is illustrated in Figure 7.

It must be noted that the collected data can change in time. However, since these changes are usually not frequent then it is considered as a long-term interest. Thus, every period of time the first and second steps of the proposed approach are repeated, in the background, in order to consider the possible changes in the long-term interest without affecting the personalization speed.

Profile matching

Whenever the developers access WCMS, in order to design the website interface, their profile is matched with all other users to personalize templates. Genetic

---

[1] Semi-structured documents are documents that have a known content without knowing where such content is placed in the document.

[2] When the word developer (or user) is said alone in this paper it would mean website developer.

100

Artificial Intelligence in the 21st Century

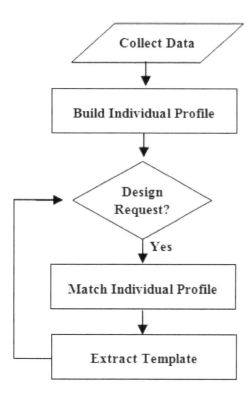

Figure 6. WCMS template personalization approach.

```
<?xml version="1.0" encoding="ISO-8859-1"?>
- <UserProfile age="kid">
  - <User ID="123456">
      <country>Any</country>
      <religion>Any</religion>
      <scale>Individual</scale>
      <language>Arabic</language>
      <gender>Any</gender>
      <ability>autism</ability>
      <nature>medical</nature>
    </User>
  + <User ID="123459">
  + <User ID="123460">
  </UserProfile>
```

Figure 7. Individual profile.

Algorithm is used to accomplish this step. It typically starts with random solutions then evolves it by repeated selection and variations of more fitted solutions. The elements of the population (chromosomes) are used to represent candidate solutions; for example, if the chromosome size is 4, then it can be represented as illustrated in Figure 8. The content of this chromosome

| "123456" | "123789" | "654321" | "987654" |

Figure 8. Solution chromosome.

represents the similar users' ID, that is, possible solution, and each gene in the chromosome will be linked to the related characteristic extracted from the XML file generated previously.

In order to produce the most fitted solution the pseudo code, illustrated in Figure 9, is applied. First, the population will be initialized by users of the same age, given the maximum number of genes; such that each chromosome will represent a solution. The maximum number of genes represents the maximum number of similar users who can be considered. Such number is specified because the repository of profiles can be very large, which tremendously increases the chromosome length to the extent that might affect the process time without much of improvement in the solution.

The fitness value of chromosome I is calculated using Equation (1), where D (I, T) is the similarity distance between the targeted user profile T and other users included in the chromosome, G is number of genes, and Ch is number of characteristic in profiles. The division used in calculating the fitness is introduced to scale its value between (0...1) and, thus, simplify the matching process. The similarity measure D (I, T) is calculated using Equation (2) for all genes in the chromosome. ChMatch is a function that calculates the similarity between two profile characteristics using Equation (3). As a result, when the similarity distance between the users increases then fitness value will also increase and, thus, the resulting solution will be more fitted.

$$F(I) = \frac{D(I,T)}{[G \times Ch]} \tag{1}$$

$$D(I, T) = \sum_{i=1}^{G} \sum_{w=1}^{Ch} ChMattch(I_{iw}, T_w) \tag{2}$$

$$ChMatch(I_w, T_w) = \begin{cases} 1 & \text{if } I_w = T_w \\ 0 & \text{if } I_w \neq T_w \end{cases} \tag{3}$$

After calculating the fitness of all users in the chromosome the population is reproduced and tested until the stop condition is reached or target solution, where the fitness is equal to one, is found.

Template extraction

In this step, templates are extracted depending on the

```
Match Profile {
Input: users profile U, target user T, population size: β, stop condition α, chromosome size γ.
Output: Solution S.

//Initialize population and calculate the fitness of each solution
P = Generate Population (U, T, β, γ);
S = best solution in P;

While (α not reached) and (F(S) ≠ 1) do
        //Crossover to produce better solutions
        P_new = Reproduce (P)
        Calculate P_new fitness;
        //Selection
        P = Select best β chromosomes from P and P_new
        S = best solution in P;
End while
Return S; }
```

Figure 9. Profile matching.

solution generated previously. Note that profiles matching and template extraction steps are repeated every time the users want to redesign their website because users and visitors' interest might change, that is, changing in the short-term interest is considered. This extraction is further divided into three steps, as follows.

Hypertext markup language (HTML) *parsing*

Parsing web pages into trees will simplify and speed up searching in such pages. Hence, in order to simplify the process of web pages matching, each website front page is parsed into a tree using DOM representation. In the proposed approach HTML documents are parsed to DOM trees where each node in the tree represents an HTML tag and associated with its attribute, if exist. Since only the template is extracted without the data then attributes and leaf nodes, which contain the text, will be removed to reduce the space. In addition, each tree will be identified by the developer (user) id and his profile fitness value to be used later. An example of the resulting tree is illustrated in Figure 10.

Tree clustering

After parsing HTML pages into DOM trees, the resulting trees are clustered into groups to identify similar templates and avoid redundant results. To accomplish this step ACC is used with CTM. In this step, each tree represents an ant, and the clusters represent the roads. The solution is represented by a vector with N elements and W values; such that N represents the number of trees, and W represents the number of clusters. For

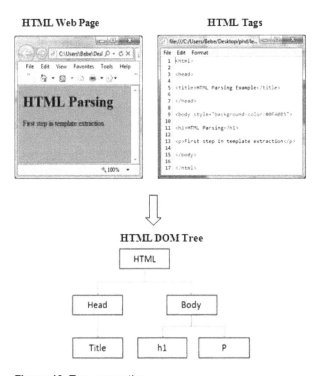

Figure 10. Tree generation.

example, if the number of trees extracted were five and the number of clusters given are three, then a solution could be as illustrated in Figure 11, which means that the second, fourth, and fifth trees belong to the same cluster while the first belong to cluster# 2, and the third tree belong to cluster# 3.

After initializing all the attributes, this step works as follows. First, each tree will be assigned randomly to a

T1	T2	T3	T4	T5
2	1	3	1	1

Figure 11. Cluster solution.

cluster, that is, ants are positioned randomly on the road. Next, while the stop condition is not reached, each tree is matched with all other trees, that is, each ant searches its neighborhood to find the most similar one. The similarity measure between two trees Ti and Tj is calculated using the TreeMatch function illustrated in Figure 12; where d(n) is the node n degree in a tree (number of first-level children), T[i] is a sub-tree of tree T starting from level i and afterwards, s(n) is the total number of siblings of a node n including itself, and M is the measure matrix. Such measure selects sub-trees, which share the same root, and analyze its tag name to return the similarity weighted measure between two trees. TreeMatch function is based on CTM, discussed previously, which calculates tree similarity recursively in a matrix and counts the weight difference between two trees.

After calculating the similarity measure it will be possible to apply the transition rule in order to update the local pheromone and decide whether to pick up a neighbor cluster or drop the current tree cluster. Usually, in the original ACC algorithm, if the current ant does not carry an object (cluster) while its neighborhood has an object, then it will take the same object as them based on a pickup probability, that is, join their cluster. On the other hand, if the current ant found to be carrying an object but its neighborhood carries a different object, then it will drop its object based on a drop-down probability, that is, it will be temporary with no cluster.

However, it has been found that such manner, in WCMS personalization, could affect the accuracy, especially if the global solution was initialized with no cluster. Thus, a slightly different transition rule has been exploited and used to improve the accuracy, as follows. If the current tree has similar clustered neighborhood then the neighborhood cluster will be picked up, based on probability P_p, and the current tree will join the same cluster. On the other hand, if the current tree has a similar cluster to none neighborhood tree, this means that the clustering is inaccurate; therefore, the target tree must drop down its cluster, that is, will not belong to a cluster, based on a certain probability P_d.

The probability of picking up (P_P) and dropping down (P_d) a tree out/in a certain cluster are calculated using Equation (4) and (5), respectively, where f is the similarity measure calculated previously, using TreeMatch function, K_p and K_d are threshold constant defined at the beginning. If f is much higher than K_p then the measured tree is already surrounded by similar neighbors, that is, the probability will be close to zero and such tree will not

```
TreeMatch {
Input: two trees T1 and T2.
Output: weighted similarity measure W.
//if root nodes then it should not matches
If T1.root ≠ T2.root
    Return 0;
//if not root then calculate the weighted similarity
Else
    m = d(T1.root);
    n = d(T2.root);
    // Initialize measure matrix
    M [i][j] = 0 for all i = (0 .. m) and (j = 0 .. n);
    //start matching sub-trees
    For i = 1 to m do
        For j = 1 to n do
            // Recursive call to measure sub trees similarities
            // starting from current node as root
            SupTreeM = TreeMatch (T1[i-1], T2[j-1]);
            M [i][j] = Max ( M[i][j-1], M[i-1][j], (M[i-1][j-1] +
SupTreeM) );
        End for
    End for
//Check if leaf nodes is reached
If m ≠ 0 and n ≠ 0 then
```

$$W = \frac{M[m][n]}{Max\ (s(T1.root), s(T2.root))};$$

```
Else
```

$$W = \frac{M[m][n]+1}{Max\ (s(T1.root), s(T2.root))};$$

```
Return W;
End if }
```

Figure 12. Tree matching.

pick up a new cluster. Alternatively, if f is much higher than K_d then the result will be close to one and, thus, the probability of dropping down the tree cluster is low because it must exceed P_d. In addition, if the similarity between two trees is zero while they have the same cluster then P_d will be equal to 1 in order to force the drop down of the cluster, since there are no shared tags between the two trees, that is, they should never belong to the same cluster. At the end, after comparing all trees together and updating their local pheromone, the global pheromone will be updated. Then, the process will be repeated in order to further improve the solution and assign trees to the most appropriate cluster or group.

$$P_P = \left(\frac{K_p}{K_p + f_{(i,j)}}\right)^2 \tag{4}$$

$$P_d = \begin{cases} \left(\frac{f_{(i,j)}}{K_d + f_{(i,j)}}\right)^2 & f \neq 0 \\ 1 & f = 0 \end{cases} \tag{5}$$

It must be noted that only one tree can update the global pheromone in each round to guarantee testing as many roads as possible. In addition, some trees might not find any similar neighborhood; thus, it has been decided to leave such trees in a separate cluster to ensure that its characteristic does not disappear. Doing such separation will ensure that unique web pages are preserved to improve the clustering in case a similar website has joined the Web. The pseudo code of the proposed clustering algorithm is illustrated in Figure 13.

Template generation

At the end, in order to extract the common templates for the developer, the resulting clusters will be examined and trees with the highest fitness in each cluster will be chosen. After that, attributes such as images and colors will be changed to random values. Then, DOM trees are parsed back to HTML files to be viewed as the personalized template.

IMPLEMENTATION

In order to test the performance of the proposed approach an experiment has been conducted. Here details of the experiment, explanation of its result, and highlights of the main issues are discussed.

Experiment settings

The proposed approach has been implemented with Java language in JBuilder environment. It was executed on a PC with Intel®Core™ i7 CPU, 2.67 GHz processes, and 6 GB RAM. In addition, different websites with different languages and characteristics have been used in the experiment. Each website has a full profile which was synthetically built in a database. The websites used to build such database are listed in Table 1. However, it has been found that almost all the websites have an unclean structure which causes some errors during the execution. Thus, an external library, called HTML Cleaner (net.sourceforge.htmlcleaner, 2010), was used to extract

```
TreeMatch {
Input: two trees T1 and T2.
Output: weighted similarity measure W.
//if root nodes then it should not matches
If T1.root ≠ T2.root
    Return 0;
//if not root then calculate the weighted similarity
Else
    m = d(T1.root);
    n = d(T2.root);
    // Initialize measure matrix
    M [i][j] = 0 for all i = (0 .. m) and (j = 0 .. n);
    //start matching sub-trees
    For i = 1 to m do
        For j = 1 to n do
            // Recursive call to measure sub trees similarities
            // starting from current node as root
            SupTreeM = TreeMatch (T1[i-1], T2[j-1]);
            M [i][j] = Max ( M[i][j-1], M[i-1][j], (M[i-1][j-1] + SupTreeM) );
        End for
    End for
//Check if leaf nodes is reached
If m ≠ 0 and n ≠ 0 then
```
$$W = \frac{M[m][n]}{Max\ (s(T1.root), s(T2.root))};$$
```
Else
```
$$W = \frac{M[m][n]+1}{Max\ (s(T1.root), s(T2.root))};$$
```
Return W;
End if }
```

Figure 13. Tree clustering.

the websites from its URL and clean the web pages, and then converts it to HTML pages.

During the experiment, all the parameters were unchanged, except for the stop condition, including population and chromosome size, pick up and drop down probability, in addition to the number of clusters. Population and chromosome size was set to "10" because only ten templates are wished to be viewed. In addition, the pickup probability (K_p) and drop down probability (K_d) have been initialized with "0.5" because it's unknown if it is better to drop or pick the cluster, thus, 50% chance is given in both cases. Lastly, the maximum number of group was set to "5".

Here, ten experiments, that have different stop conditions starting from 10 to 100, have been recorded to measure the performance of the proposed approach, where the templates are extracted for news company website that is written in English and target normal users. In each experiment, different measures have been calculated and recorded, as identified and next explained.

Evaluation measure

In order to evaluate the result of the experiment three types of measures have been calculated. The first

Table 1. Website samples.

Website
http://drupal.org
http://epda3.net/iv/mnshd-40.html
http://fcsn.org/index.php
http://games.sh3bwah.maktoob.com/3-0
http://googleblog.blogspot.com
http://gulfkids.com/ar/
http://www.children.gov.on.ca/htdocs/English/topics/specialneeds/index.aspx
http://kids.nationalgeographic.com/kids/
http://kids.yahoo.com/
http://news.google.com
http://news.maktoob.com/
http://pbskids.org/
http://science.nasa.gov/kids/
http://shopping.kelkoo.co.uk
http://wordpress.org
http://www.6abib.com/
http://www.abs-cbnnews.com/
http://www.adabatfal.com/
http://www.adpsn1.netfirms.com/
http://www.aljazeera.net/portal
http://www.Amazon.com
http://www.arabnews.com/
http://www.Ashford.com
http://www.atfaal.net/
http://www.bbc.co.uk/news/
http://www.delicious.com
http://www.ebay.com
http://www.facebook.com
http://www.feedo.net/disability/DisabilityMain.htm
http://www.Finance.yahoo.com
http://www.google.com
http://www.healthofnations.com/?gclid=CJ2J0_3m0qgCFcIMfAodL0qNgQ
http://www.housesforrent.ws
http://www.joomla.org
http://www.kids.jo/main/
http://www.kidscom.com/
http://www.msnbc.msn.com/
http://www.news.yahoo.com
http://www.officedepot.com
http://www.phpbb.com
http://www.q8sneed.com/
http://www.rentals.com
http://www.s9y.org
http://www.shopping.yahoo.com
http://www.simplemachines.org
http://www.time4learning.com/index.htm
http://www.werathah.com/special/index.htm
http://www.zdnet.com/news
http://www.bbc.com
http://health.yahoo.net/

measure is the algorithm speed, which record the time of executing the profile matching and template extraction phases of the algorithm, that is, the personalization step. The second measure, however, records the quality of the individual matching using the fitness of the extracted solution in each experiment to indicate how much the users included in the solution are similar to the target user. At the end, the clustering algorithm quality was assessed using two measures: inter-cluster and intra-cluster similarity.

Inter-cluster similarity measures the similarity degree between pages in the same cluster using TreeMatch function illustrated in Figure 12 and then divides it by the number of users in each cluster to finally divide the total of all clusters over the number of cluster; such divisions are used to scale the final value from 0 to 1. Of course if the result of such a measure is high, that is, pages in one cluster are very similar, this will indicate good quality. On the other hand, intra-cluster similarity measures the similarity between the clusters. The average pair-wise distance has been used to calculate the similarity between the clusters; which measures the distance between the most fitted trees of each cluster all together using TreeMatch function, illustrated in Figure 12, and then divide it by the number of cluster to scale its value from 0 to 1. Naturally, if the result of this measure has a low value, that is, each cluster is very dissimilar from the other; this will indicate good clustering quality. The result of these measures and its details are further discussed.

DISCUSSION

After conducting the ten experiments, using the parameters specified previously, each measure is calculated and recorded. In Figure 14, the execution time of the approach is illustrated. As it can be noted, when the stop condition increases the time will most probably increase. Such result is normal because the profile matching and tree clustering algorithms depend, partially, on this condition. Nevertheless, the time taken to execute the algorithm, in any experiment, is very low. Most of the experiments take less than one second while the maximum time it reaches was less than second and a half. This indicates that the algorithm performance, in terms of speed, is very good.

The good result was achieved because the proposed algorithm refines and normalizes the data before going into the personalization. Specifically, the dataset is refined based on the profile of the webpage that is stored as XML tags. Hence, searching in the tree data structure of XML and matching profile would not consume a lot of time. Moreover, reducing of the dataset based on the stored profile would tremendously reduce the personalization process and, consequently, increase the algorithm speed. Hence, even if the dataset was large, the proposed algorithm will reduce such data and work on the related web pages only. Hence, the proposed

Figure 14. Algorithm speed.

algorithm can be scalable over a large dataset.

Additionally, the personalization precision of the proposed algorithm was measured using the quality of the GA resulting solution, as illustrated in Figure 15. Hence, the performance of profile matching step is recorded in each experiment. As it can be noted, the increase of the stop condition did not make any major differences in the fitness value. In fact, it started to slightly decrease the quality of the solution. Nevertheless, the quality of the solution extracted in each experiment was, on average, 98% match with the target user. Thus, it can be stated that the quality of the algorithm, concerning the profile matching, is high but a fair stop condition value is recommended.

Finally, in order to measure the personalization accuracy of the proposed algorithm, clustering quality were recorded. In specific, inter/intra cluster similarities have been measured and recorded in each experiment, as illustrated in Figure 16. Inter-cluster similarity indicated high percentage (99%) while intra-cluster similarity, on the other hand, indicated low percentage (0.1%). Such result denoted that the clustering algorithm is good; it revealed that such algorithm did not group dissimilar trees together and, also, did not separate similar ones. The performance excellence was because of the data refinement and profile matching, discussed before, where only the most related web pages will be considered in the clustering step. However, it must be emphasized on the fact that increasing of the stop condition did not affect the value of the clustering quality. Thus, a fair stop condition (equal to the number of pages) is also recommended.

After understanding and testing the proposed approach, it is time to summarize its contribution and compare it with others work. First of all, on the contrary of the available work discussed previously, the proposed

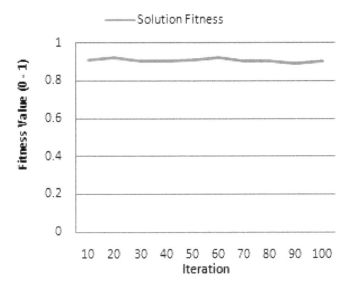

Figure 15. Personalization precision.

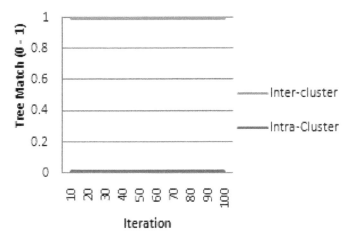

Figure 16. Personalization accuracy.

approach has further generalized web personalization. Instead of using such a personalization only on navigation and dynamic data it was applied on the static part of web pages to also consider the developer of websites rather than only the visitors. Thus, such an approach has added a value to the area of web personalization to further include providers' need, personalizing static content, and also consider the characteristics when matching rather than keywords.

Moreover, such an approach considered the long and short-term interest; it does not always update and re-execute the whole process. Only the matching and template extraction steps are repeated with every query; however, the rest is done once and updated every period of time while its result is stored in XML files. Such decision reduced the time tremendously without affecting the accuracy and, also, improved the scalability of

WCMS. In addition, the use of XML files has simplified and speeded up the process of profile matching. This is because XML content is represented as trees; thus, websites' profile will be easily searched, and information will be quickly fetched.

In addition, in order to handle web pages content, HTML was parsed to DOM trees. The uses of DOM trees have simplified and further improved the speed of web page matching and clustering. This improvement is because searching and matching trees is much better than going through the whole web page content sequentially. Moreover, such an approach is very dynamic due to the use of different parameters. Such parameters can be changed depending on the providers' need; for example, one provider could prefer only one template to be viewed; thus, the chromosome length in the matching step can be set to one. Additionally, pages were not forced to join a cluster to ensure that unique web pages are preserved in case similar websites join the Web.

Finally, as future work, ontology, which is a repository of knowledge, could be used when acquiring data; such that, instead of giving the developers limited options when entering their characteristics they can enter what they wish, and then it can be translated using the ontology's repository. For example, instead of giving the options (business, discussion forum, and medical) in nature characteristic, the user can enter (pharmaceutical) and using the ontology it will be transformed to medical. Thereby, the providers will have more flexibility when designing their websites.

Conclusion

WCMS is a powerful tool for creating, editing, organizing, and publishing content. Even though WCMS might suggest a number of templates, but it does not consider the nature of the website to be developed. It has been noticed that websites that lack in its information and structure make the visitors get lost and feel disoriented. Thus, this manuscript proposed a new approach to improve WCMS using web personalization; such that WCMS can take advantage of previous developers' knowledge to offer different template designs for each website developer depending on their need. Such an approach merged web personalization with automatic template extraction to improve the quality of WCMS and increase its flexibility and scalability. Moreover, a new technique was developed, which mixes hybrid EA (GA and ACC) with CTM. At the end of the manuscript, an experiment has been conducted to conclude that the proposed approach has a high quality, in regard of speed, precision, and accuracy. It only takes few milliseconds to accurately match users and cluster the web pages. Finally, as future work, it has been recommended to use ontology to increase the approach scalability and flexibility.

REFERENCES

Bille P (2005). A survey on tree edit distance and related problems. Theor. Comput. Sci. 337(1-3):217-239.

Carminati B, Ferrari E, Perego A (2012). A multi-layer framework for personalized social tag-based applications. Data & Knowl. Eng. 79-80(0):62-86.

Chávez F, Fernández F, Alcalá R, Alcalá-Fdez J, Olague G, Herrera F (2012). Hybrid laser pointer detection algorithm based on template matching and fuzzy rule-based systems for domotic control in real home environments. Appl. Intell. 36(2):407-423.

Christos B, Vaggelis K, Ioannis M (2004). 5-7 April 2004). Web page fragmentation for personalized portal construction. Paper presented at the Information Technology: Coding and Computing, 2004. Proceedings. ITCC 2004.

Chulyun K, Kyuseok S (2011). TEXT: Automatic Template Extraction from Heterogeneous Web Pages. Knowledge and Data Engineering. IEEE Trans. 23(4):612-626.

CoreMedia (2012). CoreMedia Introduces New Web Content Management Solution for Media and Entertainment. 2012, from http://www.coremedia.com/web-content-management/news-events/press-releases/coremedia-launches-new-web-content-management-solution-for-media-and-entertainment-/-/1602/10830/-/_11n0rb8z/-/index.html.

Crossley M, Kings NJ, Scott JR (2003). Profiles-Analysis and Behaviour. BT Technol. J. 21(1):56-66.

Deneubourg L, Goss S, Franks N, Detrain C, Chretien L (1991). *The Dynamics of Collective Sorting: Robot-Like Ant and Ant-Like Robot.* Paper presented at the from animals to animats: Proceedings of the first International Conference on Simulation of Adaptive Behavior pp. 183-192.

Dinh T, Mamun A (2004). A combination of clustering algorithms with Ant Colony Optimization for large clustered Euclidean Travelling Salesman Problem. Paper presented at the WSEAS SOSM 2004, Miami, Florida.

Eirinaki M, Mavroeidis D, Tsatsaronis G, Vazirgiannis M (2006). Introducing Semantics in Web Personalization: The Role of Ontologies. In M. Ackermann, Berendt B, Grobelnik M, Hotho A, Mladenic D, Semeraro G, Spiliopoulou M, Stumme G, Svátek V, van Someren M. (Eds.), Semantics, Web and Mining 4289:147-162 Springer Berlin / Heidelberg.

Eirinaki M, Vazirgiannis M (2003). Web mining for web personalization. ACM Trans. Internet Technol. 3(1):1-27.

ElGibreen H, El-Masri S (2012). Template Personalization and Evolutionary Algorithms. Paper presented at the GEM'12 - 9th International Conference on Genetic and Evolutionary Methods.

Eslami MZ, Zarghami A, Sapkota B, Sinderen MV (2011). Personalized Service Creation by Non-technical Users in the Homecare Domain. Proc. Comp. Sci. 5(0):409-417.

Ferrara E, Baumgartner R (2011). Automatic Wrapper Adaptation by Tree Edit Distance Matching. CoRR, abs/1103.1252.

Flesca S, Greco S, Tagarelli A, Zumpano E (2004). Non-invasive support for personalized navigation of Websites. Paper presented at the International Proceedings of Database Engineering and Applications Symposium, 2004. IDEAS '04 pp. 183-192.

Freitas A (2002). Data Mining and Knowledge Discovery with Evolutionary Algorithms. Berlin: Spinger-Verlag. Pp. 1-260.

Gui-Sheng Y, Guang-Dong G, Jing-Jing S (2010). A template-based method for theme information extraction from web pages. Paper presented at the International Conference on Computer Application and System Modeling (ICCASM), 2010. pp. V3-721-V3-725.

Haikun H, Xiaoxin C, Guoshi W, Jing L (2010). Web Data Extraction Based on Tree Structure Analysis and Template Generation. Paper presented at the International Conference on E-Product E-Service and E-Entertainment (ICEEE), 2010. pp. 1-5.

He L, Chen Y (2010). Design and implementation of Web Content Management System by J2EE-based three-tier architecture: Applying in maritime and shipping business. Paper presented at the 2nd IEEE International Conference on Information Management and Engineering (ICIME), 2010. pp. 513-517.

Hildebrandt M (2008). Defining Profiling: A New Type of Knowledge? In M. Hildebrandt & S. Gutwirth (Eds.), Profiling the European Citizen Springer Netherlands, pp. 17-45.

Ji X, Zeng J, Zhang S, Wu C (2010). Tag tree template for Web information and schema extraction. Expert Syst. Appl. 37(12):8492-8498.

Kim Y, Park J, Kim T, Choi J (2007). Web Information Extraction by HTML Tree Edit Distance Matching. pp. 2455-2460.

Laahs K, McKenna E, Vanamo VM (2008). 15 - Site Definitions and Templates Microsoft SharePoint 2007 Technologies, Burlington: Digital Press pp. 429-462.

Lu J, Ruan D, Zhang G (2007). E-Service Intelligence: An Introduction. In Lu J, Zhang G, Ruan D (Eds.), E-Service Intelligence, Springer Berlin / Heidelberg 37:1-33.

Munk M, Kapusta J, Švec P (2010). Data preprocessing evaluation for web log mining: Reconstruction of activities of a web visitor. Proc. Comp. Sci. 1(1):2273-2280.

Nasraoui O, Soliman, M, Saka E, Badia A, Germain R (2008). A Web Usage Mining Framework for Mining Evolving User Profiles in Dynamic Web Sites. Knowledge and Data Engineering. IEEE Trans. 20(2):202-215.

net.sourceforge.htmlcleaner. (2010). HtmlCleaner release 2.2. 2011, from http://htmlcleaner.sourceforge.net.

Perugini S (2010). Personalization by website transformation: Theory and practice. Information Processing &amp. Management 46(3):284-294.

Rana C (2012). A Study of Web Usage Mining Research Tools. Adv. Netw. Appl. 03(6):1422-1429.

Ravi J, Yu Z, Shi W (2009). A survey on dynamic Web content generation and delivery techniques. J. Network Comp. Appl. 32(5):943-960.

Russell S, Norvig P (2003). Artificial Intelligence: A Modern Approach (Second ed.): Prentice Hall.

Schiaffino S, Amandi A (2009). Intelligent User Profiling. In M. Bramer (Ed.), Artificial Intelligence - An International Perspective: Springer Berlin / Heidelberg 5640:193-216.

Shen Hz, Zhao Jd, Yang ZZ (2006). A Web Mining Model for Real-time Webpage Personalization. Paper presented at the International Conference on Management Science and Engineering, ICMSE '06.

Shui-Lung C, Jane Yung-jen H (2004). Tree-Structured Template Generation for Web Pages. Proceedings of the Paper presented at the International Conference on Web Intelligence, IEEE/WIC/ACM 2004.

Wan Mohd Mahidin WAMA (2003). Dynamic template for lecturers' webpages in FTMSK. Universiti Teknologi MARA.

Wei S, Jian-Chang L, Yu-Jun H, Jian-Qiang L (2005). Application of neural network model combining information entropy and ant colony clustering theory for short-term load forecasting. Proceedings of Paper presented at the International Conference on Machine Learning and Cybernetics, 2005.

What is the Document Object Model? (2004). 2011, from http://www.w3.org/TR/DOM-Level-3-Core/introduction.html.

Wool J, Woo S (2005). New Encoding/Converting Methods of Binary GA/Real-Coded GA. IEICE Trans. E88-A(6):1545-1156.

Yen BPC, Kong RCW (2002). Personalization of information access for electronic catalogs on the web. Elect. Commerce Res. Appl. 1(1):20-40.

12

Deoxyribonucleic acid (DNA) as a hypothetical information hiding medium: DNA mimics basic information security protocol

Okunoye .O. Babatunde

Department of Pure and Applied Biology, Ladoke Akintola University of Technology, P. M. B. 4000, Ogbomoso, Osun State, Nigeria. E-mail: babatundeokunoye@yahoo.co.uk.

While the computational capabilities of deoxyribonucleic acid (DNA) are now fairly known, with the building of DNA computers which utilize DNA and other sub-cellular molecules as input and output, little seems to have been investigated on the information security properties of DNA in computer science and information technology terms. The author investigated DNA as a hypothetical information hiding molecule, which employs the principles of steganography to obscure information that might be of importance to a hypothetical attacker. By employing the combinations and permutations of bases in DNA nucleotide sequences as substitutes for an English letter, the author shows that in addition to the computational capabilities of DNA, it also mimics basic information hiding and information security protocol.

Key words: Deoxyribonucleic acid (DNA) computing, information hiding, steganography, information security, biotechnology, bioinformatics.

INTRODUCTION

The recently emerging field of deoxyribonucleic acid (DNA) computing has witnessed the execution of calculations and the design of devices using sub-cellular molecules including DNA as input and output (Adleman, 1994; Quyang et al., 1997; Pirrung et al., 2000; Sakamoto et al., 2000; Wang et al., 2001; Benenson et al., 2001; Stojanovic et al., 2002; Benenson et al., 2003; Stojanovic and Stefanovic, 2003 a and b; Okamoto et al., 2004; Margolin and Stojanovic, 2005). Deoxyribonucleic acid alongside other sub-cellular molecules, have been used to perform routine calculations, while the cell is now seen as a computation (Regev and Shapiro, 2002). DNA and molecular computations have shown, in computer science terms, the computational capacity of DNA, even though detailed study of notable microbial DNA have revealed purely computational methods (Miller et al., 2003). An aspect of DNA computing the numerous literature in the expansive field, as cited previously, have laid less emphasis on the information hiding possibilities of the DNA molecule in computer science and information security terms, as distinct from the natural coding

mechanisms in the field of molecular biology. In molecular biology, deoxyribonucleic acid is known to naturally encode for twenty amino acids in sixty-four triplet bases or codons (Weaver, 2005).

These form the basis of the natural transmission of information from generation to generation in humans and all living things. There are ten nucleotide bases per turn of a DNA helix, which comprises of a sequence of ten bases. All these and other delicate arrangements in DNA structure points to subtle information processing which makes transcription, translation and protein formation possible. The objective of this paper is to examine the structure of DNA as a hypothetical information hiding medium, in computer science terms. Information hiding is a young and rapidly evolving field with many techniques which include steganography, copyright marking, fingerprinting and water marking (Petitcolas et al., 1999). Many information hiding techniques however can trace their roots back to anquity (Petitcolas et al., 1999) and have extensive applications among the military, intelligence agencies, and law enforcement.

Here, we examine hypothetical DNA steganography, as a sub-discipline of information hiding. Whereas classical cryptography is concerned about hiding the content of messages, steganography deals with concealing their existence (Anderson and Petitcolas, 1998).

Considering part of a work of cryptography (Sutton and Rubin, 2009), complicit in one of the historical events in international relations, intercepted and decoded by British Intelligence officers (The Zimmermann Telegram sent by the German Government to the Mexican Government during World War 1):

German Legation Jan 19, 1917 via Galveston
Mexico City

130 1342 13401 8501 115 3528 416 17214 6491 11310
18147 18222 21560 10247 11518 23667 13605 3494 14936
98092 5905 11311 10392 10371 0302 21290 5161 39695
23571 17504 11269 18276 18101 0317 0228 17694 4473

BERNSTORFF
Charge German Embassy
TELEGRAM RECEIVED
FROM 2nd from London # 5474

"We intend to begin on the first of February unrestricted marine warfare. We shall endeavour in spite of this to keep the United States neutral. In the event of this not succeeding, we make Mexico a proposal of alliance on the following basis..."

Many classical steganographic techniques date back to antiquity with Æneas the Tactician (Tacitus, 1990) inventing a number of such techniques. A detailed study of steganographic techniques, ancient and modern is discussed in Petitcolas et al. (1999). The general model of hiding data (Petitcolas et al., 1999) can be described as follows: The embedded data is the message one wishes to send secretly. It is usually hidden, in this case, in an innocuous message referred to as a cover-text, producing the stegotext. It is important to state that we do not imply that DNA actually hides any data of interest to a human observer. The paper aims to show that DNA can be viewed as a hypothetical stegotext, where the distribution of the combinations of its nucleotide bases per turns of DNA helix mimic the distribution of letters in a natural language such as the English language.

MATERIALS AND METHODS

The DNA used was Bacteriophage T4 DNA, obtained from GenBank, the institutional DNA depository, with accession number AF158101. With a complete genome sequence of 168,903 base pairs, Bacteriophage T4 represents the most understood model for modern genomics and proteomics (Miller et al., 2003), and has its study had revealed many insights and paradigms in molecular biology.

Advantage was taken of the mathematical combination of four nucleotides (adenine, guanine, thymine and cytosine) per turn of

the DNA helix, which consist of ten bases (Nelson and Cox, 2000). Mathematically, there are 23 possible combinations and 296 permutations of four numbers with the sum of ten (Table 1).

The combinations of nucleotides in 3,183 helical segments of Bacteriophage T4 DNA (consisting of ten bases) were recorded (Table 2).

This represents 31,830 bases, complement 168,900' to 137,070' in the 5' to 3' direction. For the related complement, 21 nucleotide combinations were discovered; the combinations 0, 0, 0, 10 and 0, 0, 1, 9 did not occur. The frequencies of the nucleotide combinations were recorded while, similarly, the frequencies of 3,183 letters of the English language from the 5th chapter of a classic English literature text, Wuthering Heights (Figures 1 and 2) (Bronte, 1965) were recorded (Table 3). Considerable reductions in text are possible in the English language without losing information due to the statistical nature of the language and high frequency of certain words. This property is called redundancy (Shannon, 1949). Redundancy is of central importance in information security, and given that there was a disparity between the number of nucleotide combinations and English letters, we omit the letters C, Q, V, X, Z to bring the symbols to numerical parity of 21 pieces. Due to the fact that we assumed, hypothetically, that the nucleotide combinations are hiding information in the English language, we set up a simple substitution table between the nucleotide symbols and English letters, in order of increasing frequency (Table 4).

RESULTS

Consider the following sequence of helical combinations from T4 Phage DNA:

3': 0055 1234 0370 1144 4411 2611 2035 1414 1333
1342 1018 1117 2224 2242 0334 6004 1045 4051
2008 3016 0316 4132 1243 3007 8110 3115 5104
2323 2332 4060 2440 1216 1711 3340 4321 4006: 5'

This is comparable with a standard work of cryptography such as the Zimmermann Telegram (Sutton and Rubin, 2009). Interception of this traffic in a security situation could raise suspicion, especially if the interceptor is oblivious of their source. It might be argued however that the traffic is trivial for a capable attacker, as it is obvious the numbers are merely a mathematical operation (combinations) on the number set (x: 0 ≤ x ≤ 10); nevertheless the robustness of the traffic is its concealment within the cell protoplasm, encoded in the arrangement of nucleotide bases in DNA helices, making it a very uncanny example of "covered writing", hence steganography. Therefore, any attempt to retrieve the message by a hypothetical attacker will involve molecular biology procedures for DNA extraction, purification and analysis.

With the substitution of each respective nucleotide combination as depicted previously in the T4 phage DNA segment with the corresponding English letter, we obtain an embedded data containing 3,183 letters in the English language. Since we assume the stegotext, T4 phage DNA is concealing a message in English language, the probable word method (Shannon, 1949), is used to recover any embedded message within the stegotext. The probable words may be words or phrases expected

Table 1. Possible helical nucleotide combinations and permutations.

Nucleotide combination	Number of permutation	Permutation
0,0,0,10	4	00010,0010,01000,10000
0,0,1,9	12	0019, 0091,0109,0190,0901,0910,1009,1090,1900,1009,9001,9100
0,0,2,8	12	0028,0082,0208,0280,0802,0820,2008,2080,2800,8200,2080,8020
0,0,3,7	12	0037,0073,0307,0370,0703,0730,3007,3070,3700,7300,7003,7030
0,0,4,6	12	0046,0064,0406,0460,0604,0640,4006,4060,4600,6004,6040,6400
0,0,5,5	6	0055,0505,0550,5005,5050,5500
0,1,2,7	24	0127,0172,0217,0271,0712,0721,1207,1270,1702,1720,2017,2071 2107,2170,2701,2710,7012,7021,7102,7120,7201,7210,1027,1072
0,1,3,6	24	0136,0163,0316,0361,0613,0631,1036,1063,1306,1360,1603,1630, 3016,3061,3106,3160,3601,3610,6013,6031,6103,6130,6301,6310
0,1,1,8	12	0118,0181,0811,1018,1081,1108,1180,1801,1810,8011,8101,8110
0,2,2,6	12	0226,0262,0622,2026,2062,2206,2260,2602,2620,6022,6202,6220
0,2,3,5	24	0235,0253,0325,0352,0523,0532,2035,2053,2305,2350,2503,2530, 3025,3052,3205,3250,3502,3520,5023,5032,5203,5230,5302,5320
0,2,4,4	12	0244,0424,0442,2044,2404,2440,4024,4042,4204,4240,4402,4420
0,3,3,4	12	0334,0343,0433,3034,3043,3304,3340,3403,3430,4033,4303,4330
1,1,1,7	4	1117,1171,1711,7111
1,1,2,6	12	1126,1162,1216,1261,1612,1621,2116,2161,2611,6112,6121,6211
1,1,3,5	12	1135,1153,1315,1351,1513,1531,3115,3151,3511,5113,5131,5311
1,1,4,4	6	1144,1414,1441,4114,4141,4411
1,2,2,5	12	1225,1252,1522,2125,2152,2215,2251,2512,2521,5122,5212,5221
1,3,3,3	4	1333,3133,3313,3331
1,2,3,4	12	1234,1243,1324,1342,1423,1432,2134,2143,2314,2341,2413,2431, 3124,3142,3214,3241,3412,3421,4123,4132,4213,4231,4312,4321
2,2,3,3	6	2233,2323,2332,3223,3232,3322
2,2,2,4	4	2224,2242,2422,4222
0,1,4,5	24	0145,0154,0415,0451,0514,0541,1045,1054,1405,1450,1504,1540, 4015,4051,4105,4150,5014,5041,5104,5140,4501,4510,5401,5410
Total	296	

Table 2. Nucleotide combinations, permutations, frequencies and probabilities in 3,183 turns of T4 phage genome.

S/N	Combination		Permutation	Frequency	Probability
1	0,0,5,5	(X18)	6	5	0.0016
2	0,0,2,8	(X19)	1 2	7	0.0022
3	0,1,1,8	(X21)	1 2	11	0.0035
4	1,1,1,7	(X14)	4	15	0.0047
5	0,0,3,7	(X1 7)	1 2	16	0.0050
6	0,0,4,6	(X2 0)	12	23	0.0072
7	0,2,2,6	(X1 6)	1 2	63	0.0198
8	0,1,2,7	(X3)	24	76	0.0239
9	0,1,3,6	(X10)	24	109	0.0343
10	1,1,4,4	(X13)	6	119	0.0374
11	0,2,4,4	(X6)	1 2	1 35	0.0424
12	0,1,4,5	(X1)	24	140	0.0440

Table 2. Cont'd.

13	1,1,2,6	(X 8)	1 2	144	0.0453
14	0,3,3,4	(X12)	1 2	145	0.0456
15	1,3,3,3	(X9)	4	181	0.0569
16	2,2,2,4	(X15)	4	188	0.0591
17	1,1,3,5	(X7)	1 2	195	0.0613
18	0,2,3,5	(X11)	24	225	0.0707
19	1,2,2,5	(X4)	1 2	290	0.0911
20	2,2,3,3	(X2)	6	295	0.0927
21	1,2,3,4	(X5)	24	800	0.2514
Total			2 7 0	31 8 3	0. 9988

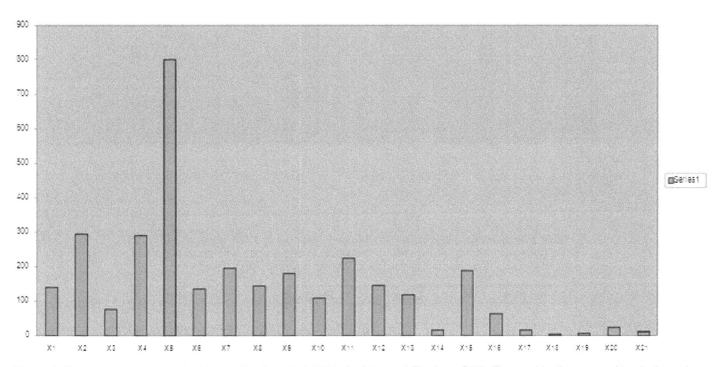

Figure 1. Frequency graph of nucleotide combinations in 3,183 helical turns of T4 phage DNA. The combinations are written in the order they appear in T4 phage DNA in the 5' to 3' direction.

in the particular message due to its source, or they may merely be common words and syllables which occur in any text in the language, such as the, and, tion, and the like in English language (Shannon, 1949). From this substitution of nucleotide combinations in T4 Phage with an English letter, over 300 words could be spelt out, phrases occurred occasionally, and a few statements could be made from the resulting text (Table 5). Reconstructions were often necessary to make sense of the statement.

DISCUSSION

Steganography, derived from the Greek, literally means "*covered writing*" (Johnson and Jajodia, 1998a). While cryptography scrambles a message so it cannot be understood, steganography hides a message so it cannot be seen (Johnson and Jajodia, 1998b).

DNA and molecular computing have ushered in a new era in computer science and information technology. The goal, however is not to compete with silicon based electronic computers, but rather to focus on areas of computation, such as combinatorics, where electronic computers are quite inefficient (Adleman, 1994). More-over, as a information hiding medium, it is noteworthy that storing information in molecules of DNA allows for an information density of approximately 1 bit/nm^3, a dramatic improvement over existing storage media such as videotapes, which store information at a density of

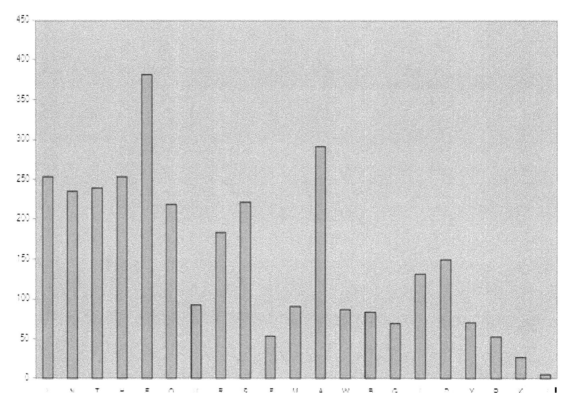

Figure 2. Frequency graph of 3,183 letters of chapter 5 of Wuthering heights. The letters are arranged in the order they appear in the text.

Table 3. Frequencies and probabilities of English letter out of 3,183 letters of an English text (Wuthering heights) in the case of the letters H and I which both occur 253 times, thereby having the same probabilities (the consonant is placed before the vowel).

S/N	Letter	Frequency	Probability
1	J	5	0.0016
2	K	26	0.0082
3	P	52	0.0163
4	F	53	0.0167
5	G	69	0.0217
6	Y	70	0.0220
7	B	83	0.0261
8	W	86	0.0270
9	M	91	0.0286
10	U	92	0.0289
11	L	131	0.0412
12	D	149	0.0468
13	R	183	0.0575
14	O	219	0.0688
15	S	221	0.0694
16	N	235	0.0738
17	T	239	0.0751
18	H	253	0.0795
19	I	253	0.0795
20	A	291	0.0914
21	E	382	0.1200
	Total	3183	1.0001

Table 4. A simple substitution table.

S/N	Nucleotide combination	English letter
1	0,0,5,5	J
2	0,0,2,8	K
3	0,1,1,8	P
4	1,1,1,7	F
5	0,0,3,7	G
6	0,0,4,6	Y
7	0,2,2,6	B
8	0,1,2,7	W
9	0,1,3,6	M
10	1,1,4,4	U
11	0,2,4,4	L
12	0,1,4,5	D
13	1,1,2,6	R
14	0,3,3,4	O
15	1,3,3,3	S
16	2,2,2,4	N
17	1,1,3,5	T
18	0,2,3,5	H
19	1,2,2,5	I
20	2,2,3,3	A
21	1,2,3,4	E

Table 5. Some words, phrases and statements found in the stegotext.

S/N	Words	Phrases	(Reconstructed) statement
1	IT	'BE HIM'	HO A SEAL
2	HE	'A SEA'	I TIRE
3	IS	'IT DIE'	WE EAT A TREE
4	ME	'LET TWO'	USE A SEA
5	US	'I READ'	HE IS WOE
6	THEIR	'AN HAT'	WOE HIT IT
7	DEN	'AS IS'	A NUN HE SEES
8	SUN	'SEE A SANE'	LET TIM'S TOE HEAL
9	MEN	'A RIDE'	HEAL US
10	ROB	'LORE DEN'	SO LET TWO LOAD
11	LIE	'USE LEG'	I READ IT SIR
12	SEED	'END IN'	IT FIT
13	AREA	'HER HAT'	BE RED ROSE
14	HEAL	'SELL BEAR'	YES HE ERRED HE SEES A NET
15	WEST	'BE OR'	
16	STAR	'I SUE'	
17	ELITE	'NUNS ARE'	
18	HEARD	'A REAL'	
19	TENET	'LET TWO'	
20	BERTH	'TEA SEED'	

approximately 1 bit/10^{12} nm^3 (Adleman, 1994). Currently, the only application of DNA in steganography is in the field of currency security, where special inks or materials with particular structure (such as fluorescent dyes or DNA) are used to write a hidden message on bank notes or other secure documents (Petitcolas et al., 1999). These materials provide a unique response to some particular excitation such as a reagent or laser light at a particular frequency.

SUMMARY AND CONCLUSION

The work is entirely hypothetical in nature, showing how DNA nucleotides mimic lettering in a natural language like the English language. While this work is purely hypothetical, the dramatic improvement in storage by DNA over conventional steganographic materials might have useful applications in the future. It is not impossible, that given the current outlay of designer molecular devices, the protocols of current molecular biology, genetic engineering and biotechnology might envision a future not unlike the skin implanted microchips, where information hiding could find a new terrain in microscopic cells, not to mention human subcutaneous cells. Presently, this work sheds new light and provides insight on the interesting way in which deoxyribonucleic acid nucleotides can be viewed as a hypothetical biochemical steganographic media, just as in standard computer science and engineering applications.

REFERENCES

Adleman LM (1994). Molecular computation of results to combinatorial problems. Science, 266:1021-1024.
Anderson RJ, Petitcolas FAP (1998). On the limits of steganography. IEEE J. Selected Areas Commun., Special Issue Copyright Privacy Protection, 16: 474-481.
Benenson Y, Adar R, Paz-Elizur T, Livneh Z, Shapiro E (2003). DNA molecule provides a computing machine with both data and fuel. Proc. Nat. Acad. Sci. USA, 100: 2191-2196.

Benenson Y, Paz-Elizur T, Adar R, Keinan E, Livneh Z, Shapiro E (2001). Programmable and autonomous computing machine made of biomolecules. Nature, 414: 430-434.
Bronte E (1965) Wuthering Heights. The Penguin English library: Middlesex.
Johnson NF, Jajodia S (1998a). Steganalysis: The analysis of hidden information. Proceedings of the IEEE Information Technology Conference, Syracuse, New York, USA.
Johnson NF, Jajodia S (1998b). Exploring steganography: seeing the unseen. IEEE Comput., 31: 26-34.
Margolin AA, Stojanovic MN (2005). Boolean Calculations made easy (for ribozymes). Nat. Biotechnol., 23: 1374-1376.
Miller ES, Kutter E, Mosig G, Arisaka F, Kunisawa T, Ruger W (2003). Bacteriophage T4. Microbiol. Mol. Biol. Rev., 67: 86-156.
Nelson DL, Cox MM (2000). Lehninger Principles of Biochemistry. New York: Worth Publishers.
Okamoto A, Tanaka K, Saito I (2004). DNA logic gates. J. Am. Chem. Soc., 126: 9458-9463.
Petitcolas FAP, Anderson RJ, Kuhn MG (1999). Information hiding: a survey. Proceed. IEEE, Special Issue Protection Multimedia Content, 87: 1062-1079.
Pirrung MC, Connors RV, Odenbaugh AL, Montague-Smith MP, Walcott NG, Tollet JJ (2000). The arrayed primer extension method for DNA microchip analysis. Molecular computation of satisfaction problems. J. Am. Chem. Soc.122: 1873-1882.
Quyang Q, Kaplan PD, Liu S, Libchaber A (1997). DNA solution of maximal clique problem. Science, 278:446-449.
Regev A, Shapiro E (2002). Cellular abstractions: cells as computation. Nature, 419: 343.
Sakamoto K, Gouzu H, Komiya K, Kiga D, Yokoyama S, Yokomori T, Hagiya M (2000). Molecular computation by DNA hairpin formation. Science, 288: 1223-1226.
Shannon CE (1949). Communication theory of secrecy systems. Bell Syst. Tech. J., 28: 656-715.
Stojanovic MN, Mitchell TE, Stefanovic DJ (2002). Deoxyribozyme-based Logic Gates. Am. Chem. Soc., 124:3555 – 3561.
Stojanovic MN, Stefanovic DJ (2003a). A deoxyribozyme based molecular automation. Nat. Biotechnol., 21: 1069-1074.
Stojanovic MN, Stefanovic DJ, (2003b). Deoxyribozyme based half-adder. J. Am. Chem. Soc., 125: 6673 – 6676.
Sutton WG, Rubin AD (2009). "Cryptography", Microsoft® Encarta® DVD, Redmond WA: Microsoft Corporation.
Tacitus A (1990). How to survive under siege/Æneas the Tactician. Oxford: Clarendon ancient history series, Clarendon press, pp. 84-90, 183-193.
Weaver RF (2005). Molecular Biology, 3rd edition, McGraw-Hill.

13

Location-aware information services platform for mobile users in Nigeria

Nnebe S. E.[1]* and Chiemeke S.C.[2]

[1]Department of Computer Science, Ambrose Alli University, Ekpoma, Edo State, Nigeria.
[2]Department of Computer Science, University of Benin, Benin city, Edo State, Nigeria.

Ongoing advances in technology and proceeding miniaturization have led to growing popularity and widespread use of mobile devices. A modern research direction is location-aware computing, which aims at providing services to users taking into consideration the location of the user in space. Apart from communication features and basic functionality like address books or organizers, users expect today's portable and handheld devices to provide more advanced features such as presenting relevant location information, a location plan or information about nearby facilities or services. The usage of location information to adapt the applications to the current location and provide the user information that is relevant to the current position is a fascinating concept. In this paper, we present a location-aware application that provides location-aware information services. Our approach presents an overview of location-aware services from a broad perspective involving application prospects. We provide here a platform for a location-aware information notification service that allows for personalized deployment of services that can be customized as regards mobile phone users in Nigeria.

Key words: Location-aware computing, location-aware services, mobile devices, technology.

INTRODUCTION

The various changes witnessed in mans' life were as a result of his conscious efforts to control his environment through the application of different technologies. From the beginning of time, man has strived to improve his way and quality of life. He has been curious to find out his location since ancient times. Ancient people used landmarks, stars and verbal queries to locate themselves. In the middle ages, man used compasses and maps to find out his locations. The mobility, portability and the ever increasing services that are being offered by mobile devices has led people living in the current world into focusing on embedding Location Based Services (LBS) into mobile devices. This is a result of the curiousity for knowing mobile user's current position. This is a feature that can be used to locate a mobile device or the user carrying the mobile device. That is to provide appropriate information and service based on the understanding of the users' location and demand.

With the fast growing nature of mobile computing devices and cheap location sensing systems, location information has become an important resource for mobile users. Location-aware computing should take advantage of the user's current location to provide him with relevant information. Information and service needs of men vary according to their immediate situation and location. A location-aware service responds to this by offering contextually relevant information. When the location of a user had been recognized, they can be communicated to others, if the user so wishes.

As the wireless networking revolution continues, computing devices are becoming more widespread and universally connected. Computing applications now operate in a variety of new settings: for instance, embedded in cars or wearable devices. Presently, the mobile phones are increasingly not aware of their mobility. Most mobile users in Nigeria still can not find answers to these questions: Where am I? Where are my friends and family? and what is around me? As these technologies and third generation mobile networks become a reality, location based information systems are thought to be a growing area. They will serve a mobile user by ex ploiting the position of a mobile terminal in order to locate objects and points of interests around him.

---

*Corresponding author. E-mail: nnebese@yahoo.com.

Today, an ill-prepared traveler in Nigeria (who does not consult the internet, buy a guide book, pick up information at the hotel or airport check-in, buy a Global Positioning System (GPS) receiver, etc) wastes a lot of time, and will not receive much help from his or her mobile device. The traveler must obtain help manually by asking questions or they are stranded. When mobile users find themselves in an environment with which they are unfamiliar, their behaviour and needs are largely predictable. In their own country or outside, in a vehicle or on foot, they need to find somewhere to eat, perhaps a pharmacy, somewhere to obtain cash, a taxi stand, locating a hotel and a foreign exchange, finding the local tourist attractions and so on. When driving, there may be other requirements, such as help with finding a route through an unknown city or details of breakdown services.

In situation such as this, location-aware applications can be of great assistance. Achieving this justifies the need for a better purpose of use of the mobile device, as it motivates the necessity, especially in cases of emergency, tourism, navigation and other relevant applicable areas.

The domain of LBS poses specific challenges that make developing services difficult especially in developing countries. These include the inherent complexity of dealing with geographical data, lack of adequate infrastructure and the necessity for making services location-aware.

The primary idea of LBS is that a portable device sends its location to a server, the server searches through its database and sends the most relevant information near the location to the device (Zhou et al., 2007). Figure 1 depicts the five basic components of LBS and their connections.

Considering the instance that somebody wants to take a dinner in a restaurant and is therefore searching a restaurant in the Internet, a useful approach to prevent that one gets as search result every restaurant web-page in the world, one could restrict the search by adding further search criteria. A good choice is the city where the mobile user is (position), the actual time (evening) or a special type of restaurant (local or Chinese or Greek).

Such kind of restaurant search with respect to position can be done by use of a Location-aware Service. They are services that are related by their information contents to a certain place or location. They are part of the larger location-based solutions (LBS) picture that comprises GPS-enabled mobile computing services (communication and computation via mobile devices). They should deliver location-based information whenever and wherever it may be needed ideally accessed via mobile phones.

Further, considering the scenario of searching a restaurant, the information chain from a service request to the reply (answer) can be described below with Figure 1 and is illustrated using our derived conceptual framework in Figure 2. The information the user wants for

instance is the availability of a restaurant nearby. Therefore the user expresses his need by selecting the appropriate function on his mobile device: e.g. menu: location information => searches => restaurants.

The information (restaurants) will now be presented to the user either as a text list ordered by distance and location. Finally, if he has chosen a specific restaurant he can ask for a route to that restaurant.

This paper discusses an architecture of LBS that is based on Java with web services; a client side, server and a back end database server. The paper encourages the provision and use of location-aware information. It therefore, focuses on the provision of location-aware system to mobile users whose locations are in constant change. It presents a framework, which can easily be implemented by network providers and easily used by the users at a reasonable cost. The platform presented here can help awaken the dormant aspects of IT in Nigeria and Africa in general and help the user integrate into his environment and other communities easily.

RELATED LITERATURE

Research within location aware services has been conducted for over a decade. Early works such as Active Badge system (Want et al., 1992) use infra-red technology but other sensor technologies have been explored as well (Hazas and Ward, 2002). The research focusing on location aware services is vast and a number of these services have been implemented, for instance the Guide project (Cheverst et al., 2002) which is the most extensive academic studies of location based services (Cheverst et al., 2000) and cyber Guide (Abowd et al., 1997).

Schilit et al. (1995) researchers at Xerox PARC, developed a suite of context aware applications for PARCTAB (Want et al., 1995), a device that combines the properties of the Active Badge System and PDA. One of the first PARCTAB applications displays team members and computing devices, such as printers, according to their proximity (Schilit et al., 1995). Another PARCTAB application is the Location Browser, an application for viewing a "location-based file system", in which directories are named after locations and contain files and programs. When a user moves within the building, the browser updates the displayed directory to match the location of the user (Lamming and Mike, 1994). Forget-Me-Not for PARCTAB was also developed. It is a portable memory aid which automatically collects data and allows users to search and display the collected information based on the context, and traverse implicit links between past events.

Similarly, AudioAura (Mynatt et al., 1998), Situational Awareness (Schmidt et al., 1999], In/Out Board (Dey, 2000), Context-Call (Schmidt et al., 2000) and Awarenex (Tang et al., 2001) are also fieldwork applications of

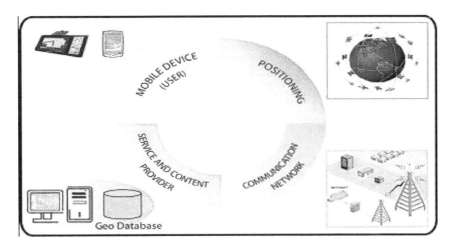

Figure 1. The basic components of LAS: User, communication network, positioning, service provider and content provider (Reichenbacher, 2004).

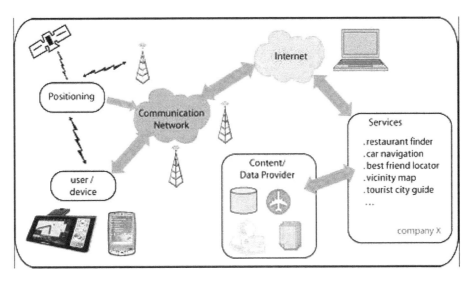

Figure 2. LBS components and information flow (Stefan, 2006).

location based services developed.

Android (2006) says location-based services platform for mobile phones is a good and conducive media for mobile phones to exchange information for the better of the users.

In cognizance with the great and immense benefit of a location based service platform, Android worked with powerful mobile phone producers such as T-mobile, HTC, Qual Comm. (QCOM), Motorola, Sony Ericsson, Nokia and others to develop an Open Handset Alliance for the mobile industry. Android is a fully integrated mobile "Software Stack" that consists of operating system, middleware, user-friendly interface and applications.

Telecgsm and Geolife UK announced the availability of the first turn-by-turn mobile navigation application NAVMII for the iphone 3Gand 3GS in Nigeria (Geolife, 2010). Navmii transforms the Apple iphone into a voice

and visual guided navigation system with detailed maps of Nigeria, covering over 30 cities. Users can search for an address by city, street or junction with Navmiis address input, or select a point on a map.

NAVMII makes navigation on the iphone incredibly simple but are only compliant with iphone 3G and 3GS and requires iphone operating system 3.0 or later. They are designed specifically for iphones and not compatible with other brands of phone as such is not popular among other brands of phones.

Starcomms Nigeria announced the launch of StarTrack- a location based family finder service in partnership with UK based Location Based Service (LBS) supplier, Creativity Software (Tushar, 2010). The LBS service enables users to locate their family and friends, through Starcomms Code Division Multiple Access (CDMA) network. The LBS solution uses real-time location of the users' mobile phones, providing their

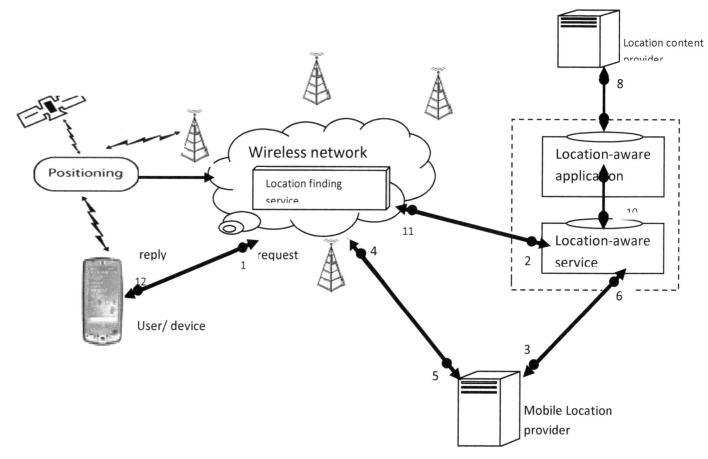

Figure 3. Conceptual framework illustrating location aware services.

location without making a call.

To register for the service, Starcomms subscribers simply send a registration SMS containing their name to the operator. Subscribers can then add a person they wish to locate, by sending a further SMS containing the name and number of that person. When a subscriber requests the location of another registered user the location information is sent to them via an SMS containing a written description of their location with the time and date. StarTrack provides the need for subscribers to be in touch without necessarily interfering in each other's activities. This makes StarTrack the service of choice, but it is SMS-based and available to only Starcomms subscribers. It does not provide Points of Interest (POIs) that we addressed here. StarTrack infringes on subscribers privacy hence they are not notified before their locations are disclosed to family and friends.

These applications or services above differ in the extent of contextual information they use as well as the services they provide to the user. The very few ones that are available in Nigeria are customised for particular brands of phones and networks and not applicable to other brands. Most of them failed to cues about how application objects should be structured to seamlessly interact with the positioning tools.

The similarities between the available technologies and our proposed technology are that they are mobile phone based. The difference is that our architecture uses both network positioning and assisted or integrated positioning. It is intended for use by all networks and mobile phones that support positioning.

The architecture presented in this paper considers a service as a specific instance of a software system that carries out a computational operation on behalf of a user. It exports its interfaces and is capable of being accessed via standard network protocols.

THE CONCEPTUAL FRAMEWORK

Figure 3 is a conceptual framework which gives an illustrative view of LAS components and services information flow as shown in Figure 4. The framework further shows how location aware services can aid in locating a nearby information service (restaurant) as considered earlier.

When the location finding service has been activated on a user's mobile phone, the actual position of mobile phone is obtained from the Positioning Service. The mobile client sends an information request via the location-aware service which contains the objective to

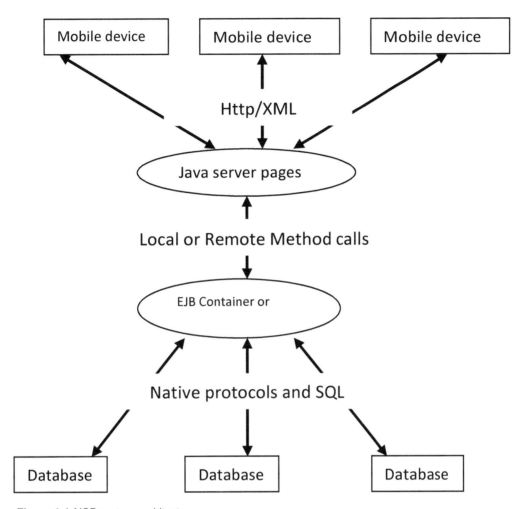

Figure 4. LAISP system architecture.

search for via the wireless network by virtue of the mobile location provider and an available location-aware application. The application server reads the request and activates the appropriate service. The server searches through its database (location-content provider) to find the most relevant information (for instance restaurants characterized by the distance and the address) near the user and sends (reply) back to the user.

The system has both a physical and logical layout shown in Figure 5 and 6. In the physical layout, a user submits a query from a mobile device to a server. The server searches through its database to find the most relevant information near the user and sends it back to him/her. Positioning is done through the use of assisted or integrated GPS or network positioning technique or a combination of the three.

COMPOSITIONS OF THE CONCEPTUAL ARCHITECTURE

The architecture of our proposed Location-aware information Services Platform (LAISP) is a client side, server and a back end database server and is depicted in Figure 3. It outlines the overall architecture and components of the system developed.

Our three-tier architecture splits the platform into:

i) The client
ii) The server
iii) The database

RESEARCH FRAMEWORK AND METHODOLOGY

We adopted three-tier architecture as depicted in Figure 5. It outlines the overall architecture and components of the system. The three-tier architecture is very attractive for developing applications because it offers benefits that the traditional two-tier architecture does not give.

Our three-tier architecture splits the platform into: the client, the server, and the database. The system has both a physical and logical layout. In the physical layout, a user submits a query from a mobile device to a server. The server searches through its database to find the most relevant information near the user and sends it back to the user. Positioning can be done via the use of assisted or integrated GPS or network positioning technique. In the logical layout, the framework is divided into: the Client

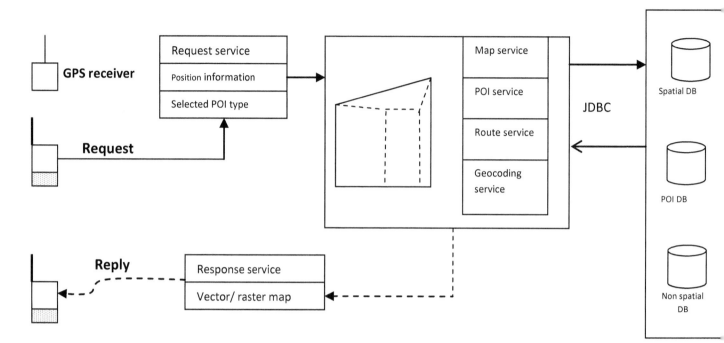

Figure 5. The physical layout of the proposed service procedure.

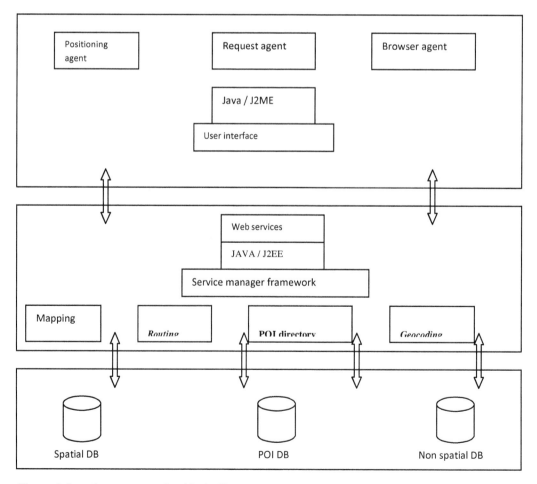

Figure 6. Location-aware services' logical layout.

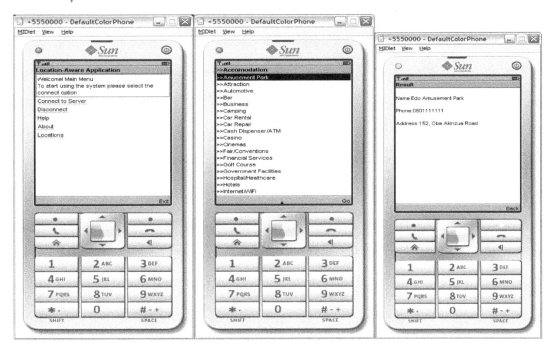

Figure 7. Screenshots from the design showing an instance of the main menu, different POIs and a sample result on Sun Microsystem's Java wireless toolkit.

application, the Application server- "middle tier", and the Database server. The Client application sends a service request to a middle-tier, which then sends the command to the database. The database processes the requests and sends then back to the middle tier, which then sends the result, back to the user. Hence, it is observed that there is no direct communication between the client application and the database.

The first tier is the user terminal, the user interface on the mobile device. This is often called the presentation tier. It is the topmost tier of the framework. The positioning agent provides real location of a user to the service (pull), the request service allows the user to select different services, while the Browser agent supports geographical view utilities, which are developed to present spatial data based on J2ME. The user interface is an important component of the platform that makes it possible for clients to personally manage the contents that appear on their device(s).

The second tier is the business mediator, which provides web services based on J2EE. It is also called the application tier and it controls an application's functionality by performing detailed processing. It serves as a 'go-between' for the client and database. Communication between the service platform and mobile user is achieved through socket proxy.

The database is the third-tier. It supports the management of information that is relevant, these may include POI, base maps, geocode sources etc. Geometrical objects are stored and managed in relational tables. The database tier is also known as data tier, information is stored and retrieved. It keeps data neutral and independent from application servers or business logic. The service platform connects to database through Java Database Connectivity (JDBC) or Open Database Connectivity (ODBC). The database used was Oracle9.

The methodology adopted is the Object Oriented Analysis and Design (OOAD). OOAD was chosen as a result of its incomparative suitability with JAVA technology. It solves problem by decomposing it into objects that can be handled separately and relatively more conveniently.

This paper involved the development of modules that were implemented as computer and phone software. The software is a client-server application as shown on the framework, with a computer as the server and mobile phone as the client. The client-side was programmed using JAVA 2 Micro Edition (J2ME), which is a set of technologies and specifications developed for small devices and very suitable for most Java enabled phones. It is suitable because it uses a subset J2SE (Java 2 Standard Edition) components such as virtual machine and leaner APIs.

The server-side is a Java Server Pages (JSP) application deployed on Apache Tomcat 4.1 application server.

IMPLEMENTATION/RESULTS

We implemented our framework on Sun Microsystems's Java Wireless toolkit and NetBeans IDE and platforms on an Intel Pentium M 1.4 GHz laptop (Figure 7). Most of the components were written in Java. The system functioned as designed in all tests that were conducted.

The service developed was optimized for use in Nokia N96, which has integrated, assisted GPS to determine the latitude and longitude in the trial. Ekpoma community in Edo state of Nigeria was used for trials and the result listed some points of interests sorted by distance as displayed in Figure 8.

CONCLUSION AND FUTURE WORK

We have presented here an architectural framework and platform for the location-aware information service that enables the delivery of personalized content to users depending on their location. The architecture uses the

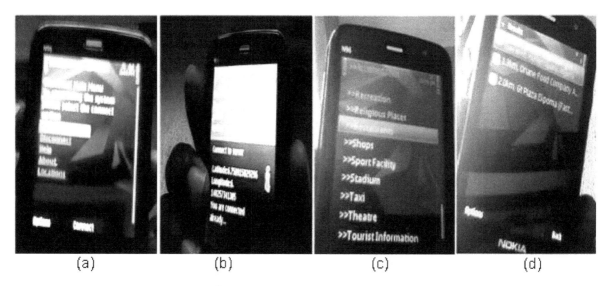

$$(a) \qquad\qquad (b) \qquad\qquad (c) \qquad\qquad (d)$$

Figures 8. (a) The front page of the location aware service application (b) The position/location (longitude/latitude) of the user terminal or device. (c) The location aware service portal and (d) Results of available restaurants sorted with distance (closeness to user) for a user position in Ekpoma, Nigeria.

request/reply infrastructure as an efficient and customizable content transportation mechanism which supports the communication between content providers and subscribers. The architecture provides service personalization by enabling users to define personal profiles.

The location-awareness was realized by designing the presence service that communicates with the location management component. We have described a conceptual framework for handling location information at different process stages, and to present locations.

We have implemented the location information service and integrated components into a prototype system for personalized location-aware information delivery. We suggest that a general and ubiquitous location service is a crucial abstraction for location-aware services. In order to achieve ubiquitous coverage, multiple location systems must be incorporated. Fine-grained access control to location information is necessary to prevent violations of people's privacy.

REFERENCES

Abowd GD, Atkeson CG, Hong J, Long S, Kooper R, Pinkerton M (1997). Cyberguide: A mobile context-aware tour guide. Wireless Network, 3: 421-433.

Cheverst K, Davies N, Mitchell K, Efstratiou C (2001). Using context as a Crystal Ball: Rewards and Pitfalls. Pers. Ubiquitous Comput., 5: 1.

Cheverst K, Mitchell K, Davies N (2002). The role of Adaptive Hypermedia in a context-aware Tourist Guide. Commun. ACM, 45(5): 47-51.

Cheverst K, Mitchell K, Davies N, Friday A, Efstratiou C (2000). Developing a context-aware electronic Tourist Guide. Some issues and experiences. In proceedings of the SIGCHI conference on Human factors in computing systems, The Hague, The Netherlands. ACM New York, pp. 17-24.

Geolife UK (2010). Turn by Turn Personal Navigation Made Simple for Nigerian iPhone Users. Navmii: The First Mobile Navigation Application for Nigeria, Geolife Ltd, PRNE.

Hazas M, Ward A (2002). An Introduction to Location-Based System. Houghton Miffin Co., Boston. www.attws.com/mmode/Location-based/ntwk_doc/it_05.pdf.

Lamming M, Mike F (1994). Forget-me-not: Intimate Computing in Support of Human Memory. In Proceedings of the FRIEND21 Symposium on Next Generation Human Interfaces, Tokyo, Japan.

Mynatt ED, Maribeth B, Roy W, Michael B, Jason BE (1998). Designing Audio Aura. In Proceeding of the Conference on Human Factors in Computing Systems (CHI 98), Los Angeles, California, USA, pp. 566-573.

Reichenbacher T (2004). Mobile Cartography -Adaptive visualisation of geographic information on mobile devices (PhD).

Schilit B, Roy W (1995). The Xerox PARCTAB. Project Website available at http://www.ubiq.com/parctab.

Schmidt A, Antti T, Jani M (2000). Context-Aware Telephony Over WAP. Pers. Ubiquitous Comput., 4(4): 225-229.

Schmidt A, Kofi AA, Antti T, Urpo T, Kristof V, Walter V (1999). Advanced Interaction in Context. In Proceedings of the First International Symposium on Handheld and Ubiquitous Computing (HUC), Karlsruhe, Germany, Springer-Verlag, pp. 89-101.

Stefan S (2006). Foundation of location-Based Services, University of Zurich.

Tang JC, Nicole Y, James B, Max VK, Francis L, Janak B (2001). Connexus To Awarenex: Extending Awareness to Mobile Users. In Proceedings of the SIGCHI Conference on Human Factors in Computing Systems. Seattle, Washington, United States, ACM Press, pp. 221-228.

Tushar M (2010). Starcomms Nigeria unveils LBS solution Thursday, March 25th, 2010 | Posted by ITNewsAfrica.com.

Want R, Andy H, Veronica F, Jonathan G (1992). The Active Badge Location System. ACM Trans. Inf. Syst. (TOIS), 10(1): 91-102.

Want R, Bill NS, Norman IA, Rich G, Karin P, David G, John RE, Mark W (1995). The ParcTab Ubiquitous Computing Experiment. Technical Report CSL-95-1, Xerox Palo Alto Research Center, Palo Alto, California, USA.

Zhou XT, Xinning F, Zhao WZ (2007). Research of Location-based Services based on JAVA and an Application Solution. Key Laboratory of Geo-Informatics of State Bureau of Surveying and Mapping, Chinese Academy of Surveying and Mapping, Beijing China.

14

Precision and repeatability analysis of Optotrak Certus as a tool for gait analysis utilizing a 3D robot

M. M. G. Mazumder[1]*, S. Kim[1] and S. J. Park[2]

[1]Kongju National University, South Korea.
[2]Korean Research Institute of Standards and Science (KRISS), South Korea.

In both scientific and clinical investigations, the precision and repeatability of instruments are demanded; however, precision of motion analysis systems has been reported in the literature rarely and studies are generally not comparable. This study introduces a new method of determining precision and repeatability of Optotrak Certus, a motion analysis tool for gait analysis using a three dimensional (3D) robot. Using 3D robot as reference of standard for distance, the angle and velocity measurement, the accuracy and precision of the Optotrak Certus in terms of angle, distance between markers were quantitated. The standard deviation (SD) and the coefficient of variation (CV) provide a measure of precision whereas the coefficient of multiple correlation (CMC) provides a measure of repeatability. Experimental results containing CMC, CV and SD values for variation of angle, volume, circular movement and speed were demonstrated to analyze the repeatability; hence the repeatability was satisfactory. Angle and distance between markers showed good agreement between measurements, and comparable measures of precision are reported as well as CMC and CV values. The investigation is ethical and practical in measurement analysis in terms of precision and repeatability.

Key words: Gait, CMC, CV, precision, repeatability, SD, 3D robot.

INTRODUCTION

Recently, the 3D motion analysis systems has been widely used in the field of gait analysis. It has been found that 3D motion analysis systems are always related to some errors and therefore, only obtained values. For 3D motion measurement systems, there are some internal and external influencing factors, which are responsible for errors such as sensor types, method application, data acquisition conditions, measurement range, object reflectance, precision, spatial resolution and measurement planning.

Optotrak Certus (OC) is a very popular tool used in industries, universities and research institutions around the world. OC obtains 3D positions utilizing infrared light-emitting diodes, which reflect light back to the sensor mounted in a stand. The markers are 16 mm in diameter and weigh 6 g. A position sensor consisting of three one-dimensional charge-coupled devices paired with three lens cells are permanently mounted in a 1.1 m long stabilized bar and calibrated by the manufacturer. The sensor captures the positions of the markers sequentially with a total sampling speed of 4600 Hz, and maximum frame rate of 400 Hz (NDI, 2007). In addition, OC can track up to 512 markers and the size and weight of OC makes it easy to move between locations. In the fields of engineering, accuracy is the degree of conformity of a measured quantity to its absolute value. Accuracy is closely related to precision, also called reproducibility or repeatability, the degree to which further measurements or calculations will show the same or similar results. The results of a measurement can be either accurate but not precise or precise but not accurate, neither or both. Accuracy is the degree of veracity while precision is the degree of reproducibility (Li, 1999; Richards, 1999; Currier, 1999). A result is called valid if it is both accurate and precise. In case of OC, precision refers to the angles and distance used between markers in gait analysis. The reliability test of motion analysis system in the aspects of

*Corresponding author. Email: mynudding@mech.uwa.edu.au, mynudding@yahoo.com.

Abbreviations: SD, Standard deviation; **CV,** coefficient of variation; **CMC,** coefficient of multiple correlation; **OC,** optotrak certus.

precision and repeatability was performed by Allard et al. (1995) in terms of the frame-to-frame repeatability of the measurement. The landmark, distance between markers and angles studies investigated using Optotrak system (Glossop et al., 1996; Li, 1999; States, 1997; Richards, 1999), suggested about the reliability of motion analysis systems. In this paper, the precision and repeatability of OC is investigated using a three 3D robot and CMC analysis based on marker position, angle, volume, circular movement and object moving at different speed. Furthermore, the repeatability analysis of dynamic objects with acceleration, constant speed and deceleration are investigated.

EXPERIMENTAL SETUP

The experimental set up includes three devices which are:

(1) 3D robot
(2) OC (Northern Digital, Waterloo, Ontario, Canada)
(3) PC with compatible softwares of OC and 3D robot

Our laboratory designed a 3D robot, which can move in the X, Y and Z coordinate in real time simultaneously. There are transmitters available which enables data transfer from the 3D robot to the remote pc. The highest limits for movement in X, Y and Z axis are 50, 30 and 50 cm, respectively. There is a flat plate available which is mounted in the Z axis that will be used later for placing markers.

Depth of the sensors measurement

For the measurement of the depth of the sensors, we did not forward to the extreme limit. We utilized one static marker at a certain distance from the sensors of the Optotrak Certus and measure the maximum and the minimum the depth of the sensors which were found at 1.5 and 6.9 m, respectively, although the manufacturer recommended the depth of the sensors between 2 and 6 m.

Precision analysis experiment

For precision experiment, we utilized the OC system with a strober along with 4 markers. One marker was placed in one corner of the flat platform where the origin of the 3D robot was placed as shown in Figure 1. From Figure 1, it can also be seen that the marker 1 is all the way static and the other three markers, that is, markers 2, 3 and 4 can move whenever the plate is moving. We measured the absolute distance of the markers 2 and 4 with the angle formed between the line formed by markers 1 and 4, and the line formed by marker 1 and marker 2. Afterwards, we measured the distance and the angle between markers 2 and 4 both in static and dynamic condition by taking three trials using OC system. The results with error (%) and standard deviation (SD) value are also provided.

Repeatability analysis experiment

In case of repeatability, we used coefficient of multiple correlation (CMC) approach being developed by Matlab program (Lee, 2006). For any measurement system for experimental design, the repeatability of data acquired by a measurement system (Portney and Watkins, 1993; Currier, 1999) is a major factor. Synonyms commonly used to describe repeatability are reliability, stability,

consistency and predictability (Currier, 1999; Hislop, 1963). Any measurement device is called a reliable system if it can measure the same values in the same quantity with repeatability for its desired application. CMC is a powerful measure of the repeatability of waveform data (Neter et al., 1989; Kadaba et al., 1989), and it is applied in some gait analysis studies previously (Kadaba et al., 1989; Growney 1997). The repeatability of any measured data can be more accurately analyzed by the CMC analysis (Neter et al., 1989; Kadaba et al., 1989; Growney, 1997). When the waveform of every data set is similar to each other, the CMC value approaches close to 1. The CMC values can be interpreted as follows:

(1) Values ranging from 0.00 to 0.25 (little or no similarity)
(2) Values ranging from 0.25 to 0.50 (fair degree of similarity)
(3) Values ranging from 0.50 to 0.75 (moderate similarity)
(4) Values ranging from 0.75 to 1 (high similarity)

The CMC analysis can provide us with the information of repeatability of measured data sets but it can't show if there is any error in the size of measurement. A useful statistical technique that addresses this issue is the coefficient of variation (CV). We perform repeatability analysis in the aspects of variation of angle, position, volume, circular movement and speed. In case of position and angle repeatability analysis, the experimental set up was same as in precision analysis. For circular movement repeatability analysis, we utilized the position of the marker 2. It may be mentioned here that our designed 3D robot can move to form a circle in two dimensional plane. Using the position of the marker 2 on the plate, the same circular movement was repeated three times which was later utilized for the repeatability analysis. Our markers (Markers 1, 2, 3 and 4) were placed in four corners of the flat plate of the 3D robot in the form of a rectangle having the same length and width as the rigid body dimension. The other four markers ((Markers 5, 6, 7 and 8) were placed in the four corners of the rigid body. Whenever the plate was moving along the Z axis the volume formed by the eight markers between the rigid body and the plate was also changing. Using the position of the markers, we calculated the volume for three trials obtained from OC and performed the repeatability analysis.

RESULTS

Precision test for distance between markers

For precision test to determine distance between markers, three trials taken from OC for both static and dynamic condition with error (%) and SD value for each trial are shown in the Tables 1 and 2.

Precision test for angles

For precision test in terms of angle, the angle data between the line formed by markers 1 and 4 and the line formed by markers 1 and 2 was taken in static condition from Optotrak Certus with SD value as well as error (%) are shown in Table 3.

Repeatability analysis for Position and object moving at different speed

The position of marker 2 was utilized for position repeatability analysis. In Figure 2, we have plotted the measured

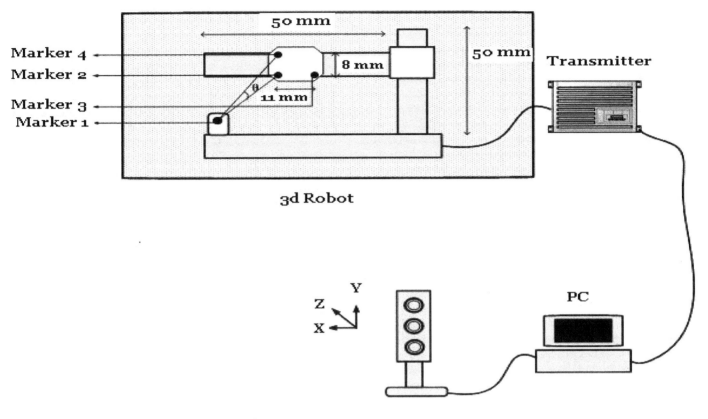

Figure 1. Experimental setup for precision analysis.

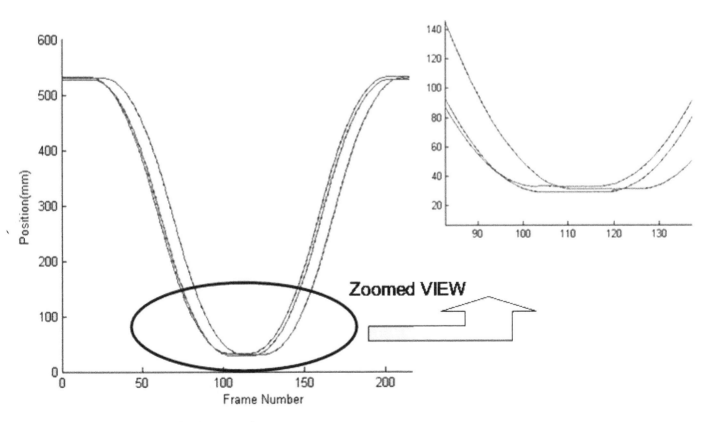

Figure 2. Three raw trail position data in the z axis.

three trial position data in the vertical axis whereas the horizontal axis contains the corresponding frame number in the Z coordinate. We also added a zoom view of each figure for better understanding of presence of three trial data. Similar figures can be plotted for the X and Y axis also. The CMC values, CV values (%) and SD values were found at 0.998, 0.7226 and 0.0161 for X axis; 0.9897, 0.3165 and 0.0017 for Y axis; 0.9897, 12.9263 and 0.1945 for Z axis, respectively which represent better repeatability and less error in position data. After this analysis, we performed the repeatability analysis for the dynamic object at difference speed. It may be mentioned that while doing the experiment, we used the trapezoidal velocity profile for the moving object which has an initial acceleration stage, the middle constant speed stage and deceleration stage. We performed the repeatability analysis for the acceleration, constant and deceleration speed, and the obtained CMC values, CV values (%) and SD values were 0.9926, 11.7747 and 7.5139 for acceleration stage; 0.6275, 1.2282 and 0.2217 for constant speed; 0.9855, 22.2025 and 7.4604 for deceleration stage. From the values, it can be seen that the constant speed profile has the low CMC value which means the repeatability was not very good for an object moving with constant speed whereas for the acceleration and deceleration stage, the CMC value were found better. But for the acceleration and deceleration stages, the CV values were found little higher which show some error in data.

Repeatability analysis for angle

As the plate was moving, the angle between markers 2 and 4 with reference to static marker was changing. Figure 3 is the plotting of the measured variation of angle between markers 2 and 4 versus corresponding frame number with a zoom view to show the presence of three trial data. The CMC, CV (%) and SD values were found as 0.9901, 1.2634 and 1.0917, respectively that prove better repeatability and less error.

Repeatability analysis for volume

For the repeatability analysis for volume, we used a rigid body. Figure 4 shows the plotting of the variation of volume between the plate and rigid body with a zoom view to show the three trial data. The CMC, CV (%) and SD values were calculated as 0.9999, 1.4151 and 0.0016 that show better repeatability and lower error.

Repeatability analysis for circular movement of markers

As the position of marker 2 was varied for the circular movement, Figure 5 shows the plotting of the measured

variation of the position of marker 2 in the X coordinate for circular movement in X-Y plane. From Figure 5, one can understand the similarity between three trial data. Besides a zoom view is provided for better understanding of the three trial data. Same plotting can be obtained for Y axis movement. The CMC, CV (%) and SD values were calculated as 0.9949, 2.8104 and 0.0944 for the X axis and for the Y axis, the values were obtained as 0.9956, 0.7761 and 0.1062, respectively that proved better repeatability and less error.

DISCUSSION

The experimental results suggested that the OC exhibits very high precision and excellent repeatability for the measurement of distance, angle, volume and speed. Although precision and repeatability were not tested under human movement, however in the case of OC, the excellent precision of the system remove doubts from the researchers mind in aspects of distance, position and the depth of the sensors as the system shows high precision. Moreover, OC also has great repeatability. There was no significant difference in the measured data taken between sessions in either distance or angle measured. In the precision analysis for the distance between markers, the errors (%) and the SD values were found between 0.569 ~ 0.57 and 0.002 ~ 0.0043, respectively for static condition whereas for the moving condition, they were found as 0.572 ~ 0.578 and 0.0058 ~ 0.0086, respectively. In case of precision of angles between markers, the error (%) and SD values were found in between 4.01 ~ 4.013 and 0.000134 ~ 0.000192. As we can see in case of angle, the error is more comparing to distance. The repeatability analysis is summarized in Table 4. Finally, the viewing area for the OC was compatible with the manufacturer's suggestion of a depth of 2 – 6 m. A larger range was available under static conditions for the system and the 3D robot, although the extreme limit was not observed. To mention our limitation, it can be stated that all the viewing areas under the system were not analyzed. Despite the trials taken for the movement of 3D robot, all the way the 3D robot was near to the center of the viewable area of the system. Recently some people suggested the availability of noise in 3D data although we did not put it into consideration. Finally, all the CMC values were close to one that shows better repeatability, the CV values were low and shows less error in measurement, and the SD values were also found very low. These results prove the reliability of OC as a motion analysis system. But as we did not deal with human motion, we cannot guarantee high reliability for any given application of human motion using OC. The reliability of a motion analysis system depends on lot of factors such as depth of the markers, motion of the markers in skin, position of the markers which means landmark, etc. From practical experience, we can say the markers sometimes go out of sight for the sensors during

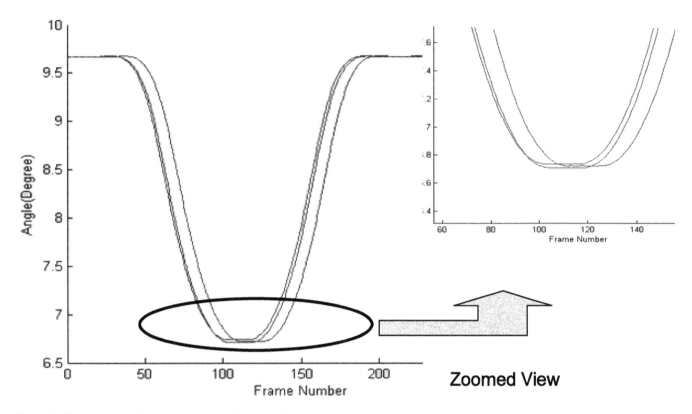

Figure 3. Variation of angle between marker 2 and marker 4.

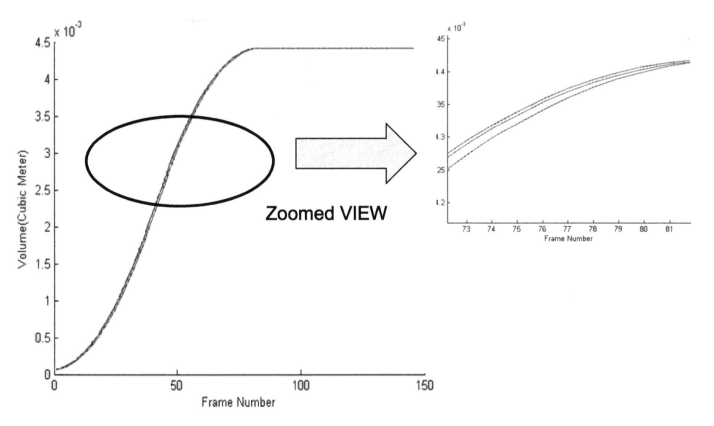

Figure 4. Variation of volume between the flat plate and the rigid body.

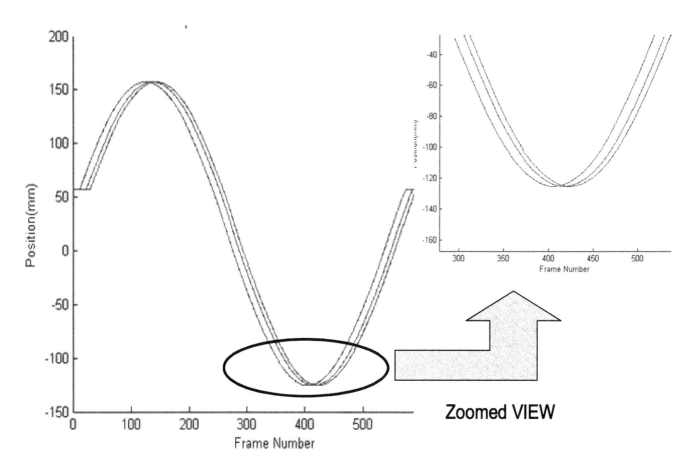

Figure 5. Position of marker 2 for circular movement in the x axis.

human motion whereas the other motion analysis systems are designed to overcome the out of sight problem better than the OC by providing cameras or sensors at various directions relative to the subject or utilizing electromagnetic device that does not care about out of sight problem. However, for any application of motion analysis system the device should be examined to find the accuracy and the reliability of the system. Finally the present study corroborated the idea that OC is an effective motion analysis tool in assessing motion of an object since they show better precision and repeatability. Regardless of these measurements, most of the motion analysis systems motion of the marker due to skin and landmarks are still the main issues to be considered. The results presented here can be used for further analysis and improvement of the performance of the motion analysis systems.

Conclusion

This study presents the analysis for assessing the performance of a commercially available motion analysis system (Optotrak Certus) utilizing a 3D robot. OC show minimal errors during our trails which suggest the

measurement will not be subjected to a significant error for gait analysis. The precision and the repeatability analysis make us believe that OC is a highly reliable motion analysis system. Further studies should deal with the noise associated with the measured 3D data as well as the larger viewing area for the position and depth of the markers to apply in human gait analysis.

REFERENCES

Allard P, Stokes I, Blanchi J (1995). Three-dimensional analysis of human. movement, Human Kinetics Champaign, IL.
Currier DP (1999). In elements of research in physical therapy. Baltimore: Williams and Wilkins (Third Edition).
Glossop N, Hu R, Randle J (1996). Motion in vertebral bodies during spine surgery. CAOS Conference, Bern, Switzerland, pp. 1 – 7.
Growney E, Meglan D, Johnson M, Cahalan T, An KN (1997). Repeated measures of adult normal walking using a video tracking system. Gait Posture, 6: 147-162.
Hislop HJ (1963). Modern instrumentation and its implications in physical therapy. J. Phys. Ther., 43: 257-262.
Kadaba MP, Ramakrishnan HK, Wootten ME, Gainey J, Gorton G, Cochran GVB (1989). Repeatability of kinematic, kinetic and electromyographic data in normal adult gait. J. Orthop. Res., 7: 849-860.
Lee RYW (2006). MatLab program for repeatability analysis of waveform data. http://biomech.brighton.ac.uk/help/cmc.
Li Q, Zamorano L, Jiang Z., Gong XJ, Pandya A, Perez R, Diaz F (1999). Effect of optical digitizer selection on the application accuracy

of a surgical localization system – A quantitative comparison between the OPTOTRAK and FlashPoint tracking systems. Comput. Aided Surg., 4: 314–321.

NDI Technical Specification Sheet (2007). Northern Digital Inc.

Neter J, Kutner MH, Nachtscheim CJ, Wasserman W (1989). Applied linear statistical models. Chicago: Irwin (Fourth Edition).

Portney LG, Watkins MP (1993). In: Foundations of clinical research: Applications to practice. Norwalk, Connecticut: Appleton and Lange.

Richards J (1999). The measurement of human motion: A comparison of commercially available systems. Hum. Mov. Sci., 18 :589–602.

States R (1997). Two simple methods for improving the reliability of joint center locations. Clin. Biomech., 12: 367–374.

15

Belief network-based acoustic emission analysis for real time monitoring in CIM environment

T. Suryasekhara Reddy[1]*, C. Eswara Reddy[2] and S. Prabhavathi[3]

[1]Department of Mechanical Engineering, R. Y. M. Engineering College, Bellary, India.
[2]Department of Mechanical Engineering, S. V. U. College of Engineering, Tirupati, India.
[3]Department of Electrical and Computer Engineering, R. Y. M. Engineering College, Bellary, India.

Machining is the most important part of the manufacturing process. Machining deals with the process of removing material from a work piece in the form of chips. Machining is necessary where tight tolerances on dimensions and finishes are required. The common feature is the use of a cutting tool to form a chip that is removed from the work part, called Swarf. Every tool is subjected to wear in machining. The wear of the tool is gradual and reaches certain limit of life which is identified when the tool no longer produce the parts to required quality. There are various types of wear a single point cutting tool may be subjected to in turning. Of these, flank wear on the tool significantly affects surface roughness. The other types of tool wears are generally avoided by proper selection of tool material and cutting conditions. On-line surface roughness measurements gained significant importance in manufacturing systems to provide accurate machining. The acoustic emission (AE) analysis is one of the most promising techniques for on-line surface roughness monitoring. The AE signals are very sensitive to changes in cutting process conditions. The gradual flank wear of the tool in turning causes changes in AE signal parameters. In the present work, investigations are carried for turning operation on mild steel material using high speed steel (HSS) tool. The AE signals are measured by highly sensitive piezoelectric element; the on-line signals are suitably amplified using a high gain pre-amplifier. The amplified signals are recorded on to a computer and then analyzed using MATLAB. A program is developed to measure AE signal parameters like ring down count (RDC), signal rise time (SRT) and root mean square (RMS) voltage. The surface roughness is measured by roller ended linear variable probe, fitted and moved along with tool turret on a CNC lathe machine. The linear movements of probe are converted in the form of continuous signals and are displayed on-line in the computer. This paper proposes to monitor tool wear and surface roughness by acoustic emissions using belief networks. The feature vectors of AE analysis and machining time were used to train the network. The overall success rate of detecting tool wear and surface roughness is high with low error.

Key words: Acoustic emission, surface roughness, turning, belief network.

INTRODUCTION

Bayesian belief networks are also known as belief networks, casual probabilistic networks, casual network, or graphical probability networks. These networks have attracted much attention recently as a possible solution to complex problems related to decision support under uncertainty. Although the underlying theory has been around for a long time, the possibility of building and executing realistic models has only been made possible because of recent improvements on algorithms and the availability of fast electronic computers.

A Bayesian network or a directed acyclic graphical model is a probabilistic graphical model that represents a set of random variables and their conditional independencies using directed acyclic graphs. Formally,

---

*Corresponding author. E-mail: tssreddy2010@gmail.com.

Abbreviations: AE, Acoustic emission; **RDC,** ring down count; **PCI,** peripheral component interconnect; **ADC,** analog digital converter; **DAC,** digital analog converter; **SRT,** signal rise time; **RMS,** root mean square; **CIM,** computer integrated manufacturing; **HSS,** high speed steel.

Bayesian networks are directed acyclic graphs whose nodes represent random variables in the Bayesian sense. They may be observable quantities such as latent variables, unknown parameters or a hypothesis which represents conditional dependencies, and nodes which are not connected represent variables which are conditionally independent of each other. Each node is associated with a probability function that takes input as a particular set of values for the node's parent variables and gives the probability of the variable represented by the node. For example, if the parents are m Boolean variables, then the probability function could be represented by a table of 2^m entries, one entry for each of the 2^m possible combinations of its parents being true or false. Efficient algorithms exist that perform inference and learning in Bayesian networks. Bayesian networks that model sequences of variables are called dynamic Bayesian networks. Generalizations of Bayesian networks that can represent and solve decision problems under uncertainty are called influence diagrams.

In machining, whether a tool needs to be changed, is decided either by a machine operator or by the life expectancy of the tool. The judgment of the machine operator is often based on the visual inspection of the tool and the surface finish produced on the work piece, both requiring a certain degree of skill. The decision based on tool-life expectancy suggests the idea of an average life for a class of tools calculated from previous data. For a particular machining condition, the tool manufacturer gives a recommended tool life for a given insert. This practice of tool replacement based on fixed tool life may not be the most economical since a tool can be replaced prematurely or only after damage has been done. Consequently, besides the unnecessary wastage of some tools, the frequent tool changes cause higher machine down time, decreasing thereby the system productivity and increasing production costs. In manufacturing, cutting cost and improving product quality are the necessary measures to adopt in an increasingly competitive world. In addition to the developments within manufacturing technology leading to the machining of larger or complicated work pieces and the use of expensive materials, the need for condition monitoring of cutting tools becomes increasingly evident. For these reasons, quality and productivity requirements through international competition have forced many manufacturers to use automated monitoring systems.

Literature review

Machine tool automation is an important aspect for manufacturing companies facing the growing demands of profitability and high quality products as a key competitiveness. The purpose of supervising machining processes is to detect interferences that would have a negative effect on the process but mainly on the product quality and production time. In the manufacturing environment, the prediction of surface roughness is of paramount importance to achieve this objective. There are two different classifications methods, Bayesian networks and artificial neural networks, for predicting surface roughness in high speed machining (Feng and Wang, 2003). A variety of tool wear and failure sensing techniques have established the effectiveness of tool failure detection in the last few decades. Optical techniques have been used to measure the progress of tool wear by using a charge-coupled device (CCD) camera (Levi et al., 1985) or a TV camera (Sata et al., 1979; Uehara, 1972).

Detected tool wear by scanning chips with an electron microprobe analyzer for wear debris removed from the cutting edge. Cook (1980) used abraded radioactive wear particles; a small amount of radioactive material was implanted in the flank of the tool. The spot was checked at the end of every cutting cycle. If the spot disappeared, the spot would be considered to be tool worn. Gomayel and Bregger (1986) used an electromagnetic sensor to measure the change in diameter of a work piece and converted it to the size of wear on the tool.

The voltage output obtained from the electromagnetic sensor was directly related to the gap between the sensor and the work piece. Cutting forces have been used to relate to tool wear and tool breakage (Tlusty and Andrews, 1983; Lan and Dornfeld, 1984). Sadat and Raman (1987) detected flank wear by using the noise spectra resulting from the rubbing action of the tool with the work piece. It was found that the noise in the frequency range of 2.75 – 3.5 kHz significantly increased from 9 to 24 dB as the tool became worn. Motor current (Liao, 1974) and motor power (Constantinides and Bennett, 1987) of the spindle was investigated for tool wear and tool breakage sensing (Turkovich and Kramer, 1986; Lin, 1995).

METHODOLOGY

The Methodology consists of the experimental set-up on CNC lathe machine. The job material mild steel is chosen and cutting tool is of HSS. The optimal cutting parameters like speed, feed and depth of cut are found by conducting number of trails at various speeds, feeds and depth of cut values. The linear variable differential transducer (LVDT) is mounted on the tool turret. It consists of a mechanical probe with high strength roller end made-up of hardened steel with nylon. As the cutting tool moves, the probe also moves along the machined surface. Thus it scans the entire surface in machining.

The deviations of the probe are displayed on digital display meter through signal converter. The signal converter consists of a series of filters, a 3-way phase detector with which positive and negative deviations are set and displayed on digital analyzer. The junction card takes the output from the signal converter and transforms the voltage within the acceptable limits of the computer. The data acquisition card takes the input from the junction card and converts the signals from analog to digital form. The digital data is thus available for the software to process further, to find digitally the surface roughness parameters like Ra, Rz and Rmax.

The PCI-02 is a 2-layer board with sufficient ground plate to give

Table 1. Levels of cutting parameters.

Parameter	Code	Unit	Level 1	Level 2	Level 3
Speed	A	Rpm	700	770	850
Feed	B	Mm/rev	0.05	0.10	0.15
Depth of cut	C	mm	0.5	1.00	1.5

Table 2. L_9 orthogonal array for flank wear.

Experiment	P1 (A)	P2 (B)	P3 (C)	SNR (db)
1	1	1	1	20.698
2	1	2	2	20.949
3	1	3	3	18.5387
4	2	1	2	18.946
5	2	2	3	19.794
6	2	3	1	19.844
7	3	1	3	18.5507
8	3	2	1	18.9091
9	3	3	2	14.8817

Table 3. Significance of flank wears with cutting parameters.

Level	A (speed)	B (feed)	C (depth of cut)
1	20.0619	19.3982	19.8170
2	19.528	19.8842	18.2589
3	17.4472	17.7548	18.9611
Δ	2.6147	2.1294	1.5581
Rank	3	2	1

high noise immunity. The card provides the bridge between the PCI bus and the peripheral bus. It provides the control, address and data interfaces for peripheral to work as a PCI compliment peripheral.

The ADC/DAC signals are brought out through a 25-pin D type of connector. Preliminary investigations are carried out to find optimum speed at which surface finish is optimum. Further predictions for tool wear, acoustic emission signal parameters and surface roughness parameters are found at this optimal cutting speed, and depth of cut and the feed is changed from 0.05 to 0.2 mm/revolution. The AE signals are measured by highly sensitive piezo sensor. The signals are suitably filtered and amplified using a high gain pre-amplifier. The amplified signals are then recorded in the computer. The signals are analyzed using MATLAB. A program is developed to measure AE signal parameters - as ring down count (RDC), signal rise time (SRT) and RMS voltage. The linear movements of roller ended high strength probe are converted to continuous signal and are displayed on computer. The tool flank wear is measured by Toolmaker's microscope. The experiments required are estimated by Taguchi method, and the experiments are conducted for different parameters of feed, depth of cut and speed. Each turning operation on CNC machines consists of 28 trails and for every trail, the AE, flank wear and surface roughness parameters are recorded. Table 1 shows levels of cutting parameters, Table 2 shows L9 orthogonal array selected according to Taguchi methodology for conducting experiments for flank wear while Table 3 Shows the significance of flank wear with cutting parameters. The signal to noise ratio (SNR) for surface roughness

is as shown in Table 4. Table 5 shows the significance of surface roughness with cutting parameters.

RESULTS AND DISCUSSION

The behavior of flank wear with cutting time shows that, initially the wear increases at faster rate, later it was consistent for some time and then increased rapidly due to sudden increase in rubbing between tool and work piece. The AE variations plotted also shows significant relation with machining time and flank wear. Initially the variations were gradual and consistent, later they changed rapidly due to sudden change in energy levels of AE signals.

The RDC is the number of times the signal amplitude crosses the preset reference threshold. Initially, the RDC value increases rapidly, drops down and then again increases. The initial increase is due to the microfracturing that takes place while the tool comes in contact with the work piece. The micro-unevenness on the cutting edge is removed producing more burst emissions. Later-on, as the machining continues, normal metal removal in the form of chips is observed resulting in

Table 4. L_9 orthogonal array for surface roughness.

Experiment	P1 (A)	P2 (B)	P3 (C)	SNR (db)
1	1	1	1	-5.3519
2	1	2	2	-5.6841
3	1	3	3	-5.7350
4	2	1	2	-9.5600
5	2	2	3	-9.4780
6	2	3	1	-8.5960
7	3	1	3	-11.4673
8	3	2	1	-11.0968
9	3	3	2	-12.6108

Table 5. Significance of surface roughness with cutting parameters.

Level	A (speed)	B (feed)	C (depth of cut)
1	-5.5903	-8.7931	-8.3482
2	-9.2113	-8.7530	-9.2850
3	-11.725	-8.9806	-8.8934
Δ	6.1347	0.2276	0.9368
Rank	3	1	2

Table 6. Consistent values of acoustic emission parameters.

Machining time range	FW	RDC	Rise time	RMS voltage
60-420	0.05-0.1	-	-	-
60-450	-	4000-5000	45,000-60,000	-
60-440	-	-	-	5000-6000

Table 7. Consistent values of surface roughness.

Machining time	R_z	R_{max}	R_a
0 - 400	1.0-2.5	5.5-14	-
0 - 380	-	-	1.2-5.0

continious emissions along with the flank face. Then the flank wears-out due to contact of tool with the job surface leading to rubbing and friction, giving rise to flank wear. The gradual increase in flank wear gives rise to burst emissions. The RMS voltage also increases beyond the critical value because of increase in contact area of the tool tip with workpiece. In general, it is expected that flank wear increases the area of contact and hence increase in RMS voltage. The rise time of the AE signal is gradual up to 0.1 mm of flank wear. Later, it decreases rapidly due to increase in frequency of signals caused due to more rubbing. The variations of surface roughness parameters such as Rz, Rmax and Ra with flank wear are consistent with gradual variation up to 400 s and up to 0.1 mm of flank wear and later increases rapidly. The inconsistency

is due to increase in intensity of rubbing action. The increase in tool wear rate causes rapid change in surface roughness beyond critical value. Tables 6 and 7 show the consistent values for AE and roughness parameters.

Conclusion

The network model was developed to investigate reliability of the working tool as it wear out gradually. The sample of the network with nodes is shown in Figure 1. To improve accuracy for predicting tool wear and surface roughness, the belief network model is utilized to prove accuracy of the results. The belief networks learns from the case data file. The network is tested for tool wear for

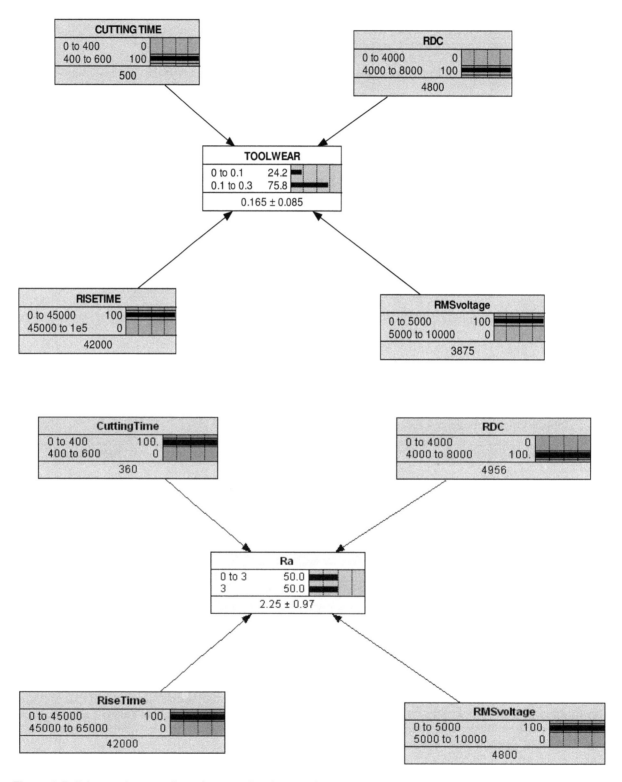

Figure 1. Belief networks to predict tool wear and surface roughness.

the best prediction to match the actual case. The same is followed to predict surface roughness. In both cases, the percentage error is neglegible and therefore, the prediction with belief network in correlation with the experimental results; hence, the validation.

REFERENCES

Constantinides N, Bennett S (1987). An investigation of methods for on- line estimation of tool wear, Int. J. Machine Tools Manuf., 27(2): 225-237.
Cook NH (1980). Tool wear sensors. Wear, 2: 49-57.

Feng CX, Wang XF (2003). Surface Roughness Predictive Modeling: Neural Networks versus Regression. Itetransactions, 35: 11-27.

Gomayel JL, Bregger KD (1986). On-line tool wear sensing for turning operations, J. Eng. Ind., 108: 44-47.

Lan MS, Dornfeld DA (1984). In-process tool fracture detection. J. Eng. Mater. Technol., 106: 111-118.

Levi R, Villa A, Quaglia G, Ghiara R, Rutelli G (1985). An Expert Control System for Tool Life Management in Flexible Manufacturing Cells. Ann. CIRP., 34: 87-90.

Liao YS (1974). Development of a monitoring technique for tool change purpose in turning operations. Proc. 15th Int. Machine Tool Des. Res. Conf., pp. 251-257.

Lin J (1995). Inverse estimation of the tool-work interface temperature in end milling. Int. J. Machine Tool Manuf., 35(5): 751-760.

Sadat AB, Raman S (1987). Detection of tool flank wear using acoustic signature analysis. Wear, 115: 265-272.

Sata T, Matsushima K, Kawabata T (1979). Recognition and Control of the Morphology of Tool Failures, Ann. CIRP., 28: 43-47.

Tlusty J, Andrews GC (1983): A critical review of sensors for unmanned machining. Ann. CIRP., 32: 536-572.

Turkovich BF, Kramer BM (1986). A comprehensive tool wear model. Ann. CIRP., 35: 67-70.

Uehara K (1972). On the Mechanism of Crater Wear of Carbide Cutting Tool. Ann. CIRP., 21: 31-32.

16

Liquid crystal-reconfigurable conformal monopole antennas structures for microwave applications

S. Missaoui* and M. Kaddour

Electronics Laboratory, Department of Physics, Faculty of Science, Tunis El Manar, Tunisia.

In this article, the design of conformal monopole antennas on a very thin layer of flexible liquid crystals (LCs) is introduced. The flexible LC substrate can be bent and folded over the module case, resulting in a tight integration of the antenna with the frontend module. Firstly, a meander monopole antenna, designed for single band operation, is presented with details of the structure, simulation and measurement results. Secondly, a method to increase the peak gain and decrease the return loss of the antenna is proposed. The simulated results are compared with measured data, and good agreement is obtained.

Key words: Liquid crystals, monopole antennas, agile structure, microwave.

INTRODUCTION

The planar-monopole antenna has been shown to be a useful candidate for wideband communications systems. The increasing demand for low cost, low profile wireless devices has resulted in a need for highly efficient, compact antennas that can integrate well into future portable wireless communication devices. Owing to their advantages in terms of weight, cost, manufacturability and compatibility with microwave circuits, electrically small planar antennas are seen as the favorable candidates to be used in such systems. In particular, printed monopole antennas are gaining in popularity due to their nearly omnidirectional far-field radiation pattern. Up to now, several approaches have been proposed to study the meander monopole antenna (Altunyurt et al., 2007; Shackelfford et al., 2003; Liang et al., 2005; Zhang et al., 2009). One of the sought properties for this device is the possibility to folded and rolled resulting in a compact design and integration of the antenna with the RF module package. For decades, enormous efforts have been deployed for using new materials which have a better functionality. Among these materials, liquid crystals (Swaminathan et al., 2005; Altunyurt et al., 2007; Zakharov and Mirantsev, 2003) are potentially useful.

This material consists on a state of matter which has properties between those of a conventional liquid and

those of solid crystals. LC is a low-cost dielectric with a combination of good electrical and mechanical properties. LC has a low dielectric constant of $\varepsilon_r = 2.95$, and a low loss tangent of 0.002 up to microwave frequencies. LC also has favorable mechanical properties such as flexible for conformal and flex circuit applications, a low coefficient of thermal expansion and low moisture absorption (Swaminathan et al., 2005; Tentzeris et al., 2004). All of these advantages make it appealing for high frequency applications (DeJean et al., 2005; Symeon et al., 2006; Negar et al., 2007; Serkan et al., 2006). Nevertheless, recent studies (Missaoui et al., 2010; 2011; Gaebler et al., 2009; Spinglart et al., 2001) have shown their dielectric anisotropy property.

In this paper, a method to enhance the performance of printed monopole antennas is presented. The proposed approach consists of placing a metal patch next to the patch in order to direct the fields in one direction by using the reflexion from the metal patch and a method to decrease the return loss will be introduced.

CONCEPTION AND SIMULATION OF A MEANDER MONOPOLE ANTENNA BASED ON LCs

Conception of a meander monopole antenna

The structure of the meander monopole antenna based on LCs as shown in Figures 1 and 2. The substrate of the

*Corresponding author. E-mail: Asayed.elmissaoui@gmail.com.

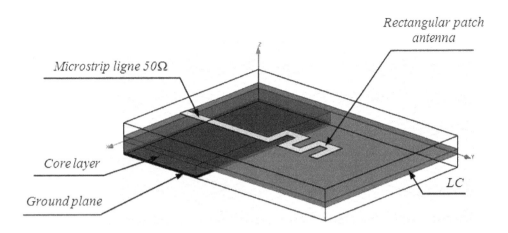

Figure 1. Structure of a meander monopole antenna based on *LCs*

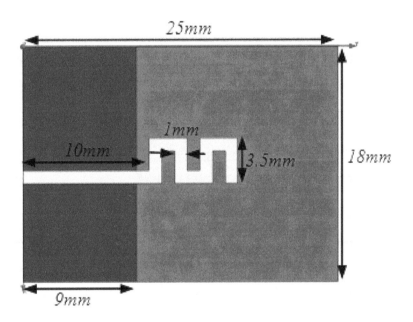

Figure 2. size of a meander monopole antenna

antenna is composed of two layers of dielectric. This meander antenna is printed on LC substrate with thickness of 25 μm and size of 18 × 25 mm, the LC is inserted by capillarity with a dielectric constant permittivity of $\varepsilon_r = 2.9$ and a loss tangent of 0.002, the bottom layer is a 508 μm rigid, glass-reinforced organic prepreg layer (core layer) with a size of 18 × 9 mm. The core layer has a loss tangent of 0.0037 with a dielectric constant of 3.48.16 mm long portion of the LC layer is not supported by the core layer and can be easily conformed due to the flexibility of LC. The antenna is printed on the flexible portion of LC.

The antenna is excited with a 50 Ω microstrip line which is printed on the rigid part of the substrate, supported by the core layer. The ground plane of the signal line covers the back side of the core layer with a size of 18 × 9 mm.

Figure 3 shows the design for the proposed meander monopole antenna with a three rectangular slots.

Simulation of a meander monopole antenna

The high frequency structure simulator (HFSS) was used to optimize the dimensions of the antenna to obtain a resonant frequency of 6 GHz.

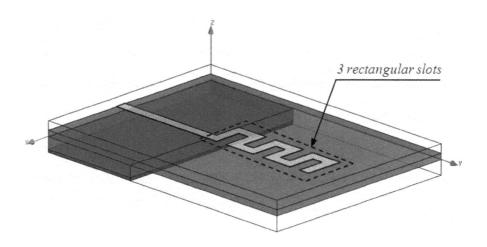

Figure 3. Structure of a meander monopole antenna based on LCs with three rectangular slots

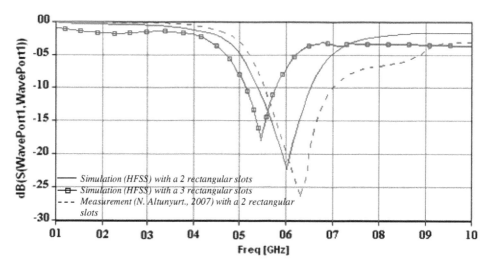

Figure 4. Simulated (HFSS) and measured (Altunyurt., 2007) return losses.

Figure 4 depict the results of simulated and measured return losses, we can see that return loss achieved -20 dB from 5.5 to 6.5 GHz for the results of simulated and measured with a patch to *2* rectangular slots. The resonance frequency variation (ΔF_r) between simulated and measured results is 300 MHz. The bandwidths simulated and measured of the monopole antenna with a two rectangular slots at -10 dB are respectively 1.19 GHz(19.8%) and 1.46 GHz (24.3%). The simulation resonant frequency for the meander monopole antenna with a 3 rectangular slots is 5.46 GHz. one notices that, if one adds a third rectangular slots, one obtained a variation of the simulation resonant frequency ($\Delta F'_r$ = 530 MHz), the return loss achieved -15 dB from 5 to 6 GHz.

Figures 5 and 6 depicts the simulated radiation patterns of the meander monopole antenna with a two slots for the plane ($\varphi = 0°$), ($\varphi = 90°$) and ($\theta = 90°$) at a resonant frequency of 6 GHz. The antenna has a nearly omnidirectional pattern like that of dipole and the simulated peak gain of the antenna was found as 2.9 dB.

CONCEPTION AND SIMULATION OF A NEW STRUCTURE TO INCREASE THE PEAK GAIN OF THE MEANDER MONOPOLE ANTENNA BASED ON LCs

Conception of a new structure antenna

In this section, a method to increase the peak gain of the monopole antenna is introduced. The new structure and size of the meander monopole antenna based on LCs as shown in Figures 7 and 8. This directly affects the

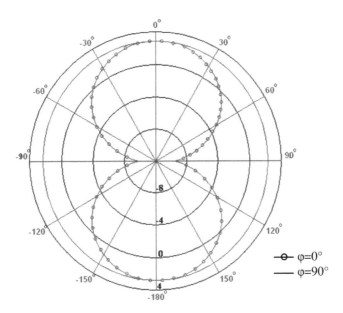

Figure 5. The simulated radiation patterns of the meander monopole antenna with a two slots for φ = 0° and φ = 90° at 6 GHz.

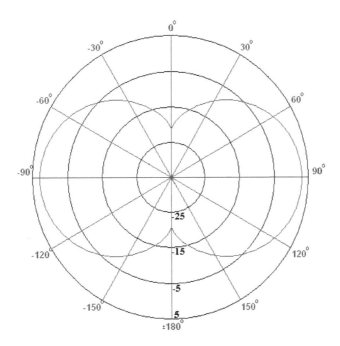

Figure 6. The simulated radiation patterns of the meander monopole antenna with a two slots for θ=90° at 6 GHz

antenna gain which has to be maximized to lower the power consumption of the wireless terminal. The proposed approach consists of placing a metal patch (Altunyurt et. al., 2007) next to the antenna in order to direct the fields in one direction by using the reflection from the metal patch. This topology provides compact antenna solutions with broader bandwidth and higher peak gain suitable for use in portable electronics. The

parameters affecting the matching and the peak gain of the antenna are:

- The horizontal length of the metal patch (7 mm) and the distance between the metal patch and the antenna (4 mm).
- The width and length of the ground plane (7.3 × 7 mm).
Figure 9 shows the new design for the proposed to

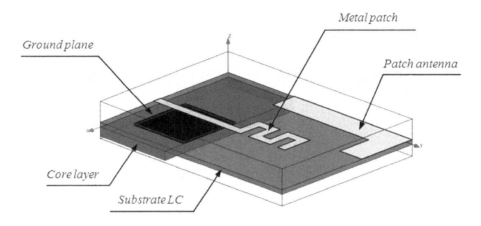

Figure 7. New structure to increase the peak gain of the meander monopole antenna based on *LCs*

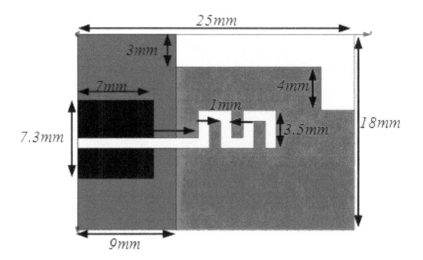

Figure 8. size of a new structure to increase the peak gain of the meander monopole antenna

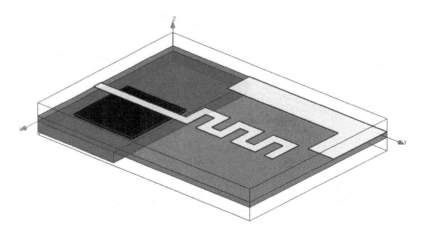

Figure 9. New structure to increase the peak gain of the meander monopole antenna based on LCs with a 3 rectangular slots.

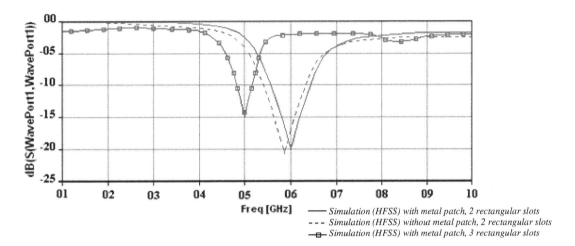

Figure 10. The comparison of the simulated return loss for with and without metal patch cases, to 2 and 3 rectangular slots.

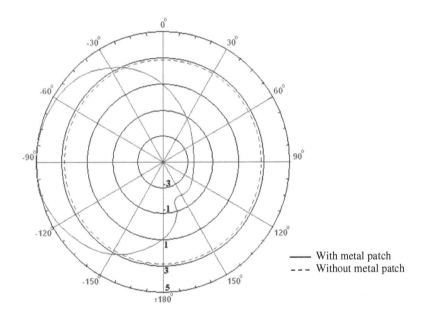

Figure 11. The simulated radiation patterns with and without metal patch of 2 slots for $\varphi = 90°$ at 6 GHz.

increase the peak gain and decrease the return loss of the meander monopole antenna based on *LCs* with a *3* rectangular slots.

Simulation of a new structure antenna

Figure 10 depict the comparison of the simulated return loss for with and without metal patch cases, to 2 and 3 rectangular slots.

We can see that return loss achieved -15 dB from 5.5 to 6.5 GHz for the results of simulated with and without metal patch to *2* rectangular slots. The resonance frequency variation (ΔF_r) is 140 MHz and the bandwidths simulated with and without metal patch at -10 dB are respectively 846.15 MHz (14.1%) and 941.17 MHz (15.68%). The simulation resonant frequency for the meander monopole antenna with metal patch to 3 rectangular slots is 5 GHz. one notices that, if one adds a third rectangular slots, one obtained a variation of the simulation resonant frequency ($\Delta F'_r = 1$ GHz), the bandwidths result at -10 dB is 346.15 MHz and the return loss achieved -10 dB from 4.5 to 5.5 GHz.

Figures 11 and 12 depicts the simulated radiation patterns of the meander monopole antenna with and without metal patch of 2 slots for the plane ($\varphi = 90°$) and

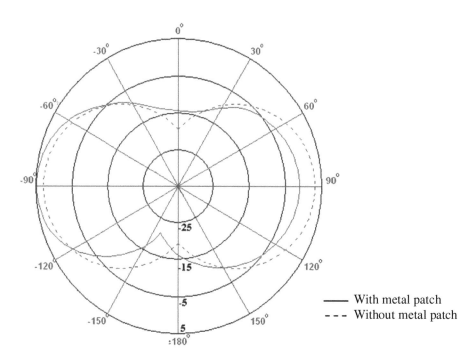

Figure 12. The simulated radiation patterns with and without metal patch of 2 slots for θ = 90° at 6 GHz.

(θ = 90°) at a resonant frequency of 6 GHz.

It is clearly seen from the radiation pattern comparison that, the fields are directed in one direction, the peak gain with and without metal patch is respectively *5 dB* and *2.9 dB*, therefore the found gain with metal patch is improved.

CONCLUSION

This paper presents the fundamentals of LC material and its applications for reconfigurable monopole antenna. To verify the performance of the proposed conformal configuration, a prototype was designed and simulated with a very thin layer of flexible LC. We have shown that the return loss of the meander monopole antenna with metal patch to *3* rectangular slots can be achieved -10 dB from 4.5 to 5.5 GHz. The meander monopole antenna based on LCs with a 2 rectangular slots gives a better performance for the bandwidth and the resonance frequency.

Therefore, for an increase of number of rectangular slots, we noticed a serious mistake of the resonance frequency and a reduction of the bandwidth. The only advantage o the antenna structure with a 3 rectangular slots is the reduction of the return loss. The results of simulated radiation patterns with and without metal patch to 2 rectangular slots have greatly improved about 2.1 dB and the fields are directed in one direction. A good agreement is obtained between measurements and numerical model results and it confirms the validity of our approach.

REFERENCES

Altunyurt N (2007). "Printed Monopole Antennas with Increased Bandwidth and Gain for Wi-Fi Applications," IEEE AP-S, June.

Altunyurt N, Swaminathan M, Sundaram V, White G (2007). "Conformal antennas on Liquid Crystalline Polymer substrates for consume applications," 2007 APMC Asia-Pacific Microwave Conference, Dec.

DeJean G, Bairavasubramanian R, Thompson D, Ponchak GE Tentzeris MM, Papapolymerou J (2005). "Liquid Crystal polyme (LCP): a new organic material for the development of multilayer dual frequency/dual-polarization flexible antenna arrays." Antennas and Wireless Propagation Lett., 4: 22 - 26.

Gaebler AM, Goelden F, Manabe A, Goebel M, Follmann R, Koether D Modes C, Kipka, M. Deckelmann, T. Rabe, B. Schulz, P Kuchenbecker, A. Lapanik, S.Mueller, Haase WA, Jakoby R (2009) "Liquid Crystal-Reconfigurable Antenna Concepts for Space Applications at Microwave and Millimeter Waves." Int. J. Antennas Propagat., Article ID 876989, p. 7.

Liang J, Chiau CC, Chen X, Parini CG (2005). "Printed circular ring monopole antennas." Microwave optical Technol. Lett., 45(n° 6) 372-375.

Missaoui S, Kaddour M, Gharbi A (2010). "Development and design o multilayer antennas based on liquid crystals," IOP Conference Series Materials Sci. Eng., 13: 1.

Missaoui S, Kaddour M, Gharbi A (2011). "Design and Simulation o Tunable Phase Shifters Based on Liquid Crystals." Electromagnetics 31(4): 285 - 293, May.

Missaoui S, Kaddour M, Gharbi A (2011). "Design and simulation reconfigurable liquid crystal patch antennas on foam substrate." J Chem. Eng. Mater. Sci., 2(7): 96-102.

Negar T, Nikolaou S, Tentzeris MM (2007). "Microwave tumor detection using a flexible UWB elliptical slot antenna with a tuning uneven U-shape stub on LCP," IEEE Antennas and Propagation Soc. Sym., pp 257-260.

Serkan B, Bhattacharya S, S, Li Y, Rida A, Tentzeris MM, Laskar J (2006). "Design of a novel high-efficiency UHF RFID antenna on flexible LCP substrate with high read-range capability," IEEE Antennas and Propagation Soc. Sym. pp. 1031-1034.

Shackelfford AK, Lee KF, Luk KM (2003). "Design of small-size wide-bandwidth microstrip-patch antennas." IEEE Antennas Propagation, Mag, 45(n° 2): 75-83.

Spinglart B, Tentillier N, Huret F, Legrand C (2001). "Liquid crystals applications to RF and microwave tunable components." Molecular Crystals and Liquid Crystals, 368: 183-190.

Swaminathan M, Bavisi A, Yun W, Sundaram V, Govind V, Monajemi P (2005). "Design and fabrication of integrated RF modules in LCP Substrates." 2005 IECON 32nd Annual Conference of IEEE Industrial Electronics Society, pp. 2346-2351.

Symeon N, Ponchak GE, Papapolymerou J, Tentzeris MM (2006). "Conformal double exponentially tapered slot antenna (DETSA) on LCP for UWB applications." IEEE Trans. Antennas and Propag., 54(6): 1663-1669.

Tentzeris MM, Laskar J, Papapolymerou J, Stéphane P, Palazzari V, Li R, DeJean G, Papageorgiou N, Thompson D, Bairavasubramanian R, Sarkar S, Lee JH (2004). "3-D-Integrated RF and millimeter wave functions and modules using liquid crystal polymer (LCP) systemon-package technology." IEEE Trans. on Advanced Packaging, 27(2): 332-340.

Zakharov AV, Mirantsev LV (2003). "Dynamic and dielectric properties of liquid crystals." Phys. Solid State, 45: 183-188.

Zhang X, Zhang T-L, Xia Y-Y, Yan Z-H, Wang X-M (2009). "Planar monopole antenna with band notch characterization for UWB applications". Progress Electromagnetics Res. Lett., 6: 149-156.

17

Statistical digital image stabilization

M. H. Shakoor* and M. Moattari

Fars Science and Research Branch, Islamic Azad University, Shiraz, Iran.

In this paper, an efficient algorithm for the statistical digital image stabilization (SDIS) is proposed to reduce the computational cost of block matching algorithm, for local motion estimation. This method is based on calculation of statistical functions, mean and variance of pixels in each block; four blocks are used in each frame. By using the statistical functions, the best block is selected then the local motion vector (LMV) of selected block is estimated by using full search algorithm. LMV of selected block is used as global motion vector (GMV) and it is used to stabilize current frame. Full search algorithm is used for motion estimation, but instead of searching points in a block for full search, it is used in the partial distortion elimination method to terminate the improper candidate blocks and reduce computation for block matching.

Key words: Digital image stabilization, motion estimation, block matching algorithm, global motion vector, statistical functions, partial distortion elimination.

INTRODUCTION

The goal of image stabilization systems is to compensate for the position offset, caused by external variations of the camera, while excluding the effects of the undesired movement vectors by irregular conditions in the image sequence.

There are many types of image stabilization systems; one method for this purpose is digital image stabilization (DIS). The process of the DIS mainly consists of two steps: the motion estimation and the motion compensation. The task of motion estimation is used to estimate the global camera movement vector from the acquired video sequence and select the general global motion vector from several local motion vectors. The current video frame can be compensated by estimated global motion vector. The motion estimation plays an important role in the whole stabilization process. Many algorithms have been proposed to obtain fast or precise local motion vectors, such as, block matching (Vella et al., 2002), edge pattern matching (Parik et al., 1992), bit-plane matching (BPM) (Jeon et al., 1999), representative point matching (RPM) (Hsu et al., 2005), etc. Among these algorithms, block matching is precise and reliable, but it is a costly computation. The RPM can greatly reduce the complexity of computation in comparison with the other methods. However, it is sensitive to irregular

conditions such as internal moving objects, low-contrast block, and texture pattern. Therefore, the reliability evaluation is necessary to screen the undesired motion vectors for the RPM method (Hsu et al., 2005). For the purpose of increasing the speed and precision of local motion estimation vectors, a fast method for digital image stabilization based on block matching is proposed. This method uses statistical properties to select one of four blocks. It is used as statistical properties (mean and variance of pixels in each block) to select the best block from four candidates. The best block has two properties; it should not have a uniform area and it should belong to the background which does not have any motion objects in it. After the selection of the block, a method of block matching must be used to calculate LMV. When the best block is selected, LMV is estimated using block matching algorithm.

There are many methods for block matching, such as three-step search (3SS) (Koga et al., 1981), new three-step search (3SS) (Li et al., 1994) and four-step search (4SS) (Po and Ma, 1996), etc. These methods have errors because of some irregular conditions such as moving objects, intentional panning, noise, and cause error. The most accurate BMA is the full search algorithm (FS) that compares every candidate blocks in the search window with the current block. Although FS predicts the most similar block, it is computationally intensive. But instead of searching points in a block for full search, it is used in the partial distortion elimination (Park et al., 2008;

---
*Corresponding author. E-mail: mhshakoor@gmail.com.

Montrucchio and Quaglia, 2005) method to terminate the improper candidate blocks and reduce computation for block matching. So, instead of matching all the pixels in a block, the partial matching error can give the opportunity to make the fast, full search, possible. The partial distortion elimination (PDE) is the most popular example of the fast matching methods. PDE can easily be combined with the fast searching approach. Generally, PDE algorithm prunes the improper blocks by comparing the current minimum distortion with the partial distortion within the block. After that, LMV is calculated by full search (only in selected block). This LMV is used as GMV to apply to frame and motion compensation.

This paper is organized as follows: Local motion vector estimation, conventional fast algorithm for calculation of LMV and partial distortion elimination (PDE) are presented subsequently, after which the proposed statistical algorithm is presented for selecting the best block. Furthermore, local motion estimation is presented, before global motion estimation and motion compensation are introduced. Thus, simulation results are given before the concluding remarks are made.

BLOCK MATCHING ALGORITHMS

Block matching algorithm (BMA) is the most popular motion estimation algorithm. BMA calculates motion vector for an entire block of pixels instead of individual pixels. The same motion vector is applicable to all the pixels in the block.

This reduces computational requirement and also results in a more accurate motion vector since the objects are typically a cluster of pixels.

BMA requires very heavy computational complexity. So, there are many methods to increase the speed of BMA calculations, such as histogram (Shakoor and Moattary, 2009) or PDE (Park et al., 2008; Montrucchio and Quaglia, 2005).

In block matching, each frame is segmented into blocks. Each block is compared against candidate blocks of the previous frame, and the best one is chosen upon the minimization of some matching criteria. The best match is chosen as a predictor for the next frame.

Conventional fast algorithms

By comparing the sum of block between current and candidate blocks, many improper candidate blocks can be eliminated with less computational costs. In other words, the calculation of the sum of absolute difference (SAD) could be reduced. SAD is a very time consuming part of each block matching algorithm. If the number of search points is decreased, the number of SAD calculations is decreased and algorithm works so fast (Shakoor and Moattai, 2009) (Figure 1).

$$SAD = \sum_{i=0}^{N-1}\sum_{j=0}^{M-1}| f_{cur}(j,i) - f_{ref}(j+v_x, i+v_y) |$$

(1)

SAD is the typical matching criterion used in local motion

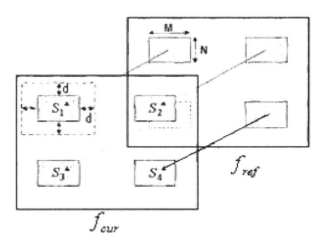

Figure 1. Four areas for the calculation of LMV.

estimation and it can be obtained through (1). N and M is the block height and width and $f_{cur}(x,y)$, $f_{ref}(x,y)$ are the pixel intensities at the current block and candidate block, respectively. i and j denote the index of horizontal and vertical directions within the block, respectively. v_x and v_y denote motion vectors of the candidate block in the reference frame. Minimum of SAD determines best block matching.

Partial distortion elimination (PDE)

One of the important methods that reduce the unnecessary computation during the SAD calculation within a block is PDE. General block matching algorithms compare the current minimum SAD (minSAD) with the final SAD, whereas PDE algorithm uses the partial sum of matching distortion to eliminate the improper candidate before finishing the matching distortion calculations. If an intermediate sum of matching distortion is larger than the minimum value of matching distortion at that time, the remaining computation for the matching distortion is unnecessary. In the PDE algorithm, the row based k-th partial SAD to check during the matching is as follows:

$$PartialSAD(k) = \sum_{i=0}^{k}\sum_{j=0}^{M-1}| f_{cur}(j,i) - f_{ref}(j+v_x, i+v_y) |$$

(2)

where k=0,1,... N-1

Here, in (2), M and k denote the block width and the number of rows already evaluated, respectively. If k is smaller than N and the partial SAD(k), calculated SAD until the k-th row, exceeds the current minSAD, then the remaining summation may be terminated. For example, if the Partial SAD(n) is larger than the minSAD at k=n, then N-1-n SAD operations could be saved. This technique can be combined with the other block matching algorithms simultaneously and helps to reduce the computational load efficiently in FS algorithms.

PROPOSED ALGORITHM FOR SELECTING BEST BLOCK

Proposed algorithm has two states so it is proposed in two ways

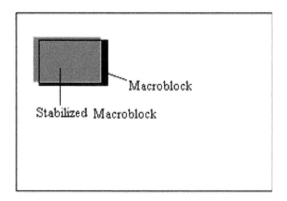

Figure 2. Block and stabilized block in an area.

and named SDIS1 and SDIS2. In these proposed method, two statistical functions are used to select the best block of four blocks. Then BMA is used only for the best block.

The first proposed algorithm for selecting best block (SDIS1)

In this method, we select four blocks of image, then calculate mean and variance (standard deviation) of pixels in each block, then, by selecting the best block and find the LMV only for this block, we can use LMV as GMV for current frame. The proposed method has flowing steps:

Step 1: Calculate mean and standard deviation of pixels in each area [m1,m2,m3,m4] and [s1,s2,s3,s4] for current frame (t-th frame).

Step 2: Calculate difference of mean for 2 previous frames (ms_i^{t-1} is the mean of t-1th (stabilized) frame in area i and m_i^{t-2} is the means of t-2nd frame of i-th area) for each area i: $mDiff_i = |m_i^{t-2} - ms_i^{t-1}|$ Sort the values of [mDiff1, mDiff2, mDiff3, mDiff4] (in increasing order).

Step 3: Select the first mDiff (the smallest remain mean) (i-th area)

if $s^i > T1$ then select i-th macroback as best block and algorithm reach to end. Else repeat Step3 for the next area.

Step 4: If there are not any areas to satisfy condition of Step3 then select the area that has the minimum of $mDiff_i / (1 + s_i)$.
T1 is a threshold value. For busy and noisy images this threshold should be large.

Hint: in Step1 Mean and Standard Deviation of the stabilized block is calculated. It does not mean current block must be shifted. According to Figure 2, it means we use some other pixels that belong to th block when it is stabilized.

If the global motion vector (GMV) of the previous frame is (v_x, v_y) :

$$m = \sum_{i=0}^{N-1}\sum_{j=0}^{M-1} f^t(j-v_x, i-v_y) \tag{3}$$

$$s = (\sum_{i=0}^{N-1}\sum_{j=0}^{M-1}|m - f^t(j-v_x, i-v_y)|)/(N*M) \tag{4}$$

Best block is selected by 3 and 4 properties:

(1) $s^i > T1$ (in SDIS1)

It means, this block should not have uniform area, because, motion estimation in uniform area usually has many errors. T1 is a threshold value which should be large for busy and noisy image.

(2) $mDiff_i < T2$ (in SDIS2)

mDiff must be lower than a threshold value T2. It means, this block should not have motion object or it should belong to the background of frame. This condition is used in SDIS2.

The second proposed algorithm for selecting the best block (SDIS2)

If in SDIS1, step 2 and step 3 are changed as here, a new method named SDIS2 is proposed:

Step 2: Calculate the difference of mean of the two previous frames. For each area $mDiff_i = |m_i^{t-2} - ms_i^{t-1}|$ then sort the values of [s1, s2, s3, s4] (in decreasing order).

Step 3: Select the first s (the biggest remain standard deviation) (in i-th area) if $mDiff_i < T2$ then select i-th block as the best block and algorithm reach to the end. Else repeat Step3 for the next area.

Step 4: If there is no area to satisfy the condition of Step 3 then select the area that has a max of $s_i / (1 + mDiff_i)$. T2 is a threshold value, for busy and noisy image, it should be much greater than zero, otherwise it should be near zero.

LOCAL MOTION VECTOR ESTIMATION

When the best block is selected, LMV is calculated only for it. Full search is used for block matching and for the best estimation. The PDE technique is used to eliminate many computations in SAD and to reduce the search points. In this part, local motion vector of selected area is calculated by block matching full search method and this local motion vector is used as global motion vector for next step. The advantage of this method is calculation of only one LMV instead of four LMV (Shakoor and Moattai, 2009), so, it increases the speed of operation.

GLOBAL MOTION ESTIMATION AND COMPENSATION

In many algorithms, the global motion vector is obtained by :

GMV^t =   median{LMV1,LMV2,LMV3,LMV4}^{t}

GMV^t is global motion vector of t-th frame and LMV1 to LMV4 are local motion vectors of each area. In the proposed method LMV that was estimated in previous parts is used as GMV of current frame:

GMV^t = LMV^t (5)

Figure 3. Bike, person, road samples.

Also, we can use this formula to smooth GMV (Accumulated GMV):

$$AccGMV^{t} = k1*AccGMV^{t-1} + k2 * LMV^{t} \qquad (6)$$

The coefficient k1 and k2 are less than 1 and depend on current GMV^{t} and it is different from GMV^{t-1}. At the end of operations, AccGMV is applied to current frame to stabilize it.

EXPERIMENTAL RESULT

Computer simulations have been performed on, for example, bike, person and road, which consist of some different motions (Figure 3). Person has large global motion vectors, bike has some smooth motions, but there are many internal motions in all of four areas of each frame and road has smooth global motion and there is also a moving object (car) only in a small area of each frame. In simulation part, the original image of the previous frame was used as a reference frame to

generate a motion compensated prediction image. Image quality was measured by the peak signal-to-noise ratio (PSNR) as defined in Equation (8):

$$MSE = (\frac{1}{NM}) \sum_{i=0}^{N-1}\sum_{j=0}^{M-1}[I_{o}(i,j) - I_{c}(i,j)]^{2} \qquad (7)$$

$$PSNR = 10 \ Log_{10}(\frac{255^{2}}{MSE}) \qquad (8)$$

Io denotes the original current frame, and Ic denotes the motion-compensated prediction frame. Block size = 16, search region = [-7, +7]. PSNR results are listed in Table 2.

In Table 1 the numbers of search points are shown. In all examples, the proposed method searches the points only in one area, but in other cases, sum of searched point's number in all four areas are used because, in proposed method, points of the best area are used not points of all

areas. In the last row, full search is used for calculation of LMV of each four areas. The number of search point for full search in each area is 225 but by using PDE some of these points are eliminated and the number of search point is less than 225. Table 1 compares the speed of proposed methods and other methods. The quality of proposed methods is compared to stabilize the frame, so, full search algorithm and proposed algorithms have approximately the same result (median method is used for calculation of GMV from LMVs for full search in the last row). In most cases, proposed methods have similar results as full search. In this simulation, T1=0.07*15*15 and T2 = 3 for all of the samples. T1 and T2 should be changed depending on the size of motion vectors and the amount of noise that exist in images. These values of T1 and T2 are good for road sample and they should be changed for other samples to produce better PNSR.

Figures 4 and 5 show accumulated LMV and

Table 1. Number of search points in each methods (all search points in each frame).

Method	Bike	Person	Road
SDIS1	215	219	208
SDIS2	215	219	208
TSS	100	100	100
NTSS	78.4	85.6	80.4
FSS	74.2	76.5	80.8
FS	900	900	900

Table 2. PSNR of each method (GMV estimated by full search method and other methods).

Method	Bike	Person	Road
SDIS1	18.93	17.59	31.72
SDIS2	19.82	17.77	31.65
TSS	18.88	16.48	29.50
NTSS	18.90	16.53	29.48
FSS	18.88	16.56	29.38
FS (median)	20.16	18.00	32.20

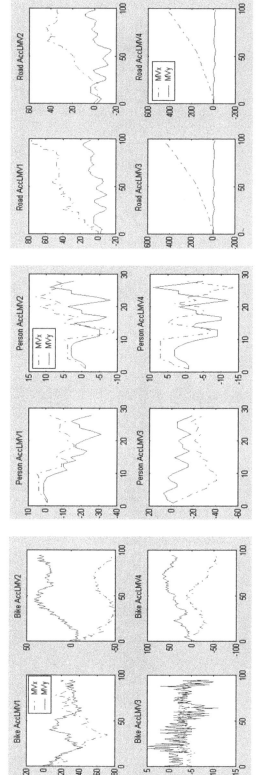

Figure 4. Result of AccLMV for SDIS2 in each area (bike, person and road samples).

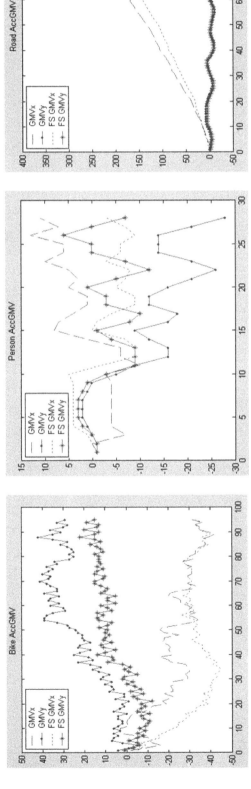

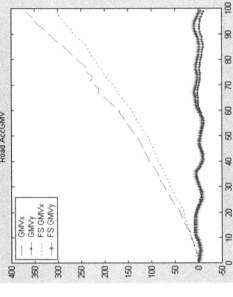

Figure 5. Result of AccGMV for SDIS2 and FS (bike, person and road samples).

Table 3. Specification of each samples.

Frame	Frames number	Size	Comment
Bike	96	256*256	Smooth motion
Person	28	320*240	Large motion
Road	99	336*224	Smooth and small motion

accumulated GMV for each sample that uses SDIS2, in these figures, accumulated vector is obtained by adding new vector to the previous accumulated vector. There are some differences between full search and the proposed plot because of the intentional panning. Some plots in Figure 4 show LMVs of each area and in many samples, they show that there are many differences between LMVs in each area. LMV of each area is calculated by FS method. But Figure 5 shows GMVs that are extracted from the best area in each frame. In some cases that intentional

panning occurred, there are some differences. In Table 3, specifications of each sample are listed

Conclusion

In this paper, a statistical digital image stabilization method is proposed that used fast block matching algorithm. A statistical method is used for selecting the best block for full search LMV. We have considered Partial SAD criteria for BMA, and also used PSNR criteria for comparing

results with traditional BMAs. The new algorithm can reduce most of the computational complexity compared to previous developed fast BMAs and has better quality than many other BMA algorithms.

ACKNOWLEDGEMENTS

We would like to thank Sang-Jun Park, Soonjong Jin and Jechang Jeong for using PDE in our paper. We also wish to thank the Islamic Azad

University, Fars Science and Research Branch for supporting this research.

REFERENCES

Hsu SC (2005). Robust Digital Image Stabilization Technique Based on Inverse Triangle Method and Background Detection, IEEE Trans. Consum. Electron., 51(2) : 335-345.

Jeon SW (1999). Fast digital image stabilizer based on Gray-coded bit-plane matching, IEEE Trans. Consum. Electron., 45(3): 598-603.

Koga T, Iinuma K, Hirano A, Iijima Y, Ishiguro T (1981). "Motion compensated interframe coding for video conferencing," In Proc. Nat . Telecommun . Conf., New Orleans, LA, pp. G. 5 .3.1-G.5.3.5.

Li R, Zeng B, Liou ML (1994). "A new three step search algorithm for block motion estimation." IEEE Trans. Circuits Syst. Video Technol., 4: 438-442.

Messina G (2002). Digital image stabilization by adaptive block motion vectors filtering, IEEE Trans. Consum. Electron., 48: 796-801.

Montrucchio B, Quaglia D (2005). "New sorting-based lossless motion estimation algorithms and a partial distortion elimination performance analysis," IEEE Trans. Circuit Syst. Video Technol., 15(2): 210-220.

Park SJ, Jin S, Jeang J (2008). "Adaptive partial distortion search algorithm using histogram-based sorting," In Proc. ICME, pp. 833-836.

Po LM, Ma WC (1996). "A novel four-step search algorithm for fast block motion estimation," IEEE Trans. Circuits Syst. Video Technol., 6(3): 313-317.

Shakoor MH, Moattary M (2009). "Digital Image Stabilization Using Histogram-Based Sorting," in Proc. KAM. 3: 266-268.

Shakoor MH, Moattai M (2009). "A Fuzzy Method Based on Bit-Plane Images for Stabilizing Digital Images", IEEE Conf. CONIELECOMP.106-108.

Vella F, Castorina A, Parik JK, Parrk YC, Kim DW (1992). An adaptive motion decision system for digital image stabilizer based on edge pattern matching, IEEE Trans. Consum. Electron., 38(3): 607-616.

18

A novel electrical model to an antenna array

A. Ferchichi[1], N. Fadlallah[2]* and A. Gharssallah[1]

[1]Unit of Research Circuits and Electronics Systems High Frequency, Faculty of Science, University El Manar Tunis, Tunisia.
[2]Radiocom Team, Lebanese University. IUT Saida, Lebanon.

In this paper, an electrical model is developed to represent the input admittance of an antenna array with a finite number of elements. This model consists of an RLC bock component to represent the input admittance of each elementary antenna element and a capacity component to represent different degrees of antenna coupling effects. The equations based on cavity model are developed to represent physical meaning of each model. Numerical results show that good accuracy for the simulation results can be obtained by using this electrical model to the results obtained by using HFSS. As the array is large and sparse, a very small amount of computation can yield good accuracy. This model is shown not only to be numerically efficient compared to the full wave analysis using the moment method, but also to give physical insight into the antenna array mutual coupling mechanism. Furthermore, this model has no limitation on antenna array geometry and excitation.

Key words: Antenna array, electrical model, coupling capacity.

INTRODUCTION

Recently, there has been a growing interest in creating low-cost, high-performance and high network capacity cellular systems by using an antenna array in the place of a single antenna (Vasquez et al., 2009).

Patch array is useful in microwave application to obtain radiation pattern which present a high directivity. Usually, this kind of antenna is used in application where we search to increasing directivity without having a limitation in the dimension offered to the antenna.

Generally, the array factor is calculated with elements independent for each other. In real life, the coupling between elements can lower the array's performances (Krusevac et al., 2006; Fu et al., 2006; Jarchi et al., 2007; Farkasvolgyi and Nagy, 2007; Fallahi and Roshandel, 2007). It is necessary to take account the coupling between elements to design accurately the array. Electrical coupling is difficult to evaluate, for this reason previous works are concentrated to analyze the array by using the numerical methods (Yuan et al., 2007; Liu et al.,

2006; Qiu et al., 2006; Uduwawala et al., 2005; Losito, 2007). From the electromagnetic results given by numerical methods they extract the electrical model in Persson et al. (2003), use the theory of diffraction combining with numerical algorithm in order to calculate the mutual coupling between circular apertures on a doubly curved surface. In (Ert"urk and Rojas (2003), a novel method is developed by the author's by combining the method of moments and the green's function to analyze antenna array.

In our research we propose a technique to calculate the RLC parameters of the array without necessary need of the numerical results. In the proposed model, we introduce the mutual coupling in the case of a planar rectangular array. In order to build our model, we began by analyzing the elementary rectangular patch, then we used two elements, finally we generalized the technique in order to build an electrical model of a 2*2 array. The introduced model is very important because in one hand it helps reducing the time of simulation. In the other hand, the proposed model can help us to display the design of an array taking in consideration all kind of coupling between different elements.

*Corresponding author. E-mail: n_fadlallah@yahoo.com.

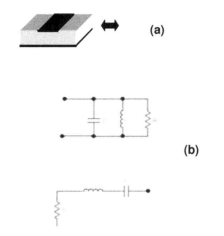

Figure 1. Electrical model of a planar antenna (a) Parallel configuration (b) Serie parallel.

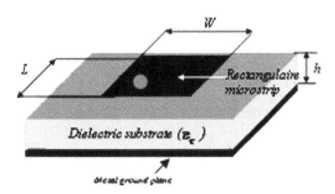

Figure 2. Rectangular patch.

In order to evaluate our model, we compared the results given by the electrical model and those obtained by using HFSS simulator which is based on FEM method (ANSYS, 2009).

This paper is organized as follow: A brief introduction on the importance of using electrical model. A development of the advantages of using electrical model. An electrical model of a rectangular patch is given. A new approach in building an electrical model for a two planar array is developed. Finally a brief conclusion and a future work consists the fifth section.

ELECTRICAL MODEL

In order to design antenna structures, many techniques are developed. Those techniques use numerical methods based on resolving electromagnetic equations in different form. For this reason, much software was used like ADS simulator, HFSS simulator, and IE3D simulator (Monti et

al., 2009). Those entire Simulators give their results by resolving electromagnetic equations in their integral or differential forms (Balanis, 1997). But those techniques have some limitation. First, we cannot take the calculation of all kinds of losses. Besides after simulating the structures, we have not the possibility to control antenna parameters like return loss, input impedance when modifying geometry of antenna, nature of substrate. That is why, replacing an antenna by an equivalent circuit will be very important in parametric analyzing of the proposed structure (Anguera et al., 2004). In this way, the model techniques have a great interest. One of those solutions is modeling an antenna by an electrical model.

Building an electrical model means replacing it by an RLC circuit, Figure 1. There were two configurations: a parallel or a series resonant model. The RLC parameters are calculating the equation developed in (Nasimuddin and Verma, 2004).

As demonstrated in previous work Ferchichi et al. (2010), the electrical model is used to know what occurred to the input impedance, the return losses when modifying the geometry of the antenna, the nature of substrate and the excitation (Celal and Kerim, 1998). In this way, analyzing an array of antenna will be very interesting.

The main idea is to replace each antenna elements by its equivalent RLC circuits, and then we must introduce the mutual coupling between different elements.

ELECTRICAL MODEL OF SINGLE RECTANGULAR PATCH

Geometry of patch

Figure 2 shows the geometry of a rectangular patch on a dielectric substrate with a ground plane. The patch is characterized by the resonant length L and the width W.

The antenna is placed on an h= 3.2 mm of NeltecNY9260 (IM) substrate material, which has a dielectric constant $\varepsilon_r = 2.6$, and loss tangent (tang δ= 0.002). The structure is excited by a cable coaxial.

Electrical model

To build the electrical model of the rectangular patch we use the same method developed in our previous work (Ferchichi et al., 2009). The model is based on the input impedance Z_{in} of a rectangular patch excited by a coax. Z_{in} is given in Nasimuddin and Verma (2004) by the equation (1):

$$Z_{in} = R + j\,X$$

$$Z_{in}\,(f) = \frac{R}{1 + Q_T^2\left[\dfrac{f}{f_r} - \dfrac{f_r}{f}\right]^2} + j\left[X_L - \frac{RQ_T\left[\dfrac{f}{f_r} - \dfrac{f_r}{f}\right]}{1 + Q_T^2\left[\dfrac{f}{f_r} - \dfrac{f_r}{f}\right]^2}\right]$$

$$(1)$$

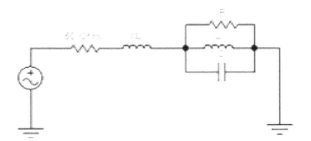

Figure 3. An electrical model of rectangular patch.

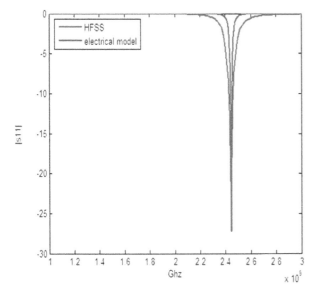

Figure 4. Return loss of rectangular patch.

Then we determine the resonant resistance R, the dynamic capacity Cdyn, the inductance L, the quality factor QT and the reactance X_L, (Nasimuddin and Verma, 2004). The antenna will be modeled by the electrical model presented in Figure 3.

Return loss results

The model proposed with the values of R, L, C and X_L calculated is simulated in order to evaluate S11 parameter. The results obtained by the model are in good agreement with those obtained by using HFSS which is based on a numerical method. Besides, the model is simulated immediately which take a short time comparing to the time simulation of the HFSS simulator which is about few minutes, Figure 4.

ARRAY OF TWO ANTENNA

Geometry of patch array

At the beginning, we analyzed a planar array that consisted of two elements. The elements of patches are a rectangular patch with the

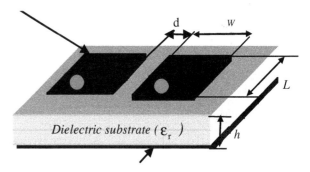

Metal ground plane

Figure 5. A two element Array of patch.

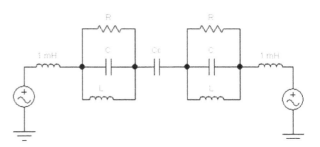

Figure 6. Electrical model of the proposed array.

same dimension and substrate characteristic of the single patch simulated in the first Figure 5.

Electrical model

The proposed electrical model is built by using two RLC block that represents the equivalent of each antenna element, the two blocks are connected by a single capacitance due to the coupling between the two patches, Figure 6.

Resonant resistance

The resonant resistance R is related essentially to the losses in the conductor, substrate and the radiation quality factor. In the case of an array of patch we use the equation as follows:

$$R = \frac{Q_T \, H}{\pi f_r \; \varepsilon_{dyn} \varepsilon_0 \; WL} \; \cos^2\left(\frac{\pi \, x_0}{L}\right) \qquad (2)$$

Q_T is the quality factor, it can be calculated by using the formulas developed in Nasimuddin and Verma, (2004), f_r is the resonant frequency, H is the dielectric thickness, W and L are the geometry dimensions of the single patch and x_0 is the distance between the excitation and the side edge.

As for ε_{dyn}, it represents the dynamic permittivity of the antenna array, it can be obtained from the equation as follows:

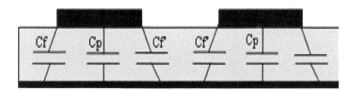

Figure 7. Dynamic capacitance of the two patch.

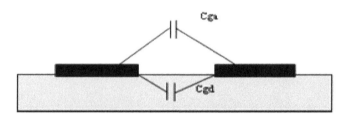

Figure 8. Coupling capacitance of the two patch.

$$\varepsilon_{dyn} = \frac{C_{dyn}(\varepsilon)}{C_{dyn}(\varepsilon_0)} \qquad (3)$$

The dynamic capacitance

As can be seen in Figure 7, the dynamic capacitance can be divided into three capacitances:

$$C_{dyn} = C_p + C_f + C_{f'} \qquad (4)$$

C_p denotes the parallel capacitance between the element patch and the ground plane; C_f is the fringe capacitance at the outer edge of the patch and $C_{f'}$ the fringe capacitance of a side due to the presence of the other Bahl (2003), Figure 7.

Parallel capacitance

$$C_p = \frac{e_0 e_r W L}{H g_n g_m} \qquad (5)$$

Fringe edge capacitance of each side C_f

The fringe capacitance C_f in the rectangular patch can be divided in two parts. Each part is related to a side:

$$C_f = C_{f_1} + C_{f_2} \qquad (6)$$

Where:

C_{f1} represents the edge capacitance on one side of a patch length L, it can be calculated using the equation as follows:

$$C_{f1}(\varepsilon) = \frac{1}{2\gamma_n}\left(\frac{\varepsilon_{reff}(\varepsilon,H,W)}{c_0 Z(\varepsilon_r=1,H,W)} - \frac{\varepsilon_0\varepsilon_r W}{H}\right)L \qquad (7)$$

C_{f2} represents the edge capacitance on one side of a patch length W, it can be calculated using the equation as follows:

$$C_{f2}(\varepsilon) = \frac{1}{2\gamma_m}\left(\frac{\varepsilon_{reff}(\varepsilon_r,H,L)}{c_0 Z(\varepsilon_r=1,H,L)} - \frac{\varepsilon_0\varepsilon_r L}{H}\right)W \qquad (8)$$

Fringe edge capacitance of side due to the presence of other $C_{f'}$

In the case of two elements patch, there is two sides where $C_{f'}$ exists. Its expression can be calculated via the expression of C_f as can be seen in equation as follows:

$$C_{f'} = \frac{C_{f'}}{1+A\left(\frac{H}{A}\right)\tanh\left(\frac{10a}{H}\right)}\left(\frac{\varepsilon_r}{\varepsilon_{reff}}\right)^{1/4} \qquad (9)$$

Where

$$A = \exp\left[-0.1\exp\left(2.33-1.5\frac{W}{H}\right)\right] \qquad (10)$$

Coupling capacitance

The coupling capacitance is derived from the odd mode capacitance Bahl (2003), Figure 8. It can be calculated using the equation as follows:

$$C_c = C_{ga} + C_{gd} \qquad (11)$$

The gap capacitance in air

It describes the gap capacitance in the air. Its value can be calculated using the equation as follows Bahl (2003):

$$C_{ga} = \varepsilon_0 \frac{K(k')}{K(k)} \qquad (12)$$

Where $K(k)$ and $K(k')$ are the elliptic function and its complement,

$$k = \frac{S}{S+2W} \qquad (13)$$

While S is the distance between the two elements of patches

and $\quad k' = \sqrt{1-k^2} \qquad (14)$

Finally, we can write the gap capacitance as follows:

$$C_{ga} = \begin{cases} \dfrac{\varepsilon_0}{\pi} \ln\left\{2\dfrac{1+\sqrt{k'}}{1-\sqrt{k'}}\right\} & \text{for } 0 \leq k^2 \leq 0.5 \\[4mm] \dfrac{\pi\varepsilon_0}{\ln\left\{2\dfrac{1+\sqrt{k}}{1-\sqrt{k}}\right\}} & \text{for } 0.5 \leq k^2 \leq 1 \end{cases} \qquad (15)$$

The gap capacitance in dielectric

C_{gd} Represents the capacitance value due to the electric flux in the dielectric region, it can be calculated using the equation as follows, Ferchichi et al. (2010):

$$C_{gd} = \frac{\varepsilon_0\varepsilon_r}{\pi} \ln\coth\left(\frac{\pi S}{4h}\right) + 0.65 C_f\left\{\frac{0.02}{S/h}\sqrt{\varepsilon_r} + \left(1-\frac{1}{\varepsilon_r^2}\right)\right\} \qquad (16)$$

Return loss

Basing on the equations developed in the previous paragraph, we have calculated the values of: R, L, C and X_L. Then when we compare simulation results obtained by the model and using HFSS, we can say that S11 are similar which prove that our model is accurate. As for S12, there is a little difference between the two results due to variation among mutual coupling calculating by the two methods, Figure 9. Besides, there is a gain in time simulation.

ARRAY OF ANTENNA: 2*2

Geometry of patch

The second application of the developed model is a bidirectional array of antenna. In this case, we use a four rectangular antenna. Each element has the same dimension and substrate as proposed single patch, Figure 10.

Electrical model

In this case the electrical model can be constructed using the same technique. First we must determine the dynamic capacitance of each element in order to calculate the dynamic permittivity and the resonant resistance. Then we calculate the coupling capacitance between the different elements. The proposed model is shown in Figure 11.

The dynamic capacitance

The introduction of two other elements modify the dynamic capacitance.

$$C_{dyn} = C_p + C_f + C_{f'} \qquad (17)$$

Where Cp and Cf still unchangeable but Cf' will change because each element have two sides in contact with two other side. Thus the fringe capacitance of side due to the presence of the presence of the other will be divided into two parts.

$$C_{f'} = C_{f_1'} + C_{f_2'} \qquad (18)$$

Where $C_{f_1'}$ and $C_{f_2'}$ can be calculated using the equation :

$$C_{f_1'} = \frac{C_{f_1'}}{1+A\left(\frac{H}{A}\right)\tanh\left(\frac{10a}{H}\right)}\left(\frac{\varepsilon_r}{\varepsilon_{reff}}\right)^{1/4} \qquad (19)$$

$$C_{f_2'} = \frac{C_{f_2'}}{1+A\left(\frac{H}{A}\right)\tanh\left(\frac{10a}{H}\right)}\left(\frac{\varepsilon_r}{\varepsilon_{reff}}\right)^{1/4} \qquad (20)$$

After calculating the dynamic capacitance, we can dedicate the dynamic permittivity ε_{dyn} by applying the Equation 3.

Coupling capacity

In this case, we have four elementary patches so there is a coupling between all those elements. As can be seen in the Figure 11 of model , the coupling capacity can be divided into two kind parts:

The coupling capacity between each two elements C_{cc}
The diagonal coupling capacity C_{ccd}

Thus, the coupling capacity can be written as follows:

$$C_c = 4C_{cc} + 2C_{ccd} \qquad (21)$$

Where:

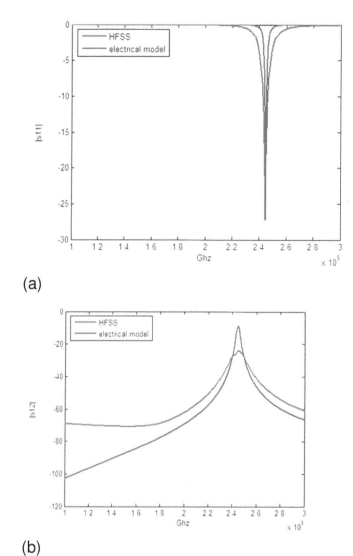

(a)

(b)

Figure 9. S-parameters of the two patch (a) S11 and (b) S12.

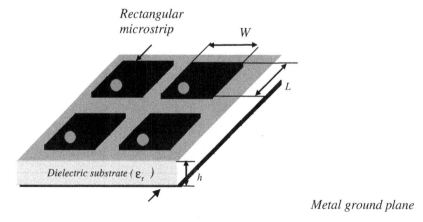

Figure 10. A four elements array of patch.

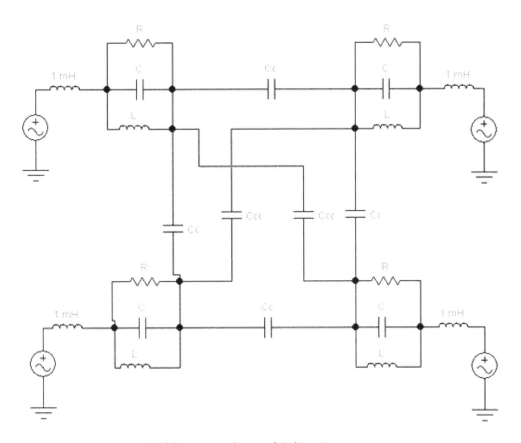

Figure 11. Electrical model of the proposed array of 4 elements.

$C_{cc} = C_{ga} + C_{gd}$, the gap capacitance in the presence of the air and the dielectric C_{ga} and C_{gd} are calculated by the equation 15 and 16.

$$C_{ccd} = C_{gad} + C_{gdd} \qquad (22)$$

To calculate the diagonal gap capacitance in the presence of the air and the dielectric C_{gad} and C_{gdd} we use the same equation of C_{ga} and C_{gd} but we change the expression S by $\sqrt{2}\,S$ which is the distance between the diagonal patch.

RETURN LOSS

After building our electrical model, the simulation results are compared to those given by HFSS. As can be seen, S11, S12 and S13 are in good agreement which means that our model is very accurate, Figure 12. Besides, the time simulation of HFSS simulator increases when adding elementary element but the electrical model keeps the same time simulation when adding element which is instantaneously.

Conclusion

In our paper, we have concentrated on the coupling between elements of an array. The couplings in the arrays are evaluated by modelling the proposed array by an electrical model. Each antenna element is replaced by the RLC equivalent block. We have described the different coupling between array elements in the case of two and four array antenna. The proposed approach can be easily implemented without complicated mathematical programming methods. The technique has shown its ability to generate reasonable results in all checked cases.

Therefore, the usage of electrical model to analyse array antenna shows very interesting and useful results, even though if, considering the approximations for different geometry of array and for different kind of excitation. Moreover, a further development will be in case of mushroom antenna were the array element are related to the GND by using via hole.

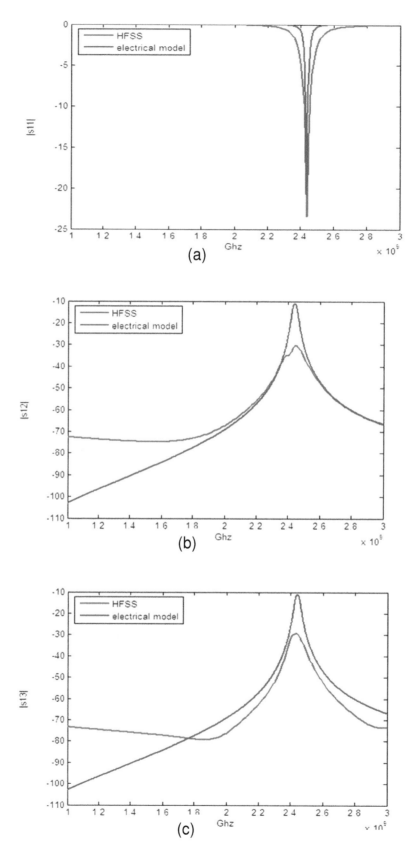

Figure 12. S-parameters of the array of 4 elements patch. (a) S11, (b) S12, (c) S13.

REFERENCES

Anguera J, Martinez E, Puentte C, Borja C, Soler J (2004). "Broad-Band Dual-Frequency Microstrip Patch Antenna With Modified Sierpinski Fractal Geometry" IEEE Trans. Antennas and Propagation, p. 52.

ANSYS, Inc. Proprietary (2009). " Ansoft HFSS, User-Guide", 3rd Edition, February.

Bahl I (2003). "Lumped Elements for RF and Microwave Circuits".

Balanis A (1997). "Antenna theory", John Wiley & Sons, Inc, pp. 379-412.

Celal Y, Kerim G (1998). "Simple model for the impedance of rectangular microstrip antenna", J. Eng. Sci., pp. 733-738,

Ert"urk VB, Rojas RG (2003). "Efficient analysis of input impedance and mutual coupling of microstrip antennas mounted on large coated cylinders," IEEE Transactions on Antennas and Propagation, 51(4): 739–748, Apr.

Fallahi R, Roshandel M (2007). "Effect of mutual coupling and configuration of concentric circular array antenna on the signalto-interference performance in CDMA systems," Progress In Electromagnetic Res., PIER, 76: 427–447.

Farkasvolgyi A, Nagy L (2007). "Mutual coupling effects on the mean capacity of MIMO antenna systems," Progress In Electromagnetic Research Symposium, 130–106, Prague, Czech Republic, Aug., pp. 27–28.

Ferchichi A, Fadlallah N, Sboui N, Gharsallah A (2009)." Analysis and design of Printed Fractal Antenna by Using an Adequate Electrical Model", Int. J. Communic. Networks and Information Security IJCNIS, 1: 3, Dec.

Ferchichi A, Sboui N, Gharsallah A (2010). "New antenna based on Triangular patch as a solution for RFID Application", App. Computat. Electromagn. Soc. ACES J., 25(3): 199-205 March.

Fu YQ, Zheng QR, Gao Q, Zhang GH (2006). "Mutual coupling reduction between large antenna array using electromagnetic bandgap (EBG) structures," J. Electromagnet. Waves Applications, 20(6): 819–825.

Jarchi S, Rashed-Mohassel J, Neshati MH (2007). "Mutual coupling of rectangular DRA in four element circular array," Progress In Electromagnetic Research Symposium 2007, 2000– 2004, Beijing, China, March, pp. 26–30.

Krusevac S, Rapajic PB, Kennedy R (2006). "Mutual coupling effect on thermal noise in multi-element antenna systems," Prog. Electromagn. Res. PIER, 59: 325-333.

Liu H-X, Zhai H-Q, Li L, Liang C-H (2006). "A progressive numerical method combined with MoM for a fast analysis of large waveguied slot antenna array," J. Electromagnet. Waves Applications, 20(2): 737–754.

Losito O (2007). "Design of conformal tapered leaky wave antenna," PIER Online, 3(8): 1316–1320.

Monti G, Catarinucci L, Tarricone L (2009). "Compact Microstrip Antenna for RFID Applications" Progress In Electromagnetic Res. Lett., 8: 191-199.

Nasimuddin AK, Verma A (2004). "Fast and accurate model for analysis of equilateral triangular patch antenna," J. Microwaves Optoelectronics, 3: 99-110, April.

Persson P, Josefsson L, Lanne M (2003). "Investigation of the mutual coupling between apertures on doubly curved convex surface: Theory and measurements," IEEE Transactions on Antennas and Propagation, 51(4): 682–692, Apr.

Qiu ZJ, Hou XY, Li X, Xu JD (2006). "On the condition number of matrices from various hyberid vector FEM-BEM for emulations for 3-D Scattering," J. Electromagn. Waves Appl., 20(13): 1797–1806.

Uduwawala D, Norgren M, Fuks P, Gunawardena A (2005). "A complete FDTD simulation of a real gpr antenna system operating above lossy and dispersive grounds," Prog. Electromagn. Res. PIER, 50: 209–229.

Vasquez C, Hotopan G, Ver Hoeye S, Fernández M Herràn LF, Las F (2009). "Microstrip Antenna Design Based On Stacked Patches for Reconfigurable Two Dimensional Planar Array Topologies" Prog. Electromagn. Res, PIER, 97: 95-104.

Yuan T, Li L-W, Leong M-S, Li J-Y, Yuan N (2007). "Efficient analysis and design of finite phased array of printed dipoles using fast algorithm: Some case studies," J. Electromagn. Wave Appl., 21(6): 737–754.

19

Electromyographic (EMG) signal to joint torque processing and effect of various factors on EMG to torque model

Khalil Ullah[1]*, Asif Khan[1], Ihtesham-ul-Islam[1] and Mohammad A. U. Khan[2]

[1]Department of Electrical Engineering, National University of Computer and Emerging Sciences, Peshawar, Pakistan.
[2]Department of Electrical and Computer Engineering, Effat University, Jeddah, Saudi Arabia.

This study present electromyographic (EMG) signal to torque model and investigates the effects of various factors on EMG signal and EMG to torque model. Pre-processing techniques are applied on EMG signal in order to remove the DC offset, 60 Hz noise and to estimate the EMG amplitude. The estimated EMG amplitude is then mapped to joint torque using a new non-linear equation. This equation uses some parameters, whose values are obtained using nonlinear regression. Ten subjects took part in the experiments and performed variable force maximal voluntary contractions (MVC) and sub-maximal voluntary contractions (SMVC). The resulting elbow joint torque and EMG signals were pre-processed and entered to the model to find value of the parameters using nonlinear regression. Once these values were obtained they were put into the model and thus joint torque was estimated. Also EMG is analysed for effect of various factors like muscle fatigue, cross talk and different joint velocity. The results obtained from this model are highly correlated with the true values of the torque and the average correlation and mean square error for different experiments are 0.9997 and 0.047 Nm respectively. This new mathematical equation can be used to design a control system for rehabilitation and wearable robots.

Key words: Electromyographic (EMG), maximal voluntary contractions (MVC), power spectral density, levenberg-marquardt algorithm, non-linear regression.

INTRODUCTION

Muscle is a source of force and joint torques in human body. In the upper limb of human body the bicep and tricep muscles consist of muscle fibres and joint movements are realized by contraction of these fibres, controlled by Central Nervous System (CNS).When the muscle fibres receive the command (electrical activity) from CNS, an electric signal is generated on the muscle surface and the signal is called EMG signal (Roberto and Philip, 2004).

The EMG signal is random, continuous and nonlinear in nature (Hogan and Mann, 1980; Siegler et al., 1985). These properties of EMG signal reveal that it should be processed in order to get a simple model for its amplitude and then map this amplitudeto joint torques. Some of the models that map the EMG to joint torque assume that the EMG signal is a band limited white noise modulated by the level of muscle contraction thusjoint torque can be derived from this signal by controlling muscle length (Rack and Westbury, 1969). According to these assumptions,

---

*Corresponding author. E-mail: khalil.ullah@nu.edu.pk.

mapping EMG signal to joint torque requires pre-processing the raw EMG signal. Numerous attempts have been made by researchers to mathematically model the joint moments and torques using EMG signal. In some of these models, first the muscle force is calculated and then joint torque is estimated. In one of these models torque is calculated on basis of response from a single motor (Fuglevand et al., 1993). Herbert and Gandevia (1999) improved this system by providing an accurate single motor response. Statistical optimization methods are also used by researcher to extract the joint torque and muscle tension from EMG signals, but these statistical methods are not robust because they use too many parameters (Hof and Van der Berg, 1981). Some researchers tried to get a signal and to extract torque for each joint of the body from this single EMG signal using low pass filtering. Low pass filtering is the easiest way to get EMG amplitude, and then using it for torque prediction. However if it is used for controlling the whole body skeleton then it is very difficult to get such set of EMG signals that will result in torque for whole body joints (Zajac, 1993). Some researchers have used Artificial Neural Networks (ANN) for estimating joint torque from EMG signal. It has been shown that ANN yield good results if it is trained for limited values of EMG and torque (Fausett, 1993). If there is large data set of EMG and torque, then ANN results are random and not well-correlated with the measured torque.

Most of these models have established a successful relationship between EMG signal and joint torque. However, the muscle fatigue is caused if the force is applied repeatedly and the contractions of muscles are sustained. This fatigue affects the capability of applying force (McComas et al., 1995). Similarly joint angular velocity and cross-talk also have effect on the EMG signal and thus affecting the EMG to torque processing. The previously mentioned models did not consider these cases of muscle fatigue, joint velocity and cross-talk, while modelling the muscle force and joint movements on the basis of EMG signal. Some of the models like Reiner and Quintern (1997) and Gait's et al. (1993) models use more than 25 parameters, making them very complex and it is very difficult to adjust these parameters for different muscle contractions and joint torques. Another major disadvantage of these models is that they use too many assumptions so they are not robust.

One of the solutions to model joint torque on the basis of EMG signal is to use a new mathematical model, which can predict joint torque from EMG signals at both the conditions of muscle fatigue and varying joint velocity. So in this study we present a new mathematical (nonlinear) model using nonlinear regression. Nonlinear regression enables us to fit a set of data to a mathematical model which represent the data in a compact form (Douglas et al., 1988). The model considers a few parameters, whose values are found and then updated until the difference between the model data and actual data is minimized. Thus, we get a single equation which represents the EMG to torque relation using a single function (Gallant, 1975). In our non-linear regression model Levenberg-Marquardt method is used for finding and adjusting value of the parameters as explained by Marquardt (1963) and Levmar (2005). The pre-processed EMG signal, recorded from the bicep muscle of the human arm, and the joint torque are used as input to our model. Then a merit function is minimized by adjusting the parameter's values until there is no more improvement in the merit function. The joint torque estimated by our model is highly correlated with the measured torque.

MODEL DEVELOPMENT METHODOLOGY

Basic physiology of motor control, muscle contraction and EMG generation

The motor unit is an important functional unit of muscle. It has motor neurons and muscle fibers which are innervated by motor neurons. This is shown in Figure 1. When a muscle fibre of a motor unit is activated an electrical potential is generated called fibre's potential. This potential spreads into the muscle fibre through the transverse tubules. In response to this action potential, the stored calcium is released that binds with troponin, altering the location of tropomyosin. This frees the active site on the actin, allowing a muscle contraction to take place (Roberto and Philip, 2004).The sum these   electric potentials in a motor unit are called motor unit action potential (MUAP). Sum of these motor unit action potentials is called electromyographic signal.This signal can be acquired by either placing electrodes on the surface of human's muscle (Non-invasio), or by inserting needle electrode into the muscle (Invasio).

Experimental setup and data collection

The robotic exoskeleton arm that was used in this experiment (Figure 2) had a link and joint corresponding to the human elbow joint. The length of the link was adjustable for different lengths of the arm. Also there was another mechanism that was fastened to the arm as shown in Figure 2. It had a potentiometer at the elbow joint. This was used to record the elbow joint angle when the subject was performing the contractions.

Ten persons without any physical disorder took part in the experiments in order to collect the EMG signal, joint angle and load data. Before starting the experiment each subject was trained how to operate the load sensor and the potentiometer. Also the skin was prepared by shaving the hair in order to place the surface EMG sensor properly on the bicep brachii muscle. Subjects were asked to stand straight and fasten the exoskeleton robotic arm. They were asked to do non-fatigue MVC and SMVC contractions and the

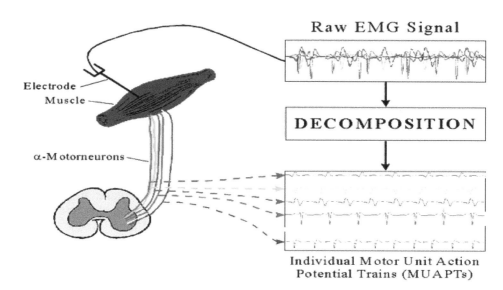

Figure 1. The motor unit, MUAPs and the electromyogram signal.

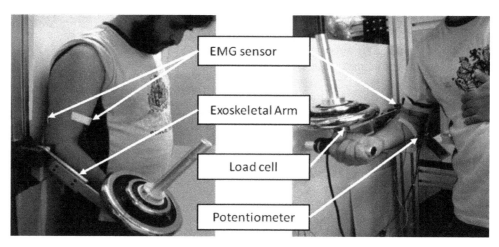

Figure 2. A view of the experimental setup, exoskeletal robotic arm with load cell for measuring load lifted by the subject and a manipulator with potentiometer for measuring joint angles.

corresponding EMG, angle and load data were recorded to a file in computer. The time duration of the experiment for one subject varied between 5 to 15 s for one contraction with rest time 10 min between two contractions. For recording the EMG signal from bicep muscle a DELSYS single differential DE-2.3 sensor was used. This sensor has detection surfaces consisting of two parallel bars. It is a band pass filter with cut-off frequencies 20-500 Hz. MNT-50L miniature load cell was used for measuring the load lifted by a subject. Data from all these sensors was sampled using 1000 Hz sampling frequency and then digitized using a NI USB-6009 A/D converter, in order to feed into the computer for analysis. NI-LabVIEW 8.5 was used for data acquisition and real time processing, while Math works-MATLAB 7.6 and Microsoft Visual

C++ 2005 were used for batch processing.

Data pre-processing

Before inputting the EMG signal to the model it was first pre-processed. DC offset was calculated for 2 s and then removed, this signal was then passed through a 5th ordered notch filter to remove the 60 Hz noise due the power supply, then full-wave rectified and finally the moving average of the EMG (of window size varying from 0.2 to 0.5 s), was found. This moving average EMG is then normalized. The normalized moving average EMG is the estimated amplitude of the EMG signal. Similarly the joint angle and load data

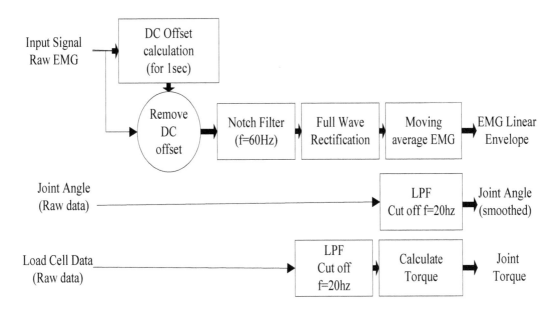

Figure 3. Schematic diagram for EMG signal, joint angle and joint torque pre-processing.

were collected and smoothed and then joint torque was calculated. Now, this torque acted as a control variable for our model because on the basis of this measured torque the parameters of our mathematical model are adjusted. The schematic diagram for pre-processing of the EMG signal, joint angle and load data is shown below in Figure 3. The EMG linear envelope obtained after pre-processing and actual torque was then entered as input to our model. The raw EMG, pre-processed EMG and joint torque data for MVC and .SMVC for two different subjects is shown in Figure 4.

EMG to torque models

In order to model joint torques from EMG signal, it is important to know the nature of the relationship between EMG and joint torque. According to these assumptions to find a best mathematical model for estimating joint torque, EMG linear envelope was plotted against joint torque and it was found that the relation is not linear and is somewhat exponential (Figure 5). Also according to Stephen and Stuart (2008) EMG producing less torque output output at higher levels of activation. Due to the nonlinear and exponential nature of the relationship, different exponential models including neural network were introduced and analyzed to get the best model. Each of these models except ANN has unknown parameters, a, b and c. The values of these parameters are obtained using nonlinear regression. The ANN and other models were analysed in two ways. The ANN and other models were analysed in two ways, batch processing and real-time processing. In the batch processing the ANN is trained and for the other models both EMG estimated amplitude, and measured joint torque were entered to the model and best fit values were found for the parameters using nonlinear regression. These values were put into the model to calculate the torque for the same EMG signal. While in real-time processing,

another different EMG signal was entered to the model and the joint torque for this new EMG was calculated using the parameters obtained from batch processing.

Table 1 shows the analysis of different candidate models. MSE and correlation coefficient were calculated for each model. The model which has least MSE and greater correlation between measured torque estimated torque in both batch and real-time processing was selected. The comparison of these models is shown in Figure 6. The selected mathematical model and the non-linear regression for finding values of the parameters are discussed in details in the next subsections. Besides the above models polynomial curve fitting was also used. The polynomial gave good results in range of the data but outside the range of the data the results were quite different from measured data. The results of our new selected model were also compared to some existing models developed by Metral and Cassar (1981) and Fleischer (2005).

The selected best mathematical model

As the relationship between EMG and joint torque is non-linear Metral and Cassar (1981). Thus a new mathematical model was introduced to map EMG to joint torque. The model which can best describe the relationship between EMG and joint torque is given in Equation. (1).

$$\tau_{es} = u^a * \exp(b - c * u) \tag{1}$$

Here in Equation 1, τ_{es} is the estimated joint torque, u is the pre-processed EMG signal and a, b, c are the unknown parameters. The problem is to estimate best fit values for these unknown parameters. For this purpose non-linear regression was used,

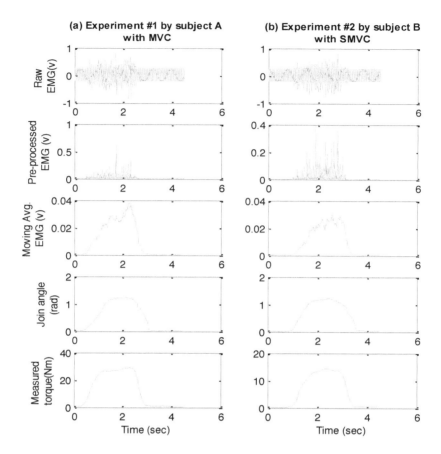

Figure 4. EMG Signals, raw EMG and denoised EMG, normalized moving averaged
EMG and the measured joint Torque for two different subjects.

where a merit function was selected and minimized. This is
explained in detail in next subsection.

Non-linear regression for finding values of the parameters

Regression analysis is a technique that fits a set of data to a
smooth continuous function (Laurene, 1998). Regression has two
types, linear and nonlinear. In non-linear regression, large number
of iterations are performed to minimize the merit function (*MF*) and
the values of the parameters are non-linearly related to the model.

The purpose of nonlinear regression is to determine the best-fit
values for the parameters for a model by minimizing the chosen *MF*
(Laurene and Fausett, 1998). In this iterative approach first initial
values were obtained using least square fitting for the parameters
and then the Levenberg-Marquardt Algorithm developed by
Marquardt (1963), was used to obtain values of the parameters for
next iteration. The newly estimated values now act as the initial
values for the following iteration. Adjusting the values of the
parameters is continued until no further improvement in the *MF*. Let
our model torque is denoted by τ_{es} and τ_{ac} is the actual measured
torque. Then our model can be written as follows in Equation 2.

$$\tau_{es} = \tau_{es}\ (u,\ a,\ b,\ c) \tag{2}$$

The *MF* minimization can be represented by Equationn. 3.

$$MF^2 = \sum_{i=1}^{N} \left[\frac{\tau_{aci} - \tau_{es}\ (u_i,\ a,\ b,\ c)}{\sigma_i} \right]^2 \tag{3}$$

The whole algorithm for merit function minimization to find values of
parameters is as follows Marquardt (1963):

(i) Estimate initial values for the unknown parameters using least
square fitting.
(ii) Using these initial values, calculate the merit function by putting
values of parameters in Equation 3.
(iii) Now to minimize the merit function, adjust the values of the
parameters using the Levenberg-Marquardt method.
(iv) Compute the merit function and compare it to its previously
obtained value.
(v) Repeat step 3 and 4 until no further minimization occurs in MF^2

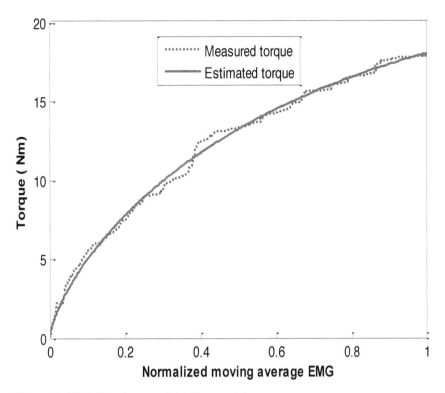

Figure 5. EMG Signal versus Joint Torque plot.

Table 1. Detail of the different models and ANN for estimating joint torque from EMG signal.

	Model	Batch analysis of the models		Real time analysis of the models	
No	The model	MSE (Nm)	R^2	MSE (Nm)	R^2
1	$\tau = a + b u^2 + ce^u$	0.094	0.997	0.382	0.993
2	$\tau = a + b\cos(u) + c\sin(u)$	0.167	0.996	0.525	0.990
3	$\tau = a + be^u + ce^{-u}$	0.116	0.997	0.442	0.992
4	$\tau = au^b$	0.128	0.997	0.311	0.994
5	$\tau = a + b\sqrt{u}$	0.497	0.988	0.301	0.997
6	Neural network	0.021	0.998	0.415	0.993
7	$\tau = u^a e^{(b-cu)}$	0.049	0.998	0.056	0.997
8	$\tau = ae^{(b/u)}$	0.413	0.981	0.527	0.987
9	$\tau = a/(1 + be^{(cu)})$	0.145	0.989	0.328	0.988

(vi) Save the final values of the parameters, and now the joint torque is calculated by putting these parameters into Eqn. 1.
(vi) Finally calculate some performance indexes (MSE, variance and correlation). Once the best fit values for the parameters were obtained, they were assigned to the parameters of our model. Now in real-time, only the EMG envelope was entered as input to the model, and it generated the estimated joint torque. The schematics for batch and real-time processing are shown in Figure 7.

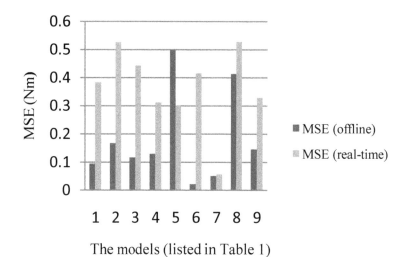

Figure 6. Comparison of the models on basis of MSE in both batch and real-time processing.

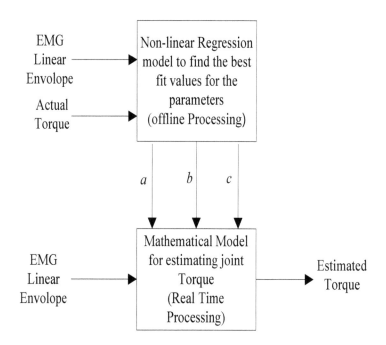

Figure 7. Schematic diagram for batch and real-time processing.

RESULTS OF THE MODEL

To validate the performance of the new model, experiments were performed using the experimental setup discussed in previous section. The experiments were performed in two groups. First group presents experiments that were performed to obtain best parameter's values. Second group presents experiment in which only EMG signal was entered as input to the model and it generated the required torque. There were several important results derived after completing the described experimental procedure.

Table 2. Values of the parameters and error analysis for 5 subjects data

No.	Values of the Parameters for model $u^a * \exp(b - c * u)$			Error analysis (Real time)		
	a	b	c	SSE (Nm)	MSE (Nm)	R^2
1	0.815	3.318	0.314	364.4	0.071	0.988
2	0.844	3.450	0.366	285.6	0.056	0.998
3	0.699	3.231	0.348	174.0	0.072	0.987
4	0.784	3.267	0.412	315.0	0.061	0.991
5	0.805	3.336	0.374	321.2	0.062	0.983

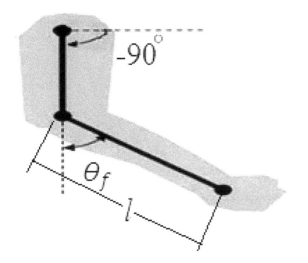

Figure 8. Shoulder joint angle and elbow joint angle (θ_f) during contractions.

During the first group of experiments, five subjects took part in the experiments. The shoulder joint angle was fixed at -90° w.r.t x-axis as shown in figure. Each subject did isometric flexion on the elbow joint. They flexed the elbow from 0 to 90° θ_f) w.r.t y-axis as in Figure 8.After flexion, they extended their arms with elbow joint angle decreased from 90 to 0° w.r.t y-axis (Figure 8). During these contractions the subjects applied variable force with maximal and submaximal contractions and the resulted joint torque was entered as input to the model for batch processing. During the batch processing the algorithm found best fit values for the unknown parameters. As the iterations of the *MF* minimization algorithm increased the values of the parameters were adjusted so the estimated torque became closer and closer to the actual torque and thus the mean square

error (MSE) was decreased. The algorithm took 29 iterations to get the best fit values for the parameters for one subject and 24 for the one of the four other subjects. The convergence time for getting best values of the parameters was 31.537 and 21.6 μ for two subject's data respectively. The estimated parameter's values and the error analysis for each of the five subjects (who took part in experiments) are listed in Table 2.

As in batch processing the best values for the parameters are obtained so now in real time processing only EMG signal is entered to the model and torque is obtained for the joint (Figure. 7). The joint torque estimated by our model is highly correlated with measured torque. The mean square error (MSE) and correlation coefficient were 0.056 Nm and 0.998, and for another subject's data were 0.061 Nm, 0.991 respectively. The results for two different subjects that participated in experiments are shown in Figure 9.

Here subject "A" performs maximal voluntary contraction (MVC) and subject "B" performs sub-maximal voluntary contractions (SMVC). Result for another subject, who perform MVC is shown in Figure 10. From Figures 9 and 10, it is clear that our model can successfully map EMG signal to the joint torque in both maximal and sub-maximal voluntary contractions

Factors affecting EMG to torque model

There are a lot of factors which can affect the EMG signal thus can affect EMG to torque model. Due muscle fatigue the EMG envelope is slightly increased. Due to this increase in EMG amplitude the EMG to torque model is affected and the values of the parameters should be adjusted to overcome this change. This change in parameters of the model is shown in Figure 11.

Similarly joint angular velocity also affects the EMG

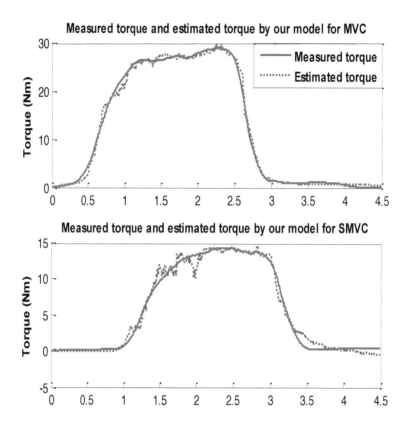

Figure 9. Results of two experiments performed by different subjects (Subject A perform MVC and subject B SMVC).

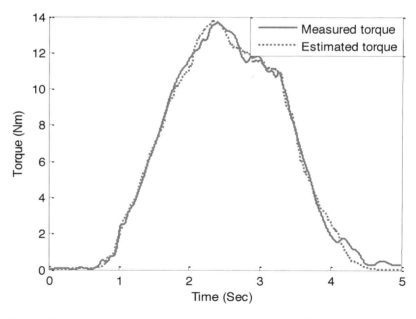

Figure 10. Results of our model for one subject data during MVC.

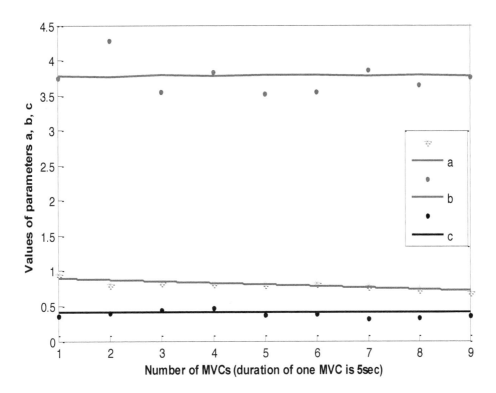

Figure 11. Change in Values of the parameters due to muscle fatigue.

signal and thus affecting the EMG to torque model. A large number of contractions were performed by subjects varying the joint velocity, and it was found during the experiments that the EMG amplitude is increasing linearly in the beginning as the joint velocity increases and after some time it changes very slightly. Now at this stage when EMG amplitude is changing, the values of the parameters were again estimated using the proposed algorithm and it was found that the new values of the parameters are changing. These changes in values of the parameters are shown in Figure 12.

DISCUSSION

In this study a new nonlinear model is introduced and then experiments were performed in order to validate the model. In the creation of the model three parameters (a, b, c) were used. The selection of the number of parameters is very critical and it can affect the predicted output. The robustness of the model is related with the values of the parameters. If optimized values are not obtained for the parameters then there may be larger errors.

In this study a new nonlinear model is introduced and then a number of experiments were performed in order to validate the model. In the creation of the model three parameters (a, b, c) were used. The selection of number of parameters is very critical and it can affect the predicted output. The robustness of the model is related with the values of these parameters. If best fit values are not obtained for the parameters then there may be large errors. As standard method (e.g. Levenberg Marquardt) is used for estimation of the parameters and the correlation coefficient and MSE values show that this model can successfully map EMG to joint torque.

Another purpose of this study was to examine the estimation of torque from EMG during maximal and submaximal contractions. Previously only torque is estimated from EMG in case of maximal voluntary contractions. As a patient with serious muscle injury can't exert maximum force so the model should be able to estimate the accurate torque from EMG in such case of sub-maximal forces. Hence in our model we calibrate EMG to torque processing for both maximum and also sub-maximal um muscle contractions. The results (Figures 9 and 10) show that our mathematical model is able to map EMG to joint torque for both maximal and

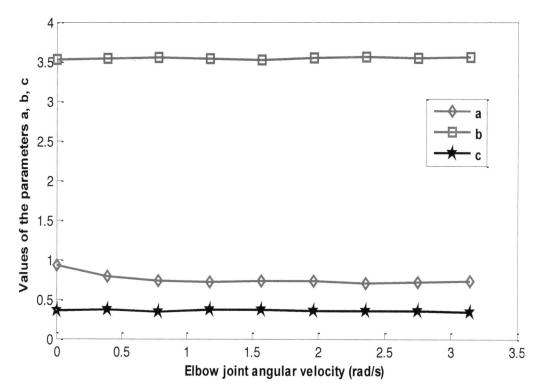

Figure 12. Change in values of the parameters of our model due to change in angular velocity of the joint.

sub- maximal voluntary contractions (Figure 9b).

Although the results of our model are good, still some MSE errors exist between target torque and our estimations. The new model is a simpler model as compare to other existing models because it takes only one EMG signal and only the muscle fatigue and joint velocity are analyzed. The model needs only one EMG signal from the bicep brachii muscle for estimating the joint torque. If torques for the shoulder joint and other joints are to be estimated, then more EMG sensors will be needed, and I hope our model may be successful in this case as well.

This model was refined by studying the EMG signal for muscle fatigue and varying joint velocity. It was found that there are slight changes in parameter's values of the model which should be considered during torque estimation.

Conclusions

This study investigates the relationship between EMG signal and joint torque and presents an EMG-to-torque model. The main aim of this research was to detect the intended motion of the human arm and then develop an EMG-to-Torque model that will be a basis for controlling the exoskeletons.

For this purpose it was required to find a relationship between the electrical activity (EMG) and joint torque. A nonlinear model which has least MSE and greater correlation with measured torque is selected.

Conceptually this mathematical model has some advantages and disadvantages. As joint torque estimated by this model directly depend on EMG signal so this model is very sensible to EMG recording. Improper placement of sensors and inaccurate experiments may result in wrong estimates, but still this model is more robust because it uses limited number of EMG sensors. From the results of the model, it can be considered that our mathematical model can be used successfully to predict joint torque from EMG signal. A standard method is used for finding parameter's values, which leads to mapping EMG to joint torque. In the experiments only healthy subjects took part due to safety reasons, but we hope that this model can help in controlling assistive devices for disabled people who have some muscular disorder.

This model will be a basis for controlling exoskeletons. In the future we hope this model can be used successfully to make an interface between human operator and the exoskeleton arm. A device (exoskeleton) and a control system may be developed which will support a human operator with extra force in the elbow joint specially and also for legs and thigh joints. The exoskeleton can be attached with human body and it should increase his or her mobility and strength by supporting the arm, leg and thigh muscles.

REFERENCES

Douglas MB, Donald GW (1988). Nonlinear Regression Analysis and Its Application, Wiley Series in probability and Statistics. ISBN-13: 978-0471816430.

Fleischer CHG (2005). Predicting the intended motion with EMG signals for an exoskeleton orthosis controller in Proceedings of the IEEE/RSJ Int.. Conf. Intelligent Robots and Systems.

Fuglevand AJ, Winter DA, Patla AE (1993). Models of recruitment and rate coding organization in motor unit pools. J. Neurophysiol., 70(6): 2470-2488.

Gallant AR (1975). Nonlinear Regression. Am. Stat., 29: 73-81.

Gait Y, Mizrahi J, Levy M (1993). A musculotendon model of the fatigue profiles of paralyzed quadriceps muscle under FES.IEEE Trans. Biomed. Eng., 40: 664–674.

Herbert RD, Gandevia SC (1999).GandeviaTwitch interpolation in human muscles: mechanisms and implications for measurement of voluntary activation. J. Neurophysiol., 82: 2271–2283.

Hof AL, Van der Berg JW (1981). EMG to force processing III: estimation of model parameters for the human triceps surae muscle and assessment of the accuracy by means of a torque plate. J. Biomech., 14: 771–785.

Hogan N, Mann R (1980). Myoelectric signal processing: Optimal estimation applied to electromyography—Part1: Derivation of the optimal myoprocessors. IEEE Transactions on Biomedical Engineering. BME-27: 7.

Laurene VF (1993). Fundamentals of Neural Networks: Architectures, Algorithms and Applications.

Levmar MIAL (2005). A brief description of the Levenberg-Marquardt algorithm implemented by Levmar," Manolis I. A. Lourakis Institute of Computer Science, Greece.

Marquardt D (1963). An algorithm for least-squares estimation of nonlinear parameters," SIAM J. Appl. Math. 11: 431–441.

McComas AJ, Miller RG, Gandevia SC (1995). Fatigue brought on by malfunction of the central and peripheral nervous systems. In Fatigue—Neural and Muscular Mechanisms.editors. PlenumPress, New York. pp. 495–512.

Metral S, Cassar G (1981). Relationship between force and integrated EMG activity during voluntary isometric anisotonic contraction. Eur. J. Appl. Physiol., 46: 185-198.

Rack PMH, Westbury DR (1969). "The effects of length and stimulus rate on tension in the isometric cat soleus muscle," J. Physiol., 204: 443-460.

Riener R, Quintern J (1997). A physiologically based model of muscle activation verified by electrical stimulation. J. Bioelectrochem. Bioenerget., 43(2): 257-264(8).

Roberto M, Philip P (2004). Electromyography, physiology, engineering and non-invasive applications. IEEE Press Engineering in Medicine and Biology Society, Sponsor, 2.

Siegler S, Hillstrom HJ, Freedman W, Moskowitz G (1985). Effect of myoelectric signal processing on the relationship between muscle force and processed EMG. Am. J. Phys Med., 64(3): 130-149.

Stephen HMB, Stuart M (2008). Co-activation alters the linear versus non-linear impression of the EMG-torque relationship of trunk muscles," J. Biomech., 41(3): 491-7.

Zajac FE (1993). Muscle coordination of movement: a perspective," J. Biomech. 26(1): 109-24.

20

Ultra low loss of a thermal arrayed waveguide grating (AWG) module in passive optical networks

Mohammed A. A., Ahmed Nabih Zaki Rashed[*], Gaber E. S. M. E. and Saad A. A.

Electronics and Electrical Communication Engineering Department, Faculty of Electronic Engineering, Menouf 32951, Menoufia University, Egypt.

In the present paper, high transmission bit rate of a thermal arrayed waveguide grating (AWG) which is composed of lithium niobate (LiNbO₃)/polymethyl metha acrylate (PMMA) hybrid materials on a silicon substrate in passive optical networks (PONs) has parametrically analyzed and investigated over wide range of the affecting parameters. We have theoretically investigated the temperature dependent wavelength shift of the arrayed waveguide grating (AWG) depends on the refractive-indices of the materials and the size of the waveguide. A thermalization of the AWG can be realized by selecting proper values of the material and structural parameters of the device. Moreover, we have analyzed the data transmission bit rate of a thermal AWG in passsive optical networks (PONs) based on maximum time division multiplexing (MTDM) technique.

Key words: Passive optical networks (PONs), arrayed waveguide gratings (AWGs), integrated optics, optical planar waveguide, optical fiber communications, maximum time division Multiplexing (MTDM) technique.

INTRODUCTION

With the explosive growth of end user demand for higher bandwidth, various types of passive optical networks (PONs) have been proposed. PON can be roughly divided into two categories such as time-division-multiplexing (TDM) and wavelength-division-multiplexing (WDM) methods (Park et al., 2004). Compared with TDM-PONs, WDM-PON systems allocate a separate wavelength to each subscriber, enabling the delivery of dedicated bandwidth per optical network unit (ONU). Moreover, this virtual point-to-point connection enables a large guaranteed bandwidth, protocol transparency, high quality of service, excellent security, bit-rate independence, and easy upgradeability. Especially, recent good progress on a thermal arrayed waveguide grating (AWG) and cost-effective colorless ONUs (Lee et al., 2006a) has empowered WDM-PON as an optimum solution for the access network. However, fiber link failure from the optical line terminal (OLT) to the ONU leads to the enormous loss of data. Thus, fault monitoring and network protection are crucial issues in network operators

for reliable network. To date (Kim et al., 2000), many methods have been proposed for network protection. In the ITU-T recommendation on PONs (G.983.1) duplicated network resources such as fiber links or ONUs are required. The periodic and cyclic properties of AWGs are used to interconnect two adjacent ONUs by a piece of fiber. In the recent years, arrayed waveguide gratings (AWGs) have appeared to be one of attractive candidates for high channel count Mux/DeMux devices to process optical signals in a parallel manner. Its low chromatic dispersion (Park et al., 2007), typically ±5 to ±10 ps/nm, makes it possibly be used for 40 Gbit/s systems. However, it is well known that manufacturing AWGs involves a series of complex production processes and requires bulky facilities (Lee et al., 2006b). Their cost remains a big issue. Further, the technical complexity leads to low yield and poor performance. The former, no doubt, further increases the production cost while the latter degrades the signal quality and system's performance (Chan et al., 2003), exhibiting high insertion loss, high channel crosstalk, low channel uniformity, and high polarization dependent loss. More vitally, AWGs require active temperature control in order to stabilize the thermal wavelength drift and temperature-dependent loss variations (Wang et al., 2005). Due to its capability to

*Corresponding author. E-mail: ahmed_733@yahoo.com.

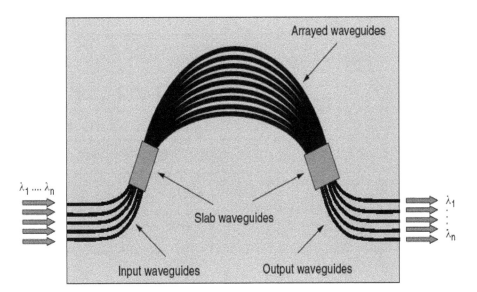

Figure 1. A schematic planning view of a thermal arrayed waveguide grating.

increase the aggregate transmission capacity of a single-strand optical fiber, the arrayed waveguide grating (AWG) multiplexer is considered a key component in the construction of a dense wavelength-division-multiplexing system (Inoue et al., 2004). However, an AWG made of silica is so sensitive to the ambient temperature that the output wavelength changes by as much as 0.66 nm/C (Kaneko et al., 2005). In the present study, a hybrid material waveguide with lithium niobate (LiNbO₃) core material and PMMA cladding material is considered as the most attractive a thermal structure because of its resistance to the thermo-optic sensitivity of the materials. First, the principle of the a thermal AWG with LiNbO₃/PMMA hybrid materials is described, and the relative formulas are derived for analyzing the temperature dependence of the AWG. Second, the theoretical analysis of the data transmission bit rate of a thermal AWG in PONs based on MTDM technique. Finally, a conclusion is reached based on the analysis and general discussion.

A THERMAL AWG MODULE IN PONS ARCHITECTURE MODEL

The network architecture is shown in Figure 1. It is based on two cascaded Athermal arrayed waveguide gratings (AWGs). The first stage is an Nx1a thermal AWG located at the optical line terminal (OLT) or central office (CO). The functionality of this a thermal AWG is to route optical signals generated by the OLT laser diodes stack to each of the network branches to which the OLT will serve (Lee et al., 2006z). The second stage is a 1× M a thermal AWG located at the remote node. Its task is to demultiplex the M incoming wavelengths to each of the output ports, which connect to optical network channels and then to the number of supported users. The entire network routing intelligence is located at the CO in order to provide easy upgradeability and easy integration with the backbone. The two cascade a thermal AWGs are connected to each other by the single mode optical fiber cables (Lee et al., 2006b).

Features of a thermal arrayed waveguide grating module

Arrayed waveguide grating (AWG) which handles the function of wavelength multiplexer/ demultiplexer is extensively used in configuring optical communication networks that are becoming more diversified. Since the transmission wavelength of an AWG is temperature dependent, it was a common practice to control its temperature using heaters or Peltier elements. The AWG consists of input waveguides, arrayed waveguide, slab waveguide and output waveguides, constituting a diffraction grating that takes advantage of the optical path difference in the arrayed waveguide. Figure 1 shows a schematic view of AWG circuitry. As ambient temperature changes, the phase front at each wavelength generated by the arrayed waveguide will tilt due to the change in the refractive index of the optical waveguide and the linear expansion of the silicon substrate, causing a shift of the focusing point on the output waveguide within the slab waveguide (Kokubun et al., 2002).

As shown in Figure 2, the arrayed waveguide grating (AWG) with cross-sections is designed as square shape with the core width a, of lithium niobate (LiNbO₃) material and PMMA polymer overcladding and undercladding material on a silicon substrate.

REFRACTIVE-INDEX OF HYBRID MATERIAL

Lithium niobate (LiNbO₃) core material

The investigation of both the thermal and spectral variations of the waveguide refractive index (n) requires Sellmeier equation. The set of parameters required to completely characterize the temperature dependence of the refractive-index (n_1) is given below, Sellmeier equation is under the form (Jundt, 1997):

$$n_1^2 = A_1 + A_2H + \frac{A_3 + A_4H}{\lambda^2 - (A_5 + A_6H)^2} + \frac{A_7 + A_8H}{\lambda^2 - A_9^2} - A_{10}\lambda^2$$

(1)

Where λ is the optical wavelength in μm and $H = T^2 - T_0^2$. T is the temperature of the material, C, and T_0 is the reference temperature and is considered as 27 °C. The set of parameters of Sellmeier equation coefficients, LiNbO₃, are recast and dimensionally adjusted as follows (Jundt, 1997):

A_1=5.35583, A_2=4.629 × 10^{-7}, A_3=0.100473, A_4=3.862 × 10^{-8}, A_5=0.20692, A_6= -0.89 × 10^{-8}, A_7=100, A_8=2.657 × 10^{-5}, A_9=11.34927, and A_{10}=0.01533.

Equation (1) can be simplified as the following expression:

$$n_1^2 = A_{12} + \frac{A_{34}}{\lambda^2 - A_{56}^2} + \frac{A_{78}}{\lambda^2 - A_9^2} - A_{10}\lambda^2$$

(2)

Where: $A_{12}=A_1+A_2H$, $A_{34}=A_3+A_4H$, $A_{56}=A_5+A_6H$, and $A_{78}=A_7+A_8H$.

Then, the differentiation of Equation (2) with respect to λ which gives:

$$\frac{dn_1}{d\lambda} = \left(\frac{-\lambda}{n_1}\right)\left[\frac{A_{34}}{\left(\lambda^2 - A_{56}^2\right)^2} + \frac{A_{78}}{\left(\lambda^2 - A_9^2\right)^2} + A_{10}\right]$$

(3)

In the same way, the second differentiation with respect to λ yields:

$$\frac{d^2n_1}{d\lambda^2} = -\frac{1}{n_1}\left[\frac{A_{34}\left[\left(\lambda^2 - A_{56}^2\right)-4\lambda^2\right]}{\left(\lambda^2 - A_{56}^2\right)^3} + \frac{A_{78}\left[\left(\lambda^2 - A_9^2\right)-4\lambda^2\right]}{\left(\lambda^2 - A_9^2\right)^3} + A_{10}\right]$$

(4)

Also, the differentiation with respect to T gives:

$$\frac{dn_1}{dT} = \left(\frac{T}{n_1}\right)\left[A_2 + \frac{\left(\lambda^2 - A_{56}^2\right)A_4 + 2A_6A_{56}A_{34}}{\left(\lambda^2 - A_{56}^2\right)^2} + \frac{A_8}{\left(\lambda^2 - A_9^2\right)}\right]$$

(5)

PMMA polymer cladding material

The Sellmeier equation of the refractive-index is expressed as the following (Ishigure et al., 1996):

$$n_2^2 = 1 + \frac{C_1\lambda^2}{\lambda^2 - C_2^2} + \frac{C_3\lambda^2}{\lambda^2 - C_4^2} + \frac{C_5\lambda^2}{\lambda^2 - C_6^2}$$

(6)

The parameters of Sellmeier equation coefficients, PMMA, as a function of temperature (Ishigure et al., 1996):

C_1=0.4963, C_2=0.07180 (T/T_0), C_3=0.6965, C_4=0.1174 (T/T_0), C_5=0.3223, and C_6=9.237.

Then the differentiation of Equation (6) with respect to T yields:

$$\frac{dn_2}{dT} = \frac{\lambda^2 (0.0718)}{n_2 T_0}\left[\frac{C_1C_2}{\left(\lambda^2 - C_2^2\right)^2} + \frac{1.635C_3C_4}{\left(\lambda^2 - C_4^2\right)^2}\right]$$

(7)

THEORETICAL MODEL AND GOVERNING EQUATIONS ANALYSIS

Model of A thermal arrayed waveguide grating (AWG)

We present a thermal condition and the relative formulas of LiNbO$_3$/

PMMA hybrid materials AWG on a silicon substrate. The temperature dependence of AWG center wavelength is expressed as (Ma et al., 2007; Kokubun et al., 2003):

$$\frac{d\lambda_c}{dT} = \frac{\lambda_c}{n_c}\left(\frac{dn_c}{dT} + n_c \alpha_{sub}\right)$$

(8)

where T is the ambient temperature, C, λ_c is the center wavelength of the arrayed waveguide grating, μm, n_c is the effective refractive-index of the arrayed waveguide grating, α_{sub} is the coefficient of thermal expansion of the Si substrate, and $\frac{dn_c}{dT}$: is the thermo-optic (TO) coefficient of the waveguide.

By integrating Equation (8), we can obtain the following expression:

$$\lambda_c = C n_c e^{\left(\alpha_{sub}T\right)}$$

(9)

Where C is an integrating constant. Assume that $\lambda_c=\lambda_0$, and $n_c=n_{c0}$ when $T=T_0$ at room temperature, we can determine C as the following:

$$C = \frac{\lambda_0}{n_{c0}}e^{\left(-\alpha_{sub}T_0\right)}$$

(10)

Substituting from Equation (10) into Equation (9), we can obtain:

$$\lambda_c = \frac{\lambda_0 n_c}{n_{c0}}e^{\left[\alpha_{sub}(T-T_0)\right]}$$

(11)

From Equation (11) we obtain the central wavelength shift caused by the temperature variation as:

$$\Delta\lambda = \lambda_c - \lambda_0 = \frac{\lambda_0}{n_{c0}}\left[n_c e^{\left(\alpha_{sub}(T-T_0)\right)} - n_{co}\right]$$

(12)

Taking Δλ = 0, from Equation (12) we can obtain a thermal condition of the AWG as:

$$\alpha_{sub}(T - T_0) = \ln\left(\frac{n_c}{n_{c0}}\right)$$

(13)

Then by differentiating Equation (13), a thermal condition of the AWG can also be expressed in another form as the following (Kokubun et al., 2003):

$$\frac{dn_c}{dT} = -\alpha_{sub} n_c$$

(14)

The effective refractive index of the arrayed waveguide grating (AWG) is given by (Kaneko et al., 2004):

$$n_c = \frac{\beta}{k} = \frac{k\left[\left(n_1^2 - n_2^2\right)b + n_2^2\right]}{k} = \left(n_1^2 - n_2^2\right)b + n_2^2 \quad ,$$

(15)

Where β is the propagation constant of the fundamental mode, k is the wave number, and b is the normalized propagation constant and is given by (Kaneko et al., 2004):

$$b(V) = \left(1.1428 - \frac{0.9660}{V}\right)^2 ,$$

(16)

Where V is the normalized frequency. For single mode step index optical fiber waveguide, the cut-off normalized is approximately V= V_c= 2.405, and by substituting in Equation (16) we can get the normalized propagation constant b at the cut-off normalized frequency approximately b ≈ 0.5, and then by substituting in Equation (15) we can obtain:

$$n_c = \frac{1}{2}\left(n_1^2 + n_2^2\right) \quad , \tag{17}$$

By taking the square root of Equation (17) yields:

$$\sqrt{n_c} = 0.7\left(n_1^2 + n_2^2\right)^{1/2} \tag{18}$$

The cut-off normalized frequency for single mode step index fiber waveguide is given by the following expression (Kaneko et al., 2004):

$$V_c = \frac{2\pi a}{\lambda_{cut-off}}\left(n_1^2 - n_2^2\right)^{1/2} \tag{19}$$

Assume that the cut-off wavelength is equal to the central wavelength to transfer the fundamental modes only, that is $\lambda_{cut-off}$ = λ_c. Equation (19) can be expressed in another form as follows:

$$\lambda_c = \frac{1.4\,\pi\, a\left(n_1^4 - n_2^4\right)^{1/2}}{2.405\sqrt{n_c}} \tag{20}$$

Equation (20) can be simplified as follows:

$$\lambda_c = \frac{1.83 a\left(n_1^4 - n_2^4\right)^{1/2}}{\sqrt{n_c}} \tag{21}$$

Equation (21) can be expressed in another form as follows:

$$n_c = \frac{3.35\, a^2\left(n_1^4 - n_2^4\right)}{\lambda_c^2} \tag{22}$$

By substituting from Equation (22) into Equation (14) yields:

$$\frac{dn_c}{dT} = -\frac{3.35\,\alpha_{sub}\, a^2\left(n_1^4 - n_2^4\right)}{\lambda_c^2} \quad . \tag{23}$$

The effective refractive index n_c is dependent on the refractive indices of the materials and on the size and shape of the waveguide, then by selecting proper materials and structural parameters of the waveguide to satisfy Equation (23), the A thermal arrayed waveguide grating (AWG) can be designed.

Theoretical model analysis of high data transmission bit rate

The total B.W is based on the total chromatic dispersion coefficient D_t (Zhud et al., 2002), where:

$$D_t = D_m + D_w \tag{24}$$

Where D_m is the material dispersion coefficient in s/m², and D_w is the waveguide dispersion coefficient in m²/s. Both D_m, D_w are given by Kuznetsov et al. (2005) (for the fundamental mode):

$$D_m = -\frac{\lambda}{C}\left(\frac{d^2 n_1}{d\lambda^2}\right), \quad \text{s/m}^2 \tag{25}$$

$$D_w = -\left(\frac{n_2}{C n_1}\frac{\Delta n}{\lambda}\right)Y , \quad \text{s/m}^2 \tag{26}$$

Where C is the velocity of the light, 3 ×10⁸ m/s, n_1 is the core refractive-index, n_2 is the cladding refractive-index, Y is a function of wavelength, λ (Kuznetsov et al., 2005).

The relative refractive-index difference Δn is defined as (Kuznetsov et al., 2005).

$$\Delta n = \frac{n_1^2 - n_2^2}{2n_1^2} \tag{27}$$

The total pulse broadening due to total chromatic dispersion coefficient D_t is given by (Kuznetsov et al., 2005):

$$\Delta\tau = D_t\, L\,\Delta\lambda, \quad \text{ns} \tag{28}$$

Where Δλ is the spectral line-width of the optical source, nm, and L is the length of single-mode fiber waveguide, m. The maximum time division multiplexing (MTDM) transmission bit rate is given by (Kuznetsov et al., 2005).

$$B_{rm} = \frac{1}{4\Delta\tau} = \frac{0.25}{\Delta\tau}, \quad \text{Gbit/s} \tag{29}$$

The optical signal wavelength span 1 μm ≤ λ_{si}, optical signal wavelength≤ 1.65 μm is divided into intervals per link as follows:

$$\Delta\lambda_0 = \frac{\lambda_f - \lambda_i}{N_L} = \frac{0.65}{N_L}, \quad \mu m\,/\,link \tag{30}$$

Then the MTDM bit rates per fiber cable link is given by the following expression:

$$B_{rLink} = \frac{0.25\, x\, N_{ch}}{\Delta\tau}, \quad \text{Gbitsec/link} \tag{31}$$

Where N_{ch} is the number of optical network channels in the fiber cable link, and N_L is the number of links in the fiber cable core and is up to 24 links/core.

RESULTS AND DISCUSSION

The center wavelength at room temperature T_0=27ºC is selected to be λ_0= 1.550918 μm, which is one of the standard wavelengths recommended by the International Telecommunication Union (ITU) (Zhud et al., 2002). This

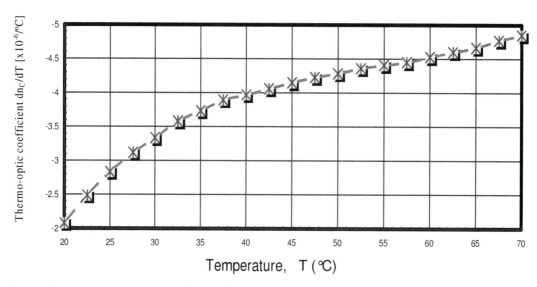

Figure 2. Variation of thermo-optic (TO) coefficient versus temperature when n_1=2.33, n_2=1.52, a= 5 μm.

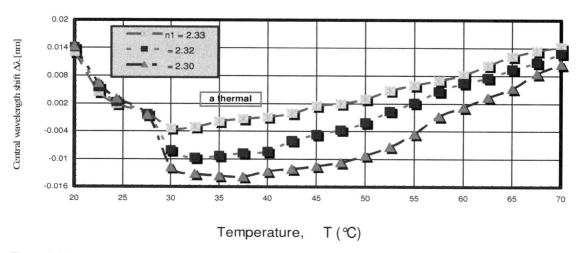

Figure 3. Variation of the central wavelength shift versus temperature for different core refractive-indices.

AWG device is made on the silicon substrate have a coefficient of thermal expansion of α_{sub}= 2.63 × 10^{-6}/ºC (Zhud et al., 2002). Because the environmental temperature of an AWG is usually changed from 20 t0 70ºC. We discuss the central wavelength shift Δλ in this range of temperature variation. The subsequent relations between wavelength shift and refractive-indices of core, and cladding n_1, n_2 as well as the core width are discussed as follows. Also, we discuss the maximum transmission bit rate of AWG device model in the operating wavelength range from 1 μm to 1.64 μm as follows.

Figure 3 has indicated the dependence of the thermo-optic (TO) coefficient dn/dT on the temperature T.

We can find that dn/dT is not constant with the variation of temperature which nonlinearly increases as

temperature increases. Therefore, this behavior of dn/dT will obviously affect the shifts of the central wavelength caused by the variation of temperature.

As shown, Figures 4 to 7 have demonstrated the dependence of the central wavelength shift Δλ on the refractive-indices of the core, and cladding n_1, n_2 as well as the core width for the designed thermal hybrid material AWG, which are calculated from Equation (12). We can find that there exists an optimal operation condition of the AWG, which should guarantee the central wavelength shift Δλ to be small enough in a sufficiently large range of the temperature variation. To be precise, when we select n_1=2.33, n_2=1.52, and a=5 μm, the central wavelength shift is within the range of 0.012 to 0.015 nm as the temperature increases from 20 to 70ºC. In this case, we can presume that the thermalization is realized in the designed AWG.

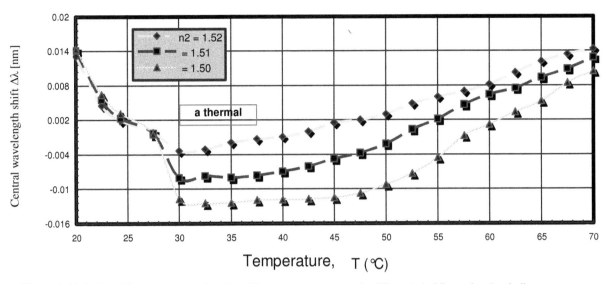

Figure 4. Variation of the central wavelength shift versus temperature for different cladding refractive-indices.

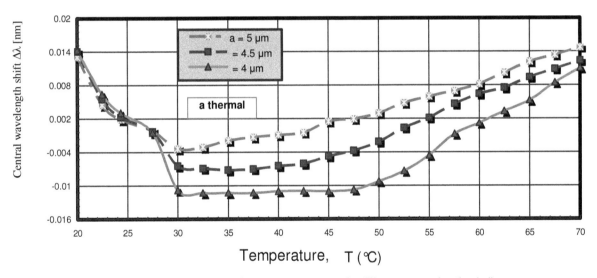

Figure 3. Variation of the central wavelength shift versus temperature for different core refractive-indices.

Figure 7 has demonstrated the variation of the total chromatic dispersion D_t against the variation of optical signal wavelength within the range from 1 to 1.64 µm for different relative refractive-index difference Δn. We can find that the smaller Δn, the smaller $|D_t|$ within the same variation of the optical signal wavelength.

As shown in Figure 8, the variation of the MTDM transmission bit rate, against the variation of optical signal wavelength within the range from 1 to 1.64 µm for different relative refractive-index difference Δn. We can find that the smaller Δn, the larger the bit rate within the same variation of the optical signal wavelength.

Figures 9 and 10 have indicated that as the numbers of links in the fiber cable core increase, MTDM bit rate either per link or per channel increases at the same

relative refractive index difference Δn. While the smaller of Δn, the higher of bit rates either per link or per channel at the same number of links in the fiber cable core.

Figures 10 and 11 have indicated that as the number of links in the fiber cable core increase, MTDM bit rate either per link or per channel increases at the same ambient temperature. While the smaller of T, the slightly higher of bit rates either per link or per channel at the same number of links in the fiber cable core.

Conclusions

We have presented a novel technique for theoretical simulation and optimum design of the A thermal AWG

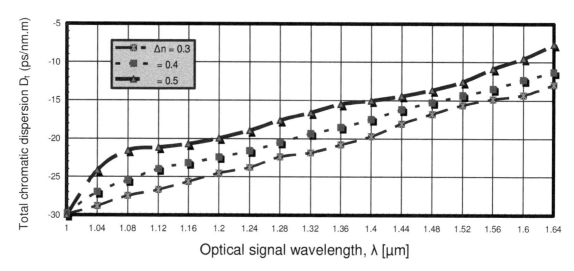

Figure 6. Total chromatic dispersion coefficient versus optical signal wavelength at the assumed set of parameters.

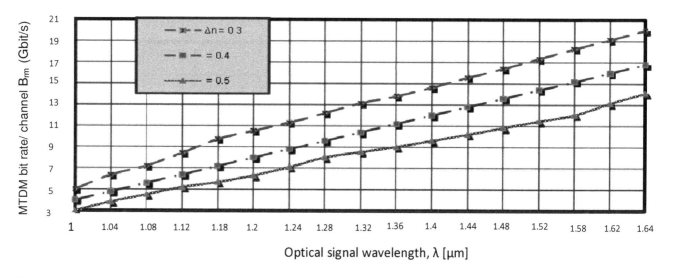

Figure 7. MTDM transmission bit rate/ channel versus optical signal wavelength the assumed set of parameters.

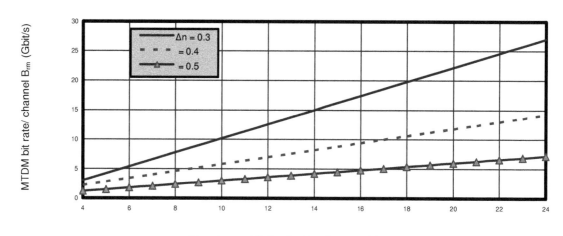

Figure 8. MTDM transmission bit rate/channel versus number of links in the fiber cable core at the assumed set of parameters.

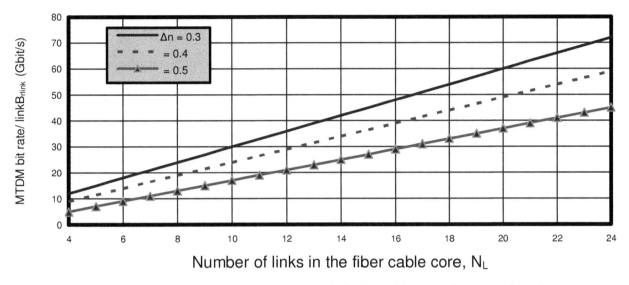

Figure 9. MTDM transmission bit rate/link versus number of links in the fiber cable core at the assumed set of parameters.

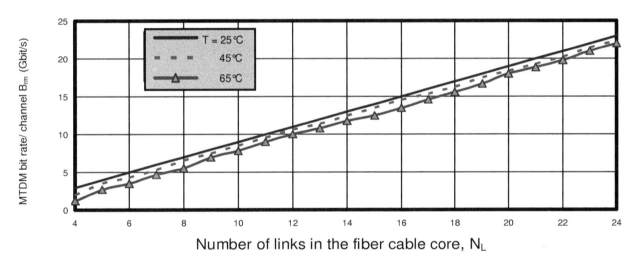

Figure 10. MTDM transmission bit rate/ channel versus number of links in the fiber cable core at the assumed set of parameters.

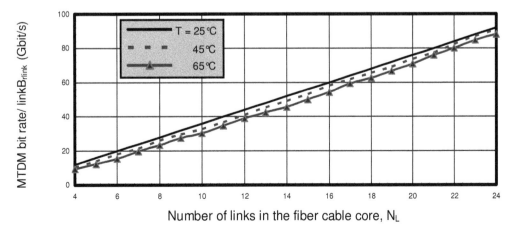

Figure 11. MTDM transmission bit rate/link versus number of links in the fiber cable core at the assumed set of parameters.

with LiNbO$_3$/PMMA hybrid materials. By selecting the proper values of the refractive-indices of the materials and the core size of the waveguide, the a thermalization can be realized. To be precise, the central wavelength shifts of the designed a thermal hybrid material AWG only increases to 0.027 nm/C, while that of the conventional silica-based AWG increases to 0.66 nm/C (Kaneko et al., 2005), our designed a thermal hybrid material AWG showed a good performance with $\Delta\lambda$ = ~ 0.027 nm/C over the temperature range of 20 C to 70ºC. Finally, we can conclude that the smaller Δn, and the lower ambient temperature T, The higher transmission bit rate of our a thermal hybrid material AWG model either per link or per channel which is appropriate for passive optical networks standards.

REFERENCES

Chan TJ, Chan CK, Chen LK, Tong F (2003). A self-Protected Architecture for Wavelength-Division-Multiplexed Passive Optical Networks. IEEE Photon. Technol. Lett., 15: 1660–1662.

Inoue Y, Kaneko A, Hanawa F, Hattori K, Sumida K (2004). A thermal Silica-Based Arrayed-Waveguide Grating Multiplexer. Electron. Lett., 33: 5-7.

Ishigure T, Nihei E, Koike Y (1996). Optimum Refractive Index Profile of The Grade-Index Polymer Optical Fiber, Toward Gigabit Data Link. Appl. Optics, 35: 2048-2053.

Jundt DH (1997). Fabrication Techniques of Lithium Niobate Waveguides. Optics Lett., 22: 1553-1555.

Kaneko A, Kamei S, Inoue Y, Takahashi H (2004). A thermal Silica-Based arrayed Waveguide Grating (AWG) Multi/Demultiplexer With New Low Loss Groove Design. Electronics Lett., 23: 3-5.

Kaneko A, Kamei S, Sugita AA (2005). A thermal Silica-Based Arrayed-Waveguide Grating (AWG) Multi/Demultiplexer With New Low Loss Groove Design. Electron. Lett., 36: 318–319.

Kim HD, Kang S-G, Lee C-H (2000). A low-Cost WDM Source with an ASE Injected Fabry–Pérot Semiconductor Laser. IEEE Photon. Technol. Lett., 12: 1067–1069.

Kokubun Y, Yoneda S, Matsuura S (2003). Temperature-Independent Optical Filter at 1.55 μm Wavelength Using A silica-Based A thermal Waveguide. Electron. Lett. 34: 367–369.

KokubunY, Funato N, Takizawa M (2002). A thermal Waveguide for Temperature-Independent Lightwave Devices. IEEE Photon. Technol. Lett., 5: 1297–1300.

Kuznetsov M, Froberg N, Henlon R, Reinke C, Fennelly C (2005). Dispersion-Induced Power Penalty in Fiber-Bragg-Grating WDM Filter Cascades Using Optically Preamplified and Nonpreamplified Receivers. IEEE Photon. Technol. Lett., 12: 1406-1408.

Lee C-H, Sorin WV, Kim BY (2006a). Fiber to the Home using a PON Infrastructure. J. Lightw. Technol., 24: 4568–4583.

Lee K, SBK, Lim DS, Lee HK, Sorin WV (2006b). Fiber Link Loss Monitoring Scheme in Bidirectional WDM Transmission using ASE-Injected FP-LD. IEEE Photon. Technol. Lett., 18: 523–525.

Ma CS, Qin ZK, Zhang HM (2007). Design of A thermal Arrayed Waveguide Grating (AWG) Using Silica/Polymer Hybrid Materials. Optica Applicata J., XXXVII: 305-312.

Park J, Baik J, Lee C (2007). Fault-Detection Technique in a WDM-PON. Opt. Express., 15: 1461–1466.

Park S-J, Lee C-H, Jeong K-T, Park H-J, Ahn J-G, Song K-H (2004). Fiber-to-the-Home Services Based on Wavelength-Division-Multiplexing Passive Optical Wetwork. J. Lightw. Technol., 22: 2582–2591.

Wang Z, Sun X, Lin C, Chan C-K, Chen LK (2005). A novel Centrally Controlled Protection Scheme for Traffic Restoration in WDM Passive Optical Networks. IEEE Photon. Technol. Lett., 17: 717–719.

Zhud Q, Xu Z, Lu D (2002). An A thermal AWG with hybrid material structure Waveguide. Proc. SPIE, 4904: 5-9.

21

Investigation of self-similar nature of video streaming traffic in corporate network

Shalangwa D. A.[1] and Malgwi D. I.[2]

[1]Department of Physics, Adamawa State University, Mubi, Adamawa State, Nigeria.
[2]Department of Physics, University of Maiduguri, Borno State, Nigeria.

In this work, a model of the corporate network had been developed, simulated and implemented using an optimized network engineering tool in a simulation area of 1.5 × 1.5 km enterprise topology network to stream video between each other. Total of 14,670 video traffic (traffic load) is streamed from different sources and destinations at random. The video streaming traffic is monitored, analyzed in view of identifying traffic self-similarity in the network. The results of the analysis show that video traffic is highly self-similar in the network using Abry-Veitch and smoothing algorithms method. The effect of self-similarity in the network is reduced with the help of 1D wavelet technique.

Key words: Smoothing algorithms, video, traffic, optimized network engineering tools (OPNET), self-similar.

INTRODUCTION

Today, the increasing demand in telecommunication service make the structure of network traffic very complex more especially with the introduction of multimedia service such as audio and video streaming over IP network in addition to the traditional web browsing, file transfer protocol, email and so on. Due these massive demands it is then predicted that traffic in most telecommunication network becomes inherently self-similar in nature. Traffic monitoring is a very difficult task because one would not know exactly when input characteristics will change (Karagiannis et al., 2002). Unfortunately they are limited mathematical model to capture the traffic behavior while traffic volume continuous to grow in its exponential form.

When we want to study traffic of all kinds in telecommunication network usually question of constructing a model of input characteristics (volume of the traffic) arises. However, to design a suitable model for any network and to develop fast algorithms of free flow of

information across a network from source to destination, understanding network traffic become a critical issue because the fundamental aim of network monitoring is to deliver an outstanding quality of service to the end user with little or no interference.

Many researches in this field show that in general, telecommunication traffic are self-similar or fractal in nature (Adas, 1997; Chaoming, 2005; John, 1981; Oleg et al., 2007; Nikolai, 1995; Nagurney, 2008; Walter, 1997) been global system for mobile communication [GSM], GPRS or Ethernet. The presence of self-similarity in a network may be associated with amplified queing delay, packet loss rate, bottle neck or affect buffer capability (Beryes, 2007; Hamibindu et al., 2007).

In order to investigate the presence of self-similarity in our developed simulated network model, we imposed high-resolution video traffic statistics and we monitored video streaming traffic for several minutes. The behavior of internet traffic is usually time dependent and they are

Table 1. Simulation metrice parameter.

Simulation size	1.5 × 1.5 km
Traffic monitored	Video
Simulation time	30 min
Application configuration setting	High-resolution Video
2 LANs	3 host users each

Table 2. Sample statistics of all the observations for video streaming.

	Sample mean(s)	Min value(s)	Max value(s)	Range
All Observations	1 4,670 145.25	0	121	121

usually considered being long range dependence (LRD) while self-similar behavior of network traffic is best described in terms of long range dependence and autocorrelation function of the time series (Guaghui et al., 2004; Karagiannis et al., 2002).

There are various popular methods in which self-similar nature of internet traffic can be identified for example using time-variable plot, periodogram, ratio variance residuals, wavelet, absolute moment, whittle, and R/S method. While in this work we used two techniques to check the presence of self-similarity in our simulated network model. That is log plot of Abry-Veitch and smoothing algorithms while in second method we closely observed the autocorrelation function (ACF) and fast Fourier transform energy spectrum behavior to validate our results.

This work considers two separate corporate networks located at a remote locations to each other with at least three host users in each corporate network streaming video to one another.

IMPLEMENTATION OF THE SIMULATION MODEL

An optimized network engineering tools (OPNET) is used to realize the entire structure of the network in a simulation area of 1.5 km × 1.5 km enterprise topology network. The simulation model is first created using a startup wizard. The topology of each corporate network is then created. The required number of the nodes is dragged into the empty space base on number of nodes required per corporate network, then the nodes fields are adjusted as follows to enable them stream video to each other. The application configuration attribute is set to video to enable us stream video across the network, profile configuration attribute is also set to match with application configuration attribute while the personal computer attributes at each corporate network are set to support the profile as given in the simulation matrices parameter of Table 1.

Collection of statistics

In OPNET, there are two major statistics available that is global statistics and nodes statistics; global statistics tell us about the statistics of the entire network while node statistics tell us about the statistics of an individual node. Appropriate statistics are ther imposed on the model. Simulation is run, and the result is taking.

Mathematical relationship between LRD and self-similarity

If we assume X (t) is a second order stochastic stationary process. Let's consider $\beta(x)$, $\rho(x)$ be the ACF and spectrum of the second order stochastic stationary process. There is a close relationship that exist between LRD and self-similarity given by:

$$\beta = 2H - 1 \text{ when } \frac{1}{2} < H < 1 \text{ is valid}$$

$$\beta x(p) \_ k_\beta |p|^{-\infty} \text{ as } |p| \quad where \ \infty \in (0,1)$$

$$\rho x(q) \_ k_\rho |q|^{-|1-\infty|} \text{ as } |q| \quad where \ \infty \in (0,1)$$

$\beta x(p)$ Usually goes to zero slowly called LRD;

If Z(t) is said to be self-similar If and only if $k^{-H} Z(kt) = Z(t)$, $when \ k > 0$

RESULTS AND DISCUSSION

The result given in Table 2, is video streaming for the length of simulation assumed to be the same with video streaming data traffic in real life network as shown in Figure 1 shows the video streamed data traffic for the length of the simulation, on the vertical axis is the video traffic sent in packet per second against time in second on the horizontal axis. It seems that slightly close to 60 s no packet is transmitted thereafter the video packets were transmitted continuously with an increase in packets, slightly above 60 s, the packets exhibit stochastic stationary behavior. Stochastic stationary process is one of condition of suspecting self-similarity in a network (Higuchin, 1988). Figure 2 present log plot of the video data traffic; for the process to be LRD the logscale plot will exhibit a region where by the log scale plot will be approximately linear with time axis while remain constant with the video traffic axis then the H

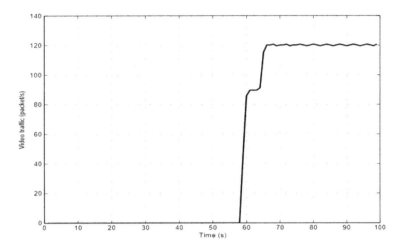

Figure 1. Video streamed data traffic.

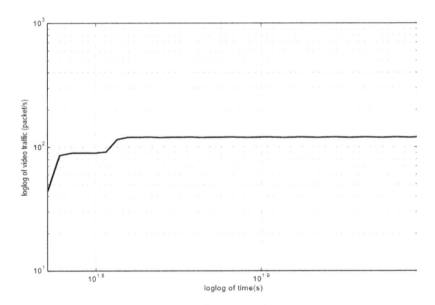

Figure 2. Loglog plot of video data traffic streamed.

exponent can be estimated from logscale plot by $\{H=(slope+1)/2\}$ (Abry et al., 1998). The slope is calculated as 14.32 while the Hurst exponent is evaluated as 7.66; this evident that in this work video data traffic is highly self-similar considering the fact that for traffic in the network to become self-similar Hurst exponent must falls within $0.5<H<1$; the degree of the self-similarity increases as H get close to 1 (Oleg et al., 2007).

In the second method, we used smoothing algorithms. Smoothing algorithms has shown sufficient performance over different sets of data (Umer et al., 2008). Having known that the process is stochastic stationary, we then apply the smoothing algorithms technique; this technique involve different decomposition and reconstruction levels of a signal (video data traffic) using 1D wavelet (Rami, 2011) also taking into consideration ACF which is believed, that its coefficient decay slowly to zero with

LRD which describe the intensity of self-similarity in network (Karim, 2007). Next we decomposed, de-noised and reconstructed the stochastic stationary video data traffic step by step up to 5 levels using db 10 wavelet type to validate the ACF and FFT energy spectrum property as given in Figure 3 to 5. When a process is decomposed and reconstructed up to 5 levels it means the process is highly LRD because the maximum decomposition and reconstruction level of db wavelet type is 7; the higher the level of the decomposition and reconstruction stronger the LRD as well as self-similarity (Xiaomo et al., 2004).

In Figure 3 the ACF coefficient is almost zero, FFT has less energy indicating strong relationship with LRD, Figure 4, ACF coefficient move slightly from zero. FFT energy increases showing a decrease in relationship with LRD while Figure 5, ACF coefficient increase significantly,

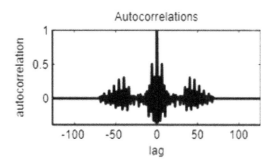

Figure 3a. ACF after level 1 reconstruction.

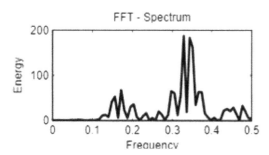

Figure 3b. FFT after level 1 reconstruction.

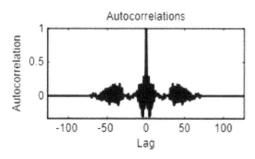

Figure 4a. ACF after level 3 reconstruction.

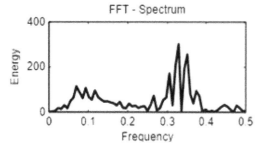

Figure 4b. FFT after level 3 reconstruction.

FFT energy increase tremendously showing poor relationship with LRD as well as self-similarity. Figure 6 present the original data traffic and de-noised data traffic assuming the LRD and self-similarity are not applicable

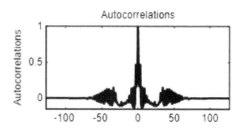

Figure 5a. ACF after level 5 reconstruction.

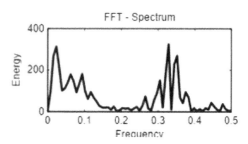

Figure 5b. FFT after level 5 reconstruction.

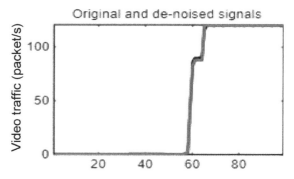

Figure 6. Original and de-noised video traffic data.

to the network. Therefore, it is expected that minimal delay, packet loss, packet retransmission and high buffer capacity will be the feature of the simulated network.

Conclusion

A video traffic had been monitored, analyzed in a model of simulated network developed with a view of checking presence of self-similarity in the network using Abry-Veitch and smoothing algorithms method. Both methods revealed that video traffic is highly LRD and self-similar. The presences of self-similarity in any telecommunication network change the characteristics or behavior of the network by affecting the overall network quality of service (QoS). This work is centered on checking and reducing self-similar properties of network, but does not take into consideration the causes of self-similarity in the network. Hope this work has provided some basic information on how to investigate self-similarity of video traffic in telecommunication network and reduce its effects. Further recommends that another research work should be conducted to identify the causes of the self-similar process in telecommunication network.

Conflict of Interests

The author(s) have not declared any conflict of interests.

REFERENCES

Abry P, Veitch D (1998). Wavelet analysis of long range dependence traffic. IEEE Trans. Inf. Theory 44(1):2-15. http://dx.doi.org/10.1109/18.650984

Adas A (1997). Traffic models in broadband network. IEEE Communication Magazine. http://dx.doi.org/10.1109/35.601746

Beyers D (2007). Packet radio network research, development and application.Proceeding SHAPE Conference on packet radio, Amsterdam.

Chaoming S, Shlomo H, Hernan AM (2005). Self-Similarity of complex network. Nature. 433:392. http://dx.doi.org/10.1038/nature03248

Hamibindu P, Ying Z, Morley ZM, Charlie YH (2007). Understanding network delay changes by routing events. Proceeding of ACM SIGMETRICS.

Higuchin T (1988). Approach to an irregular time series on the basis of the fractal theory. Physica B. 30:277-283. http://www.sciencedirect.com/science/article/pii/0167278988900814

John EH (1981). Fractal and self-similarity. J. Math. Univ. Indiana 30(5):713-747. http://dx.doi.org/10.1512/iumj.1981.30.30055

Karagiannis T, Faloutsos M, Riedi RH (2002). Long range dependence: Now you see it, now you don't. IEEE Global Internet.

Karim MR (2007). Identifying long range dependence of network traffic through autocorrelation function. Proceeding of 32nd Annual Conference on Local Computer Network pp. 15-18.

Nagurney A, Qiang Q (2007). A Network efficiency measure for congested network. Europhys. Lett. 79(38005):1-5. http://supernet.isenberg.umass.edu/articles/nagurney-epl_final.pdf

Nikolai L, Boris T (1995). An analysis of an ATM buffer with self-similarity (fractal) input traffic 14th Annual IEEE Conference. http://www.psu.edu/

Oleg IS, Sergey MS, Andrey VO (2007). Self-similar process in Telecommunications. John Wiley and Sons, Ltd.

Rami C (2011). Signal denoising using wavelets. Project report. http://tx.technion.ac.il/~rc/SignalDenoisingUsingWavelets_RamiCohen.pdf

Umer H, Mohammed SA (2008). Statistical properties of white. LUMS School of Science Engineering.

Walter W, Murad ST, Robert S, Daniel VW (1997). Self-Similarity through high-variability: Statistical analysis of Ethernet LAN traffic at the source level. IEEE Trans. 5(1):71-86.

Xiaomo J, Hojjat A (2004). Wavelet packet autocorrelation method for traffic flow pattern analysis. Computer Aided Civil Inf. Eng. 19:327-337.

22

Computational screening of ionic liquids as solvents for reprocessing of spent nuclear fuel

Yusuf A. Z.[1] , Zakir A.[2], Mustapha S. I.[3], Halima S. A.[3] and Nuhu M.[3]

[1]Nigerian National Petroleum Cooperation (NNPC), Nigeria.
[2]Human Physiology Department, Ahmadu Bello University Zaria.
[3]Chemical Engineering Department, Ahmadu Bello University Zaria.

COSMO-RS method was used in screening 2106 ionic liquids as alternate solvents to volatile n-dodecane used in PUREX. The distribution coefficients of uranylnitrate in ionic liquids/aqueous nitric acid biphasic system and the solubility of the ionic liquids in water were determined using COSMO-RS. Seventeen ionic liquids based on tetrafluoroborate BF_4, were the most hydrophobic than others screened with hexamethylguanidiumtetrafluoroborate having the highest distribution coefficient. Their distribution coefficients were higher than that of the convention n-dodecane used for separation of uranium and plutonium from spent nuclear fuel but having more hydrophilicity than n-dodecane. This shows that ionic liquids can be used as alternate solvents in PUREX.

Key words: Ionic liquids, spent nuclear fuel (SNF), conductor-like screening model (COSMO-RS), Plutonium uranium extraction (PUREX), COSMOtherm, n-dodecane, n-tributylphosphate (TBP).

INTRODUCTION

The products contained in SNF are radioactive with half-lives from days to millions of years which give a lot of threat to human health and environment (Terry, 2008). Uranium and Plutonium are conventionally recovered through PUREX process. PUREX, an abbreviation for Plutonium (P) Uranium (UR) Extraction (EX), makes use of about 30% tri-n-butyl phosphate (TBP) with Kerosene or pure n-Dodecaneas diluents (Sung et al., 2010). In this process, Uranium and Plutonium are extracted as UO_2^{2+} and Pu^{4+} and then converted to UO_2 and PuO_2. Aside from uranium and plutonium, various fission products can be recovered from SNF. Thus some extraction processes have been developed using different extracting agents to recover fission products from PUREX raffinate. The extraction processes developed for SNF treatment and recovery, utilize organic solvents that are volatile, hazardous, toxic, flammable, and unstable towards the radiation and heat generated by the SNF (Sung et al., 2010). Since the undesirable properties of these conventional solvents may pose several threats and problems both to plant operation and to environment, several researches are ongoing in search of alternate safer solvents such as ionic liquids (ILs) which have unique physical and chemical properties, such as specific solvent abilities, negligible vapor pressures, non flammability, thermal and radiological stability and broad liquid temperature ranges among many. They have led to promising applications as environmentally benign solvents that can be possible candidates to replace conventional organic solvents (Sung et al., 2010).

During the past 10 years, ionic liquids (ILs) have received increased attention. They are organic salts, and their chemical and physical properties can be tailored by the selection of an anion and cation (Wasserscheid, 2000). Therefore, it is possible to generate a huge number of different ionic liquids, each with specific properties. Despite the interest, accurate thermodynamic data of ionic liquids and their mixtures are still rare and to exploit the potential of these new substances, it would be of great value to have prediction methods that can reliably predict the thermodynamic properties of ionic liquids and their mixtures. This would help to scan the growing set of already known ILs in order to find suitable candidates for a certain task or to design new ILs for special applications (Geetanjali and Kumar, 2008). Group contribution methods, which are the most widely used theoretical models are not applicable because group interactions parameters are not available at present for ionic liquids and the group contribution concept is not suitable to handle the long-range interactions in ionic compounds (Hamad and Sumon, 2008). Monte Carlo simulations and molecular dynamics need appropriate force-fields for the treatment of ionic liquids, which have to be developed (Hamad and Sumon, 2008). This work will present the application of a continuum solvation based thermodynamic prediction model, Conductor-like Screening Model for Real Solvents, COSMO-RS for prediction of thermo-physical data which is a computational approach independent of experimental data and with general applicability (Eckert and Klamt, 2002).

The aim of the research is to computationally screen suitable hydrophobic ionic liquids as solvents for the extraction of Uranium from spent nuclear fuel using COSMO –RS method by determining the distribution coefficients of uranyl nitrate in hydrophobic ionic liquids/ aqueous nitric acid biphasic solution and determination the solubilityof the ionic liquids in water. The work will be limited to the application of COSMO-RS, a thermodynamic model which uses statistical thermodynamic approach in determination of thermodynamic properties based on results obtained from quantum chemical/COSMO computation for the screening of ionic liquids for Uranium Extraction from spent nuclear fuel.

MATERIALS AND METHODS

The following are the materials used in carrying out the research work:

a) System Softwares
i) Linux operating system
ii) Windows 7 operating system

b) Application Softwares
i) Chem draw 3D ultra 8.0/ Marvin sketch software.
ii) TURBOMOLE 5.6 Program Package (LINUX VERSION).
iii) COSMOthermSoftware.

The following are the methods used in carrying out the research work:

1) The Marvin sketch software is first used in sketching the structure of each individual molecule. The environment has a drawing kit including all elements in the periodic table and heterocyclic structures for easy sketch of the molecular structures. Marvin sketch software operates on windows. The file generated is saved in xyz format and is used as an input file for TURBOMOLE to perform the quantum chemical/COSMO calculation.

2) The TURBOMOLE uses the xyz file generated from Marvin sketch to perform quantum chemical/COSMO calculation to generate the screening charge densities of the molecules. The screening charge is a microscopic property of a molecule like internal energy and it is the main parameter used in the COSMO-RS model. The quantum chemical/COSMO computation on TURBOMOLE 5.6 is parameterized using DFT-level of computation utilizing BP-functional on TZVP basis set. The file is saved as a COSMO file and an input file to COSMOtherm to perform the statistical thermodynamics and to determine the screening charge density profiles and chemical potentials of the individual molecules (Klamt, 1995). The higher the specification of the computer machine, the faster the computation of the screening charges of the molecules.

3) A database is created for all the COSMO files generated using the TURBOMOLE program software.

4) The screening charge density profiles and the chemical potentials of the molecules are determined using COSMOtherm. The COSMOtherm is the software that solves the COSMO-RS model based on self consistency field algorithm (SCF) to statistically determine the screening charge density profiles and the chemical potentials of the molecules (Klamt, 1995).

5) The 81 cations and 26 anions were combined to generate 2106 ionic liquids (Table 1).

6) The solubility of the ionic liquids in water is determined from COSMOtherm using the equation;

$$Log_{10} (x_j^{sol}) = [\mu_j^{(p)} - \mu_j^{(t)} - max(0, \Delta G_{fus})] / (RT \ln(10))$$

Where ΔG_{fus} is the heat of fusion per mole. If the compound is solid, the energy change of a compound from the super cooled liquid state to the ordered solid state has to be taken into account, that is, the solutes Gibbs free energy of fusion ΔG_{fus} (or equivalently its Gibbs free energy of crystallization $\Delta G_{cryst} = -\Delta G_{fus}$) has to be either given and computed from experimental data or estimated by COSMOtherm. For a liquid, it is automatically specified but for solids it has to be determined using QSPR and then specified manually.
T = Temperature in degree Celsius
R = molar gas constant in KJ/mol/Kelvin
$\mu_j^{(i)}$ = chemical potential of solute j in solvent i in energy/mole
$\mu_j^{(P)}$ = chemical potential of pure compound j in energy/mole
x_j = mole fraction of the solubility of solutes in water (dimensionless).

7) The distribution coefficient and octanol-water partition coefficients are determined from COSMOtherm using the equation:

$$Log_{10} (p) = Log_{10}[exp(\mu_j^{(1)} - \mu_j^{(t)})] / RT) . V_1/V_2)$$

Where v_1 and v_2 are volume quotients of phase 1 and phase 2
$\mu_j^{(1)}$ = chemical potential of uranyl nitrate in phase 1 in energy/mole
$\mu_j^{(2)}$ = chemical potentials of uranyl nitrate in phase 2 in energy/mole
P = partition coefficient (dimensionless).

Table 1. List of cations and anions.

S/N	Cations		
1	1,1-dimethyl-pyrrolidinium	42	methyl-trioctyl-ammonium
2	1,1-dipropyl-pyrrolidinium	43	tetra-methyl ammonium
3	1-ethyl-1-methyl-pyrrolidinium	44	tetra-ethyl ammonium
4	1-butyl-1-methyl-pyrrolidinium	45	tetra-n-butyl ammonium
5	1-butyl-1-ethyl-pyrrolidinium	46	benzyl-triphenyl-phosphonium
6	1-hexyl-1-methyl-pyrrolidinium	47	tetrabutyl-phosphonium
7	1-octyl-1-methyl-pyrrolidinium	48	trihexyl-tetradecyl-phosphonium
8	3-methyl-imidazolium	49	triisobutyl-methyl-phosphonium
9	1-butyl-imidazolium	50	guanidinium
10	1,3-dimethyl-imidazolium	51	hexamethylguanidinium
11	1-ethyl-3-methyl-imidazolium	52	N,N,N,N,N-pentamethyl-N-isopropyl-guanidinium
12	1-butyl-3-methyl-imidazolium	53	N,N,N,N,N-pentamethyl-N-propyl-guanidinium
13	1-pentyl-3-methyl-imidazolium	54	N,N,N,N-tetramethyl-N-ethylguanidinium
14	1-hexyl-3-methyl-imidazolium	55	S-ethyl-N,N,N,N-tetramethylisothiouronium
15	1-octyl-3-methyl-imidazolium	56	O-ethyl-N,N,N,N-tetramethylisouronium
16	1-decyl-3-methyl-imidazolium	57	O-methyl-N,N,N,N-tetramethylisouronium
17	1-dodecyl-3-methyl-imidazolium	58	N-butyl-isoquinolinium
18	1-tetradecyl-3-methyl-imidazolium	59	morpholinium
19	1-hexadecyl-3-methyl-imidazolium	60	methylmorpholinium
20	1-octadecyl-3-methyl-imidazolium	61	dimethylmorpholinium
21	1-benzyl-3-methyl-imidazolium	62	N-fluoropropoxy-methylmorpholinium
22	1-ethyl-2-3-methyl-imidazolium	63	O-ethyl-tetrapropylisouronium
23	1-propyl-2-3-methyl-imidazolium	64	O-hydro-tetraethylisouronium
24	1-butyl-2-3-methyl-imidazolium	65	O-hydro-tetramethylisouronium
25	1-hexyl-2-3-methyl-imidazolium	66	O-methyl-tetraethylisouronium
26	1-hexadecyl-2-3-methyl-imidazolium	67	O-methyl-tetrapropylisouronium
27	1-methyl-3-(3-phenyl-propyl)-imidazolium	68	O-propyl-tetramethylisouronium
28	4-methyl-n-butylpyridinium	69	O-propyl-tetrapropylisouronium
29	1-ethyl-pyridinium	70	O-butyl-tetramethylisouronium
30	1-butyl-pyridinium	71	O-ethyl-tetraethylisouronium
31	1-hexyl-pyridinium	72	diethyl-dimethylammonium
32	1-octyl-pyridinium	73	dimethylammonium
33	1-butyl-3-ethyl-pyridinium	74	ethyl-trimethylammonium
34	1-butyl-3-methyl-pyridinium	75	methyl-triethylammonium
35	1-butyl-4-methyl-pyridinium	76	tetra-ethyl ammonium
36	1-hexyl-3-methyl-pyridinium	77	tetramethylammonium
37	1-hexyl-4-methyl-pyridinium	78	trimethylammonium
38	3-methyl-1-octyl-pyridinium	79	n-methyldiazabicyclo-undec-7-enium
39	4-methyl-1-octyl-pyridinium	80	n-ethyldiazabicyclo-undec-7-enium
40	1-butyl-3,4-dimethyl-pyridinium	81	n-hexyldiazabicyclo-undec-7-enium
41	1-butyl-3,5-dimethyl-pyridinium		

S/N	Anions		
1	Tetrafluoroborate	14	bissalicylatoborate
2	Hexafluorophosphate (vi)	15	tetracyanoborate
3	methyl sulfate	16	bis(2,4,4-trimethylpentyl)phosphinate
4	chlorate	17	bis-pentafluoroethyl-phosphinate
5	bromate	18	bis(trifluoromethylsulfonyl)methane
6	Iodide	19	decanoate
7	formate	20	tosylate

Table 1. Contd.

8	toluene-4-sulfonate	21	bis(pentafluoroethylsulfonyl)imide
9	trifluoromethane-sulfonate	22	n-methyl-n-butylcarbamate
10	tris(nonafluorobutyl)trifluorophosphate	23	n-methyl-n-propylcarbamate
11	tris(pentafluoroethyl)trifluorophosphate	24	Nitrate
12	bisbiphenyldiolatoborate	25	Thiocyanate
13	bisoxalatoborate	26	Methylphosphonate

Post processing

From the properties determined, criteria for the selection of suitable ionic liquids were imposed. These are based on the following criteria;

Hydrophobicity

Out of the 2106 ionic liquids, those with mole fraction solubility of 1 are considered hydrophilic while those with mole fraction solubility of zero are considered as hydrophobic ionic liquids.

Comparable partition coefficient with n-dodecane

Those ionic liquids with distribution coefficient greater than or equal to that of n-dodecane were recommended for screening. Similarly, those with solubility mole fraction of less than 1 are considered partially miscible with water while those with solubility mole fraction of 1 are considered fully miscible with water (hydrophilic). Those ionic liquids that satisfy criteria 1 and 2 were recommended. Using these criteria, 111 ionic liquids were screened out of the in the database. 17 ionic liquids based on BF_4 are the most hydrophobic. The 17 ionic liquids are given below:

1) 1,1-dimethyl-pyrrolidinium tetrafluoroborate
2) 1-ethyl-1-methyl-pyrrolidinium tetrafluoroborate
3) tetra-ethylammoniumtetrafluoroborate
4) hexamethylguanidiniumtetrafluoroborate
5) N,N,N,N,N-pentamethyl-N-isopropyl-guanidiniumtetrafluoroborate
6) N,N,N,N,N-pentamethyl-N-propyl-guanidiniumtetrafluoroborate
7) S-ethyl-N,N,N,N-tetramethylisothiouroniumtetrafluoroborate
8) O-ethyl-N,N,N,N-tetramethylisouroniumtetrafluoroborate
9) O-methyl-N,N,N,N-tetramethylisouroniumtetrafluoroborate
10) O-methyl-tetraethylisouroniumtetrafluoroborate
11) O-propyl-tetramethylisouroniumtetrafluoroborate
12) O-butyl-tetramethylisouroniumtetrafluoroborate
13) O-ethyl-tetraethylisouroniumtetrafluoroborate
14) methyl-triethylammoniumtetrafluoroborate
15) n-methyldiazabicyclo-undec-7-eniumtetrafluoroborate
16) n-ethyldiazabicyclo-undec-7-eniumtetrafluoroborate
17) tetra-methylammoniumtetrafluoroborate

RESULTS AND DISCUSSION

Data validation of solubility

The experimental solubility in water values of some solvents determined was compared with that of COSMO-RS method. The correlation factor obtained was 0.994 which shows a good correlation between the experimental and that of the model. This is a validation of the model for determination of solubility of compounds in water. Figure 1 gives the comparison between the experimental and the model results. The experimental results were obtained from Laurie (2004) and Felicia et al. (2009).

Evaluation of the distribution coefficient and solubility of n-dodecane and the screened ILs

The distribution coefficient of uranylnitrate in n-dodecane /aqueous nitric acid biphasic system and that of uranylnitrate in ionic liquids/aqueous nitric acid biphasic system was determined using COSMO-RS method. The solubility of the n-dodecane and ionic liquids in water was also determined to determine the hydrophobicity of the ionic liquids and the n-dodecane. As shown in Figure 2, the solubility of n-dodecane in water is 0.0072 and is the most hydrophobic among the solvents and this gives its advantage of easier recycle and recovery. This is because the more hydrophobic the solvent is, the better the separation with the aqueous phase. Among the ionic liquids screened, 17 of them are the most hydrophobic closest to n-dodecane with solubility mole fraction of less than 0.1. Although they have comparable or higher distribution coefficient with the conventional solvent, n-dodecane. The advantage of higher distribtution coefficient is the use of less number of stages during continuous extraction. It can also be seen that some ionic liquids give high distribution coefficient but more miscible with water. It has been reported that hydrophilic ionic liquids forms complex with uranyl nitrate via anionic and cationic complexes with contamination of the aqueous phase and this is a limitation in the application of these types of ionic liquids for this application despite the high distribution coefficient (Binnemans, 2007). Hydrophobic ionic liquids on the other hand, forms complex via neutral complexes without contamination of the aqueous phase (Binnemans, 2007).

Effect of nitric acid concentration

Nitric acid concentration affects the distribution coefficient

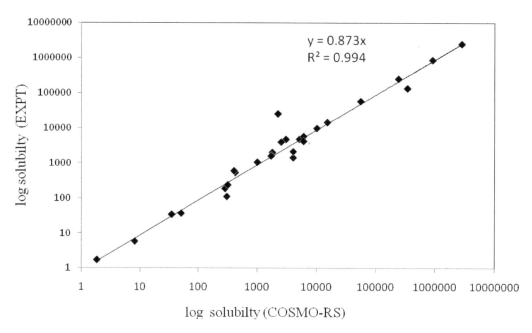

Figure 1. Comparison of experimental solubility values against COSMO-RS.

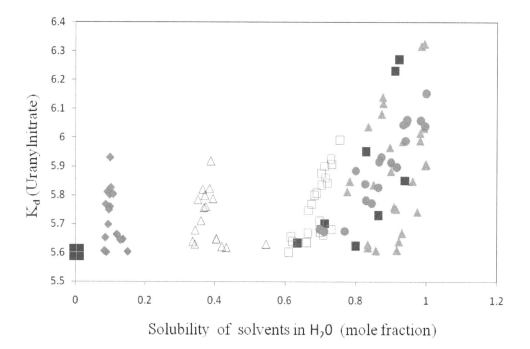

Figure 2. K_d (Uranyl nitrate) against the solubility of solvents in water.
◆ Bf$_4$ based ILs   △ TF$_2$N based ILs   ● Thiocyanate based ILs
■ Iodo based ILs   ☐ pentafluoroethylphosphinate based ILs
▲ Methylsulfate based ILs   ■ n-dodecane (Reference Solvent).

of the uranyl nitrate in the ionic liquid/aqueous nitric acid biphasic system as can be seen in Figure 3. The distribution coefficient increases with increase in nitric acid concentration from 0.2 to 4 molar and then slightly decreases to 8 molar. This is because with increase in nitric acid concentration, the solubility of the solute in the

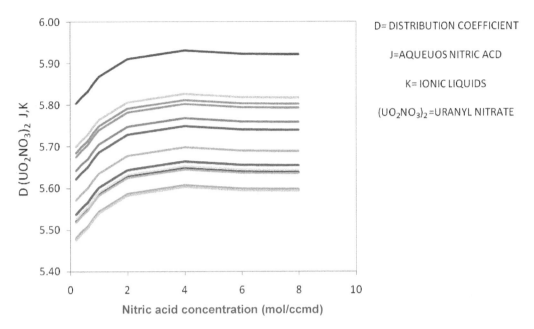

Figure 3. Effect of nitric acid concentration on the D $(UO_2NO_3)_2$ J, K of the 17 selected ionic liquids.

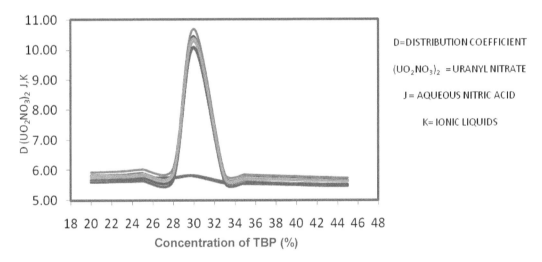

Figure 4. Effect of TBP concentration on the D $(UO_2NO_3)_2$ J, K of the selected ionic liquids.

aqueous phase decreases as a result of poor coordination of the nitrate ions with the uranyl nitrate while its solubility in the ionic liquid phase increases. Conversely, the solubility of the solute increases with the increase in nitric acid concentration as a result of its good coordination with the nitrate ions.

Effect of TBP concentration on distribution coefficient

TBP is the universally accepted extractant used in the PUREX process for the extraction of uranium and plutonium from spent nuclear fuel. It forms complex with elements at the +vi and +iv oxidation states. Uranium with the most stable oxidation state of +vi forms complex with the TBP while plutonium at the +iv oxidation state also forms complex with the TBP. They are extracted together to the organic phase and then separated to obtain uranium and plutonium. As shown in Figure 4, the distribution coefficient of uranyl nitrate in ionic liquids/aqueous nitric acid biphasic system, increases with increase in TBP concentration from 20 to 30% and then decreases with increase in TBP concentration from

30 to 45%. The maximum distribution coefficient is obtained at 30% TBP concentration. This is also reported by Binnemans (2007) that optimum distribution coefficient is obtained at 30% TBP concentration from the range of percentage application of the TBP concentration from 20 to 40%.

Conclusion

1) There are many potential ionic liquids that display higher distribution coefficient than n-dodecane.

2) 17 ionic liquids based on BF_4 are the most recommended hydrophobic ionic liquids of the 111 screened.

3) Tributyl-phosphate TBP has effect on thedistribution coefficient. The highest distribution coefficient is obtained at 30% TBP by volume and four (4) molar concentration trioxonitric (vi) acid.

4) The effect of temperature with the distribution coefficients was also investigated. The distribution coefficients of all the ionic liquids/nitric acid biphasic system were decreasing with temperature from 25 to 100°C.

REFERENCES

Binnemans K (2007).Lanthanides and Actinides Chemistry in ionic liquids. Chem.Rev.

Eckert F, Klamt A (2002). Fast solvent screening via quantum chemistry COSMO-RS approach. AIChE J. 48(2):369.

Felicia S, Alice M, Petre I, Adrian B, Titus C, Alexandru T B (2009). New alternatives for estimating the Octanol/water partition coefficient and water solubility for volatile organic compounds using GLC data (Kovàts retention indices). ARKIVOC (10):174-194.

Hamad EM, Sunon KZ (2008). Computational screening of ionic liquids for aromatic extraction using COSMO-RS.

Klamt A (1995). Conductor-like Screening Model for Real Solvents: A New Approach to the Quantitative Calculation of Solvation Phenomena. J. Phys. Chem. 99:2224.

Sung HH, Russel MN, Yoon MK (2010). Reprocessing of spent nuclear fuel using ionic liquid. Korean J. Chem. Eng. 27950:1360-1365

Wasserscheid P, Keim W (2000). Ionic liquids - New solutions for transition metal catalysis. Angew. Chem.-Int. Edit. 39(21):3773-3789.

23

A comparative study of meta-heuristics for identical parallel machines

M.O. Adamu[1] and A. Adewunmi[2]

[1]Department of Mathematics, University of Lagos, Lagos, Nigeria.
[2]School of Computer Science, University of Kwazulu-Natal, Durban, South Africa.

This paper considers the scheduling problem of minimizing the weighted number of early and tardy jobs on identical parallel machines, $Pm||\sum w_j(U_j + V_j)$. This problem is known to be NP complete and finding an optimal solution is unlikely. Six meta-heuristics including hybrids are proposed for solving the problem. The meta-heuristics considered are genetic algorithm, particle swarm optimization and simulated annealing with their hybrids. A comparative study that involves computational experiments and statistical analysis are presented evaluating these algorithms. The results of the research are very promising.

Key words: Parallel machine, heuristics, just-in-time, meta-heuristics, NP-complete.

INTRODUCTION

Scheduling Just-In-Time (JIT) jobs is of great importance in both manufacturing and service industries. Production wastages are reduced and profitability is improved when JIT is applied. Its application cuts across medical, machine environment, distribution network and other environments. In this paper, we consider the comparative study of various heuristics for scheduling weighted jobs on identical parallel machines. The objective is to minimize the weighted number of early and tardy jobs on identical parallel machines.

During the past few decades, a considerable amount of work has been done on scheduling on multiple machines to minimize the number of tardy jobs (Adamu and Adewunmi, 2012b) and on single machine (Adamu and Adewunmi, 2012c). Garey and Johnson (1979) have shown our problem to be NP-complete and finding an optimal solution appears unlikely. Using the three-field notation of Graham et al. (1979), the problem is represented as $Pm||\sum w_j(U_j + V_j)$. Scheduling to minimize the (weighted) number of tardy jobs have been considered by Ho and Chang (1995), Süer et al. (1993), Süer (1997), Süer et al. (1997), Van der Akker (1999),

Chen and Powell (1999), Liu and Wu (2003), and M'Hallah and Bulfin (2005). Sevaux and Thomin (2001) addressed the NP-hard problem to minimize the weighted number of late jobs with release time $(P|r_j|\sum w_jU_j)$. They presented several approaches for the problem including two MILP formulations for exact resolution and various heuristics and meta-heuristics to solve large size instances. They compared their results to that of Baptiste et al. (2000) which performed averagely better. Baptiste et al. (2000) used a constraint based method to explore the solution space and give good results on small problems (n < 50). Dauzère-Pérès and Sevaux (1999) determined conditions that must be satisfied by at least one optimal sequence for the problem of minimizing the weighted number of late jobs on a single machine. Sevaux and Sörensen (2005) proposed a variable neighbourhood search (VNS) algorithm in which a *tabu* search algorithm is embedded as a local search operator. The approach was compared to an exact method by Baptiste et al. (2000). Li (1995) addressed the $P|$agreeable due dates $|\sum U_j$ problem. Where the due dates and release times are assumed to be agreeable. A heuristic algorithm is presented and a dynamic programming lower bounding procedure developed. Hiraishi et al. (2003) addressed the non preemptive scheduling of n jobs that are completed exactly at their due dates. They showed this problem is polynomially solvable even if positive set-up is allowed. Sung and Vlach (2001) showed that when the number of machines is fixed, the weighted problem considered by Hirashi et al. (2003) is solvable in polynomial time (exponential in the number of machines) no matter whether the parallel machines are identical, uniform or unrelated. However, when the number of machines is part of the input, the unrelated parallel machine case of the problem becomes strongly NP-hard. Lann and Mosheiov (2003) provided a simple greedy $O(n \log n)$ algorithm to solve the problem of Hiraishi et al. (2003) greatly improving in the time complexity. Čepek and Sung (2005) considered the same problem of Hiraishi et al. (2003) where they corrected the greedy algorithm of Lann and Mosheiov (2003) that was wrong and presented a new quadratic time algorithm which solved the problem. Adamu and Abass (2010) proposed four greedy heuristics for the $Pm||\sum w_j (U_j + V_j)$ problem and extensive computational experiments performed. Janiak et al. (2009) studied the problem of scheduling n jobs on m identical parallel machines, in which for each job a distinct due window is given and the processing time is unit time to minimize the weighted number of early and tardy jobs. They gave an $O(n^5)$ complexity for solving the problem ($Pm|p_j = 1 |\sum w_j(U_j + V_j)$). They also consider a special case with agreeable earliness and tardiness weights where they gave on $O(n^3)$ complexity ($Pm|p_j = 1$, r_j, agreeable ET weights$|\sum w_j(U_j + V_j)$). Adamu and Adewunmi (2012a) compared the heuristics of Adamu and Abass (2010) with some metaheuristics.

PROBLEM FORMULATION

A set of independent jobs $N = \{1,2, \ldots, n\}$ has to be processed on m parallel identical machines, which are simultaneously available from time zero, each having an interval rather than a point in time, called due window of the job. The left end and the right end of the window are respectively called the earliest due date (that is, the instant at which a job becomes available for delivery), and the latest due date (that is, the instant by which processing or delivery of a job must be completed). There is no penalty when a job is completed within the due window, but for earliness or tardiness, penalty is incurred when a job is completed before the earliest due date or after the latest due date. Each job j ε N has a processing time p_j, earliest due date a_j, latest due date d_j and a weight w_j. it is assumed that there is no preemptions and only one job is allowed to be processed on a given machine at any given time. For any schedule S, let t_{ij} and $C_{ij}(S) = t_{ij} + p_j$ represent the actual start time on a given machine and completion time of job j on machine i,

respectively. Job j is said to be early if $C_{ij}(S) < a_j$, tardy i $C_{ij}(S) > d_j$ and on-time if $a_j \le C_{ij}(S) \le d_j$. For any job j, the weighted number of early and tardy jobs (Liu and Wu 2003)

$$ w_j U_j = w_j \operatorname{int}\left\{ \frac{1}{2} sign[C_{ij}(S) - p_j] + \frac{1}{2} \right\} $$

Where we define that

$$ sign[C_{ij}(S) - p_j] = $$
$$ \begin{cases} 1, & if \ a_j > C_{ij}(S) \quad OR \quad C_{ij}(S) > d_j \\ -1, & a_j > C_{ij}(S) \quad OR \quad C_{ij}(S) > d_j \end{cases} $$

and that int is the operation of making an integer Obviously,

$$ U_j = \begin{cases} 1, & if \ a_j > C_{ij}(S) \quad OR \quad C_{ij}(S) > d_j \\ 0, & a_j > C_{ij}(S) \quad OR \quad C_{ij}(S) > d_j \end{cases} $$

Therefore, the scheduling problem of minimizing the weighted number of tardy jobs on identical paralle machines can be formulated as G.

$$ G = \sum_{i=1}^{m} \sum_{j=1}^{n} w_j U_j = \sum_{i=1}^{m} \sum_{j=1}^{n} w_j \operatorname{int}\left\{ \frac{1}{2} sign[C_{ij}(S) - p_j] + \frac{1}{2} \right\} \quad (1) $$

$$ \operatorname{Min} G = \sum_{i=1}^{m} \sum_{j=1}^{n} w_j U_j = \min \sum_{i=1}^{m} \sum_{j=1}^{n} w_j \operatorname{int}\left\{ \frac{1}{2} sign[C_{ij}(S) - p_j] + \frac{1}{2} \right\} $$
$$ (2) $$

HEURISTIC AND META-HEURISTICS

Greedy heuristic

Adamu and Abass (2010) have proposed four greedy heuristics which attempt to provide near optimal solutions to the parallel machine scheduling problem. In this paper the fourth heuristic (DO2) would be use. It entails sorting the jobs according to their latest due date (that is, latest due time - processing time) and ties broken by the highest weighted processing time is used (that is, weight / processing time).

Results of these greedy heuristics are encouraging; however it will be further investigated whether using meta-heuristics and their hybrids can achieve better results.

Genetic algorithm

Genetic algorithms (GAs) are one of the best known meta-heuristics for solving optimization problems. GAs are loosely based on evolution in nature and use strategies such as survival of the fittest, genetic crossover and mutation. Since GAs usually have a high performance and also use a population based technique, it was decided to investigate their comparative performance with the greedy heuristics.

Problem representation

Deciding on a suitable representation is one of the most important aspects of a GA. It was decided that each job would be fixed to a gene in the chromosome – implying that the chromosome has length n (where n is the number of jobs). Each gene would also have a machine number (the number of the machine to which the job will be assigned) and an order (a value between 1 and n representing the order in which jobs assigned to the same machine will be executed). Genetic operators would then need to be applied to both the machine number and the order.

Algorithm

A basic pseudo code of the genetic algorithm found in Adamu and Adewunmi (2012a) was used.

Fitness function

The fitness function calculates the sum of the weights of jobs which could not be assigned onto any of the machines so that they would finish within the earliest due and latest due dates. For each machine, jobs which are assigned to it are placed in a priority queue (which bases priority on their respective order). Each job is then removed from the queue and placed on the machine. If the job was to finish early, then it would be scheduled to begin later (at earliest due date -processing time) in order to avoid the earliness penalty. However, if the job was to finish past the end time, then it would not be scheduled at all and instead would have its weight added to the total penalty (fitness). One final, important aspect to note is that a lower fitness function implies a better performance.

Genetic operators

Genetic algorithms have a large number of operators available to them as well as different implementations of the operators which may be useful in different situations. In the initial version of the GA, the following operators were used: 1-point crossover for machines, conventional mutation for machines (that is, choose a random machine between 0 and m-1 inclusive), swap mutation for the execution order (since naturally this is permutation based) and tournament selection. However, since there are no guarantees that these operators allowed for the best performance, further experimentation with variations of these operators was performed. More details will be given subsequently.

Particle swarm optimization (PSO)

Particle swarm optimization was chosen to attempt to solve the parallel machine scheduling problem. It is a population based technique derived from the flocking behaviour of birds which relies on both the particle's best position found so far as well as the entire population's best position to get out of local optimums and to find the global optimum. PSO is appropriate to use for parallel machine scheduling because not much is known about the solution landscape and so PSO may be useful to get out local optimums to find the global optimum.

Problem representation

The PSO algorithm requires that a representation of the solution (or encoding of the solution) is chosen. Each particle will be instances of the chosen representation. A complication is that PSO works in the continuous space whereas the scheduling problem is a discrete problem. Thus, a method is needed to convert from the continuous space to the discrete space. The representation is as follows:

(i) Each particle contains a number between 0 (inclusive) and the number of machines (exclusive). This number represents the machine on which the particle is scheduled and is simply truncated to convert to the discrete space.
(ii) Each particle contains a number between 0 (inclusive) and 1 (exclusive). This number represents the order of scheduling relative to the other particles on the same machine where a lower number indicates that that job will be scheduled before the jobs with higher numbers.

Algorithm

A basic pseudo code of the PSO found in Adamu and Adewunmi (2012a) was used.

Fitness function

Finally, a method is needed to convert the encoding into a valid schedule (this is performed when calculating the fitness).

This is performed by separating the jobs into groups based on the machine to which they are assigned. Within a group, the jobs are sorted by their order parameter and organized into a queue. The schedule for a particular machine is then formed by removing jobs from the queue and scheduling them as early as possible without breaking the earliness constraint. The weights of jobs that cannot be scheduled are totaled as the fitness of the solution (which would ideally be as small as possible).

Simulated annealing

Simulated annealing (SA) was chosen as a meta-heuristic which could solve the parallel machine scheduling problem. Simulated annealing is based on real-life annealing, where the heating of metals allows for atoms to move from their initial position and the cooling allows for the atoms to settle in new optimal positions. SA is not a population based heuristic – thus only one solution is kept at any one stage. Since SA should result in less operations being performed with respect to a population based technique, execution times may be quicker. It is this reason why SA was chosen for investigation.

It should also be noted that simulated annealing will in all likelihood achieve better results than a simple hill-climbing technique. This is because SA can take downward steps (that is, accept worse solutions) in order to obtain greater exploration. Thus, it is less likely to become stuck in a local minimum (a very real problem given the complex solution space).

Problem representation

The representation is remarkably similar to that used in the GA. A solution consists of n elements (where n is the number of jobs). Each element has a specific job as well as the machine onto which it will be assigned and the order of assignment. Perhaps the major difference between them is that the GA has a population of solutions (chromosomes) whereas SA focuses on a single solution.

Algorithm

A basic algorithm used in the SA [found in Adamu and Adewunmi (2012a)] technique:

Fitness function

Since, the solution is represented in virtually the exact same manner as a chromosome in the GA and a particle in PSO, the fitness function is calculated in the same manner. That is, jobs pertaining to a particular machine are placed in a priority queue before being assigned onto the machine. Those which cannot be assigned contribute towards the penalty.

Operators

Although, simulated annealing does not really have operators (in the sense of a GA having genetic operators), the SA algorithm does has to select a neighbor. The particular neighbor selection strategy that is used updates only a single element of the solution. The element is given a new randomly chosen machine and a new order (done by swapping with the order of another randomly chosen element). By allowing for a high level of randomness when selecting the neighbor, it will be ensured that good exploration will be achieved and that a local best is not found too early.

COMPUTATIONAL ANALYSIS AND RESULTS

Date generation

The program was written in Java using Eclipse. It actually consists of a number of programs, each one implementing a different type of solution. The output of each of these programs gives the final fitness after the algorithm has been performed and the time in milliseconds that the algorithm took to run.

The heuristics were tested on problems generated with 100, 200, 300 and 400 jobs similar to Adamu and Abass (2010), Ho and Chang (1995), Baptiste et al. (2000), and M'Hallah and Bulfin (2005). The number of machines was set at levels of 2, 5, 10, 15 and 20. For each job j, an integer processing time p_j was randomly generated in the interval (1, 99). Two parameters, k1 and k2 (levels of Traffic Congestion Ratio) were taken from the set {1, 5, 10, 20}. For the data to depend on the number of jobs n, the integer earliest due date (a_j) was randomly generated in the interval (0, n / (m * k1)), and the integer latest due date (d_j) was randomly generated in the interval ($a_j + p_j$, a_j + p_j + (2 * n * p) / (m * k2)).

For each combination of n, k1 and k2, 10 instances were generated, that is, for each value of n, 160 instances were generated with a weight randomly chosen in interval (1, 10) for 8000 problems of 50 replications. The meta-heuristics were implemented on a Pentium Dual 1.86 GHz, 782 MHz, and 1.99 GB of Ram. The following meta-heuristics were analyzed GA, PSO, SA, GA Hybrid, PSO Hybrid, PSOGA Hybrid and SA Hybrid.

Improvements

Genetic algorithms are different from many other meta-heuristics in that they have different genetic operators which can be tried and tested – rather than simply changing parameters. The original GA which was tested used 1-point crossover, random mutation for machines, swap mutation for order and tournament selection. It was decided to try other combinations of operators in order to see if performance could be increased. For this reason, roulette-wheel selection, uniform crossover and insert mutation (for order) were all programmed. A user would then be able to choose any combination of operators to use for their own GA. More information on the optimal combination of genetic operators will be mentioned subsequently in the parameters.

Greedy hybrids

Once the meta-heuristics (GA, PSO and SA) had been programmed, it was thought that improvements on them could potentially be made if they somehow included aspects or features from the greedy heuristic used by Adamu and Abass (2010). It was clear from the works of Adamu and Abass (2010) that the key to the greedy heuristics was in the order in which jobs were assigned to machines. So the mechanisms of ordering in DO2 needed to be incorporated in the meta-heuristics (GA, PSO, SA).

To implement the hybridization in the 3 meta-heuristics, the order field was removed from Gene, Dimension and Element respectively. Also, any code in Chromosome, Particle and Solution which dealt with the order (for example, swap mutation in Chromosome) was removed.

Parameters

For each solutions strategy, there are a number of different parameters that affect the performance of the algorithm such as population size, mutation rate, initial temperature, etc. These parameters needed to be experimentally determined and so the algorithms were run manually on a subset of all the testing data in order to determine the optimal parameters. This involved experimenting with the full range of each parameter and recording and tabulating the results achieved. The combination of parameters that gave the best performance was selected as the optimal parameters.

The optimal parameters for the genetic algorithm are:

(i) A population size of 10.
(ii) Random mutation (for machines) used at a rate of 0.01.
(iii) Swap mutation (for order) used at a rate of 0.01.
(iv) Uniform crossover at a rate of 0.5.
(v) Tournament selection with a k set at 40% of the population size.
(vi) The number of iterations of the algorithm was set at 2000.

Further to the above parameters, the genetic algorithm hybrid achieved best results when hybridized with the DO2 greedy heuristic.

The optimal parameters for particle swarm optimization are:

(i) A population size of 50.
(ii) A w (momentum value) of 0.3.
(iii) A c1 of 2.
(iv) A c2 of 2.
(v) The number of iterations of the algorithm was set at 2000.

Further to the above parameters, the particle swarm optimization hybrid achieved best results when hybridized with the DO2 greedy heuristic.

The optimal parameters for simulated annealing are:

(I) An initial temperature of 25.
(ii) A final temperature of 0.01.
(iii) A geometrical decreasing factor (beta) of 0.999.

Further to the above parameters, the simulated annealing hybrid achieved best results when hybridized with the DO2 greedy heuristic.

DISCUSSION

In this part of the work, the results of the algorithms are shown, including the hybridizations. In the four columns shown in Table 1, each cell consists of two numbers. The top number is the weight of the schedule that is produced, averaged over 50 runs. The bottom number is the average time in milliseconds that the algorithm takes to complete.

Also included are four charts each for the performance of the meta-heuristics in relation to the penalty (Figure 1) and time (Figure 2) for N= 100, 200, 300 and 400. Figure 1 compares the relative performance (penalty) of each of the 6 algorithms compared to the number of machines used. Again, four charts are given to show the computational times of the meta-heuristics for various values of N. It should be clear from both the Table 1 and the charts that the Simulated Annealing Hybrid (SAH) out performed the other meta-heuristics in almost all points and the over all lowest time averagely less than a second. It was observed the various hybrids performed better than their meta-heuristic without it. It further proves the effectiveness of hybridization on the meta-heuristics.

The Genetic algorithm (GA) performed worst compared to other meta-heuristics in all of the categories considered for all N jobs and M machines. The GA time is averagely 2.8 s, far slower than the SAH – notably because it keeps track of a population of individual solutions. Results show it to be in the region of 2.8 times slower compared to SAH.

The genetic algorithm which is hybridized with DO2 (GAH) achieves better results (Table 1 and Figure 1) compared to the simple genetic algorithm (GA) on all of the test cases. In all cases considered, the GAH outperform the ordinary GA and as the value of N

increases the performance rate of GAH over GA widens. For larger values of N the performance of GAH is almost equivalent if not better than SAH. GAH takes on average about 2.77 s. GAH would be ideal for larger values of N where an optimal solution is not readily feasible.

The particle swarm optimization (PSO) and the hybrid PSO (PSOH) produce lower weight compared to the GA. Furthermore, they are far slower than all the meta-heuristics considered (over 14.4 times slower for PSO and 10.5 for PSOH in relation to SAH). This is understandable since PSO is a population-based algorithm so there is a lot of work being done at each step. Hybridizing particle swarm optimization with the DO2 greedy heuristic produces results which are better than PSO for all cases. The PSOH is also about 1.37 times faster than PSO.

The results for simulated annealing (SA) are far better on the average than those GA, PSO and PSOH both in performance of penalty and time (Tables 1 and 2 and Figures 1 and 2). On average, SA takes 1 s to run. However, it is about 2.8, 2.77, 14.4 and 10.5 times quicker than the GA, GAH, PSO and PSOH respectively (Table 5).

Hybridizing simulated annealing with the DO2 greedy heuristic (SAH) produces results that are slightly better than the SA solution for all cases considered. It produces the overall best results among the meta-heuristics in terms of performance in relation to penalty and time. The average timing is a little less than a second.

Further statistical analysis are carried out for both the penalty and timing of the various algorithms. Test of homogeneity of variances, ANOVA test, multiple comparisons test and homogeneous subsets are considered. Tables 2 to 4 are for the penalty performance and time performance. For the penalty performance, it is discovered that the variances of the penalties are not significantly different. Table 2 presents the ANOVA table for penalties. The means of the meta-heuristics are significantly different from one another, that is, they do not have equal means. Due to equality of their variances, subsets of homogeneous groups are displayed in Table 3 using Scheffe's method. Four groups are obtained: group 1—SAH, GAH and SA, group 2—GAH, SA and PSOH, group 3 – PSOH and PSO, and group 4 – GA. These groups are arranged in decreasing order of their effectiveness. The worst among them is the GA. Similarly, for the time performance, Table 4 shows the ANOVA table for the test of equality of the mean time of the meta-heuristics which are also significantly different.

This implies that timings for the various algorithms are not the same. PSO and PSOH have the highest time of 14. 4 and 10.5 s respectively. While the lowest of about 1 s for both SA and SAH.

Conclusion

This paper presents results on scheduling on identical

Table 1. Performance of Meta-heuristics for different N.

	M=2			M=5			M=10			M=15			M=20		
	MIN	AVE	MAX	MIN	AVE	MAX	MIN	AVE	MAX	MIN	AVE	MAX	MIN	AVE	MAX
N=100															
GA	593 / 1906	655.72 / 3404.18	730 / 5844	525 / 4265	610.68 / 4962.46	700 / 5921	510 / 4218	558.06 / 4897.44	628 / 5937	458 / 4235	522.42 / 4942.52	557 / 5938	444 / 4328	519.22 / 5091.82	603 / 6218
GAH	313 / 2750	374.78 / 2947.88	444 / 3266	257 / 2640	340.22 / 2826.58	397 / 3125	244 / 2485	304.78 / 2667.54	385 / 2953	197 / 2484	261.2 / 2674.44	323 / 3078	202 / 2843	268.76 / 3048.78	309 / 3360
PSO	385 / 13516	459.9 / 14506.84	559 / 29969	339 / 13188	482.84 / 14182.52	583 / 25578	352 / 13047	470.16 / 14038.78	559 / 27688	419 / 13218	455.74 / 14291.92	512 / 26968	425 / 13516	477.48 / 14554.38	549 / 28578
PSOH	309 / 10125	374.76 / 10785.3	474 / 11531	289 / 9750	432.4 / 10357.54	511 / 11172	308 / 9390	450.56 / 10139.38	550 / 13453	304 / 9578	438.08 / 10346.24	484 / 19688	342 / 10735	413.22 / 11605.54	472 / 20531
SA	330 / 421	378.38 / 470.08	441 / 547	294 / 406	348.6 / 884.64	417 / 1375	242 / 875	297.02 / 1083.78	366 / 1359	188 / 907	247.92 / 1092.8	292 / 1344	216 / 937	262.94 / 1127.8	317 / 1531
SAH	342 / 532	397.94 / 584.36	473 / 657	246 / 500	315.14 / 529.52	380 / 578	200 / 453	258.44 / 487.22	329 / 563	167 / 453	211.82 / 495.32	274 / 562	173 / 531	231.52 / 574.1	282 / 656
N=200															
GA	535 / 3297	605.24 / 5051	717 / 6188	475 / 1843	544.34 / 1982.46	635 / 2265	418 / 1812	482.1 / 1967.26	538 / 2328	387 / 1812	439.78 / 1963.82	535 / 2156	357 / 1859	408.18 / 2011.86	465 / 2329
GAH	124 / 2734	180.22 / 2956.4	247 / 3313	99 / 2625	163.72 / 2796.28	240 / 3078	92 / 2453	146.74 / 2650.34	220 / 2953	75 / 2468	129.24 / 2629.22	171 / 2875	69 / 2484	107.22 / 2673.74	161 / 3015
PSO	285 / 13406	345.68 / 14314.02	410 / 19063	312 / 13172	358.06 / 13979.1	448 / 15266	188 / 13078	361.34 / 13795.56	438 / 14829	225 / 13172	354.64 / 13949.72	420 / 14921	300 / 13484	354.52 / 14203.38	409 / 15062
PSOH	127 / 10187	181.36 / 10841.88	225 / 16500	190 / 9672	257.36 / 10437.5	318 / 19250	184 / 9422	301.18 / 10144.36	344 / 17766	197 / 9484	302.32 / 10185.36	360 / 18485	265 / 9562	303.38 / 10376.2	341 / 17328
SA	157 / 984	231.2 / 1174.36	289 / 1438	162 / 922	206.5 / 1116.52	272 / 1469	93 / 875	170.5 / 1074.72	230 / 1328	103 / 891	139.48 / 1103.5	189 / 1390	78 / 937	108.22 / 1121.2	155 / 1422
SAH	138 / 547	190.74 / 1232.94	277 / 1672	93 / 1093	144.18 / 1331.58	210 / 1656	58 / 453	116.5 / 510.6	173 / 1282	60 / 431	91.4 / 488.72	140 / 578	35 / 453	66.74 / 880.02	115 / 1375
N=300															
GA	475 / 1906	591.46 / 2064.98	665 / 2359	463 / 1859	520.6 / 1987.52	583 / 2438	386 / 1813	449.34 / 1961.62	540 / 2531	319 / 1812	400.3 / 1993.14	469 / 2281	323 / 1875	371.86 / 2036.58	451 / 2922
GAH	33 / 2750	85.06 / 2964.08	146 / 3437	23 / 2594	68.24 / 2837.8	120 / 4672	27 / 2469	61.5 / 2649.78	139 / 3735	25 / 2453	50.16 / 2657.44	95 / 4594	16 / 2453	42.72 / 2653.4	78 / 3359
PSO	228 / 13422	304.32 / 14430.36	392 / 25984	210 / 13234	298.02 / 14209.66	383 / 27000	162 / 13109	306.24 / 14092.14	379 / 28438	234 / 13281	306.7 / 14214.64	377 / 26313	165 / 13453	309.72 / 14439.7	384 / 25375

Table 1. Contd.

PSOH	36	84.14	165	100	154.42	211	70	196.2	268	144	209.3	267	167	215.44	264
	10000	10703.48	11547	9656	10202.08	10984	9344	9937.72	10734	9375	9990.48	10766	9516	10167.48	11062
SA	96	164.22	237	92	130.72	195	53	102.34	169	50	79.16	136	33	61.74	87
	984	1185.98	1453	922	1115.34	1375	875	1079.92	1438	906	1079.66	1406	937	1142.32	1407
SAH	23	88.68	171	24	61.22	112	13	43.28	108	12	30.54	65	5	21.24	42
	1219	1445.26	1672	1078	1329.92	1656	1016	1216.54	1547	1000	1200.98	1563	1031	1216.58	1484

N=400

GA	483	573.08	668	413	496.28	589	316	424.66	485	308	368.82	483	290	340.28	410
	1906	2056.46	2625	1843	2002.46	3218	1813	1980.1	3125	1828	1994.6	2718	1875	2035.32	2610
GAH	0	28.42	67	0	17.86	45	1	16.04	81	0	9.76	29	0	9	29
	2719	2939.6	3718	2609	2802.28	3453	2422	2609.76	2750	2485	2643.16	4157	2454	2684.06	4500
PSO	204	285.2	362	183	257.7	349	119	262.04	356	187	265.8	330	228	274.32	319
	13406	14165.64	15157	13172	15126.54	27078	13015	14900	36375	13203	15070.32	36969	13468	15490.76	32828
PSOH	2	25.84	56	27	80.52	122	6	116.62	189	32	135.3	195	33	146.64	199
	9937	10654.98	11625	9594	10375.08	18703	9344	11234.38	27438	9266	11292.5	28157	9453	10294.68	18750
SA	82	124.62	184	29	82.3	157	22	58.46	98	12	39.42	64	6	29.5	59
	985	1109	1453	921	1112.82	1547	875	1064.52	1282	907	1106.44	1484	937	1149.38	1500
SAH	1	29.48	84	2	16.44	48	0	11.36	53	0	4.9	19	0	2.62	15
	1219	1459.4	1781	1093	1320.86	1735	1015	1192.86	1453	1016	1188.22	1609	1015	1220.66	1625

Table 2. ANOVA.

Penalty	Sum of squares	df	Mean square	F	Sig.
Between groups	2170218.657	5	434043.731	37.688	0.000
Within groups	1312911.671	114	11516.769		
Total	3483130.328	119			

parallel machines with the objective of minimizing the weighted number of early and tardy jobs. Six meta-heuristics including hybridization are proposed for solving the problem. Extensive computational experiments are performed to analyze these meta-heuristics. It was observed that the simulated annealing hybrid gives the best result both in performance and timing while the genetic algorithm was the worst among them in performance. Further research will focus on comparing these results with optimal solutions and considering other machine environment like

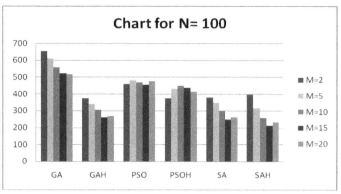

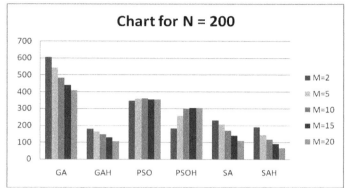

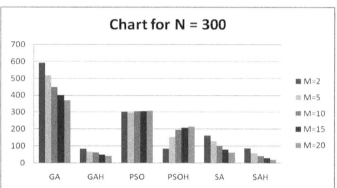

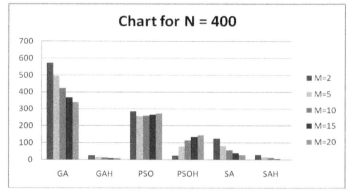

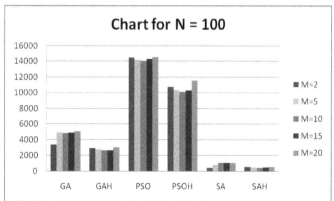

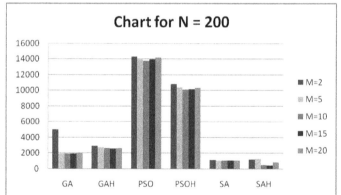

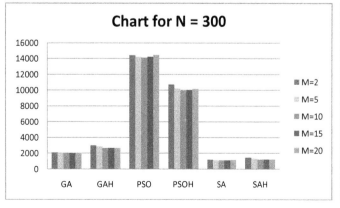

Figure 1. Meta-heuristics performance in relation to penalty.

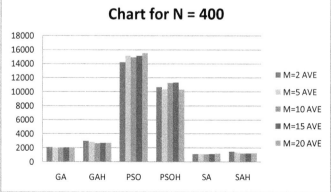

Figure 2. Performance time of the meta-heuristics.

Table 3. Homogeneous subsets using Scheffe's method (Harmonic mean sample size = 20.000).

Heuristics	N	Penalty			
		Subset for alpha = 0.05			
		1	**2**	**3**	**4**
SAH	20	116.7090			
GAH	20	133.2820	133.2820		
SA	20	163.1620	163.1620		
PSOH	20		240.9520	240.9520	
PSO	20			349.5210	
GA	20				494.1210
Sig.		0.865	0.082	0.077	1.000

Means for groups in homogeneous subsets are displayed.

Table 4. ANOVA.

Time	Sum of Squares	df	Mean square	F	Sig.
Between Groups	3.175E9	5	6.350E8	1634.682	0.000
Within Groups	4.429E7	114	388468.477		
Total	3.219E9	119			

Table 5. Post Hoc tests (multiple comparisons) using Scheffe's method.

(I) Heuristics	(J) Heuristics	Mean difference (I-J)	Penalty			
			Std. Error	Sig.	95% Confidence Interval	
					Lower bound	Upper bound
GA	GAH	360.83900*	33.93637	0.000	245.9076	475.7704
	PSO	144.60000*	33.93637	0.004	29.6686	259.5314
	PSOH	253.16900*	33.93637	0.000	138.2376	368.1004
	SA	330.95900*	33.93637	0.000	216.0276	445.8904
	SAH	377.41200*	33.93637	0.000	262.4806	492.3434
GAH	GA	-360.83900*	33.93637	0.000	-475.7704	-245.9076
	PSO	-216.23900*	33.93637	0.000	-331.1704	-101.3076
	PSOH	-107.67000	33.93637	0.082	-222.6014	7.2614
	SA	-29.88000	33.93637	0.978	-144.8114	85.0514
	SAH	16.57300	33.93637	0.999	-98.3584	131.5044
PSO	GA	-144.60000*	33.93637	0.004	-259.5314	-29.6686
	GAH	216.23900*	33.93637	0.000	101.3076	331.1704
	PSOH	108.56900	33.93637	0.077	-6.3624	223.5004
	SA	186.35900*	33.93637	0.000	71.4276	301.2904
	SAH	232.81200*	33.93637	0.000	117.8806	347.7434
PSOH	GA	-253.16900*	33.93637	0.000	-368.1004	-138.2376
	GAH	107.67000	33.93637	0.082	-7.2614	222.6014
	PSO	-108.56900	33.93637	0.077	-223.5004	6.3624
	SA	77.79000	33.93637	0.392	-37.1414	192.7214
	SAH	124.24300*	33.93637	0.025	9.3116	239.1744
SA	GA	-330.95900*	33.93637	0.000	-445.8904	-216.0276
	GAH	29.88000	33.93637	0.978	-85.0514	144.8114
	PSO	-186.35900*	33.93637	0.000	-301.2904	-71.4276
	PSOH	-77.79000	33.93637	0.392	-192.7214	37.1414
	SAH	46.45300	33.93637	0.865	-68.4784	161.3844

Table 5. Contd.

	GA	-377.41200*	33.93637	0.000	-492.3434	-262.4806
	GAH	-16.57300	33.93637	0.999	-131.5044	98.3584
SAH	PSO	-232.81200*	33.93637	0.000	-347.7434	-117.8806
	PSOH	-124.24300*	33.93637	0.025	-239.1744	-9.3116
	SA	-46.45300	33.93637	0.865	-161.3844	68.4784

* The mean difference is significant at the 0.05 level.

uniform and unrelated machines.

REFERENCES

Adamu M, Abass O (2010). Parallel machine scheduling to maximize the weighted number of just-in-time jobs. J. Appl. Sci. Technol. 15(1&2):27–34.

Adamu M, Adewunmi A (2012a). Metaheuristics for Scheduling on Parallel Machines to minimize the Weighted Number of Early and Tardy Jobs. Int. J. Phys. Sci. 7(10):1641-1652.

Adamu M, Adewunmi A (2012c). Single Machine Review to Minimize Weighted Number of Tardy Jobs. J. Ind. Manag. Optim. Submitted for publication.

Adamu MO, Adewunmi A (2012b). Minimizing the Weighted Number of Tardy Jobs on Multiple Machines: A Review. Asian J. Oper. Res.

Baptiste P, Jouglet A, Pape CL, Nuijten W (2000). A Constraint Based Approach to Minimize the Weighted Number of Late Jobs on Parallel Machines. Technical Report 2000/228, UMR, CNRS 6599, Heudiasyc, France.

Čepek O, Sung SC (2005). A Quadratic Time Algorithm to Maximize the Number of Just-In-Time Jobs on Identical Parallel Machines. Comput. Oper. Res. 32:3265-3271.

Chen Z, Powel WB (1999). Solving Parallel Machine Scheduling Problems by Column Generation. INFORMS J. Comput. 11(1):78-94.

Dauzère-Pérès S, Sevaux M (1999). Using Lagrangean Relation to Minimize the (Weighted) Number of Late Jobs on a Single Machine. National Contribution IFORS 1999, Beijing, P.R. of China (Technical Report 99/8 Ecole des Minesdes Nantes, France).

Garey MR, Johnson DS (1979). Computers and Intractability, A Guide to the Theory of NP Completeness. Freeman, San Francisco.

Graham RL, Lawler EL, Lenstra TK, Rinnooy Kan AHG (1979). Optimization and Approximation in Deterministic Sequencing and Scheduling: A Survey. Ann. Discrete Math. 5:287-326.

Hiraishi K, Levner E, Vlach M (2002). Scheduling of Parallel Identical Machines to Maximize the Weighted Number of Just-In-Time Jobs. Comput. Oper. Res. 29:841-848.

Ho JC, Chang YL (1995). Minimizing the Number of Tardy Jobs for *m* Parallel Machines. Eur. J. Oper. Res. 84:343-355.

Janiak A, Janiak WA, Januszkiewicz R (2009). Algorithms for Parallel Processor Scheduling with Distinct Due Windows and Unit-Time Jobs. Bull. Pol. Acad. Sci. Technol. Sci. 57(3):209-215.

Lann A, Mosheiov G (2003). A Note on the Maximum Number of On-Time Jobs on Parallel Identical Machines. Comput. Oper. Res. 30:1745-1749.

Li CL (1995). A Heuristic for Parallel Machine Scheduling with Agreeable Due Dates to Minimize the Number of Late Jobs. Comput. Oper. Res. 22(3):277-283.

Liu M, Wu C (2003). Scheduling Algorithm based on Evolutionary Computing in Identical Parallel Machine Production Line. Robot Comput. Integr. Manuf. 19:401-407.

M'Hallah R, Bulfin RL (2005). Minimizing the Weighted Number of Tardy Jobs on Parallel Processors. Eur. J. Oper. Res. 160:471-484.

Sevaux M, Sörensen K (2005). VNS/TS for a Parallel Machine Scheduling Problem. MEC-VNS: 18th Mini Euro Conference pm VNS.

Sevaux M, Thomin P (2001). Heuristics and Metaheuristics for a parallel Machine Scheduling Problem: A Computational Evaluation Proceedings of 4th Metaheuristics Int. Conf. pp. 411-415.

Süer GA (1997). Minimizing the Number of Tardy Jobs in Multi-Period Cell Loading Problems. Comput. Ind. Eng. 33(3&4):721-724.

Süer GA, Czajkiewicz Z, Baez E (1993). Minimizing the Number of Tardy Jobs in Identical Machine Scheduling. Proceedings of the 15[t] Conference on Computers and Industrial Engineering, Cocoa Beach Florida.

Süer GA, Pico F, Santiago A (1997). Identical Machine Scheduling to Minimize the Number of Tardy Jobs when Lost-Splitting is Allowed Comput. Ind. Eng. 33(1&2):271-280.

Sung SC, Vlach M (2001). Just-In-Time Scheduling on Parallel Machines. The European Operational Research Conference Rotterdam, Netherlands.

Van Den Akker JM, Hoogeveen JA, Van De Velde SL (1999). Parallel Machine Scheduling by Column Generation. Oper. Res. 47(6):862-872.

24

Simulation of a sachet water processing plant using an analogous electrical model

Ani Vincent Anayochukwu

Department of Electronic Engineering, University of Nigeria, Nsukka. Enugu State, Nigeria.

This paper presents an electrical model for studying the process behaviour of a sachet water production plant. In this model, the mechanical components of the plant such as the connecting pipes, the water tanks and the water filter were represented by resistors, capacitors and an inductor, respectively. A state equation was developed as a mathematical model of the electrical circuit. In this equation, resistors, capacitors and inductor representing the restriction of the pipes, the capacity of the tanks and the filtration of the filter respectively, were used as variable parameters to generate the state variables of the state equation. This mathematical model was used to simulate the effects of varying the electrical parameters ($R, C,$ and L) on the state variables (v and i) representing the restriction of the connecting pipes, the water levels (h) in the water tanks and the filtration of the water filter, respectively. Insight into the response curves will indeed form the basis for studying the process control of the sachet water processing plant.

Key words: Mathematical model, analogous system, state equation, control, modeling, simulation

INTRODUCTION

Over the years, man has constantly searched for reliable methods of controlling things around him to suit his purpose. The successful operation of a system under changing conditions often requires a control system. The flow of water in a Production Plant was previously monitored by having an operator take a pressure reading in the treatment plant once or twice a day. Obviously, this daily routine was wasteful and hardly accurate. It was impossible to maintain a stable flow even with nearly continuous operator intervention. The correct amount of water needed to sachet was very difficult, if not impossible, to ascertain from a pressure reading and thus overshooting of desired flow was common.

Sachet water plants without process control are likely to experience problems, such as the water level in the filter cells in the tanks tend to fluctuate widely and create the potential for partial drainage, overflow, and potential initial turbidity breakthrough at the beginning of the filtration cycles thereby causing most of the products not to fill properly.

The necessary condition for achieving efficient process control resides in a thorough understanding of the dynamics of water flow through the plant. If the internal conditions would be predictable through modeling and simulation, we could design a process control that would operate continuously to supply properly filled water sachets at a predetermined sachet plant. Therefore, the mathematical model representing the dynamic behaviour of the process is developed and the system variables expressed in state variable form. In this way, the entire analysis is fashioned in such a way that it is amenable to computer simulation.

In this paper, an Analogous Electrical model for sachet water processing plant is developed. A step-by-step analogous model strategy as proposed by Ani (2007) is adopted: the development of an electrical model of the sachet water production plant, computer simulation of the electrical model and the analysis of the results of the simulation time. This paper spotlights the effects of process control modeling on the treatment of simple water.

Water

Water is one of the prime natural resources, an essential commodity for the living systems that constitute the biosphere (Casey, 2006); unique in its properties – the only substance to exist in all three phases, solid, liquid and gaseous, within the temperature range of the natural environment, continually renewed by the natural hydrological cycle of evaporation, vapour transportation and precipitation. Water conservation opportunities arise in increased efficiency through improvements in flow rates, pressure, temperature, chemistry, filtration or timing (Le Chevallier and Kwok-Keung, 2004). Metering both inflow and outflow from the system provides the operator information to determine if the system is meeting design efficiencies. Process control is often an area where increased efficiency can be obtained. Many operations can also increase efficiency by recirculating water or by filtering contaminants and reclaiming water for reuse internally. Thus the engineering associated with water resources management and use is multi-faceted (Ani, 2013b). This treatise deals with the technologies used to control the treatment process and its related use in industrial manufactures. It deals with the range of treatment processes used in the production of drinking and other high quality water. In general, the presentation of the subject matter proceeds sequentially from basic principles through analytical/experimental methods to the development of process design methodologies. Processes are treated as unit operations, emphasizing those process fundamentals which can be applied to all process applications.

Physical components describing the sachet water plant

The basic physical parameters used in describing the properties of the sachet water production plant are: Pipe (restriction), tank (capacity) and filter (water filteration).

These parameters from the basis of a conceptual design were used in constructing the passive resistance, capacitance and inductance electrical network for the analog model. To accurately stimulate

the process, these parameters should be known at all locations throughout the area being modeled. The general boundary of the model is the demarcation between where recharge enters and discharge leaves the plant. The boundary was chosen so that cause-and-effect relations outside the model area would not affect the process data of the sachet water production system which are useful in preparing an analog model. The better defined the process is, the more accurate the working model (Hardt, 1971). Figure 1 shows the physical setup with all the various regulating devices.

ANALOGOUS SYSTEMS

Analog models are physical models in a different physical system used to model the original model. An analog model can be the use of electrical circuits to represent mechanical systems such as automobile suspensions. An example of an analog model is a direct analog model where series mechanical elements are replaced by analogous series electrical elements and parallel mechanical elements are replaced by equivalent electrical elements in parallel (Ani, 2013a; Hardt, 1971). The use of electric analog model in fluid flow is possible because of the mathematical similarity between the flow of electricity in conducting materials and the flow of fluid in porous media (Walton and Prickett, 1963; Pattern, 1965). Electric analog methods are now regarded as one of the powerful computing tools available to the hydrologist. Direct simulation of the hydrologic system by electrical methods simplifies the computational process. Once the analog model is verified through the use of field data, all electrical phenomena observed on the model can be directly related to hydrologic factors. Any theoretical set of water flow conditions, including alternative solutions, can be modeled, and the effects observed (Hardt, 1971).

The electrical conductivity of the resistors is proportional to the hydraulic conductivity of the plant, and the electrical capacitance is directly related to the storage coefficient of the plant. A resistor impedes the flow of electricity in the same way as the piping materials impede the flow of water through the plant; likewise, capacitor stores electricity in a manner similar to the way water is stored in a tank. If such a model is quantified, the electrical units of potential, charge, current, and model time correspond to the hydraulic units of head, volume, flow rate, and real time. The concept of analogous system is a very useful and powerful technique for system modeling (Ani, 2013a; Dorf and Bishop, 1998).

To develop fully an analog model requires detailed analysis of the process parameters. The flow system

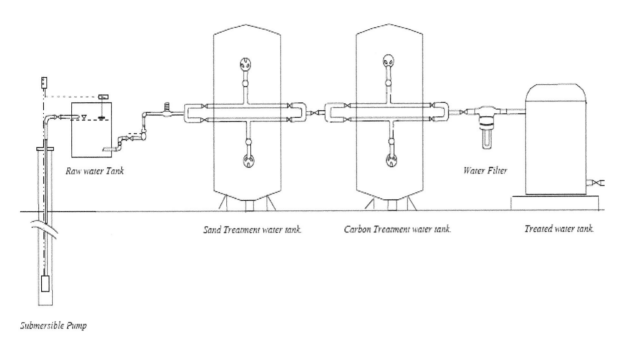

Figure 1. Flow sheet of a water treatment plant (Ani, 2007).

under equilibrium or steady-state conditions (before development) is described by a form of law of conservation of mass (fluid flow continuity).

$$\dot{m} = q_i - q_o \tag{1}$$

This simply states that the time rate of change $\dot{m}$ of mass in a container must equal the total mass inflow rate minus the total outflow rate. The quantity of water moving into the plant (recharge) is about equal to the quantity of water moving out of the plant (discharge). Water levels in the plant are a function of the magnitude of inflow and outflow and the characteristics of the materials through which the water is moving.

In liquid flow system, the differential equation describing liquid flow is derived by law of conservation of mass.

$$C\frac{dh}{dt} = \frac{h}{R} \tag{2}$$

Where:

C = storage coefficient (dimensionless)

$\dfrac{dh}{dt}$ = change in water level with time, in metre per seconds.

h = water level, in meters

R = restriction in piping

t = time, in hours

The equivalent equation for field in electricity is derived by Kirchhoff's voltage and current laws as:

$$C\frac{dv}{dt} = \frac{v}{R} \tag{3}$$

Where:

C = electrical capacitance, in farads

$\dfrac{dv}{dt}$ = change in voltage with time

t = time, in seconds

R = electrical resistance, in ohms

v = electrical potential, in volts

The similarity between these two equations indicates that the cause-and-effect response in a hydrologic system can be duplicated in an electrical system, provided the two are dimensionally equivalent (Hardt, 1971). Mathematically, a solution to the response of developed plant requires use of equations that are too complex for ordinary solution. However, an electric analog model can be constructed that closely approximates the actual flow system because the flow of fluid through porous media is analogous to the flow of current through conducting material. A model that is quantitatively proportional to the liquid flow system can be built by selecting proper electrical components.

Comparison of these two equations show that the behaviour of the two systems is determined by the same basic differential equation. The systems are analogous and there is a one-one correspondence between the elements of the two systems. The analogy is very close. The effect of variations in L, C and R on the water-levels in the hydraulic system can thus be determined by simply observing the effect on the voltages in the electric circuit of variation in L, C and R. The voltage across the capacitor and the current in the circuit vary in the same way as the water-Level and velocity of the mass (Ord-Smith and Stephenson, 1975). In complex water-flow systems, it is impractical to measure all these parameters in great detail or with high accuracy. If, however, they are known approximately, initial tests can be made with an analog model. Usually model response on the first few trails bears little resemblance to actual water-level changes.

Through evaluation of model response and reconsideration of the original plant parameters, the model design is revised until the water-level change computed by the model agrees with observed changes (Hardt, 1971). However, electrical analogies have the advantage that they can be easily set up in the laboratory. A change in a particular parameter can be accomplished very easily in the electric circuit to determine its overall effects and the electric circuit can be approximately adjusted for the desired response.

Afterwards, the parameters in the liquid level system can be adjusted by an analogous amount to obtain the same desired response (Schwedes, 1995).

Volumetric flow rate as analogous to current

Volumetric flow rate Q is defined as the quantity of fluid passing a given area per unit time and current i is defined as the rate of flow of charge across a given area, often the cross-sectional area of a wire.

Mathematically:

$$Q = \frac{dV}{dt} \qquad (4)$$

$$i = \frac{dQ}{dt} \qquad (5)$$

When two parts or elements of a fluid system are connected by a section of pipe, the principle of conservation of mass states that the amount of fluid leaving element A must enter element B. This principle also requires that the net flow rate of mass into any fluid system must equal the rate of increase of mass inside the system.

As the fluid is incompressible, the preceding statement also applies to volume flow rate and fluid volume.

In electrical system, when two elements are connected together, the principle of conservation of electric charge requires that the net charge-leaving element A must enter element B. This principle also requires that the charge entering an element minus the charge leaving the element must equal the change of net charge stored within the element.

Analogous components and variables

Analogous systems are physical systems that are identical; each can be replaced by the other system by deduction of dynamic behaviour of one of these systems from the dynamic behaviour of the other. Just like the deduction of electrical system behaviour from the hydraulic system behaviour.

The model generally starts as an analytical model, that is, a set of differential equations.

Using principle of analogy, which states that two different physical systems can be described by the same mathematical model, these equations are converted into an electrical circuit. This permits a generalization of ideas specific to a particular field in order that a broader understanding of a variety of apparently unrelated situations can be achieved.

The electrical circuit analogy is a force (flow) to current analogy as outlined in Tables 1 and 2.

The analogous components and variables are thus:

$i_i = Q_i$ (Input current; water flow into the process).

$i_o = Q_o$ (Output current; water flow from the process).

$C_1 =$ (Capacitance of capacitor 1; Capacity of tank 1 (sand treatment tank)).

$C_2 =$ (Capacitance of capacitor 2; Capacity of tank 2 (carbon treatment tank)).

$L =$ (Inductance of the inductor; filteration of the filter).

$C_3 =$ (Capacitance of capacitor 3; Capacity of tank 3 (Treated water tank)).

$v_{c1} = h_1$ (voltage across capacitor 1; water level of tank 1).

$v_{c2} = h_2$ (voltage across capacitor 2; water level of tank 2).

$v_{c3} = h_3$ (voltage across capacitor 3; water level of tank 3).

$i_1 = Q_1$ (flow of current through the inductor; rate of water flow through the filter).

$R_1 =$ (Resistance of the resistor 1; Restriction of pipe 1).

$R_2 =$ (Resistance of the resistor 2; Restriction of pipe 2).

Table 1. Describing differential equations for ideal elements of an analog system (Pattern, 1965; Dorf and Bishop, 1998).

Types of element	Physical element	Describing equation
Inductive storage	Electrical Inductance L	$v = L\dfrac{di}{dt}$
	Fluid Inertia I	$p = I\dfrac{dQ}{dt}$
Capacitive storage	Electrical Capacitance C	$i = C\dfrac{dv}{dt}$
	Fluid Capacitance C_f	$Q = C_f\dfrac{dp}{dt}$
Energy dissipator	Electrical Resistance R	$i = \dfrac{1}{R}v$
	Fluid Resistance R_f	$Q = \dfrac{1}{R_f}p$

Table 2. Through-and-across-variable for an analog system (Pattern, 1965; Dorf and Bishop, 1998).

System	Variable through element	Variable across element	Integrated through variable
Electrical	Current, i	Voltage, v	Charge, q
Liquid-level	Liquid flow rate, Q	water level, h	Liquid flow, q

R_3 = (Resistance of the resistor 3; Restriction of pipe 3).

The Liquid – Levels, h_1, h_2, and h_3 of the flow system are directly analogous to the node voltages v_1, v_2 and v_3 of the electrical circuit. Therefore, an electrical circuit is analogous to fluid flow system/plant, implying that the process control of a sachet water plant can be model by means of an electrical model.

Figure 1 shows the physical arrangement of how the system components function and it forms the basis for an analytical study. The electrical circuit representation of the system is shown in Figure 3.

Using the method of analogy for which Kirchhoff's voltage and current laws are utilized, we obtain the state equation. The network has four energy storage elements: three capacitors C_1, C_2, C_3, and an inductor L, and this network are specified by the voltage across the capacitors and current through the inductor. Since there are potential differences across the capacitors as well as current through the inductor, this electrical picture leads to ordinary differential equations. History of the network is completely specified by the voltages across the capacitors and current through the inductor at t = 0 (Nise, 2003). This involves the identification of individual system components as well as identification and idealization of their interconnection.

Interconnection of the elements imposes constraints on the variation of system variables, and the convenient way of specifying these constraints is by a mathematical statement of the way in which the various through-variables are related and the way in which the various across-variables are related. This package of equations is a complete mathematical description of the system (Shearer et al., 1971). The essence of the model is to provide the medium in which the controlled process can be analyzed without practically meddling with the operations of the real system.

MATHEMATICAL MODEL DEVELOPMENT

In order to develop the mathematical model of the system in Figure 1, the following assumptions are made (Ani, 2007):

1. Pressure differences at various stages of the process (water flow), which implies an adoption of a positive-flow direction through the Interconnected elements.
2. The input flow is equal to output flow if and only if the water level at each stage (capacitance) in the plant remains constant, which agrees with the law of conservation of mass.

3. Fluid's density remains constant despite changes in the fluid pressure (Model fluid behaviour as incompressible).
4. Laminar flow exists (the model for the tank height is linear).
5. The walls of the treatment tank and the reservoir are rigid.

Based on the assumption that the inflow minus outflow during the small time interval dt is equal to the additional amount stored in the tank, we see that

$$cdh = (q_i - q_0)dt \text{ or } c\frac{dh}{dt} = q_i - q_0 \qquad (6)$$

Where:

$\frac{dh}{dt}$ is the dependent variable reflecting the system's behaviour, C is a parameter representing a property of the system, and $q_i - q_o$ represent the independent variable along which the system's behaviour is being determined.

From the definition of resistance, the relationship between q_0 and h is given by

$$q_0 = \frac{h}{R} \qquad (7)$$

This is a model that relates water flow rate to the height of water in each tank in the plant. For each tank a flow continuity equation can be written in which the rate of change of fluid volume is equated to the rate of inflow of fluid.

The model generally starts as an analytical model, which is a set of differential equations. Using principle of analogy, which states that two different physical systems can be described by the same mathematical model, these equations are converted into an Electrical circuit. This permits a generalization of ideas specific to a particular field in order that a broader understanding of a variety of apparently unrelated situations can be achieved.

The development of these two models (Fluid and Electrical) follows a very similar process. Their respective relations in both cases enable one to relate the two-coupled sets of physical variables: Hydraulic and Electrical.

An electrical model of process control of a sachet water plant conveys a mental picture of the process control's actual behaviour in a variety of circumstances.

The developed mathematical model of process control of sachet water based on the equivalent

circuit shown in Figure 2 is stated below:
From the circuit diagram, selection of the state variables is thus:

$x_1 = v_{c1} = h_1$ (voltage across the capacitor 1 (C_1); water level of tank 1 (h_1)).

$x_2 = v_{c2} = h_2$ (voltage across the capacitor 2 (C_2); water level of tank 2 (h_2)).

$x_3 = i_1 = Q_1$ (current through the inductor and rate of water flow through the filter).

$x_4 = v_{c3} = h_3$ (voltage across the capacitor 3 (C_3); water level of tank 3 (h_3)).

Where v_c is the state variable representing voltage capacitor across each and h is an equivalent state variable representing the height of water in the tank.

The system of differential equations which govern and describes the dynamic behaviour of the model under transient conditions is presented (Ani, 2013b).

$$C_1 \frac{d(v_{c1})}{dt} = i - \left(\frac{v_{c1} - v_{c2}}{R_1}\right) \qquad (8)$$

$$C_2 \frac{d(v_{c2})}{dt} = \left(\frac{v_{c1} - v_{c2}}{R_1}\right) - i_1 \qquad (9)$$

$$L\frac{d(i_1)}{dt} = \frac{L}{R_2}\frac{d(v_{c2})}{dt} + v_{c2} - v_{c3} \qquad (10)$$

$$C_3 \frac{d(v_{c3})}{dt} = \frac{L}{R_2}\frac{d(v_{c2})}{dt} + v_{c2} - \frac{v_{c3}}{R_3} \qquad (11)$$

Rearranging the equations:

From Equation (8)

$$C_1 \frac{d(v_{c1})}{dt} = i - \left(\frac{v_{c1} - v_{c2}}{R_1}\right)$$

$$C_1 \frac{d(v_{c1})}{dt} = i - \frac{(v_{c1} - v_{c2})}{R_1}$$

$$C_1 \frac{d(v_{c1})}{dt} = \frac{iR_1 - v_{c1} + v_{c2}}{R_1}$$

$$R_1 C_1 \frac{d(v_{c1})}{dt} = iR_1 - v_{c1} + v_{c2}$$

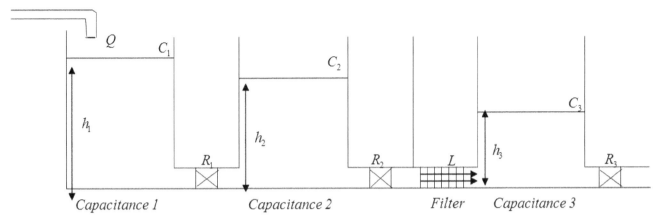

Figure 2. Coupled tank flow system.

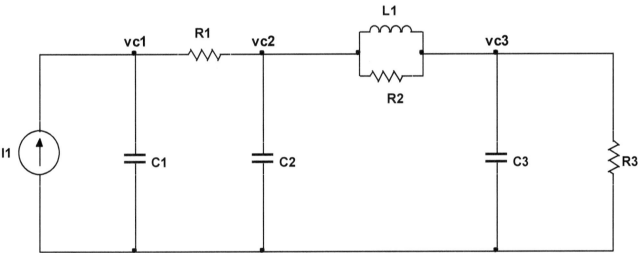

Figure 3. Electrical circuit equivalent.

$$\frac{d(v_{c1})}{dt} = \frac{iR_1}{R_1C_1} - \frac{v_{c1}}{R_1C_1} + \frac{v_{c2}}{R_1C_1}$$

$$\frac{d(v_{c1})}{dt} = \frac{i}{C_1} - \frac{v_{c1}}{R_1C_1} + \frac{v_{c2}}{R_1C_1}$$

$$\frac{d(v_{c1})}{dt} = -\frac{v_{c1}}{R_1C_1} + \frac{v_{c2}}{R_1C_1} + \frac{i}{C_1} \qquad (12)$$

From Equation (9)

$$C_2\frac{d(v_{c2})}{dt} = \left(\frac{v_{c1} - v_{c2}}{R_1}\right) - i_1$$

$$C_2\frac{d(v_{c2})}{dt} = \frac{(v_{c1} - v_{c2})}{R_1} - i_1$$

$$C_2\frac{d(v_{c2})}{dt} = \frac{v_{c1} - v_{c2} - R_1i_1}{R_1}$$

$$R_1C_2\frac{d(v_{c2})}{dt} = v_{c1} - v_{c2} - R_1i_1$$

$$\frac{d(v_{c2})}{dt} = \frac{v_{c1}}{R_1C_2} - \frac{v_{c2}}{R_1C_2} - \frac{R_1i_1}{R_1C_2}$$

$$\frac{d(v_{c2})}{dt} = \frac{v_{c1}}{R_1C_2} - \frac{v_{c2}}{R_1C_2} - \frac{i_1}{C_2} \qquad (13)$$

From Equation (10),

$$L\frac{d(i_1)}{dt} = \frac{L}{R_2}\frac{d(v_{c2})}{dt} + v_{c2} - v_{c3}$$

Substituting $\frac{d(v_{c2})}{dt}$ in Equation (13) gives:

$$L\frac{d(i_1)}{dt} = \frac{L}{R_2}\left(\frac{v_{c1}}{R_1 C_2} - \frac{v_{c2}}{R_1 C_2} - \frac{i_1}{C_2}\right) + v_{c2} - v_{c3}$$

$$L\frac{d(i_1)}{dt} = \frac{Lv_{c1}}{R_1 R_2 C_2} - \frac{Lv_{c2}}{R_1 R_2 C_2} - \frac{Li_1}{R_2 C_2} + v_{c2} - v_{c3}$$

$$L\frac{d(i_1)}{dt} = \frac{Lv_{c1} - Lv_{c2} - R_1 Li_1 + R_1 R_2 C_2 v_{c2} - R_1 R_2 C_2 v_{c3}}{R_1 R_2 C_2}$$

$$\frac{d(i_1)}{dt} = \frac{Lv_{c1} - Lv_{c2} - R_1 Li_1 + R_1 R_2 C_2 v_{c2} - R_1 R_2 C_2 v_{c3}}{R_1 R_2 C_2 L}$$

$$\frac{d(i_1)}{dt} = \frac{Lv_{c1} - Lv_{c2} + R_1 R_2 C_2 v_{c2} - R_1 Li_1 - R_1 R_2 C_2 v_{c3}}{R_1 R_2 C_2 L}$$

$$\frac{d(i_1)}{dt} = \frac{Lv_{c1} - (L - R_1 R_2 C_2)v_{c2} - R_1 Li_1 - R_1 R_2 C_2 v_{c3}}{R_1 R_2 C_2 L}$$

$$R_1 R_2 C_2 L\frac{d(i_1)}{dt} = Lv_{c1} - (L - R_1 R_2 C_2)v_{c2} - R_1 Li_1 - R_1 R_2 C_2 v_{c3}$$

$$\frac{d(i_1)}{dt} = \frac{Lv_{c1}}{R_1 R_2 C_2 L} - \frac{(L - R_1 R_2 C_2)v_{c2}}{R_1 R_2 C_2 L} - \frac{R_1 Li_1}{R_1 R_2 C_2 L} - \frac{R_1 R_2 C_2 v_{c3}}{R_1 R_2 C_2 L}$$

$$\frac{d(i_1)}{dt} = \frac{v_{c1}}{R_1 R_2 C_2} - \frac{(L - R_1 R_2 C_2)v_{c2}}{R_1 R_2 C_2 L} - \frac{i_1}{R_2 C_2} - \frac{v_{c3}}{L} \quad (14)$$

From Equation (11)

$$C_3\frac{d(v_{c3})}{dt} = \frac{L}{R_2}\frac{d(v_{c2})}{dt} + v_{c2} - \frac{v_{c3}}{R_3}$$

Substituting $\frac{d(v_{c2})}{dt}$ in Equation (13) gives:

$$C_3\frac{d(v_{c3})}{dt} = \frac{L}{R_2}\left(\frac{v_{c1}}{R_1 C_2} - \frac{v_{c2}}{R_1 C_2} - \frac{i_1}{C_2}\right) + v_{c2} - \frac{v_{c3}}{R_3}$$

$$C_3\frac{d(v_{c3})}{dt} = \frac{Lv_{c1}}{R_1 R_2 C_2} - \frac{Lv_{c2}}{R_1 R_2 C_2} - \frac{Li_1}{R_2 C_2} + v_{c2} - \frac{v_{c3}}{R_3}$$

$$C_3\frac{d(v_{c3})}{dt} = \frac{R_3 Lv_{c1} - R_3 Lv_{c2} - R_1 R_3 Li_1 + R_1 R_2 R_3 C_2 v_{c2} - R_1 R_2 C_2 v_{c3}}{R_1 R_2 R_3 C_2}$$

$$\frac{d(v_{c3})}{dt} = \frac{R_3 Lv_{c1} - R_3 Lv_{c2} - R_1 R_3 Li_1 + R_1 R_2 R_3 C_2 v_{c2} - R_1 R_2 C_2 v_{c3}}{R_1 R_2 R_3 C_2 C_3}$$

$$\frac{d(v_{c3})}{dt} = \frac{R_3 Lv_{c1} - R_3 Lv_{c2} + R_1 R_2 R_3 C_2 v_{c2} - R_1 R_3 Li_1 - R_1 R_2 C_2 v_{c3}}{R_1 R_2 R_3 C_2 C_3}$$

$$\frac{d(v_{c3})}{dt} = \frac{R_3 Lv_{c1} - R_3 Lv_{c2} + R_1 R_2 R_3 C_2 v_{c2} - R_1 R_3 Li_1 - R_1 R_2 C_2 v_{c3}}{R_1 R_2 R_3 C_2 C_3}$$

$$\frac{d(v_{c3})}{dt} = \frac{R_3 Lv_{c1} - R_3(L - R_1 R_2 C_2)v_{c2} - R_1 R_3 Li_1 - R_1 R_2 C_2 v_{c3}}{R_1 R_2 R_3 C_2 C_3}$$

$$\frac{d(v_{c3})}{dt} = \frac{R_3 Lv_{c1}}{R_1 R_2 R_3 C_2 C_3} - \frac{R_3(L - R_1 R_2 C_2)v_{c2}}{R_1 R_2 R_3 C_2 C_3} - \frac{R_1 R_3 Li_1}{R_1 R_2 R_3 C_2 C_3} - \frac{R_1 R_2 C_2 v_{c3}}{R_1 R_2 R_3 C_2 C_3}$$

$$\frac{d(v_{c3})}{dt} = \frac{Lv_{c1}}{R_1 R_2 C_2 C_3} - \frac{(L - R_1 R_2 C_2)v_{c2}}{R_1 R_2 C_2 C_3} - \frac{Li_1}{R_2 C_2 C_3} - \frac{v_{c3}}{R_3 C_3} \quad (15)$$

The resulting state equations are given by:

$$\begin{cases} \dfrac{d(v_{c1})}{dt} = -\dfrac{v_{c1}}{R_1 C_1} + \dfrac{v_{c2}}{R_1 C_1} + \dfrac{i}{C_1} \\[2mm] \dfrac{d(v_{c2})}{dt} = \dfrac{v_{c1}}{R_1 C_2} - \dfrac{v_{c2}}{R_1 C_2} - \dfrac{i_1}{C_2} \\[2mm] \dfrac{d(i_1)}{dt} = \dfrac{v_{c1}}{R_1 R_2 C_2} - \dfrac{(L - R_1 R_2 C_2)v_{c2}}{R_1 R_2 C_2 L} - \dfrac{i_1}{R_2 C_2} - \dfrac{v_{c3}}{L} \\[2mm] \dfrac{d(v_{c3})}{dt} = \dfrac{Lv_{c1}}{R_1 R_2 C_2 C_3} - \dfrac{(L - R_1 R_2 C_2)v_{c2}}{R_1 R_2 C_2 C_3} - \dfrac{Li_1}{R_2 C_2 C_3} - \dfrac{v_{c3}}{R_3 C_3} \end{cases} \quad (16)$$

The state equation's equivalent in x form is thus:

$$\begin{cases} \dot{x}_1 = -\dfrac{x_1}{R_1 C_1} + \dfrac{x_2}{R_1 C_1} + \dfrac{u}{C_1} \\[2mm] \dot{x}_2 = \dfrac{x_1}{R_1 C_2} - \dfrac{x_2}{R_1 C_2} - \dfrac{x_3}{C_2} \\[2mm] \dot{x}_3 = \dfrac{x_1}{R_1 R_2 C_2} - \dfrac{(L - R_1 R_2 C_2)x_2}{R_1 R_2 C_2 L} - \dfrac{x_3}{R_2 C_2} - \dfrac{x_4}{L} \\[2mm] \dot{x}_4 = \dfrac{Lx_1}{R_1 R_2 C_2 C_3} - \dfrac{(L - R_1 R_2 C_2)x_2}{R_1 R_2 C_2 C_3} - \dfrac{Lx_3}{R_2 C_2 C_3} - \dfrac{x_4}{R_3 C_3} \end{cases} \quad (17)$$

In vector-matrix form, the process control equation is given as:

$$\begin{bmatrix} \dot{x}_1 \\ \dot{x}_2 \\ \dot{x}_3 \\ \dot{x}_4 \end{bmatrix} = \begin{bmatrix} -\dfrac{1}{R_1 C_1} & \dfrac{1}{R_1 C_1} & 0 & 0 \\ \dfrac{1}{R_1 C_2} & -\dfrac{1}{R_1 C_2} & -\dfrac{1}{C_2} & 0 \\ \dfrac{1}{R_1 R_2 C_2} & -\dfrac{(L-R_1 R_2 C_2)}{R_1 R_2 C_2 L} & -\dfrac{1}{R_2 C_2} & -\dfrac{1}{L} \\ \dfrac{L}{R_1 R_2 C_2 C_3} & -\dfrac{(L-R_1 R_2 C_2)}{R_1 R_2 C_2 C_3} & \dfrac{L}{R_2 C_2 C_3} & \dfrac{1}{R_3 C_3} \end{bmatrix} \begin{bmatrix} x_1 \\ x_2 \\ x_3 \\ x_4 \end{bmatrix} + \begin{bmatrix} \dfrac{1}{C_1} \\ 0 \\ 0 \\ 0 \end{bmatrix} [u] \qquad (18)$$

The output equation is thus:

$$y = \begin{bmatrix} 0 & 0 & 0 & 1 \end{bmatrix} \begin{bmatrix} x_1 \\ x_2 \\ x_3 \\ x_4 \end{bmatrix} \qquad (19)$$

x is the state vector while y is the response or output vector.

STATE VARIABLES REPRESENTATION

The merit of the state-variable method is that it results easily to the form amendable to digital and/or analog computer methods of solution (Perdikaris, 1996). Sachet water processing plant can be represented in state variable form as:

$$\dot{x} = A * x + B * u \qquad (20)$$

$$y = Cx \qquad (21)$$

Where

$$\dot{x} = \begin{bmatrix} \dot{x}_1 \\ \dot{x}_2 \\ \dot{x}_3 \\ \dot{x}_4 \end{bmatrix} \quad A = \begin{bmatrix} -\dfrac{1}{R_1 C_1} & \dfrac{1}{R_1 C_1} & 0 & 0 \\ \dfrac{1}{R_1 C_2} & -\dfrac{1}{R_1 C_2} & -\dfrac{1}{C_2} & 0 \\ \dfrac{1}{R_1 R_2 C_2} & -\dfrac{(L-R_1 R_2 C_2)}{R_1 R_2 C_2 L} & \dfrac{1}{R_2 C_2} & -\dfrac{1}{L} \\ \dfrac{L}{R_1 R_2 C_2 C_3} & -\dfrac{(L-R_1 R_2 C_2)}{R_1 R_2 C_2 C_3} & \dfrac{L}{R_2 C_2 C_3} & -\dfrac{1}{R_3 C_3} \end{bmatrix} ; \quad x = \begin{bmatrix} x_1 \\ x_2 \\ x_3 \\ x_4 \end{bmatrix}$$

$$B = \begin{bmatrix} \dfrac{1}{C_1} \\ 0 \\ 0 \\ 0 \end{bmatrix} ; \qquad y = x; \quad C = \begin{bmatrix} 0 & 0 & 0 & 1 \end{bmatrix};$$

Table 3. Sachet water processing plant parameters.

R_1	R_2	R_3	L	C_1	C_2	C_3
0.1	0.1	1.0	1.0	1e-03	1e-03	1000e-03
0.3	0.3	3.0	3.0	3e-03	3e-03	1300e-03
0.5	0.5	5.0	5.0	5e-03	5e-03	1500e-03
0.7	0.7	7.0	7.0	7e-03	7e-03	1700e-03
0.9	0.9	9.0	9.0	9e-03	9e-03	1900e-03

x is the state vector while y is the response or output vector. A is the coefficient matrix of the process and is of order $(m \times m)$. B is the driving matrix of order $(n \times p)$, and C is the output matrix of order $(q \times n)$, which satisfied the rules of matrix multiplication. The above defined matrix operations are carried out on a digital computer using MATLAB software (Mathworks, 2002).

METHODOLOGY

Solution of resulting state equation is achieved numerically thus, the computer study of a modified mathematical model description involving the problem variables are instrumented on the computer and the parameter values are adjusted, thereby varying the matrices A, B, C so as to obtain/predict the behaviour of the actual system. From the model equation above, output y depends on the state equation x which is

x_4, that is $y = x_4$.

Therefore, x and y are dependent variables to be simulated.

The above equations contain all that we need to know about the theory of process control (flow) in a sachet water plant being studied. Solving the time domain $\dot{X}(t) = Ax(t) + Bu(t)$ and $Y(t) = Cx(t) + Du(t)$ where D=0. Using Ordinary Differential Equation (ODE 45) of MATLAB Software, the results will be obtained graphically.

SIMULATION AND RESULTS

Table 3 shows the sachet water processing plant parameters used for the simulation.

In order to study the dynamic behaviour of the process, the state-variable form of Equation (18), were solved numerically using the differential method. By incorporating the developed algorithm into the MATLAB m-file (MATLAB, 1997), the system time response curves for the voltage across capacitor, and flow of current through the inductor at various coordinate systems are developed.

Response of voltages across the capacitors graphs are shown in Figures 4 to 18 and 24 to 38, while Figures 19 to 23 show the Response of current through the inductor graph for the system.

The following is applicable to Figures 4 to 38.

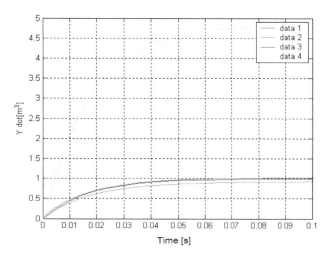

Figure 4. Effect of Restriction to flow on the Process, with R_1 =0.1.

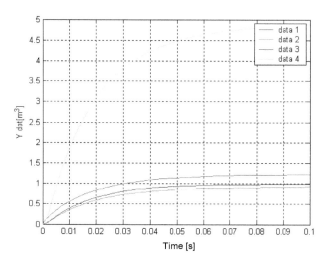

Figure 5. Effect of Restriction to flow on the Process, with R_1 =0.3.

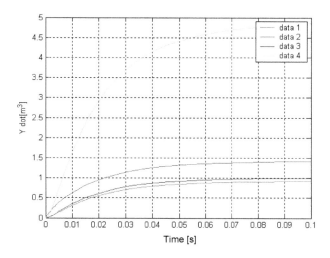

Figure 6. Effect of Restriction to flow on the Process, with R_1 =0.5.

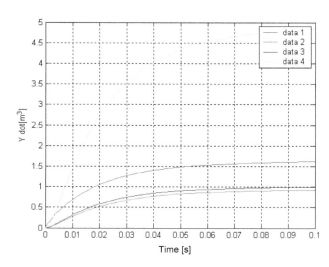

Figure 7. Effect of Restriction to flow on the Process, with R_1 =0.7.

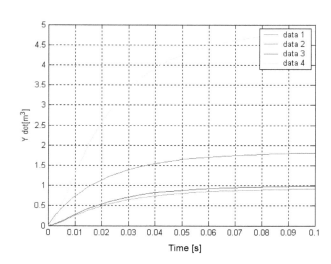

Figure 8. Effect of Restriction to flow on the Process, with R_1 =0.9.

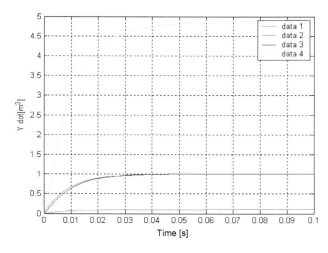

Figure 9. Effect of Restriction to flow on the Process, with R_2 =0.1.

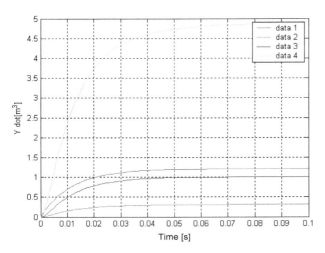

Figure 10. Effect of restriction to flow on the process, with R_2 =0.3.

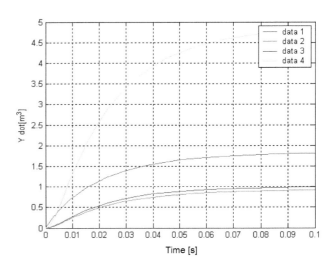

Figure 13. Effect of restriction to flow on the Process, with R_2 = 0.9.

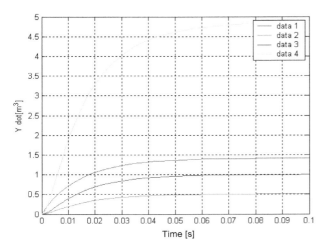

Figure 11. Effect of restriction to flow on the process, with R_2 =0.5.

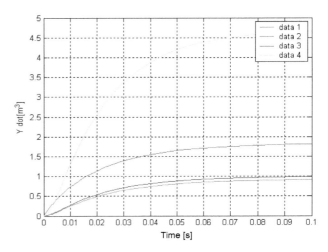

Figure 14. Effect of restriction to flow on the process, with R_3 =1.0.

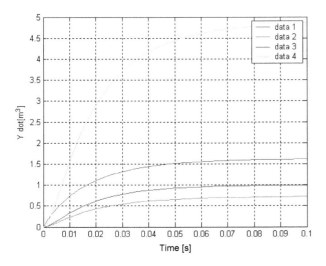

Figure 12. Effect of restriction to flow on the process, with R_2 =0.7.

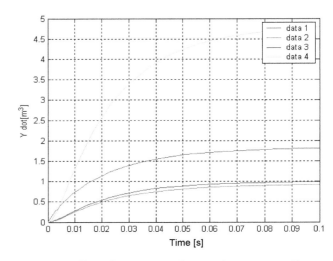

Figure 15. Effect of restriction to flow on the process, with R_3 = 3.0.

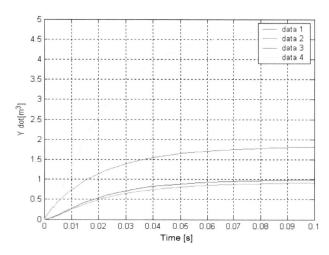

Figure 16. Effect of restriction to flow on the process, with R_3 = 5.0.

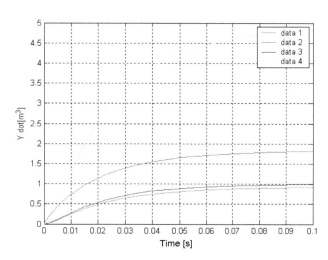

Figure 17. Effect of restriction to flow on the process, with R_3 =7.0.

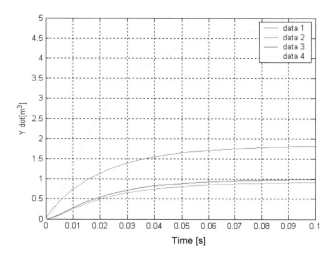

Figure 18. Effect of restriction to flow on the process, with R_3 =9.0.

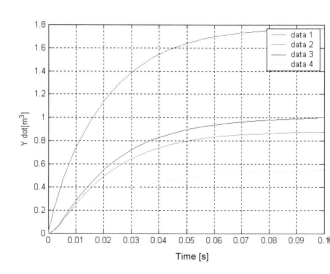

Figure 19. Effect of wound string on the process, with L =1.0.

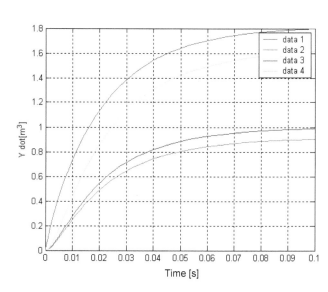

Figure 20. Effect of wound string on the process, with L =3.0.

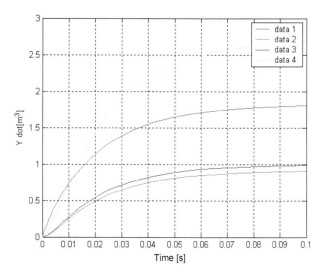

Figure 21. Effect of wound string on the process, with L =5.0.

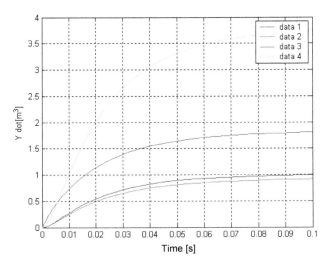

Figure 22. Effect of wound string on the process, with L =7.0.

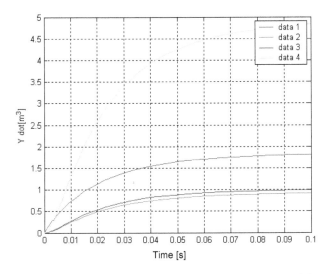

Figure 23. Effect of wound string on the process, with L =9.0.

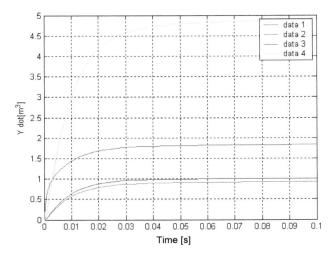

Figure 24. Effect of the capacity of tank on the process, with C_1 =1e-03.

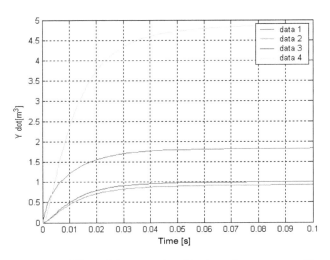

Figure 25. Effect of the capacity of tank on the process, with C_1 =3e-03.

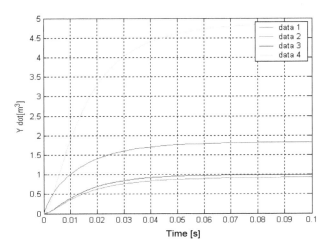

Figure 26. Effect of the capacity of tank on the process, with C_1 =5e-03.

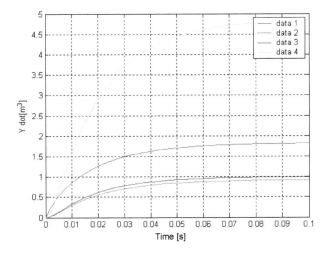

Figure 27. Effect of the capacity of tank on the process, with C_1 =7e-03.

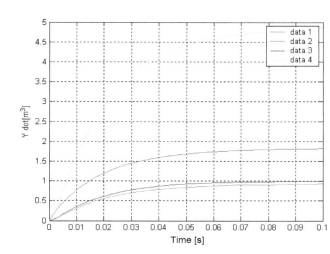

Figure 28. Effect of the capacity of tank on the process, with C_1 =9e-03.

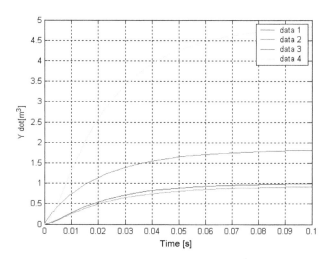

Figure 29. Effect of the capacity of tank on the process, with C_2 =1e-03.

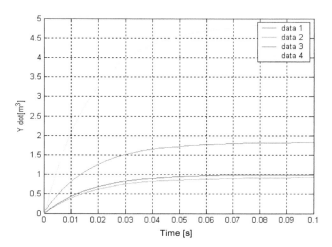

Figure 30. Effect of the capacity of tank on the process, with C_2 =3e-03.

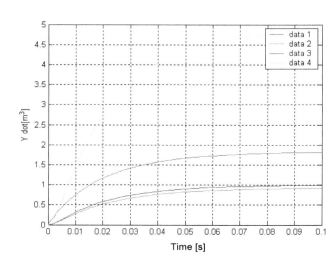

Figure 31. Effect of the capacity of tank on the process, with C_2 =5e-03.

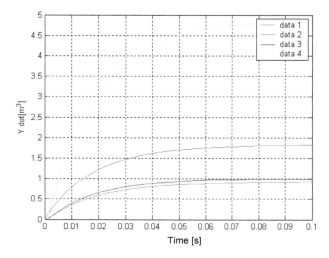

Figure 32. Effect of the capacity of tank on the process, with C_2 =7e-03.

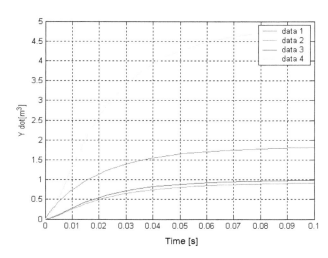

Figure 33. Effect of the capacity of tank on the process, with C_2 =9e-03.

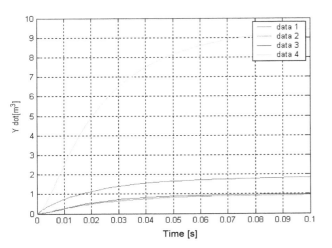

Figure 34. Effect of the capacity of tank on the process, with C_3 =1000e-03.

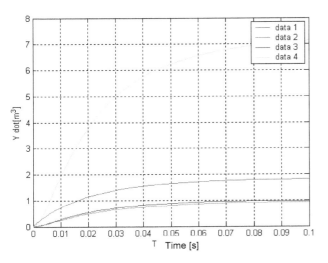

Figure 35. Effect of the capacity of tank on the PROCESS, with C_3 =1300e-03.

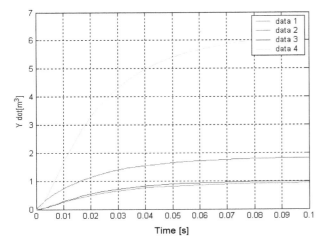

Figure 36. Effect of the capacity of tank on the process, with C_3 =1500e-03.

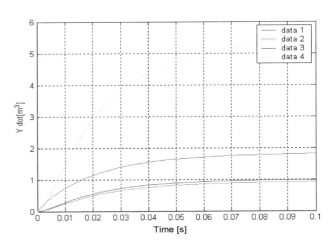

Figure 37. Effect of the capacity of tank on the process, with C_3 =1700e-03.

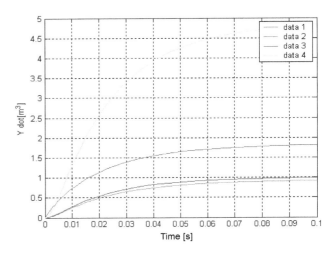

Figure 38. Effect of the capacity of tank on the process, with C_3 =1900e-03.

Data 1

v_{c1} = h_1 (voltage across capacitor 1, as water level of tank 1).

Data 2

v_{c2} = h_2 (voltage across capacitor 2, as water level of tank 2).

Data 3

i_1 = Q_1 (flow of current through the inductor, as rate of water flow through the filter).

Data 4

v_{c3} = h_3 (voltage across capacitor 3, as water level of tank 3).

Vertical Line

Ydot[m³]=(Response of voltages[v] and current[A] to change(s) in the RLC circuit;
as Response of water levels[m] and rate of water flow[cub-m/min] to
change(s) in system parameters).

Horizontal Line

Time[s]=(model time; real time).

Table 4. Table of values with R_1 varied while other parameters were kept constant.

R_1	R_2	R_3	L	C_1	C_2	C_3	v_{c1}	v_{c2}	i	v_{c3}
0.1	0.9	9.0	9.0	9e-03	9e-03	1900e-03	1.0232	0.9237	0.9904	4.8779
0.3	0.9	9.0	9.0	9e-03	9e-03	1900e-03	1.2206	0.9222	0.9895	4.8698
0.5	0.9	9.0	9.0	9e-03	9e-03	1900e-03	1.4168	0.9200	0.9878	4.8577
0.7	0.9	9.0	9.0	9e-03	9e-03	1900e-03	1.6121	0.9175	0.9858	4.8442
0.9	0.9	9.0	9.0	9e-03	9e-03	1900e-03	1.8055	0.9142	0.9830	4.8269

Table 5. Table of values with R_2 varied while other parameters were kept constant.

R_2	R_1	R_3	L	C_1	C_2	C_3	v_{c1}	v_{c2}	i	v_{c3}
0.1	0.9	9.0	9.0	9e-03	9e-03	1900e-03	1.0042	0.1046	0.9991	4.9362
0.3	0.9	9.0	9.0	9e-03	9e-03	1900e-03	1.2108	0.3122	0.9971	4.9184
0.5	0.9	9.0	9.0	9e-03	9e-03	1900e-03	1.4144	0.5171	0.9945	4.8975
0.7	0.9	9.0	9.0	9e-03	9e-03	1900e-03	1.6133	0.7183	0.9901	4.8683
0.9	0.9	9.0	9.0	9e-03	9e-03	1900e-03	1.8055	0.9142	0.9830	4.8269

Analysis of the results of the simulation

The analysis of the results of the seven (7) simulations made by varying the values of the parameters of the model, one after the other, and the interpretations of the observed values of the variables (v_{c1}, v_{c2}, i, and v_{c3}) as related to the rate of water flow, are given below:

First simulation

An increase in the Restriction (R_1) to flow between tanks 1 and 2 (as shown in Figure 1) (while keeping the other parameters constant, Table 4), caused reasonable increase in the water level of tank 1; water levels of tanks 2 and 3 decreased and flow (i_1) through the filter (L) also decreased, as demonstrated by the graphs shown in Figures 4, 5, 6, 7 and 8. In essence, this may be regarded as attempting to fine tune the process so as to influence the overall rate of water flow into the sachet bag (since varying 1 R has an effect on the water levels of tanks 1, 2, 3 and water flow (i_1) through the filter).

Second simulation

An increase in the restriction (R_2) of water flow between tank 2 and filter (while keeping the other parameters constant, Table 5) caused reasonable increase in water levels of tanks 1 and 2, with tank 2 affected most, while the flow of water through the filter and the water level of tank 3 decreased. This could be interpreted to mean that an increase in R_2 decreased the water levels in tank 3, thereby decreasing the water flow into the sachet bag. These observations are demonstrated by the graphs shown in Figures 9, 10, 11, 12 and 13. As stated above, this can also be interpreted as attempting to fine tune

the process so as to influence the overall rate of water flow into the sachet bag.

Third simulation

An increase in the restriction, (R_3) (while keeping the other parameters constant, Table 6) caused an increase in the water levels of all the tanks 1, 2, 3 [minimal changes (increase) in water levels of tanks 1, 2 and reasonable changes (increase) in water level of tank 3], while flow of water through the filter decreased. This observation was demonstrated by the graphs shown in Figures 14, 15, 16, 17 and 18.

The essence of this is to fine tune the process so as to get the right flow of water from the plant into the sachet bag. More specifically, this parameter is used to control the rate of water flow into the sachet bag.

Fourth simulation

Varying L (the inductance) and keeping other parameters constant (Table 7), caused minimal changes (increase) in the water levels of all the tanks 1, 2, 3, while the flow (i_1) of water through the filter decreased showing that at high filtration, the flow of water through the filter lessened (decreased).

This observation is demonstrated by the graphs shown in Figures 19, 20, 21, 22 and 23. This could be interpreted as indicating that at high filtration (indicating increase in number of wound string of the conductor), the flow (i_1) of water through the filter decreases, thereby affecting the overall output of water flow into the sachet bag.

Fifth simulation

Varying C_1 (increasing the capacity of tank 1) and keeping

Table 6. Table of values with R_3 varied while other parameters were kept constant.

R_3	R_1	R_2	L	C_1	C_2	C_3	v_{c1}	v_{c2}	i	v_{c3}
1.0	0.9	0.9	9.0	9e-03	9e-03	1900e-03	1.8051	0.9138	0.9832	4.6573
3.0	0.9	0.9	9.0	9e-03	9e-03	1900e-03	1.8054	0.9141	0.9830	4.7839
5.0	0.9	0.9	9.0	9e-03	9e-03	1900e-03	1.8055	0.9142	0.9830	4.8096
7.0	0.9	0.9	9.0	9e-03	9e-03	1900e-03	1.8055	0.9142	0.9830	4.8207
9.0	0.9	0.9	9.0	9e-03	9e-03	1900e-03	1.8055	0.9142	0.9830	4.8269

Table 7. Table of values with L varied while other parameters were kept constant.

L	R_1	R_2	R_3	C_1	C_2	C_3	v_{c1}	v_{c2}	i	v_{c3}
1.0	0.9	0.9	9.0	9e-03	9e-03	1900e-03	1.7680	0.8714	0.9949	0.5428
3.0	0.9	0.9	9.0	9e-03	9e-03	1900e-03	1.7959	0.9033	0.9860	1.6138
5.0	0.9	0.9	9.0	9e-03	9e-03	1900e-03	1.8018	0.9099	0.9843	2.6851
7.0	0.9	0.9	9.0	9e-03	9e-03	1900e-03	1.8043	0.9127	0.9835	3.7562
9.0	0.9	0.9	9.0	9e-03	9e-03	1900e-03	1.8055	0.9142	0.9830	4.8269

Table 8. Table of values with C_1 varied while other parameters were kept constant.

C_1	C_2	C_3	L	R_1	R_2	R_3	v_{c1}	v_{c2}	i	v_{c3}
1e-03	9e-03	1900e-03	9.0	0.9	0.9	9.0	1.8313	0.9316	0.9960	4.9213
3e-03	9e-03	1900e-03	9.0	0.9	0.9	9.0	1.8282	0.9293	0.9951	4.9085
5e-03	9e-03	1900e-03	9.0	0.9	0.9	9.0	1.8241	0.9263	0.9933	4.8919
7e-03	9e-03	1900e-03	9.0	0.9	0.9	9.0	1.8170	0.9215	0.9896	4.8660
9e-03	9e-03	1900e-03	9.0	0.9	0.9	9.0	1.8055	0.9142	0.9830	4.8269

other parameters constant (Table 8), caused changes (decrease) in all the water levels of tanks 1, 2, 3 and flow (i_1) through the filter, as demonstrated by the graphs shown in Figures 24, 25, 26, 27 and 28.

The essence of this variation is to study the effects of C_1 (capacity of tank 1) on the process (flow of water into the sachet bag) and its interaction with the other parameters of the model. In this circumstance, the increase in the value of C_1 could be interpreted as decreasing the rate of water flow into the sachet bags.

Sixth simulation

Varying C_2 (capacity of tank 2) and keeping other parameters constant (Table 9), caused changes (decrease) in all the water levels of tanks 1, 2, 3 and flow (i_1) through the filter, as demonstrated by the graphs shown in Figures 29, 30, 31, 32 and 33.

This is also to study the effects of C_2 (capacity of tank 2) on the process (flow of water into the sachet bag) and its interaction with the other parameters of the model.

Seventh simulation

Varying C_3 (capacity of tank 3) and keeping other parameters constant (Table 10), caused changes (decrease) in all the water levels of tanks 1, 2, 3, while it caused an increase in flow (i_1) through the filter, showing that any variation of the capacity of tank 3 affects all the water levels of tanks 1, 2, 3 (decrease) and flow (i_1) of water through the filter (increase). This observation is demonstrated by the graphs shown in Figures 34, 35, 36, 37 and 38. The essence of this variation is to study the effects of C_3 (capacity of tank 3) to the process (flow of water into the sachet bag) and its interaction with other parameters of the model.

Observations

Connecting pipes

It was observed that varying the restriction of the connecting pipes implies that either the radius (size) of the pipe is decreased/increased or the length of the pipe is increased/decreased which significantly influences the flow of

Table 9. Table of values with C_2 varied while other parameters were kept constant.

C_2	C_1	C_3	L	R_1	R_2	R_3	v_{c1}	v_{c2}	i	v_{c3}
1e-03	9e-03	1900e-03	9.0	0.9	0.9	9.0	1.8211	0.9265	0.9935	4.8929
3e-03	9e-03	1900e-03	9.0	0.9	0.9	9.0	1.8185	0.9243	0.9918	4.8810
5e-03	9e-03	1900e-03	9.0	0.9	0.9	9.0	1.8143	0.9212	0.9891	4.8641
7e-03	9e-03	1900e-03	9.0	0.9	0.9	9.0	1.8106	0.9182	0.9866	4.8479
9e-03	9e-03	1900e-03	9.0	0.9	0.9	9.0	1.8055	0.9142	0.9830	4.8269

Table 10. Table of values with C_3 varied while other parameters were kept constant.

C_3	C_1	C_2	L	R_1	R_2	R_3	v_{c1}	v_{c2}	i	v_{c3}
1000e-03	9e-03	9e-03	9.0	0.9	0.9	9.0	1.8287	0.9408	0.9753	9.4005
1300e-03	9e-03	9e-03	9.0	0.9	0.9	9.0	1.8173	0.9278	0.9791	7.1447
1500e-03	9e-03	9e-03	9.0	0.9	0.9	9.0	1.8124	0.9221	0.9807	6.1590
1700e-03	9e-03	9e-03	9.0	0.9	0.9	9.0	1.8085	0.9177	0.9820	5.4122
1900e-03	9e-03	9e-03	9.0	0.9	0.9	9.0	1.8055	0.9142	0.9830	4.8269

water through the filter, but caused varying effects on the water levels in all the tanks. It is an attempt to fine tune the process so as to influence the rate of water flow (to get the right water flow from the plant).

Capacity of the tanks

It was observed that varying the value of the capacities (capacitances) of any of the tanks in the process significantly influences (decreases/increases) the water levels in all the tanks, but caused varying effects on the flow of water through the filter. This implies that an increase in the value of C (capacity of tank) decreases the water level (h) in the tank and hence the rate of water flow in the process, while a decrease in the value of C (capacity of tank) increases h and hence the rate of water flow in the process depending on the type and size of pipe used which must obey the relations stated in Equations 8 – 11.

Inductance of the filter

It was observed that varying the inductance (L) of the filter influences the water levels in all the tanks, but caused changes (decrease) in the flow of water through the filter, implying that an increase in the inductance (L) (number of wound string on the filter cartridge) increases filteration. An increase in filteration tends to decrease the flow of water through the filter, and this in turn tends to influence the rate of water flow in the process.

DISCUSSION

From these results, it was observed that by varying the electrical parameters (resistors, capacitors,

inductor), it is possible to study the way the manipulation of equivalent parameters of the analogous mechanical components (the connecting pipes, the water tanks and the water filter) of the sachet water plant could influence the rate of water flow in the production process of sachet water. This work demonstrates the possibility and advantage of using electrical model to study any analogous mechanical and other system types.

Conclusion

From the analysis, it is observed that varying any of the values of the parameters of the model (Table 3) has an effect on the water levels in the various tanks and the flow of water through the filter. All these variations affect the overall rate of water flow into the sachet bag.

Of particular note is that varying the capacity of any of the tanks (1,2,3) significantly decreases the water levels in all the tanks, but causes varying effects on the flow through the filter. The analysis of this paper on modeling a water sachet production plant is a very simple way of knowing from the beginning the various sizes of pipes, tanks and filter to be used and how these will affect the flow of water in the plant before going into the physical construction of the plant. This method could be used in a more complex system.

This paper also has shown that it is possible to use the commercially available software package, MATLAB®, to model and simulate the dynamic behaviour of sachet water processing plant. By using the developed program, it becomes simple to compute and study the effect of the state variables on the system during transient state.

The program, although it is specific for sachet water processing plant, can easily be modified and adopted for any water processing plant of interest. The analysis and simulation results presented in this paper will be of immense benefit in the development and realization of a simple sachet water processing plant.

REFERENCES

Ani VA (2007). Simulation of a Sachet Water Processing Plant Using an Analogous Electrical Model. (M.Sc thesis) Department of Electronic Engineering, University of Nigeria Nsukka.

Ani VA (2007). Simulation of a Sachet Water Processing Plant Using an Analogous Electrical Model. (M.Sc thesis) Department of Electronic Engineering, University of Nigeria Nsukka.

Ani VA (2013a). Analogous Electrical Model of Water Processing Plant as a Tool to Study "The Real Problem" of Process Control. Int. J. Control Theory Comput. Model. (IJCTCM) 3:1.

Ani VA (2013b) Process Control Model of a Simple Water Treatment Plant. Trends in Mechanical Engineering and Technology (TMET)

Casey TJ (2008). Unit Treatment Processes in Water and Wastewater Engineering Aquavarra Research Limited www.aquavarra.ie/publications.

Dorf RC, Bishop RH (1998). "Modern Control Systems". Addison-Wesley Longman, Inc., New York, 8th edition, p. 38.

Hardt WF (1971). Hydrologic Analysis of Mojave River Basin, California, using Electric Analog Model. U.S. Geological Survey Open-file Report No. 97.

LeChevallier MW, Kwok-Keung AU (2004). Water Treatment and Pathogen Control: Process Efficiency in Achieving Safe Drinking Water. IWA Publishing, London, UK. http://www.who.int/water_sanitation_health/dwq/en/watreatpath6.pdf.

MATLAB (1997). "The MATLAB Compiler User's Guide". In: Mathworks Handbook. Matheworks: Natick.

Nise SN (2003). Control Systems Engineering. John Wiley & Sons, New York.

Ord-Smith JR, Stephenson J (1975). Computer Simulation of Continuous Systems. Cambridge University Press, London.

Patten PE (1965). Design, Construction and use of electric analog models in A.L.Wood and K.R.Gabrysch. Analog model study of ground water in the Houston District, Texas: Texas water Comm. Bull. 6508:41-60.

Perdikaris GA (1996). Computer Controlled Systems: Theory and Applications. Kluwer Academic Publishers: Netherlands.

Schwedes H (1995). Teaching with Analogies. In Psillos D. (Ed) Proceedings of the second PhD Summer School on European Research in Science Education, Thessaloniki. www.physics.ohio-state.edu/ICPE/TOC.html.

Shearer JL, Murphy AT, Richardson HH (1971). Introduction to System Dynamics. Addison-Wesley Publication Co., Inc., London, pp. 82-84, 102-165.

The Mathworks Inc (2002) Natick, MA, USA. Using MATLAB (v6.5).

Walton WC, Prickett TA (1963). Hydrogeologic Electric Analog Computer: American Society of Civil Engineers. J. Hydraul. Div. V.89, no.HY6, Proc. Paper 3695:67-91.

25

New technique based on uterine electromyography nonlinearity for preterm delivery detection

Safaa M. Naeem, Ahmed F. Seddik and Mohamed A. Eldosoky

Department of Biomedical Engineering, Helwan University, Helwan, Egypt.

Detecting uterine electromyography (EMG) signals can yield a promising approach to determine and take actions to prevent preterm deliveries. This paper objective is to predict this risk using such uterine signals. Previous classification studies have used only linear signal processing which depends on the spectral characteristics of the uterine EMG signals that did not give clinically acceptable results. On the other hand some studies have made linear and non-linear analysis for the signals and have found that the non-linear parameters can distinguish the preterm delivery in better way than the linear parameters. In this research, two methods will be taken; the first method is to take some linear parameters to a suitable neural network and the second one is to take some non-linear parameters to the same network. Then, the two results are compared by calculating parameters False Positive Rate, False Negative Rate, True Positive Rate, True Negative Rate and Accuracy to evaluate the classification performance. Besides, a linear parameter, discrete cosine transform, which depends on the spectral characteristics of the signals, is taken as an additional feature to the same network so the research will have a third method to illustrate the difference between the traditional previous classification method and the proposed ones. Applying the second method gives better results than the first and the third methods. The paper can propose a method depends on the uterine EMG nonlinearity which gives best results to detect preterm delivery compared with those used in previous studies.

Key words: Uterine electromyography (EMG) signals, term-preterm deliveries prediction, neural network performance evaluation, discrete cosine transform.

INTRODUCTION

A most urgent challenge in healthcare currently is the phenomenon of preterm labor, or labor prior to 37 completed weeks of gestation. Preterm labor leaves serious impacts on economy and society as a whole. The complications of preterm birth include significant neurological, mental, behavioral and pulmonary problems in later child's life (Diab et al., 2010). So any promising technique that could improve the chances of preterm birth prediction is required. Analysis of uterine electromyography (EMG), termed as electrohysterogram (EHG), records is one such technique.

Uterine EMG has been the subject of research for many years from 1950. The uterine EMG has been proved to be of interest for pregnancy and parturition monitoring (Diab et al., 2007). Uterine EMG classification, in previous researches, depends on the spectral characteristics of EMG activity. Wavelet transform is a tool that has been used to describe the uterine EMG activity and Power Spectral Density (Diab et al., 2007) as well as the Wavelet Packet Transform (Moslem et al., 2012). Most of the used signal-processing techniques were linear which rely on the changes in the frequency power spectrum of the uterine activity and included the following: the peak frequency of the power spectrum (Garfield et al., 2005); the burst energy levels (Maul et al., 2004); the mean power frequency (Hassan et al., 2010), the use of the peak frequency, the duration and number of bursts, the means and deviations of the frequency spectrum (Maner and Garfield, 2007); and the approaches of analyzing contractions using multiple techniques such as the kurtosis and skewness coefficient. Other approaches included calculating the root mean square of the signals and the median frequency of the power spectrum and the autocorrelation zero-crossing (Fele-Žorž et al., 2008).

It is known that the underlying physiological mechanisms of biological systems are non-linear processes (Akay, 2001). As the uterus is composed of billions of intricately interconnected cells whose responses are non-linear, it may be regarded as a complex, non-linear dynamic system. To analyze the outputs of such a system, non-linear signal processing techniques are applicable. Therefore, one can hypothesize that non-linear signal processing techniques may yield better results in analysis of the EHG than linear ones (Naeem et al., 2013). These techniques included time reversibility and approximate entropy (Hassan et al., 2010), another research estimated Max-Lyapunov exponent, correlation dimension and sample entropy (Fele-Žorž et al., 2008).

In this research, a combination between most of these previous techniques is done as some of the linear techniques and some of non-linear techniques are used in order to estimate their ability to recognize uterine EMG records of term and preterm deliveries using artificial neural networks ANNs.

The following linear features are chosen: the mean power frequency, the root mean square, the peak and median frequencies of the power spectrum and the autocorrelation zero-crossing and taking them into a suitable ANN to calculate the classifier parameters; while the non-linear features are: time reversibility, approximate entropy, the Max-Lyapunov exponent, the correlation dimension, phase space reconstruction based on the derivatives approach and singular spectrum analysis, adjusted amplitude Fourier transform and the sample entropy of the signal and also taking them into the same ANN to calculate the classifier parameters. Finally, compare the results to estimate the ability of linear and non-linear techniques to differentiate uterine EMG records of term and preterm deliveries. It is expectable

that the classification method depends on the nonlinear uterine EMG features gives better results.

In addition that, using a linear parameter discrete cosine transform (DCT) which depends on the spectral characteristics and the frequency contents of the uterine EMG signals and is taken as an additional linear feature to the same ANN to illustrate the difference between the traditional previous classification method and the proposed ones. The results show that this method is better than the linear method but the non-linear one is still the best.

MATERIALS AND METHODS

Database description

This research uses Term Preterm ElectroHysteroGram Data Base (TPEHG DB). The records were obtained during regular check-ups either around the 22nd week or around the 32nd week of gestation at the University Medical Centre Ljubljana, Department of Obstetrics and Gynecology, Slovenia (PhysioBank database Website [Online], 2011) and used for studies by Ivan Verdenik (Fele-Žorž et al., 2008). The DB used contains 300 uterine EMG records of which:

(i) 262 records were obtained where delivery was on term
(ii) 143 before the 26th week of gestation.
(iii) 119 during-after the 26th week of gestation.
(iv) -38 records were obtained during pregnancies which ended prematurely
(v) 19 before the 26th week of gestation.
(vi) 19 during-after the 26th week of gestation.

Each record is composed of three channels, recorded from four electrodes as shown in Figure 1. The differences in the electrical potentials of the electrodes produced three channels: S1 = E2–E1, S2 = E2–E3 andS3 = E4–E3.
In this paper, used records were digitally filtered using band pass filter (0.3 to 3 Hz) neglecting either these records were taken after or before the 26th week of gestation but the research uses them generally to make a classification into two classes, term and preterm signals.

Feature extraction

Linear features

Mean power frequency: The mean power frequency (MPF) is the frequency at which the average power within the epoch is reached (Frequency signal analysis-BIOPAC Systems Inc. [Online] (2012) and computed from the power spectral density (PSD) of the signal obtained by Welsh's averaged periodogram method (Hassan et al., 2010).

Peak frequency: The peak frequency is the frequency at which the maximum power occurs during the epoch (Maner and Garfield, 2007). For each signal, $x(t)$, the peak frequency, f_{max}, is calculated as following (Akay, 2001):

$$f_{max} = arg\left(\frac{f_s}{N}max_{i=0}^{N-1}P(i)\right)$$

(1)

Where f_s and N denotes the sampling frequency and the number of samples, respectively. P is the frequency-power spectrum.

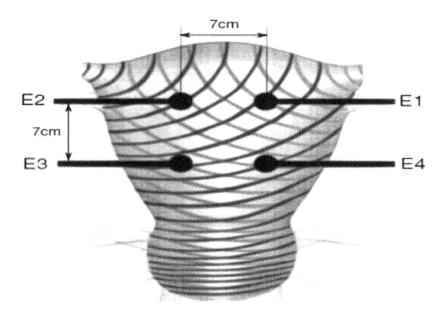

Figure 1. The placement of the electrodes on the abdomen, above the uterine surface.

Root mean square: The root mean square value (RMS) of a signal, $x(i)$, with length N is the root of the mean of the squares of all samples in a signal (Fele-Žorž et al., 2008):

$$RMS = \sqrt{\frac{1}{N}\sum_{i=0}^{N-1} x(i)^2}$$

(2)

Median frequency: The median frequency was defined as the frequency just above where the sums of the parts above and below in the frequency-power spectrum, P, are the same (Fele-Žorž et al., 2008) or it is the frequency at which 50% of the total power within the epoch is reached (Frequency signal analysis-BIOPAC Systems Inc. [Online] (2012).

Autocorrelation zero-crossing: The autocorrelation zero-crossing, τ_{Rxx}, is defined as the first zero-crossing starting at the peak in the autocorrelation, $R_{xx}(\tau)$, of the signal $x(t)$ (Fele-Žorž et al., 2008):

$$R_{xx}(\tau_{Rxx}) = 0 , R_{xx}(\tau) = \sum_{i=0}^{N-1} x(i)\,x(\tau + i)$$

(3)

Discrete cosine transform (DCT): DCT generates real spectrum of a real signal and thereby avoids redundant data and computation. The DCT of a real sequence, $x(n)$, with length N is defined as:

$$y(k) = w(k)\sum_{n=1}^{N} x(n)\cos\frac{\pi(2n-1)(k-1)}{2N} \quad , k = 1,...,N$$

(4)

$$w(k) = \begin{cases} 1/\sqrt{N} & , \quad k = 1 \\ \sqrt{2/N} & , \quad 2 \leq k \leq N \end{cases}$$

(5)

Non-linear features

Approximate entropy: As mentioned by Pincus (1991) the approximate entropy, ApEn, is defined as a measure that quantifies the regularity and predictability of the signals. The ApEn value is low for regular time series and high for complex, irregular ones (Hassan et al., 2010). This paper uses the method applied in [6] to compute the ApEn.

$$ApEn(m,r,\tau,N) = \Phi^m(r) - \Phi^{m+1}(r)$$

(6)

$$\Phi^m(r) = \frac{1}{N-(m-1)\tau} \sum_{i=1}^{N-(m-1)\tau} \log C_i^m(r)$$

(7)

Where r, the filter parameter value, is r=0.2*SD, SD is the standard deviation of the signal and $C_i^m(r)$ is the correlation sum.

Sample entropy: The sample entropy, SampEn, is a measure of complexity that can be easily applied to any type of time series data. It is conceptually similar to approximate entropy (ApEn), but SampEn does not depend on the data size as much as ApEn does (Lee, 2010).

Phase space reconstruction

Reconstruction based on derivative approach: The phase space dimension or reconstruction dimension, usually symbolized by letter d or E, is defined as the number of states that can be displayed in phase space. Phase space in d- dimensions will display a number of points $\{x(n)\}$ of the system, where each point is given by:

$$\vec{x}(n) = [x(n),x(n+T),...,x(n+(d-1)T)]$$

(8)

Where n is a moment in time of a system variable, and T is a period between two consecutive measurements of the variable. There is a problem with the phase space graphical presentation, if it has more than three dimensions (Jovic and Bogunovic, 2007). Phase space reconstruction is a standard procedure when analyzing chaotic systems. It shows the trajectory of the system in time. Here the phase space reconstruction is obtained by a method based on derivatives approach (Packard et al., 1980) that is, by taking $\vec{x}'(n)$, $\vec{x}''(n)$,...etc.

Reconstruction based on the singular spectrum approach (SSA):

SSA is a method of decomposition of time-series into the sum of a small number of independent components. The basic SSA algorithm has two stages: decomposition and reconstruction. The decomposition stage requires embedding and singular value decomposition (SVD). Embedding decomposes the original time series into the trajectory matrix; SVD turns the trajectory matrix into the decomposed trajectory matrices which will turn into the trend, seasonal, monthly components, and white noises according to their singular values. The reconstruction stage demands the grouping to make subgroups of the decomposed trajectory matrices and diagonal averaging to reconstruct the new time series from the subgroups that is, the concept of SSA consists of four steps: embedding, SVD, grouping, and diagonal averaging and all these steps mentioned in details (Yung, 2009).

Amplitude adjusted Fourier transform (AAFT)

The AAFT algorithm generates surrogate data set and this paper takes the same steps mentioned in Garfield et al. (2005) to create the AAFT for uterine EMG data. The idea is to first rescale the value in the original time series so they are Gaussian. Then the FT algorithm can be used to make surrogate time series which have the same Fourier spectrum as the rescaled data. Finally, the Gaussian surrogate is then rescaled back to have the amplitude distribution as the original time series.

Time reversibility

A time series is said to be reversible only if its probabilistic properties are invariant with respect to time reversal (Hassan et al., 2010). In this research a simple equation described in Hassan et al. (2010) is used to calculate the time reversibility T_R for a signal X:

$$T_R(\tau) = \frac{1}{N-\tau} \sum_{n=\tau+1}^{N} (X_n - X_{n-\tau})^3 \tag{9}$$

Where N is the signal length and in this paper we used $\tau=1$. Time irreversibility can be taken as a strong signature of nonlinearity.

Maximal Lyapunov exponent and correlation dimension

To calculate both parameters a practical method in Fele-Žorž et al. (2008) is used which is based on input data, represented in a phase space. The phase space is a construct which demonstrates or visualizes the changes of the dynamical variables of a system. For any time series, the phase space which is the same as original phase space of the system is reconstructed by using time-delayed samples as the coordinates of the new system.

The maximal Lyapunov exponent estimates the amount of chaos in a system and represents the maximal velocity with which different, almost identical states of the system, diverge (Fele-Žorž et al., 2008). Then the Lyapunov exponent can be calculated as the following equation as the maximum Lyapunov exponent, λ, is a measure of how fast a trajectory converges from a given point into some other trajectory:

$$\lambda = \lim_{t \to \infty} \lim_{\|\Delta y_0\| \to 0} \frac{1}{t} \log \frac{\|\Delta y_t\|}{\|\Delta y_0\|} \tag{10}$$

Where $\|\Delta y_0\|$ represents the Euclidean distance between two states of the system at some arbitrary time t_0 and $\|\Delta y_t\|$ represents the Euclidean distance between the two states of the system at some later time t.

In chaos theory, the correlation dimension, D_{corr}, is a measure of the dimensionality of the space occupied by a set of random points, often referred to as a type of fractal dimension. It is proportional to the probability of the distance between two points on a trajectory being less than some r [8]:

$$D_{corr} = \lim_{r \to 0} \frac{\log(C(r))}{\log(r)} \tag{11}$$

Where $C(r)$ is the correlation integral.

Principal component analysis

PCA is an orthogonal linear transformation that transforms the original time series by projecting it to a new set of coordinates in order of decreasing variance. The transformation is by definition an optimum transformation in the least squares sense. This method reduces the dimension of the representation space to keep only the most important information represented in fewer dimension space domains (The iPredict website [Online], 2012).

The PCA is applied for the parameters (AAFT, derivative phase space reconstruction, SSA and DCT) to obtain only ten features from 24001, 24000, 23999 and 24001 features respectively. To explain why only 10 features are chosen, two notes must be taken in consideration. First, the principal component coefficients for a M×N matrix - where M is the number of patterns and N is the number of features- are a N×N matrix. Second, the condition for classifier pattern matrix construction is that the term and preterm signals must have the same number of features. An explanation example, a 150×24001 matrix is the PCA input obtained from applying the AAFT on the training term signals and a 19×24001 matrix from the training preterm ones. After applying the PCA, a 24001×24001 matrix is obtained from the term AAFT spectrum and a 24001×24001 matrix from the preterm one. Then we can take only the first ten most principal components that have the highest variance into the ANN pattern matrix.

Artificial neural network

An important step is the classification step and actually, in this research, three types of artificial neural network ANNs are used to reach best results. One of them is unsupervised learning method (Kohonen self-organizing network) (Goyal and Goyal, 2011) and the others are supervised learning methods (feed-forward back propagation network and trainable cascade-forward back propagation network) (Goyal and Goyal, 2011). Each one of the previous networks is used for linear and non-linear features separately and gives its own parameters to compare. In the research a training data of 150 term signals and 19 preterm ones are used in addition to testing data of 111 term signals and 19 preterm ones.

RESULTS AND DISCUSSION

For each classifier, some parameters can be calculated to evaluate its performance. These parameters are:

Table 1. Resulting values of the used classifiers (linear).

Used classifier	Resulting values			
	FP	FN	TP	TN
Kohonen	12	52	7	59
Feed-forward	19	0	0	111
Cascade-forward	19	0	0	111

Table 2. Comparison of calculated parameters for the three used classifiers (linear).

Used classifier	Calculated parameter				
	FPR	FNR	TPR	TNR	ACC (%)
Kohonen	0.17	0.88	0.12	0.83	50.7
Cascade-forward	0.15	0.00	0.00	0.85	85.3
feed-forward	0.15	0.00	0.00	0.85	85.3

$$FPR = \frac{FP}{FP + TN}, \quad FNR = \frac{FN}{FN + TP} \tag{12}$$

$$TPR = \frac{TP}{TP + FN}, \quad TNR = \frac{TN}{TN + FP} \tag{13}$$

$$ACC = \frac{TP + TN}{TP + TN + FP + FN} \tag{14}$$

Where *TP*, *TN*, *FP* and *FN* stand respectively for True Positive, True Negative, False Positive and False Negative values. The values of *FPR*, *FNR*, *TPR*, *TNR* and *ACC* stand respectively for False Positive Rate, False Negative Rate, True Positive Rate (Sensitivity), True Negative Rate (Specificity) and Accuracy.

In the linear method as shown in Table 1 the Kohonen network can recognize 59 signals from 111 and seven signals from 19 for term and preterm uterine EMG respectively while the feed-forward and the cascade-forward networks cannot recognize any preterm uterine EMG signal. From these values Table 2 can be created and it indicates that the Kohonen network has a low sensitivity (0.12) which is higher than the feed-forward and cascade-forward networks' sensitivities (0.00) and it also has high FNR (0.88) while it is the opposite for the other classifiers with no FNR (0.00). From these values, we can observe that no one of the three used classifiers can separate between term and preterm deliveries in a perfect way where the Kohonen network can recognize some of the preterm records but also it classifies many term records as preterm ones. On the other hand the feed-forward and the cascade-forward networks cannot recognize any preterm record although they classify all the term records correctly. Figure 2 shows the representation of the results on the ROC graph.

In the non-linear method as shown in Table 3, the Kohonen network can recognize 80 signals from 111 and

nine signals from 19 for term and preterm uterine EMG respectively and the feed-forward network can recognize 107 signals from 111 and seven signals from 19 for term and preterm uterine EMG respectively while the cascade-forward networks can recognize 110 from 111 term signals and ten from 19 preterm ones. From these values, Table 4 can be created and it indicates that the Kohonen network has a low sensitivity (0.22) and high specificity (0.89) but it also has high FNR (0.78) while the feed-forward network has moderate sensitivity (0.64), high specificity (0.90) and low FNR (0.36). The cascade-forward network has high sensitivity (0.91) and high specificity (0.92) which are higher than the other used classifiers and it also has low FNR (0.09) and low FPR (0.08) which are lower than the others. From these values, we can observe that the cascade-forward network gives the best results where the Kohonen network can recognize some of the preterm records but also it classifies many term records as preterm ones. On the other hand the feed-forward network recognizes term and preterm records with lower errors than the Kohonen network but higher than these for the cascade-forward network. Figure 3 shows the representation of the results on the ROC graph.

In the additional linear method as shown in Table 5, the Kohonen network can recognize 77 signals from 111 and seven signals from 19 for term and preterm uterine EMG respectively and the feed-forward network can recognize 108 signals from 111 and five signals from 19 for term and preterm uterine EMG respectively while the cascade-forward networks can recognize 109 from 111 term signals and eight from 19 preterm ones. From the above values, Table 6 can be created and it indicates that the Kohonen network has a low sensitivity (0.17) and high specificity (0.87) but it also has high FNR (0.83) while the feed-forward network has moderate sensitivity (0.63), high specificity (0.89) and moderate FNR (0.37).

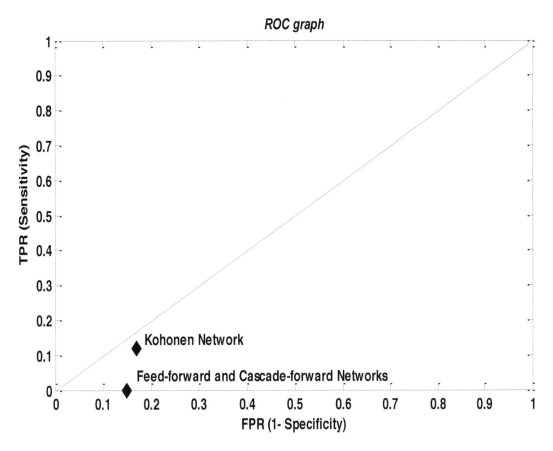

Figure 2. Representation of the results on ROC (Linear).

Table 3. Resulting values of the used classifiers (non-linear).

Used classifier	Resulting values			
	FP	FN	TP	TN
Kohonen	10	31	9	80
Feed-forward	12	4	7	107
Cascade-forward	9	1	10	110

Table 4. Comparison of calculated parameters for the three used classifiers (non-linear).

Used classifier	Calculated parameter				
	FPR	FNR	TPR	TNR	ACC (%)
Kohonen	0.11	0.78	0.22	0.89	68.5
Cascade-forward	0.10	0.36	0.64	0.90	87.7
Feed-forward	0.08	0.09	0.91	0.92	92.3

For the cascade-forward network, a sensitivity of (0.80) is obtained which is better than that in the previous linear method as it can recognize eight preterm signals from 19 ones and also it has low FNR (0.20) which is higher than that shown in Table 2 as it cannot recognize two term signals from 111 ones. In spite of that, the non-linear method shown in Table 4 is still the best. Figure 4 shows the representation of the results on the ROC graph.

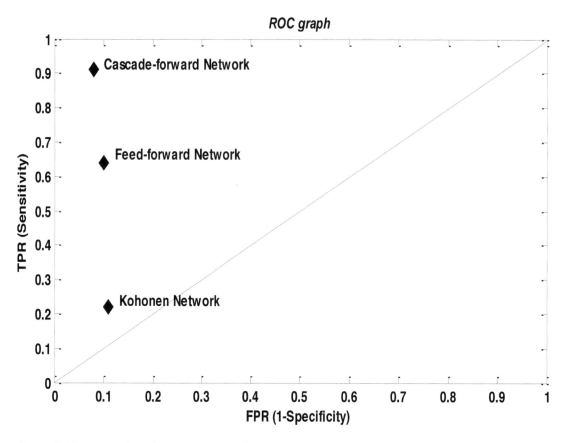

Figure 3. Representation of the results on ROC (Non- Linear).

Table 5. Resulting values of the used classifiers (linear+ DCT feature).

Used classifier	Resulting values			
	FP	FN	TP	TN
Kohonen	12	34	7	77
Feed-forward	14	3	5	108
Cascade-forward	11	2	8	109

Table 6. Comparison of calculated parameters for the three used classifiers (linear+ DCT feature).

Used classifier	Calculated parameter				
	FPR	FNR	TPR	TNR	ACC (%)
Kohonen	0.13	0.83	0.17	0.87	64.6
Cascade-forward	0.11	0.37	0.63	0.89	86.9
feed-forward	0.09	0.20	0.80	0.91	90

Conclusion

From the above results presented in this research some observations can be inferred. Firstly, using non-linear parameters of uterine EMG signals as ANN features can separate between term and preterm uterine EMG signals with results which are better than these for linear ones even if a spectral characteristic linear parameter (DCT) is used. Secondly, to get best classification accuracy with minimum error, you should use the trainable cascade-

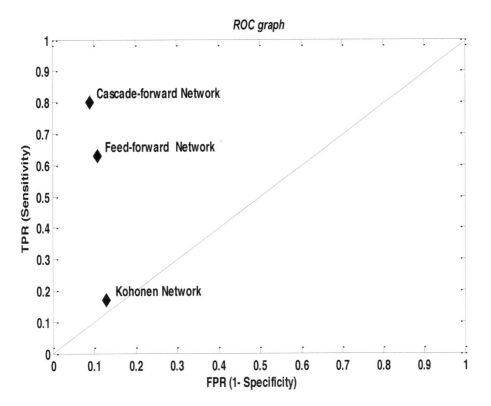

Figure 4. Representation of the results on ROC (Linear+ DCT feature).

forward back propagation network. Finally, the Kohonen network gives worse results in using both linear and non-linear parameters.

Conflict of Interest

The authors have not declared any conflict of interest.

REFERENCES

Diab MO, El-Merhie A, El-Halabi N, Khoder L (2010). "Classification of uterine EMG signals using supervised classification method," JbiSE, 3:837-842.

Diab MO, Marque C, Khalil MA (2007). "Classification for Uterine EMG Signals: Comparison between AR Model and Statistical Classification Method," IJCC.

Moslem B, Diab MO, Khalil MA, Marque C (2012). "Combining data fusion with multiresolution analysis for improving the classification accuracy of uterine EMG signals," EURASIP Journal on Advances in Signal Processing.

Garfield RE, Maner WL, MacKay LB, Schlembach D, Saade GR (2005). "Comparing uterine electromyography activity of antepartum patients versus term labor patients," Am. J. ObstetGynecol, 193:23-29.

Maul H, Maner WL, Olson G, Saade GR, Garfield RE (2004). "Non-invasive transabdominal uterine electromyography correlates with the strength of intrauterine pressure and is predictive of labor and delivery," J Matern Fetal Neonatal Med. 15:297-301.

Hassan M, Terrien J, Alexandersson A, Marque C, Karlsson B (2010). "Nonlinearity of EHG signals used to distinguish active labor from normal pregnancy contractions," In Proceedings of the 32nd Annual International Conference of the IEEE EMBS: 31 August- 4 September 2010; Buenos Aires, Argentina.

Maner WL, Garfield RE (2007). "Identification of human term and preterm labor using artificial neural networks on uterine electromyography data," Ann. Biomed. Eng. 35:465-473.

Fele-Žorž G, Kavšek G, Novak-Antolič Z, Jager F (2008). "A comparison of various linear and non-linear signal processing techniques to separate uterine EMG records of term and pre-term delivery groups," Med. Biol. Eng. Comput. 46:911-922.

Akay M (2001). Nonlinear biomedical signal processing. In dynamic analysis and modeling, IEEE Inc. New York. 2.

Naeem SM, Ali AF, Eldosoky MA (2013). "Comparison between Using Linear and Non-linear Features to Classify Uterine Electromyography Signals of Term and Preterm Deliveries," In Proceedings of the 30th National Radio Science Conference NRSC: 16-18 April 2013; Cairo, Egypt. pp. 488-498.

Pincus SM (1991). "Approximate entropy as a measure of system complexity," Proc. Natl. Acad. Sci. U S A, 88:2297-301.

Lee K (2010). File exchange – Mathworks. [Online]. Available: http://www.mathworks.com/matlabcentral/fileexchange/35784-sample-entropy.

Jovic A, Bogunovic N (2007). "Feature extraction for ECG time-series mining based on chaos theory," In Proceedings of the ITI 29th Int. Conf. on Information Technology Interfaces: 25-28June 2007; Cavtat, Croatia.

Packard NH, Cruchfield JP, Farmer JD, Shaw RS (1980). "Geometry from a Time Series," Physical Rev. Lett, 45:712-715.

Yung NK (2009). Singular Spectrum Analysis, Master's Thesis. University of California, Los Angeles.

Nielsen F (2001). Neural Networks – algorithms and applications, Niels Brock Business College.

Goyal S, Goyal GK (2011). Cascade and Feed-forward Backpropagation Artificial Neural Network Models for Prediction of Sensory Quality of Instant Coffee Flavoured Sterilized Drink," Can. J. Artificial Intelligence, Mach. Learn. Pattern recognition.

26

Relocation of source of sporadic production using genetic algorithm in distribution network

Shirin Farhadi[1] and Reza Dashti[2]

[1]Azad University of Jasb, Iran.
[2]Iran University of Science and Technology, Iran.

Today, due to the development of distribution systems and increase of demand and load, the use of the source of scattered production has developed. The establishment of the installation place and the size of the source of scattered production decrease network loss, lead to best action of network as well as the recovery of the voltage profile. In this article, we use the genetic algorithm for relocating and finding the best sources of scattered production with active power production and reactive power production by arranging and using them. Also in this article, in addition to decreased loss, balanced voltage, stabilization and recovery of profile have purpose function. The results show that the system of 33 bass is the power and effectiveness of the method.

Key words: Scattered production, optimization, genetic logs.

INTRODUCTION

The main shave of loss in one power system is related to the distribution system. The study shows that distribution system loses because of the high relation of R/X and high decrease of voltage in this system.

Today, increased demand and load leads to the development of the distribution system and its aspects; and this agent causes more loss of voltage and increases casualty. As a result, there is decreased voltage stability of knots and load imbalance.

Different methods created for determining the capacity of decomposed granite (DG) are presented in this work. Willis (2000) showed the famous legal 2/3 methods used for determining the optimum place of condenser, which in turn determines the optimum place of DG.

DG of 2/3 length lower than the post was installed.

Kashem et al. (2008) offered a number of methods for determining the optimum size of DG based on the sensation of the loss of power. The method based on the minimum casualty power in the presence of DG was established. The methods chosen were tested on the practical network in Tasmania and Australia. Acharya et al. (2007) used the increasing change in casualty power related to the change of the sensation factor of the real power injected; it was developed by Elgerd (1970). The factor this article was used to determine the bass that caused the casualty at the time the DG was installed on it, by arranging the offered method based on factor sensation.

The problem of this method is the length used in determining the place of optimum installation of DG in distribution network. It was also the only place to optimize the DG, and the only way to install a DG in the distribution network is proposed. Kean and Omalley (2006) also solve the DG optimum size on one of the line program (LP) on the Ireland network. In the literature, Rosehart and Nowicki (2007) presented a new model to determine location of DGs for economical distribution system and voltage improvement.

The purpose function was solved by using interpolation method (IP). The later output is the other rank of bass for DG installation.

The size of the optimum DG in this installation is not studied in this investigation. Hedayati et al. (2009) presented the method of load distribution for bass that is sensitive to reversal. The sensitive bass in this article is an appropriate place for DG installation.

The repeated method used for determining the place of DG optimum installation was used at first for one of the distinct capacity of DG that connected to the network the program of load distribution and the casualty of real power; voltage profile and the capacity of passing power of line are calculated. In the literature, MIthulananthan et al. (2006) determined the decreased casualty of real power of distribution network by using genetic algorithm (GA) containing the size of DG without considering any condition.

NR was used to calculate the casualty. Only one DG is investigated in this work. In the literature, Nara et al. (2001) hypothesized clearly the place of DG installation and used the method of Taboo to determine the size of DGs for the purpose of designing system network casualty.

Load is the source of fixed current generated by the coefficient of fixed power. Golshan and Arefifar (2007) have propounded the Taboo method for the size recovery of DG, where the source of reactive power like condenser and reactor or both in the distribution system is considered.

The purpose function decreases the cost of the reactive power, line load and the cost of the added reactive source.

In this investigation, the place of DG and source of reactive are not optimal.

PURPOSE FUNCTION

The aim of this study is to recover the technical function of network formulated in the form of recovery of two terms of technical network that include casualty and arrangement of the voltage of network distribution. So the presented purpose function is introduced in the form of one of the two purpose functions. In addition, the problem has equal condition, protection and functional condition which will be introduced later.

Relation 1 is description of the presented purpose function.

$$\text{Min.} f = f_1 + k_1 f_2 \qquad (1)$$

The function f_1, f_2 is also introduced by the following arrangement,

$$\text{Min.} f_1 = \min \{ P_{loss}(P_{d1}, P_{d2}, ..., P_{dn_{DG}}) \} \qquad (2)$$

P_{loss} in above relation is the casualty of real power. P_{dai} is the amount of the power of distributed production source in bass i.

f_2 is related to the index of deviation voltage that is introduced in the following form,

$$f_2 = \sqrt{\frac{\sum_{i=1}^{N_n}(V_i - V_{rated})^2}{N_n}} \qquad (3)$$

V_{rated} in Relation 3 is related to the bass voltage name, that is, one per unit. V_i the voltage of bass of system and N_n is the number of the bass of the network.

EQUAL CONDITIONS

The presentation of DG in the network should be in one way, in which all of the control and system variables in the equations of load distribution is applied. The active and reactive power based on the famous equation of load distribution in Relations 4 and 5 is shown thus (MIthulananthan et al., 2006),

$$P_{gi} - P_{di} - V_i \sum_{j=1}^{N} V_j Y_{ij} \cos(\delta_i - \delta_j - \theta_{ij}) = 0 \qquad (4)$$

$$Q_{gi} - Q_{di} - V_i \sum_{j=1}^{N} V_j Y_{ij} \sin(\delta_i - \delta_j - \theta_{ij}) = 0 \qquad (5)$$

In the above relation P_{ij} and Q_{gi} are related to the active and reactive power of load in shin i in arrangement. Also, δ_i, V_{ij} are the angle and the size of the shins voltage in arrangement. θ_{ij} and Y_{ij} are the elements that are extracted from the admittance Matrix.

Operational and protective constraints

Voltage condition

For the purpose of the observation of the quality of delivery to consumer, the voltage of every shin in distribution network should be in the minimum and defined maximum limit.

So in every condition, in the DG installation, the condition of voltage in accordance to the Relation 6 should be checked until the voltage of the bass place is in their allowed field.

$$V_i^{min} < V_i < V_i^{max} \quad I = 1...N_n \tag{6}$$

In the relation above, V_i is the voltage as bass i, V_i^{min} is the minimum allowed voltage at bass i, V_i^{max} is the maximum allowed voltage in bass I and N_n is the amount of bass in the network.

The condition of passing power line in distribution

Systems use the conductor by different segment surfaces, where the limit of the passing power is different. So during the time of installing DG in the network, subsidiary feeder should be investigated, that the power of every angle according to Relation 7 should not be more than the allowed amount (that is based on the kind of connector used).

$$|S_i| \leq |S_i^{max}| \quad i=1...N_b \tag{7}$$

In Relation 7, S_i is the passing power of branch i, S_i^{max} is the maximum passing power of branch i and N_L is the amount of the branch of the tested systems.

MODELING OF THE SPORADIC PRODUCTION

Source of sporadic production generally can be divided into four groups as follows:

1) The source of sporadic production that has the ability of producing real power (fotoveltaik). In recovery program, it is related to the limited power production, which in the form of DG, governs the condition on this kind of formulation.

$$P_{gi}^{min} \leq P_{gi} \leq P_{gi}^{max} \tag{8}$$

The minimum power p_{gi}^{min} and maximum power p_{gi}^{max} production of generator, and p_{gi} in Relation 8 are the outputs produced by generator.

2) Sporadic production source that only has the ability to produce of reactive power (synchronous condenser). Governing condition on this equation is written thus,

$$Q_{gi}^{min} \leq Q_{gi} \leq Q_{gi}^{max} \tag{9}$$

Q_{gi}^{min} and maximum power Q_{gi}^{max} are the reactive power of the generator; Q_{gi} in Relation 9 is the minimum reactive power of the generator.

3) Sporadic production source that produces active power and consumes reactive power (induction generator and winding turbin). DG is the governing condition of this kind,

$$P_{gi}^{min} \leq P_{gi} \leq P_{gi}^{max} \tag{10}$$

$$Q_{DG_i} = -(.08 + .04 P^2_{DG_i}) \tag{11}$$

4) Sporadic production source that is known as the synchronous generator as follows:

a) Has the ability of fixing reactive or any kind of pY
b) Sets voltage or any kind of pV

In this article, we use four kinds of DGs (Yanjun and Yun, 2008; Vinothkumar and Selvan, 2009).

GENETIC ALGORITHM (GA)

We can call the genetic algorithm as an explorer method. This is based on the specification and choosing of the children of sequential generation based on the principles of the best programmed genetic algorithm (from the answer to the problem in one step) This simulates the laws in genetic algorithm and their use leads to the production of children with the best quality.

In every generation, using appropriate choices in reproducing children, better approximated final answers are achieved. This process causes the new generation to be more compatible with the problem condition. This competition between generations, the victory of dominant generations and side tracking of beaten ones are effective methods for solving complex and hard problem (Golberg, 1989).

The methods of solving the problem GA are as follows,

Step 1: (the amount of first overall) we equal the counter to zero (t = 0) and produce the chromosome accidentally $[x_j(.), j = 1,...,n]$ where $x_j(.) = [x_{j1}(0), x_{j2}(0),...,x_{jm}(0)]$. $X_{jk}(0)$, in the form of accidental chromosome in the searching space, is produced.

Step 2: (evaluation) every chromosome in the first population is evaluated by the use of j purpose function, and to choose the best amount, we search for J_{BST} and arrange the chromosome that is proportional to the J_{BEST} for best amount of X_{BEST}.

Step 3 (change of counter) = in this step t=t+1

Step 4: (production of new population) = by repeating the following step, we the complete the new population.

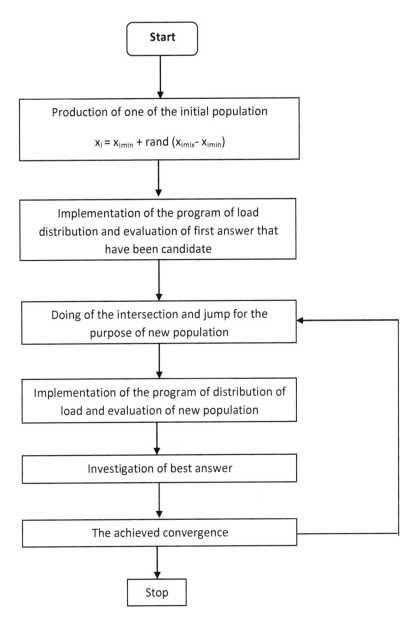

Figure 1. Flowchart of the relocation of decomposed granite (DG) sources production by genetic algorithm (GA).

a) Choice: We took an amount of parent chromosomes based on their suitability (the ones with better suitability have better chance of being chosen).

b) Intersection: By one probability, we apply the intersection operator on the chosen parent to produce the new children. If the intersection is not doing well, every branch of population is precisely copy as a parent.

c) Mutation = by one probability, we change every gene in one chromosome.

d) Acceptance = we put the new chromosome in the population.

Step 5: (replacement) = We used the new population produced to do the algorithm again.

Step 6: (stop) if the amounts of repeats are the distinct amounts needed, the program will stop, but if not, we will go to the next stop as shown in Figure 1.

NUMBER STUDY

The network includes one network of 12.66 radial KW. As shown in Figure 2, the whole active load is 3.2 MVAR and active casualty is about 210 KW before the installation of DG (Chakravorty and Das, 2001; Abumouti, 2010).

The appropriate initial population has direct effect on the speed of answer convergence and can directly affect

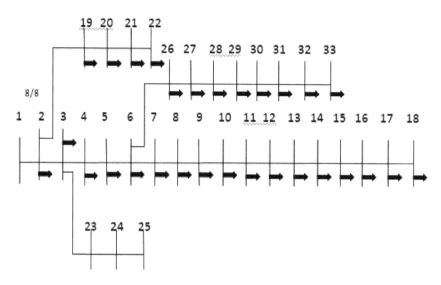

Figure 2. The study of the network by 33 bass.

Table 1. Genetic algorithm parameter.

Population	Method of choice	Intersection	Jump	End condition
300	Accidental	One point	Binary	100 repeated

Table 2. comparison between GA and PSO method for DG installation of type one.

	Basic casualty of system			
	210. 99 KW		143. 128 KVAR	
Kind of method	Active casualty (KW)	Reactive casualty (KVAR)	Place	MW
GA	72. 9601	50. 7721	13	0. 7571
			24	1. 0429
			30	1. 0429
PSO (Li et al., 2005)	72. 8214	50. 6729	14	0. 7707
			30	1. 0359
			24	1. 0966
Reload flow (EPRI, Palo Alto, CA, 2003)	116. 26	85. 42	12	2. 4939

the time of convergence.

The initial population DG created by 300 chromosomes and in every field shows the capacity and place of the installation of DG. Another information that is related to the genetic algorithm program is shown in Table 1.

In Table 2, there is a comparative between genetic method and movement algorithm of birds for installation of DG that has the ability to produce one active power.

In Table 2, the first column introduces the kinds of method, the second column introduces the casualty of the active power according to KW, the third column introduces the light reactive casualty according to KVAR, the fourth column shows the installation place of DG and the final column shows the capacity amount of DG installation on candidate bass. The place of DG installation in every three initial method is same; the only difference is in the DG capacity amount using the GA method in relation to the two other methods, which decrease the casualty a little more. Figure 3 shows the purpose function diagram.

Table 3 shows the comparison between the three methods used for DG installation, with the ability to

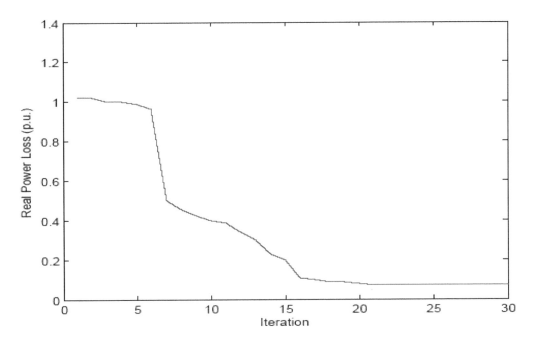

Figure 3. Minimum of the real power casualty by genetic algorithm (GA) method.

Table 3. Comparison between GA and PSO method of DG installation of type second.

Basic casualty of system				
210. 99 KW		**143. 128 KVAR**		
Kind of method	Active casualty (KW)	Reactive casualty (KVAR)	Place	MVAR
GA	140. 6558	95. 7170	10	0. 3201
			24	0. 2143
			30	1. 0714
PSO (Li et al., 2005)	139. 6957	95.2258	14	0.3092
			30	0. 8938
			6	0. 5691
Reload flow (EPRI, Palo Alto, CA, 2003)	158. 6782	108. 7812	22	1. 2092

produce reactive power only (type two).

Table 4 shows the comparison between the three methods used for DG installation, with the ability to produce active power and consume reactive power (type three).

Table 5 shows the comparison between every DG 3 method used for the installation of synchronous generator by stabilizing power (type four).

Looking at the charts and graphs of voltage profile presented in the previous section, the following points may be noted:

GA method presented to determine location and installed capacity of the four types of distributed generation sources has similar results with the GA and particle swarm optimization (PSO) methods, whose installation places are the same. The only difference could be found in installed DG capacity that causes less calculated loss in this method than the three other methods. The point is: As the search space and unknown parameters increase, GA method can be more useful. Looking at the calculated active and reactive power losses in the tables, we can conclude that, installed DG of fourth type, that is, synchronous generators have greater role in reducing losses than the other types of DG. After this type of DG, distributed generation sources from the type of photo voltaic systems, induction generator (active power generation and reactive power consumption) and the synchronous condensers decrease losses in distribution companies. Another point about the system voltage profile diagrams (Figures 4 to 7) on the

Table 4. Comparison between method GA, PSO for decomposed granite (DG) installation of type 3.

	Basic casualty of system			
210. 99 KW		**143. 128 KVAR**		
Kind of method	**Active casualty (KW)**	**Reactive casualty (KVAR)**	**Place**	**MVA**
GA	90. 1837	62. 2631	12	0. 8746
			24	1.04701
			30	1. 04701
PSO (Li et al., 2005)	90. 029	95.2258	13	0. 7899
			24	1. 0759
			30	1. 0193
Reload flow (EPRI, Palo Alto, CA, 2003)	148. 18	105. 61	12	2. 4494

Table 5. Comparison between DA and PSO for installation of DG kind 4.

	Basic casualty of system				
210. 99 KW		**143. 128 KVAR**			
Kind of method	**Active casualty (KW)**	**Reactive casualty (KVAR)**	**Place**	**MW**	**MVAR**
GA	11.914	9.876	14	0.7371	0.3485
			24	0.9872	0.4889
			30	1.0714	1.0369
PSO (Li et al., 2005)	11.8411	9.8065	30	1.0687	0.9956
			24	1.01268	0.5273
			13	0.7982	0.3960
Reload flow (EPRI, Palo Alto, CA, 2003)	71.396	57.431	12	2.5013	1.5822

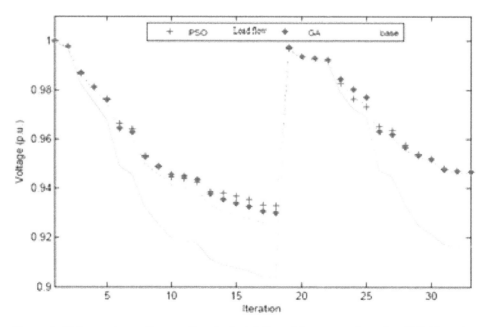

Figure 4. 33-Bus system voltage profile after installation of decomposed granites (DGs) type 2.

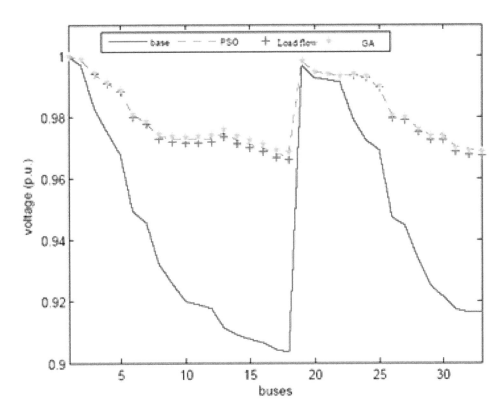

Figure 5. 33-Bus system voltage profile after installation of decomposed granites (DGs) type 2.

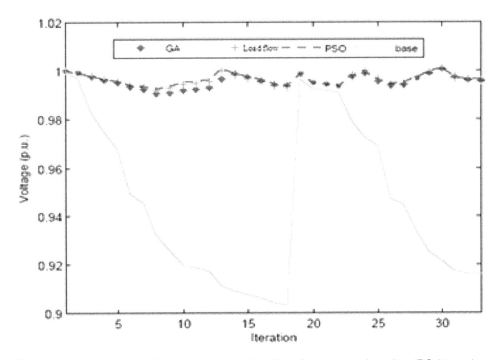

Figure 6. 33-Bus system voltage profile after installation of decomposed granites (DGs) type 4.

bass 33 system after installation of DG is that changes in bus voltage magnitude can be seen at the bass 33

system. As seen, the DG of the synchronous generator (PV), photo voltaic systems (P), induction generator and

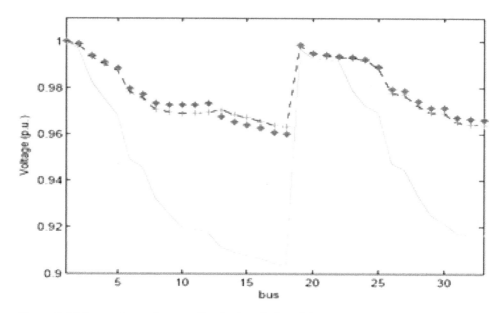

Figure 7. 33-Bus system voltage profile after installation of decomposed granites (DGs) type 3.

synchronous condenser ultimately are effective in improving network profiles.

Conclusion

GA approach was formulated to solve the problem of determining the size and location of DG and in this method, the location and capacity was nominated by GA. in spite of that, object function has two terms that improve Network voltage losses and profile. Also, DG impact of four models in the 33 bus network is evaluated and it could be seen that type of distributed generation sources will have a better impact to generate active and reactive power to reduce losses in the distribution network. Also, after installing the four types of distributed generation sources, loses reduced and the network voltage profile has been improved significantly.

Conflict of Interest

The author(s) have not declared any conflict of interest.

REFERENCES

Abu-mouti FS (2010). A Priority-Ordered Constrained search technique for Optimal distributed generation Allocation In Radial Distribution Feeder systems.

Acharya N, Mahat P, Mithulananthan N (2007). An analytical approach for DG allocation in primary distribution network. Int. J. Elect. Power Energy Syst. 28(10):669-678.

Chakravorty M, Das D (2001). Voltage stability analysis of radial distribution networks. Int. J. Elect. Power Energy Syst. 23(2):129-135.

Elgerd OI (2007). Electric Energy Systems Theory: An Introduction McGraw-Hill Inc.

Golberg DE (1989). Genetic Algorithms in search, optimization and machine learning. Longman.

Golshan MEH, Arefifar SA (2007). Optimal allocation of distributed generation and reactive sources considering tap positions of voltage regulators as control variables. European Transaction on Electrical Power, p. 17.

Hedayati H, Nabaviniaki SA, Akbarmajid A (2006). A method for placement of DG units in distribution networks. IEEE Transactions on Power Delivery, p. 23.

Installation, operation, and maintenance costs for distributed generation technologies, EPRI, Palo Alto, CA, 2003.

Kashem MA, Le ADT, Negnevitsky M, Ledwich G (2008). Distributed generation generation for minimization of power losses in distribution systems. IEEE Power Engineering Society General Meeting, p. 8.

Kean A, Omalley M (2006). Optimal allocation of embedded generation on distribution networks. IEEE Transactions on Power Systems.

Li Y, Yao D, Chen W (2005). Adaptive Particle Swarm Optimizer for Beam Angle Selection in Radiotherapy Planning. IEEE International Conference on Mechatronics & Automation,July2005, pp.421-425.

Mlthulananthan N, Oo T, Phu LV (2006). Distributed generator placement in power distribution system using genetic algorithm to reduce losses. Thammasat Int. J. Sci. Technol. 9(3):55-62.

Nara K, Hayashi Y, Ikeda K, Ashizawa T (2001). Application of tabu search to optimal placement of distributed generators. IEEE Power Engineering Society Winter Meeting.

Rosehart W, Nowicki E (2007). Optimal placement of distributed generation. 14th Power System Computation Conference, Sevilla Spain.

Vinothkumar K, Selvan MP (2009). Planning and Operation of Distributed Generations in Distribution Systems for Improved Voltage Profile. IEEE Power Engineering Society.

Willis HL (2000). Analytical methods and rules of thumb for modeling DG-distribution interaction. IEEE Power Eng. Soc. Summer Meet 3(3):143-1644.

Yanjun W, Yun Z (2008). Optimal Algorithm of Distribution Network Planning Including Distributed Generation. Nanjing China, DRPT, pp 6-9.

27

Evaluation of bandwidth performance in a corporate network by using simulation model

Shalangwa D. A.

Department of Physics, Adamawa State University, Mubi. Nigeria.

In this work a corporate network model consists of two separate buildings with four departments on different virtual local area network (VLAN) for the security purpose had been developed. The implementation was achieved using OPNET technology which really helped to reveal the traffic characteristics of network just like in a real life network. The central idea of this work is focused on the choice of likely bandwidth suitable for a corporate network design; this work categorically suggested that larger bandwidth is more preferable which is capable of handling large volume of traffic compare to the narrow bandwidth which usually suffers from delay and congestion that limits the number of the throughput at the destination.

Key words: Virtual local area network (VLAN), bandwidth, IP address, Traffic and OPNET technology.

INTRODUCTION

Years ago, telecommunication service use different technologies to achieve their communication means. However, today most of the technologies are harmonized in a single modern technology with the aim of achieving the same purpose with the separate technologies (Jeannine et al., 2008). Due to this massive demand imposed on a single communication technology, the structure of telecommunication infrastructure and traffic become more complex (http://sss-mag.com/pdf/802_11tut.pdf) and as a result of that, communication technologies needs adequate design and proper traffic monitoring to ensure better quality of service (QoS) more especially the bandwidth (Adas, 1997).

When studying general communication bandwidth, usually the question of constructing a model of input characteristics [number of users] arises; therefore to effectively choose a suitable bandwdth for any network and to develop fast algorithms of free flow of information across a network from source to destination, concept of bandwidth technology must be critically understood. This

is because the fundamental aim of any service provider is to deliver an outstanding quality of service to the end user with little or no interference.

Many researches in this field show that most communication networks, such as global system for mobile communication [GSM], GPRS, Ethernet and others suffer network congestion and delay (Abhinav et al., 2008; Beyers, 2007; Hamibindu et al., 2007; Nagurney and Qiang, 2007).

In order to address the congestion and delay problems that are inherent in most networks, a simulation model of corporate network had been designed using OPNET Technology(http://www.esat.kuleuven.be/telemic/networking/opnetwork02_johan.pdf) to test the free flow of information [packets] in dedicated channels with the same traffic volume on different bandwidth sizes. The simulation method is chosen because it can help us design the network structure, provide information about the traffic structure and save us from the cost of buying equipments and building the entire physical network structure.

This work consider corporate network that consist of two separate buildings and four separate departments; each building consist of two floors with at least one department on a floor. The departments are Administrative, Sale, Technical and Information with the total of 50 host users.

EXPERIMENTAL DESIGN AND SIMULATION

The entire corporate network may utilize the following (http://sss-mag.com/pdf/802_11tut.pdf; Behrouz, 2007); four segments with backbone (for example one segment on each floor or wing of different buildings), more than one network protocols, area configured with Open Shortest Path First (OSPF) (Beyers, 2007), Dial-up connections for users who connect from home or while traveling, Leased-line connections to branch offices, Demand-dial connections to branch offices and Internet connections; the implementation could be achieved using the following equipments below (www.cisco.com/en/US).

Materials and reasons for choosing the major network equipments

The equipments consist of edge router, switches, application configuration, profile configuration, personal computers and links of different types; 100 Kb/s, 10 Mb/s and 1 Gb/s. Switch is chosen because it has less collision domain and support scalability, while Edge Router is used to forward packets to the appropriate destination (www.cisco.com/en/US).

Network implementation

The simulation model of the corporate network is implemented in Figure 1 which consists of two switches separated by edge router connected together by crossover cable at Fa0/0 – Fa0/23 and Fa0/1 and Fa0/20 ports; thereafter each switch is connected to PCs by straight through cables at the appropriate port.

Address planning

Here address planning scheme with a starting IP address of 192.168.0.0/24 was used, which also creates a virtual local area network (VLAN) for the purpose of management and security on each segment (www.cisco.com/en/US).

Starting Address	192.168.0.0	255.255.254.0
VLAN 1 Building 1 Floor 1	192.168.1.2-12	255.255.255.0
VLAN 2 Building 1 Floor 2	192.168.1.13-27	255.255.255.0
VLAN 3 Building 2 Floor 1	192.168.2.1-21	255.255.255.0
VLAN 4 Building 2 Floor 2	192.168.2.23	255.255.255.0

Router configuration

```
R1 > En
R1#conf t
R1[conf]#interface fa0/0
R1[conf if]# ip add 192.168.1.2 255.255.255.0
R1[conf if]# no shut
R1[conf if]# exit
R1[conf]#interface fa0/1
R1[conf if]# ip add 192.168.2 255.255.255.0
```

```
R1[conf if]# no shut
R1[conf if]# exit
R1[conf if]# exit
```

Switch configuration for VLAN

```
Switch > En
Switch#conf t
Switch[conf]#hostname S1
S1[conf]#int Vlan1
S1[conf if]# ip add 192.168.2.100
S1[conf if]# no shut
S1[conf if]# int fa0/23
S1[conf if]# switchport mode access
S1[conf if]# switchport access Vlan1
S1[conf if]# exit
S1[conf if]# exit
```

Other Vlan can also be configured in the same manner (www.cisco.com/en/US).

SIMULATION RESULTS AND DISCUSSION

The address used in the address plan is called internet protocol version 4 [IPv4] which are usually derived from 16 bits binary number from 0000.0000.0000.0000 to 1111.1111.1111.1111; the zeros part represents the network address and the host number while ones' part represents the subnet mask which allows multi network creation from single address scheme. After achieving the IP address plan which play key role in directing the packets to their respective destinations, an OPNET Modeler was used to realize the entire structure of the corporate network as shown in Figure 1. The application configuration and its properties were set to defaults to enable us get any application that will be needed. Profile configuration and the server attributes were also set to support the application configuration while the personal computers were adjusted to support the profile. In order to evaluate the bandwidth performance, three separate scenarios were considered with the bandwidth of 100 Kb/s, 10 Mb/s and 1 Gb/s.

In the first scenario, 100 Kb/s bandwidth was used on the developed corporate network where some global statistics were imposed to see how the traffic are successfully sent and received at their respective destinations. For example database, email, file transfer protocols and delay in the transmission was also noted while in the second and third scenarios, 10 Mb/s and 1 Gb/s bandwidth were used respectively with the same volume of traffic and statistics as in the first scenario; the detailed observations are as shown in Figures 2, 3 and 4. Figure 2 described the amount of the packets received for email, the blue color graph represent the packets received through 100 Kb/s, red color graph represent packets received through 10 Mb/s and light green color represent packets received through 1 Gb/s bandwidth. It can be seen clearly that the packets received through 100 Kb/s bandwidth were not all successfully delivered

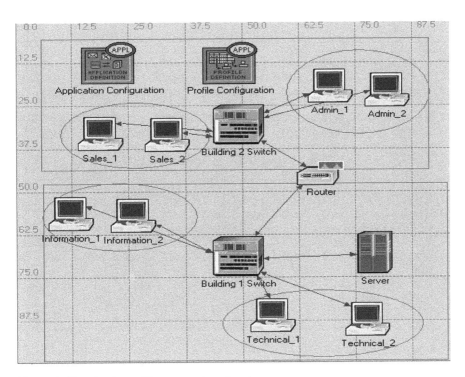

Figure 1. The structure of the corporate network.

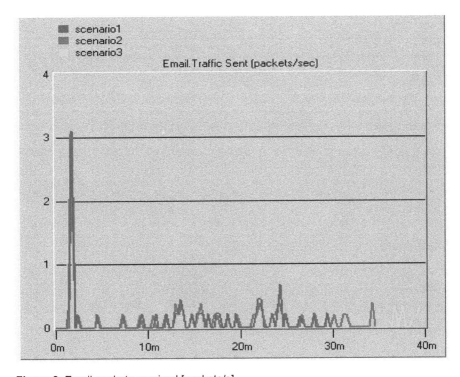

Figure 2. Email packets received [packets/s].

(Oleg et al., 2007); this is followed by packet through 10 Mb/s while packets through 1 Gb/s were tremendous at the destination (Nagurney and Qiang 2007).

Figure 3 represents ethernet delay during the transmission in all the scenarios as we can see that on average the packets were more delayed through 100 Kb/s, followed by 10 Mb/s, then 1 Gb/s bandwidth with an average delay of 0.003 bits/s in 1 Gb/s and others above

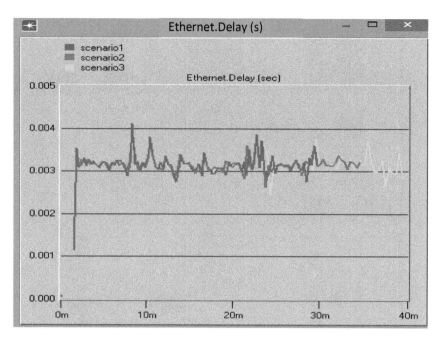

Figure 3. Ethernet delay [s].

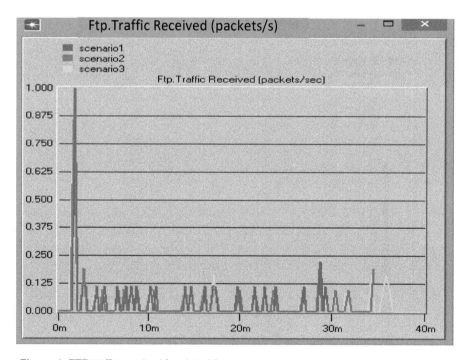

Figure 4. FTP traffic received [packets/s].

0.003 bits/s. Thus, packets that arrive through 1 Gb/s show almost no delay.

Figure 4 represents the file transfer protocol received. It also shows that packets that come through 100 Kb/s are more likely to drop than the packets that come through 10 Mb/s, then 1 Gb/s bandwidth. While Figure 5 shows the total amounts of packets forwarded during transmission,

it can also be seen that more packets are forwarded in 1 Gb/s followed by 10 Mb/s, then 100 Kb/s.

Conclusion

A corporate network had been implemented, simulated

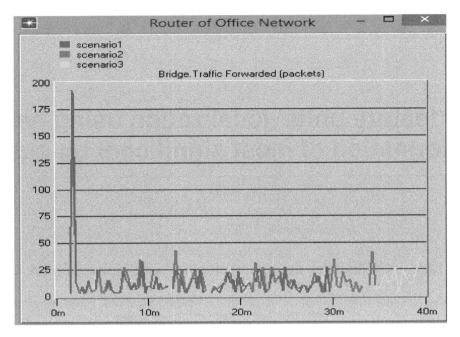

Figure 5. Traffic forwarded (packets).

using OPNET modeler and various traffic such as email, ethernet delay and file transfer protocol had been monitored. This research revealed that packets are less delivered in narrow bandwidth than wide bandwidth although in telecommunication narrow bandwidth is usually used. Therefore when choosing bandwidth, wider should be considered while not ignoring the cost. This research work provide some useful information on a choice of bandwidth when implementing a network and recommends that further research be carried out to investigate other factors that could hamper fast flow of packets in wider bandwidth.

REFERENCES

Abhinav P, Hamibindu P, Ying Z, Charlie YH (2008). A measurement study of internet delay asymmetry. web.eecs.umich.edu/~zmao/Papers/pam08_owd.
Adas A (1997). Traffic models in broadband network IEEE Communication Magazine A Technical Tutorial on the IEEE 802.11 Protocol http://sss-mag.com/pdf/802_11tut.pdf.
Behrouz AF (2007). Data communication and Computer network. McGraw Hill Higer.
Beyers D (2007). Packet radio network research, development and application. Proceeding SHAPE Conference on packet radio, Amsterdam.
Hamibindu P, Ying Z, Morley ZM Charlie YH (2007). Understanding network delay changes by routing events. Proceeding of ACM SIGMETRICS.
Jeannine S, Pat K, Lisa M, John M (2008). The value of harmonizing multiple improvement technology. Carnegien Mellon University.
Mohand Y, Louiza BM, Djamil A (2013). Throughput analysis and improvement of the 802.11 network in non ideal channel condition. J. Netw. Technol. pp. 75-85.
Nagurney A, Qiang Q (2007). An efficiency measure for congested network. Epl Journal.
Oleg IS, Sergey MS, Andrey VO (2007). Self-similar process in Telecommunications. John Wiley and Sons, Ltd.
OPNET in Advanced Networking Education http://www.esat.kuleuven.be/telemic/networking/opnetwork02_johan.pdf.
www.cisco.com/en/US.

28

Facial feature units' localization using horizontal information of most significant bit planes

Asif Khan[1]*, Khalilullah[1], Ihtesham-Ul-Islam[1] and Mohammad A. U. Khan[2]

[1]FAST National University of Computer and Emerging Sciences, Peshawar, Pakistan.
[2]Effat University, Jeddah, Saudi Arabia.

We present here an approach to find the exact position of some feature units related to human face images. We use the horizontal information in most significant bit planes of images to accomplish the task. Finding location of facial feature units is of importance as most human face recognition approaches take it as initial point. The prominent feature units in a face are eyes, nostrils and lips which are usually oriented in horizontal direction and visually significant in face image. The majority of the visually significant data in image can be extracted using higher order bits of that image. Our four step method consists of bit planes processing, separating horizontal information using wavelet transform (WT), binary thresholding and appropriate combination of Dilation and Erosion. The proposed method shows high accuracy in the presence of all real world situations like various gestures, illumination variations, closed eyes, and eyes with glasses.

Key words: Bit planes, feature localization, facial features, face recognition and wavelet transform.

INTRODUCTION

For several decades, extracting facial features and feature units localization are some of the most important research areas in image processing research community as explained by Yang et al. (2002), Lanzarotti et al. (2001), and Yuille et al. (1992). For the success of many applications such as, facial expression analysis, teleconferencing, animation, video surveillance, man machine interfacing, human performance prediction by Jabon et al. (2011), face recognition, lip reading for the deaf and some other tasks, this pre-processing step is essential. In facial expression analysis very high accuracy is required and even very small errors can be interpreted differently and can lead to wrong facial expression recognition. To locate the exact position of facial feature units is imperative in three dimensional modelling, texture mapping and the subsequent animation. For a complete facial image processing system to work, it should be able to do some tasks in a sequence. Detection of faces in a given image, extraction of facial features, recognizing people and describing facial expressions are some of those tasks. In this paper, our focus is on finding the location of various facial features which is important for the remaining two components of the system. Factors that add up to the computational cost for facial feature unit localization are locating the face region, complexity of the evaluation of cost functions, and the searching for the feature points.

*Corresponding author. E-mail: asif.khan@nu.edu.pk.

However face region extraction is no more a problem as there are many robust face detection algorithms available such as Viola and Jones (2001).

In surveys, there are four classes of facial features extraction starting with the use of geometrical information of facial features as first class, proposed by Xhang and Lender (2000) and Rizon et al. (2000). Spors and Rabenstein (2001) and Perez et al. (2001) proposed the spatio-temporal information-based techniques to extract the features from the image sequence. For the third class, the color information of each facial feature is used by Hsu et al. (2002) and Xin et al. (1998). In fourth class, important parameter for detection is intensity of the image as stated by Mariani (1999) and Chandrasekaran et al. (1997). Most facial features extraction methods are not robust and are sensitive to noise, uneven illumination, variations in orientation, colour space used and gestures. The existing algorithms for facial features extraction such as stated by Lavagetto and Curinga (1994), Desilve et al. (1995), Huang et al. (1993), Hess and Martinez (2004), Yuille et al. (1992), Zuo et al. (2004) and Majumder et al. (2011) are unable to solve the problem completely in an efficient way. Due to its high complexity, feature units localization is still under research by a lot of researchers in this area. A related work has been performed by Jun et al. (2003) but that cannot take all the real world situations.

Our objective in the current research and this paper is to find the estimated position of eyes, nose and lips in a facial image taken in any of the real world situation. The idea is to utilize the horizontal information in most significant bit planes after decomposing the face image into bit planes. The decomposition of grey image in to bit planes shows that majority of the visually significant data are available in higher order bits. In a typical face image the visually significant data are eyes, nose and mouth. It is also evident that these feature units are also horizontal information in face image. Our method consists of extracting information contained in upper bit planes of the image, concentrating on horizontal information, binary thresholding and appropriate combination of Dilation and Erosion. This method detects the eyes, nose and mouth in a digital photograph of human face. The main advantage of our method is to remove trade-off between complexity and tackling all real world situations. In section 2, we provide explanation of our proposed method. Section 3 provides simulation results and discussion about our work and section 4 provides conclusion.

MATERIALS AND METHODS

Our proposed method revolves around the idea that facial feature units are significant and horizontal data in a face image. As described in introduction that facial feature units are visually significant data in face image and we can extract this data using Most Significant Bit (MSB) planes of the image. Second part of the idea is that these feature units are horizontally oriented. We can use Wavelet Transform (WT) for the extraction of this horizontal information. Our proposed method can be divided in to four steps. First step consists of extracting MSB planes of the face image. We combine some MSB planes and use the resultant image for facial features extraction. The image obtained in the first step is processed using Wavelet Transform (WT), and this is the second step. In this step we retain only those WT coefficients which represent horizontal information and discard other coefficients to focus on mouth, nose and eyes in the image. Third step consists of thresholding to find the estimated regions of stated features in the image. Fourth step consists of combination of dilation and erosion as post-processing for increasing accuracy of the estimation. After the four steps, we draw bounding boxes around the eyes, nostrils and mouth regions in the original image.

Image or 2D signal is represented in digital form as a matrix with pixels having one of 2^N possible values, defined by N bits. Each pixel can be decomposed into N binary values from MSB to LSB and thus the whole image can be treated in this way, thus forming N bit planes, explained by Pratt (1978). These bit planes are loosely related with N subband images, where subband image with lowest spatial frequencies correspond MSB plane, and LSB plane corresponds to that of highest spatial frequencies. Depending on the values of N bits, each pixel will have corresponding value in each bit plane. Original image, $x(i,j)$, can be reconstructed from its bit planes $b_i(i,j)$ as:

$$x(i, j) = \sum_{k=j}^{N} 2^{N-K} \cdot b_k(i, j).$$

(1)

The number of planes that can be obtained with N = 8 bits per pixel are 8, each of them having the size of the original image and with pixels having two values: either 0 or 1. In our experiments the size of the original image is 256 x 256. For demonstration purposes the decomposition of image Lena in to bit planes is shown in Figure 1. The bit planes are arranged in the ascending order from MSB $b_1(i,j)$ to LSB $b_8(i,j)$. The fact is clear that MSB image $b_1(i,j)$ has large areas with uniform values (0 or 1). It is also evident that all the main features of the image are present in four MSB images and the lesser significant bit planes tend to have no characteristics and do not contribute much information.

Image analysis and processing through bit planes in such a way that extract bit planes with main horizontal features in face image is the basic idea in this paper. In a typical face image the features are eyes, nose and mouth and they are also horizontal. The other features like hair, ears etc. are not very useful for most of applications and we do not detect them in this work. We can use one or combination of more than one MSB planes for facial features extraction. Extensive experiments have shown that combining two

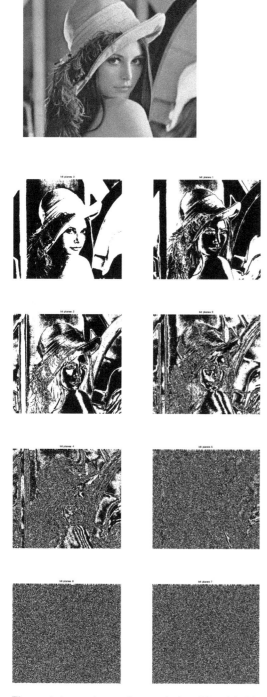

Figure 2. A typical face image with glasses from Yale atabase.

Figure 3. Combination of two MSB planes for the face image in Figure 2.

MSB planes concentrate only on the visually significant features in face image. Thus we combine the two MSB images and process i further for accurately identifying eyes, nose and mouth regions. A typical face image from Yale database is given in Figure 2 and image formed by combining its two MSB images is shown in Figure 3. Removal of glasses without disturbing eyes is one of the major achievements of this step.

Extracting horizontal information

Combining two MSB planes discards all the irrelevant components and intensities from the face image and retains significant feature

Figure 1. Lenna image (top centre) and its eight bit planes, from MSB plane (upper left) to LSB plane (bottom right).

We can then define the continuous wavelet transform (CWT) of a signal x(t) as:

$$CWT_\psi x(a,b) = \frac{1}{\sqrt{|a|}} \int_{-\infty}^{\infty} x(t)\psi^*\left(\frac{t-b}{a}\right)dt \qquad (3)$$

Where ψ(t) is called the mother wavelet with a and b are called the scaling and translation parameters, respectively. Discrete Wavelet

Figure 6. Result of binary thresholding.

Transform (DWT) is given by

$$DWT_\psi x(m,n) = \int_{-\infty}^{\infty} x(t)\psi_{m,n}^*(t)dt \qquad (4)$$

Where

$$\psi_{m,n}(t) = a_0^{-m/2}\psi\left(a_0^{-m}t - nb_0\right) \qquad (5)$$

The transforms in one-dimensional form are easily extended to transforms in two-dimensional forms like images. We require a two-dimensional scaling function, φ(x, y), and three two-dimensional wavelets, ψ^H(x, y), ψ^V(x, y), ψ^D(x, y) in two-dimensional case. The wavelets have the ability to measure variations along columns, rows, and diagonals respectively. A three-scale WT can be seen in Figure 4. We retain horizontal information in Figure 3 and discard other coefficients of WT. Then we recover the intensity image which contains only the horizontal information, as can be seen in Figure 5.

Thresholding

By using thresholding we convert image to black and white where

Figure 4. A three scale wavelet transform (WT) of face image.

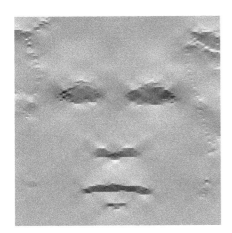

Figure 5. Horizontal information of face image in Figure 3, after WT processing.

units. Now its turn for the second part of our idea, which states, that lips, nostril and eyes are all horizontal features in a face. Now, we need to eliminate all features except horizontal features from the image obtained in first step. We can do this using Fourier Transform (FT), Wavelet Transform (WT) or Gabor Transform (GT). We have more control over WT coefficients; therefore, we use WT in this paper for extracting horizontal information. Wavelet is, basically, a function $\psi \in L^2(R)$ with zero average:

$$\int_{-\infty}^{\infty} \psi(t)dt = 0 \qquad (2)$$

Figure 7. Result of dilation on thresholded image.

Figure 8. Result of erosion on dilated image.

black components represents feature units of interest i.e. eyes, nose and mouth. We also crop some number of upper and lower rows and left and right columns form this binary image because we know that eyes and mouth remain in the center part of the face. The result of thresholding can be seen in Figure. 6. In this step some small irrelevant spots appear near eyes, nose and mouth. We can remove these small areas by appropriate use of dilation and erosion.

Dilation and erosion

In a typical face image only the edges of eyes, nostrils and lips contain the horizontal information. But due to illumination variationsand various gestures there are some false horizontal information on the face. This false horizontal information is small as compared to eyes, nose and mouth. To remove this false

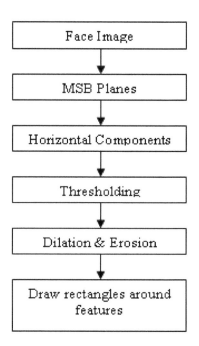

Figure 9. Sequential block diagram of the proposed method.

information we use combination of two morphological operations, first dilation and then erosion in the next step.

If A and B are two sets in Z^2, the dilation of A by B, denoted as $A \oplus B$, is defined as:

$$A \oplus B = \left\{ z \mid \left(\hat{B} \right)_z \cap A \neq \varnothing \right\} \qquad (6)$$

Set B is usually called as the structuring element for dilation.

The erosion of A by B, denoted as $A \otimes B$, is defined as:

$$A \otimes B = \left\{ z \mid (B)_z \subseteq A \right\} \qquad (7)$$

Figure 7 show the result of dilation where the black areas exactly represent the eyes, nostrils and mouth regions in face image of Figure 2. Figure 8 shows the effect of erosion on Figure 7. In our case, Erosion connects the separated parts of features. Now there are only four connected components in Figure 8 which are our desired feature units. Figure 9 shows all the steps of our proposed method.

SIMULATION RESULTS

In all of our experiments, we used the frontal pose face images of Yale face database (1997), Yale face database B

Table 1. Successful results (%).

Database	Single feature unit detected	All feature units detected
Yale	93	91
BioID	91	90
Yale B	90	87

Georghiades et al. (2001), and BioID face database Jesorsky et al. (2001). There are 165 GIF images for 15 persons in Yale Face Database. For 15 persons, there are eleven images per person, one per different facial expression or configuration. These configurations are center-light, w/glasses, happy, left-light, w/no glasses, sad, normal, right-light, sleepy, surprised, and wink. The Yale face database B consists of 5850 images for 10 subjects, each taken under 576 viewing conditions (nine poses and sixty-four illumination conditions). We used only frontal pose face images for our experiments. The BioID dataset contains 1521 grey level images for 23 different persons. Each one shows the frontal view of a face with resolution of 384x286 pixels. These databases are considered the difficult one because they contain various illumination conditions. In the experiments we used WT up to fifth level and at each level we retained only the horizontal information and discarded the other coefficients. The size of structuring element used is 3x5 for horizontal information. This size may vary for different images. The simplest value for thresholding is the mid value of minimum and maximum intensities in the image of previous step.

We have also done our experiments on faces with glasses and found successful results of our proposed method. The method gives accurate results even in the presence of various gestures of eyes and mouth and also for closed eyes. Table 1 shows the outcome of our proposed method on the above mentioned three databases. Figure 10 shows some of the successful results.

DISCUSSION

The purpose in this study is to find the location of eyes, nose and lips in a facial image taken in any of the real world situation. The idea is to utilize the horizontal information in most significant bit planes after decomposing the face image into bit planes. Our method

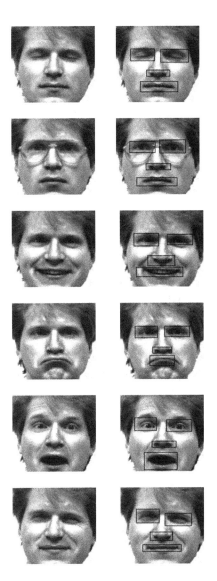

Figure 10. Some successful results of features extraction in face images, before processing (Left) and after processing (Right).

consists of extracting information contained in upper bit planes of the image, concentrating on horizontal information. Conceptually this work has some advantages and disadvantages. The main advantage of our method is to remove trade-off between complexity and tackling most of the real world situations. The disadvantage is that its accuracy is greatly affected by a variation in face pose. In the future, we hope that, this work can be used successfully to develop more efficient and robust techniques.

REFERENCES

Chandrasekaran V, Liu ZQ (1997). Facial features detection using compact vector field canonical templates. IEEE Int. Conf. on Systems, Man and Cybernetics, 3: 2022-2027.

Desilve LC, Aizawa K, Hatori M (1995). Detection and tracking of facial features in SPIE Symp. Visual Communications and Image Processing, Taipei, Taiwan, R.O.C, pp. 1161-1172.

Georghiades AS, Belhumeur PN, Kriegman DJ (2001). From Few to Many: Illumination Cone Models for Face Recognition under Variable Lighting and Pose," IEEE Trans. PAMI, 23(6): 643–660.

Hess M, Martinez G (2004). Facial features extraction based on the smallest univalue segment assimilating neuclus (susan) algorithm. Picture Coding Symposium, California, USA.

Hsu RL, Abdel-Mottaleb M, Jain AK (2002). Face detection in color images. IEEE Trans. PAMI, 24(5): 696-706.

Huang HC, Ouhyoung M, Wu JL (1993). Automatic feature point extraction on a human face in model-based image coding. Optical. Engineering, 32: 1571-1580.

Jabon ME, Sun JA, Bailenson JN (2011). Automatically Analyzing Facial-Feature Movements to Identify Human Errors. IEEE Intelligent Systems, 26: 54 - 63.

Jesorsky O, Kirchberg K, Frischholz R (2001). Robust Face Detection Using the Hausdorff Distance," In J. Bigun and F. Smeraldi, editors, AVBPA 2001, 90-95. Springer. Available: http://bioid.com.

Lanzarotti R, Campadelli P, Borghese NA (2001). Automatic Features Detection for Overlapping Face Images on Their 3D Range Model. Proceedings of the IEEE 11th Int. Conf. on Image Analysis and Proceeding (ICIAP2001), Palermo, Italy, 26-28, 316-321.

Jun M, Hong L, Wen G, Hongming Z, Gang D, Xilin C (2003). A System for Human Face and Facial Feature Location. Int. J. Image Graphics. 3(3): 461-479.

Lavagetto F, Curinga S (1994). Object-Oriented scene modeling for interpersonal video communications at very low bit-rate. Signal Processing, Image Communication, 6: 379-395.

Majumder A, Behera L, Subramanian VK (2011). Automatic and Robust Detection of Facial Features in Frontal Face Images. UK Sim 13th International Conference on Computer Modelling and Simulation, UK.

Mariani R (1999). Subpixellic eyes detection. IEEE Int. Conf. on Image Anal. Proc., pp. 496-501.

Perez CA, Palma A, Holzmann CA, Pena C (2001). Face and ey tracking algorithm based on digital image processing. IEEE Int. Con on Systems, Man and Cybenetics, 2: 1178-1183.

Pratt W (1978). Digital Image Processing, J.W. & Sons, New York.

Rizon M, Kawaguchi T (2000). Automatic eye detection using intensit and edge information. TENCON 2000. Proceeedings, 2: 415-420.

Spors S, Rabenstein R (2001). A real-time face tracker for colour videc IEEE Int. Conf. on Acoustics, Speech and Signal Processing, 3 1493-1496.

Viola P, Jones M (2001). Rapid Object Detection Using a Booste Cascade of Simple Features. Computer Vision and Patter Recognition Conf., pp. 511-518.

Xhang L, Lender P (2000) Knowledge-based eye detection for huma face recognition. 4th IEEE Int. Conf. on Knowledge-Based Intelliger Eng. Sys. Allied Tech., 1: 117-120.

Xin Z, Yanjun X, Limin D (1998). Locating facial features with colo information. IEEE Int. Conf. on Sig. Processing, 2: 889-892.

Yale   face   database   (1997) http://cvc.yale.edu/projects/yalefaces/yalefaces.html.

Yang MH, Kreigman DJ, Ahuja N (2002). Detecting Faces in Images: / Survey. IEEE Transactions on PAMI, 24(1): 34-58.

Yuille A, Hallinan P, Cohen D (1992). Feature extraction from face using deformable templates. Int. J. Comp. Vision, 8(2): 99-111.

Zuo F, de With PHN (2004). Real-time facial feature extraction b cascaded parameter prediction and image optimization. Proc. ICIAR pp. 651-659.

Permissions

List of Contributors

Abd El–Naser A. Mohamed
Electronics and Electrical Communications Engineering Department, Faculty of Electronic Engineering, Menouf 32951, Menoufia University, Egypt

Ahmed Nabih Zaki Rashed
Electronics and Electrical Communications Engineering Department, Faculty of Electronic Engineering, Menouf 32951, Menoufia University, Egypt

Mohammed A. Metwae'e
Electronics and Electrical Communications Engineering Department, Faculty of Electronic Engineering, Menouf 32951, Menoufia University, Egypt

Amira I. M. Bendary
Electronics and Electrical Communications Engineering Department, Faculty of Electronic Engineering, Menouf 32951, Menoufia University, Egypt

Dhiraj Ahuja
Department of Electrical and Electronics Engineering, YMCA University of Science and Technology, Faridabad-121006 (Haryana), India

Bharat Singh
Department of Electrical and Electronics Engineering, YMCA University of Science and Technology, Faridabad-121006 (Haryana), India

M. M. Abdelrahman
Accelerators and Ion Sources Department, Nuclear Research Center, Cairo Egypt

N.I. Basal
Accelerators and Ion Sources Department, Nuclear Research Center, Cairo Egypt

S.G. Zakha
Accelerators and Ion Sources Department, Nuclear Research Center, Cairo Egypt

M. N. LAKHOUA
Department of Electrical Engineering, ESTI, University of Carthage, Tunisia Laboratory of Analysis, Design and Command of Systems, ENIT, Tunisia

Sepehr Sadighi
Catalysis and Nanotechnology Division, Catalytic Reaction Engineering Department, Research Institute of Petroleum Industry (RIPI), Iran

S. Reza Seif Mohaddecy
Catalysis and Nanotechnology Division, Catalytic Reaction Engineering Department, Research Institute of Petroleum Industry (RIPI), Iran

Govind Sharma
ECE Department, Jaypee Institute of Information Technology, Noida, Uttar Pradesh, India-201307

Ankit Agarawal
ECE Department, Jaypee Institute of Information Technology, Noida, Uttar Pradesh, India-201307

Vivek K. Dwivedi
ECE Department, Jaypee Institute of Information Technology, Noida, Uttar Pradesh, India-201307

Hossam M. Abd El-rahman
Sohag University, Sohag, Egypt

R. M. El-Zahry
Mechanical Engineering Department, Faculty of Engineering, Assiut University, Assiut, Egypt

Y. B. Mahdy
Dean of Faculty of Computer Information Science, Assiut University, Egypt

O. K. Ogidan
Department of Electrical Engineering, Cape Peninsula University of Technology, South Africa

Bamisaye
Department of Electrical and Electronics Engineering, Federal University of Technology, Akure, Nigeria

A. J.
Department of Electrical and Electronics Engineering, Ekiti State University, Ado Ekiti, Nigeria

Adeloye V. S. A.
Department of Electrical and Electronics Engineering, Ekiti State University, Ado Ekiti, Nigeria

Medhat H. A. Awadalla
Communications and Electronic Department, Faculty of Engineering, Helwan University, Egypt

I. I. Ismaeil
Communications and Electronic Department, Faculty of Engineering, Helwan University, Egypt

M. Abdellatif Sadek
Information Technology Department, High Institute of Engineering, Shorouk Academy, Egypt

Nasr-Eddine BOUHENNA
Department of Electrical and Electronics Engineering Technology, Higher Colleges of Technology, ADMC - United Arab Emirates

Hebah ElGibreen
Information Technology Department, College of Computer and Information Sciences, King Saud University, Saudi Arabia

Samir El-Masri
Information Systems Department, College of Computer and Information Sciences, King Saud University, Saudi Arabia

Okunoye .O. Babatunde
Department of Pure and Applied Biology, Ladoke Akintola University of Technology, P. M. B. 4000, Ogbomoso, Osun State, Nigeria

S. E. Nnebe
Department of Computer Science, Ambrose Alli University, Ekpoma, Edo State, Nigeria

S.C. Chiemeke
Department of Computer Science, University of Benin, Benin city, Edo State, Nigeria

M. M. G. Mazumder
Kongju National University, South Korea

S. Kim
Kongju National University, South Korea

S. J. Park
Korean Research Institute of Standards and Science (KRISS), South Korea

T. Suryasekhara Reddy
Department of Mechanical Engineering, R. Y. M. Engineering College, Bellary, India

C. Eswara Reddy
Department of Mechanical Engineering, S. V. U. College of Engineering, Tirupati, India

S. Prabhavathi
Department of Electrical and Computer Engineering, R. Y. M. Engineering College, Bellary, India

S. Missaoui
Electronics Laboratory, Department of Physics, Faculty of Science, Tunis El Manar, Tunisia

M. Kaddour
Electronics Laboratory, Department of Physics, Faculty of Science, Tunis El Manar, Tunisia

M. H. Shakoor
Fars Science and Research Branch, Islamic Azad University, Shiraz, Iran

M. Moattari
Fars Science and Research Branch, Islamic Azad University, Shiraz, Iran

A. Ferchichi
Unit of Research Circuits and Electronics Systems High Frequency, Faculty of Science, University El Manar Tunis, Tunisia

N. Fadlallah
Radiocom Team, Lebanese University, IUT Saida, Lebanon

A. Gharssallah
Unit of Research Circuits and Electronics Systems High Frequency, Faculty of Science, University El Manar Tunis, Tunisia

Khalil Ullah
Department of Electrical Engineering, National University of Computer and Emerging Sciences, Peshawar, Pakistan

Asif Khan
Department of Electrical Engineering, National University of Computer and Emerging Sciences, Peshawar, Pakistan

Ihtesham-ul-Islam
Department of Electrical Engineering, National University of Computer and Emerging Sciences, Peshawar, Pakistan

Mohammad A. U. Khan
Department of Electrical and Computer Engineering, Effat University, Jeddah, Saudi Arabia

A. A. Mohammed
Electronics and Electrical Communication Engineering Department, Faculty of Electronic Engineering, Menouf 32951, Menoufia University, Egypt

Ahmed Nabih Zaki Rashed
Electronics and Electrical Communication Engineering Department, Faculty of Electronic Engineering, Menouf 32951, Menoufia University, Egypt

Gaber E. S. M. E.
Electronics and Electrical Communication Engineering Department, Faculty of Electronic Engineering, Menouf 32951, Menoufia University, Egypt

A. A. Saad
Electronics and Electrical Communication Engineering
Department, Faculty of Electronic Engineering, Menouf
32951, Menoufia University, Egypt

D. A. Shalangwa
Department of Physics, Adamawa State University, Mubi,
Adamawa State, Nigeria

D. I. Malgwi
Department of Physics, University of Maiduguri, Borno
State, Nigeria

A. Z. Yusuf
Nigerian National Petroleum Cooperation (NNPC),
Nigeria

A. Zakir
Human Physiology Department, Ahmadu Bello
University Zaria

S. I. Mustapha
Chemical Engineering Department, Ahmadu Bello
University Zaria

S. A. Halima
Chemical Engineering Department, Ahmadu Bello
University Zaria

M. Nuhu
Chemical Engineering Department, Ahmadu Bello
University Zaria

M.O. Adamu
Department of Mathematics, University of Lagos, Lagos,
Nigeria

A. Adewunmi
School of Computer Science, University of Kwazulu-
Natal, Durban, South Africa

Ani Vincent Anayochukwu
Department of Electronic Engineering, University of
Nigeria, Nsukka, Enugu State, Nigeria

Safaa M. Naeem
Department of Biomedical Engineering, Helwan
University, Helwan, Egypt

Ahmed F. Seddik
Department of Biomedical Engineering, Helwan
University, Helwan, Egypt

Mohamed A. Eldosoky
Department of Biomedical Engineering, Helwan
University, Helwan, Egypt

Shirin Farhadi
Azad University of Jasb, Iran

Reza Dashti
Iran University of Science and Technology, Iran

D. A. Shalangwa
Department of Physics, Adamawa State University,
Mubi. Nigeria

Asif Khan
FAST National University of Computer and Emerging
Sciences, Peshawar, Pakistan

Khalilullah
FAST National University of Computer and Emerging
Sciences, Peshawar, Pakistan

Ihtesham-Ul-Islam
FAST National University of Computer and Emerging
Sciences, Peshawar, Pakistan

Mohammad A. U. Khan
Effat University, Jeddah, Saudi Arabia

Printed in the USA
CPSIA information can be obtained
at www.ICGtesting.com
JSHW051430221024
72173JS00006B/1424